THE SECOND MOUNTAIN

THE
SECOND
MOUNTAIN

The Quest for a Moral Life

DAVID BROOKS

ALLEN LANE
an imprint of
PENGUIN BOOKS

ALLEN LANE

UK | USA | Canada | Ireland | Australia
India | New Zealand | South Africa

Allen Lane is part of the Penguin Random House group of companies
whose addresses can be found at global.penguinrandomhouse.com.

First published in the United States of America by Random House,
an imprint and division of Penguin Random House LLC 2019
First published in Great Britain by Allen Lane 2019
004

Grateful acknowledgment is made to the following for permission
to reprint previously published text:
Alfred A. Knopf, an imprint of the Knopf Doubleday Publishing Group,
a division of Penguin Random House LLC: "Married" from *The Great Fire:
Poems, 1982–1992* by Jack Gilbert, copyright © 1994 by Jack Gilbert. Used by
permission of Alfred A. Knopf, an imprint of the Knopf Doubleday Publishing
Group, a division of Penguin Random House LLC. All rights reserved.
Random House, an imprint and division of Penguin Random House LLC:
Excerpt from "Leap Before You Look" from *Collected Poems* by W. H Auden,
copyright © 1945 and copyright renewed 1973 by W. H. Auden.
Used by permission of Random House, an imprint and division
of Penguin Random House LLC. All rights reserved.

Printed and bound in Great Britain by Clays Ltd, Elcograf S.p.A.

A CIP catalogue record for this book is available from the British Library

ISBN: 978–0–241–40063–0

www.greenpenguin.co.uk

MIX
Paper from
responsible sources
FSC
www.fsc.org   FSC® C018179

Penguin Random House is committed to a
sustainable future for our business, our readers
and our planet. This book is made from Forest
Stewardship Council® certified paper.

To Anne,
who has brought boundless joy

CONTENTS

Every once in a while, I meet a person who radiates joy. These are people who seem to glow with an inner light. They are kind, tranquil, delighted by small pleasures, and grateful for the large ones. These people are not perfect. They get exhausted and stressed. They make errors in judgment. But they live for others, and not for themselves. They've made unshakable commitments to family, a cause, a community, or a faith. They know why they were put on this earth and derive a deep satisfaction from doing what they have been called to do. Life isn't easy for these people. They've taken on the burdens of others. But they have a serenity about them, a settled resolve. They are interested in you, make you feel cherished and known, and take delight in your good.

When you meet these people, you realize that joy is not just a feeling, it can be an outlook. There are temporary highs we all get after we win some victory, and then there is also this other kind of permanent joy that animates people who are not obsessed with themselves but have given themselves away.

I often find that their life has what I think of as a two-mountain shape. They got out of school, began their career or started a family, and identified the mountain they thought they were meant to climb:

I'm going to be a cop, a doctor, an entrepreneur, what have you. On the first mountain, we all have to perform certain life tasks: establish an identity, separate from our parents, cultivate our talents, build a secure ego, and try to make a mark in the world. People climbing that first mountain spend a lot of time thinking about reputation management. They are always keeping score. How do I measure up? Where do I rank? As the psychologist James Hollis puts it, at that stage we have a tendency to think, I am what the world says I am.

The goals on that first mountain are the normal goals that our culture endorses—to be a success, to be well thought of, to get invited into the right social circles, and to experience personal happiness. It's all the normal stuff: nice home, nice family, nice vacations, good food, good friends, and so on.

Then something happens.

Some people get to the top of that first mountain, taste success, and find it . . . unsatisfying. "Is this all there is?" they wonder. They sense there must be a deeper journey they can take.

Other people get knocked off that mountain by some failure. Something happens to their career, their family, or their reputation. Suddenly life doesn't look like a steady ascent up the mountain of success; it has a different and more disappointing shape.

For still others, something unexpected happens that knocks them crossways: the death of a child, a cancer scare, a struggle with addiction, some life-altering tragedy that was not part of the original plan. Whatever the cause, these people are no longer on the mountain. They are down in the valley of bewilderment or suffering. This can happen at any age, by the way, from eight to eighty-five and beyond. It's never too early or too late to get knocked off your first mountain.

These seasons of suffering have a way of exposing the deepest parts of ourselves and reminding us that we're not the people we thought we were. People in the valley have been broken open. They have been reminded that they are not just the parts of themselves that they put on display. There is another layer to them they have been neglecting, a substrate where the dark wounds, and most powerful yearnings live.

Some shrivel in the face of this kind of suffering. They seem to get more afraid and more resentful. They shrink away from their inner depths in fear. Their lives become smaller and lonelier. We all know old people who nurse eternal grievances. They don't get the respect they deserve. They live their lives as an endless tantrum about some wrong done to them long ago.

But for others, this valley is the making of them. The season of suffering interrupts the superficial flow of everyday life. They see deeper into themselves and realize that down in the substrate, flowing from all the tender places, there is a fundamental ability to care, a yearning to transcend the self and care for others. And when they have encountered this yearning, they are ready to become a whole person. They see familiar things with new eyes. They are finally able to love their neighbor as themselves, not as a slogan but a practical reality. Their life is defined by how they react to their moment of greatest adversity.

The people who are made larger by suffering go on to stage two small rebellions. First, they rebel against their ego ideal. When they were on their first mountain, their ego had some vision of what it was shooting for—some vision of prominence, pleasure, and success. Down in the valley they lose interest in their ego ideal. Of course afterward they still feel and sometimes succumb to their selfish desires. But, overall, they realize the desires of the ego are never going to satisfy the deep regions they have discovered in themselves. They realize, as Henri Nouwen put it, that they are much better than their ego ideal.

Second, they rebel against the mainstream culture. All their lives they've been taking economics classes or living in a culture that teaches that human beings pursue self-interest—money, power, fame. But suddenly they are not interested in what other people tell them to want. They want to want the things that are truly worth wanting. They elevate their desires. The world tells them to be a good consumer, but they want to be the one consumed—by a moral cause. The world tells them to want independence, but they want interdependence—to be enmeshed in a web of warm relationships.

The world tells them to want individual freedom, but they want intimacy, responsibility, and commitment. The world wants them to climb the ladder and pursue success, but they want to be a person for others. The magazines on the magazine rack want them to ask "What can I do to make myself happy?" but they glimpse something bigger than personal happiness.

The people who have been made larger by suffering are brave enough to let parts of their old self die. Down in the valley, their motivations changed. They've gone from self-centered to other-centered.

At this point, people realize, Oh, that first mountain wasn't my mountain after all. There's another, bigger mountain out there that is actually my mountain. The second mountain is not the opposite of the first mountain. To climb it doesn't mean rejecting the first mountain. It's the journey after it. It's the more generous and satisfying phase of life.

Some people radically alter their lives when this happens. They give up their law practices and move to Tibet. They quit their jobs as consultants and become teachers in inner-city schools. Others stay in their basic fields but spend their time differently. I have a friend who built a successful business in the Central Valley of California. She still has her business but spends most of her time building preschools and health centers for the people who work in her company. She is on her second mountain.

Still others stay in their same jobs and their same marriages, but are transformed. It's not about self anymore; it's about a summons. If they are principals, their joy is in seeing their teachers shine. If they work in a company, they no longer see themselves as managers but as mentors; their energies are devoted to helping others get better. They want their organizations to be thick places, where people find purpose, and not thin places, where people come just to draw a salary.

In their book *Practical Wisdom*, psychologist Barry Schwartz and political scientist Kenneth Sharpe tell a story about a hospital janitor named Luke. In the hospital where Luke worked, there was a young man who'd gotten into a fight and was now in a coma, and he wasn't coming out. Every day, his father sat by his side in silent vigil, and had done so for six months. One day, Luke came in and cleaned the young man's room. His father wasn't there; he was out getting a smoke. Later that day, Luke ran into the father in the hallway. The father snapped at Luke and accused him of not cleaning his son's room.

The first-mountain response is to see your job as cleaning rooms. "I did clean your son's room," you would snap back. "It was just that you were out smoking." The second-mountain response is to see your job as serving patients and their families. It is to meet their needs at a time of crisis. That response says, This man needs comfort. Clean the room again.

And that's what Luke did. As he told an interviewer later, "I cleaned it so that he could see me cleaning it. . . . I can understand how he could be. It was like six months that his son was there. He'd been a little frustrated, and I cleaned it again. But I wasn't angry with him. I guess I could understand."

Or take Abraham Lincoln. As a young man, Lincoln had a ferocious hunger for fame and power, to the point where he was scared by the intensity of his own hunger. But preserving the Union was a summons so great that considerations of self no longer mattered. He left personal reputation behind and set off on his second mountain.

One day in November 1861, he paid a call to the home of General George McClellan, hoping to press him, in person, to take the fight to the Confederacy more aggressively. When Lincoln arrived, McClellan was not at home, so Lincoln told the butler that he, Secretary of State William Seward, and an aide, John Hay, would wait in the parlor. An hour later, McClellan arrived home and walked past the room where the president was waiting. Lincoln waited another thirty minutes. The butler returned to say that McClellan had decided to retire for the night and would see Lincoln some other time. McClellan was playing power games with Lincoln.

Hay was incensed. Who has the gall to treat the president of the United States with such disrespect? Lincoln, however, was unruffled. "Better at this time," he told Seward and Hay, "not to be making points of etiquette and personal dignity." This wasn't about him. His pride was not at stake. He would be willing to wait forever if he could find a general who would fight for the Union. By this point Lincoln had given himself away. The cause was the center of his life. His ultimate appeal was to something outside, not inside.

That's the crucial way to tell whether you are on your first or second mountain. Where is your ultimate appeal? To self, or to something outside of self?

If the first mountain is about building up the ego and defining the self, the second mountain is about shedding the ego and losing the self. If the first mountain is about acquisition, the second mountain is about contribution. If the first mountain is elitist—moving up—the second mountain is egalitarian—planting yourself amid those who need, and walking arm in arm with them.

You don't climb the second mountain the way you climb the first mountain. You conquer your first mountain. You identify the summit, and you claw your way toward it. You are conquered by your second mountain. You surrender to some summons, and you do everything necessary to answer the call and address the problem or injustice that is in front of you. On the first mountain you tend to be ambitious, strategic, and independent. On the second mountain you tend to be relational, intimate, and relentless.

It's gotten so I can recognize first- and second-mountain people. The first-mountain people are often cheerful, interesting, and fun to be around. They often have impressive jobs and can take you to an amazing variety of great restaurants. The second-mountain people aren't averse to the pleasures of the world. They delight in a good glass of wine or a nice beach. (There's nothing worse than people who are so spiritualized they don't love the world.) But they have surpassed these pleasures in pursuit of moral joy, a feeling that they have aligned their life toward some ultimate good. If they have to choose, they choose joy.

Their days are often exhausting, because they have put themselves out for people, and those people fill their days with requests and demands. But they are living at a fuller amplitude, activating deeper parts of themselves and taking on broader responsibilities. They have decided that, as C. S. Lewis put it, "The load, or weight, or burden of my neighbor's glory should be laid daily on my back, a load so heavy that only humility can carry it, and the backs of the proud will be broken."

I've come to recognize first- and second-mountain organizations, too. Sometimes you work at a company or go to a college, and it doesn't really leave a mark on you. You get out of it what you came for, and you leave. Second-mountain organizations touch people at their depths and leave a permanent mark. You always know when you meet a Marine, a Morehouse man, a Juilliard pianist, a NASA scientist. These institutions have a collective purpose, a shared set of rituals, a common origin story. They nurture thick relationships and demand full commitment. They don't merely educate; they transform.

THE PLAN

The first purpose of this book is to show how individuals move from the first to the second mountain, to show what that kind of deeper and more joyful life looks like, step-by-step and in concrete detail. Everybody says you should serve a cause larger than yourself, but nobody tells you how.

The second purpose is to show how societies can move from the first to the second mountain. This is ultimately a book about renewal, how things that are divided and alienated can find new wholeness. Our society suffers from a crisis of connection, a crisis of solidarity. We live in a culture of hyper-individualism. There is always a tension between self and society, between the individual and the group. Over the past sixty years we have swung too far toward the self. The only way out is to rebalance, to build a culture that steers people toward relation, community, and commitment—the things we most deeply yearn for, yet undermine with our hyper-individualistic way of life.

In the first section I'm going to give a fuller account of how the two-mountain life happens. I'll take us up the slope of the first mountain, down the back slope into the valley, and then up the second mountain. Please don't take this metaphor too literally. There is, of course, no one formula that covers how all lives happen. (My wife, for example, seems to have climbed her second mountain first. Unlike most of us, she was raised in an environment that emphasized moral commitment, not individual success.) I'm using this two-mountain metaphor to render in narrative form two different moral ethoses by which people can live—a life lived for self and a life lived as a gift for others. I want to show how this first mode, which is common in our culture, doesn't satisfy. I'll describe some of the experiences people have on their way to more fulfilling lives, and share the important truths they discover. Most of us get better at living, get deeper and wiser as we go, and this book seeks to capture how that happens.

In the second half of the book, I'll describe how people live with a second-mountain mentality. People on the first mountain have lives that are mobile and lightly attached. People on the second mountain are deeply rooted and deeply committed. The second-mountain life is a committed life. When I'm describing how second-mountain people live, what I'm really describing is how these people made maximal commitments to others and how they live them out in fervent, all-in ways. These people are not keeping their options open. They are planted. People on the second mountain have made strong commitments to one or all of these four things:

A vocation
A spouse and family
A philosophy or faith
A community

A commitment is making a promise to something without expecting a reward. A commitment is falling in love with something and then building a structure of behavior around it for those moments when love falters. In this second section of this book I will try to describe commitment making: how people are called by a vocation and then live it out; how they decide who to marry and thrive in marriage; how they come up with their philosophy of life and how they experience faith; how they are seized by a desire to serve their community; and how they work with others to help their communities prosper.

The fulfillment of our lives depends on how well we choose and live out those sometimes clashing commitments.

Some of the people I'll be describing in these pages lived their lives at a very high level. Realistically, you and I are not going to live as self-sacrificially as they did. We'll fall short because we're ordinary human beings, and we're still going to be our normal self-centered selves more than we care to admit. But it is still important to set a high standard. It is still important to be inspired by the examples of others and to remember that a life of deep commitments is possible. When we fall short, it will be because of our own limitations, not because we had an inadequate ideal.

WHAT I'VE LEARNED

The first- and second-mountain distinction might sound a little like the résumé virtues versus eulogy virtues distinction I made in my last book, *The Road to Character*. And now I should confess that I'm writing this book in part to compensate for the limitations of that one. The people I described in *The Road to Character* have a lot to teach us. But a book is written in a particular time, at a particular spot on one's journey. The five years since I finished that book have been the most tumultuous years of my life. Those years—sometimes painful, sometimes joyous—have been an advanced education in the art and pitfalls of living. They have taken me a lot further down the road toward understanding.

When I wrote *The Road to Character*, I was still enclosed in the prison of individualism. I believed that life is going best when we take individual agency, when we grab the wheel and steer our own ship. I still believed that character is something you build mostly on your own. You identify your core sin and then, mustering all your willpower, you make yourself strong in your weakest places.

I no longer believe that character formation is mostly an individual task, or is achieved on a person-by-person basis. I no longer believe that character building is like going to the gym: You do your exercises and you build up your honesty, courage, integrity, and grit. I now think good character is a by-product of giving yourself away. You love things that are worthy of love. You surrender to a community or cause, make promises to other people, build a thick jungle of loving attachments, lose yourself in the daily act of serving others as they lose themselves in the daily acts of serving you. Character is a good thing to have, and there's a lot to be learned on the road to character. But there's a better thing to have—moral joy. And that serenity arrives as you come closer to embodying perfect love.

Furthermore, I no longer believe that the cultural and moral structures of our society are fine, and all we have to do is fix ourselves individually. Over the past few years, as a result of personal, national, and global events, I have become radicalized.

I now think the rampant individualism of our current culture is a catastrophe. The emphasis on self—individual success, self-fulfillment, individual freedom, self-actualization—is a catastrophe. I now think that living a good life requires a much vaster transformation. It's not enough to work on your own weaknesses. The whole cultural paradigm has to shift from the mindset of hyper-individualism to the relational mindset of the second mountain.

WHY WE ARE HERE

I've written this book, in part, to remind myself of the kind of life I want to live. Those of us who are writers work out our stuff in public, even under the guise of pretending to write about someone else. In other words, we try to teach what it is that we really need to learn. My first mountain was an insanely lucky one. I achieved far more professional success than I ever expected to. But that climb turned me into a certain sort of person: aloof, invulnerable, and uncommunicative, at least when it came to my private life. I sidestepped the responsibilities of relationship. My ex-wife and I have an agreement that we don't talk about our marriage and divorce in public. But when I look back generally on the errors and failures and sins of my life, they tend to be failures of omission, failures to truly show up for the people I should have been close to. They tend to be the sins of withdrawal: evasion, workaholism, conflict avoidance, failure to empathize, and a failure to express myself openly. I have two old and dear friends who live 250 miles from me, for example, and their side of the friendship has required immense forbearance and forgiveness, for all the times I've been too busy, too disorganized, too distant when they were in need or just available. I look at those dear friendships with a gratitude mixed with shame, and this pattern—not being present to what I love because I prioritize time over people, productivity over relationship—is a recurring motif in my life.

The wages of sin are sin. My faults accumulated and then crashed down upon me in 2013. In that year, life put me in the valley. The realities that used to define my life fell away. Our marriage of twenty-seven years ended, and, in the wake of that failed commitment, I moved into an apartment. My children were emerging into adulthood and had either left home for college or were preparing to. I still got to see them when we went out to dinner and such, but I missed those fifteen-second encounters in the hallway or kitchen at home. I had spent my adult life in the conservative movement, but my conservatism was no longer the prevailing conservatism, so I found myself intellectually and politically unattached, too. Much of my social life had been spent in conservative circles, and those connections drifted away. I realized I had a lot of friendships that didn't run deep. Few people confided in me, because I did not give off a vibe that encouraged vulnerability. I was too busy, on the move.

I was unplanted, lonely, humiliated, scattered. I remember walking through that period in a state that resembled permanent drunkenness—my emotions were all on the surface, my playlists were all Irish heartbreak songs by Sinéad O'Connor and Snow Patrol. I was throwing myself needily upon my friends in ways that are embarrassing now if I stop to remember them, which I try not to. I was unattached, wondering what the rest of my life should be, confronting the problems of a twenty-two-year-old with the mind of a fifty-two-year-old.

Having failed at a commitment, I've spent the ensuing five years thinking and reading about how to do commitments well, how to give your life meaning after worldly success has failed to fulfill. This book is a product of that search. Writing it was my attempt to kick myself in my own rear, part of my continual effort to write my way to a better life. "A book must be the axe for the frozen sea within us," Kafka wrote. It should wake us up and hammer at our skull. Writing this book has served that purpose for me.

I've also written it, I hope, for you. When it comes to what we writers do, I like to apply an observation by D. T. Niles: We are like beggars who try to show other beggars where we found bread. You have to get only a few pages into this book to realize that I quote a lot of people wiser than myself. I mean a *lot* of people. I'm unapologetic about this. It's occurred to me many times over the course of writing this book that maybe I'm not really a writer. I'm a teacher or middle-man. I take the curriculum of other people's knowledge and I pass it along.

Finally, I write it as a response to the current historical moment. For six decades the worship of the self has been the central preoccupation of our culture—molding the self, investing in the self, expressing the self. Capitalism, the meritocracy, and modern social science have normalized selfishness; they have made it seem that the only human motives that are real are the self-interested ones—the desire for money, status, and power. They silently spread the message that giving, care, and love are just icing on the cake of society.

When a whole society is built around self-preoccupation, its members become separated from one another, divided and alienated. And that is what has happened to us. We are down in the valley. The rot we see in our politics is caused by a rot in our moral and cultural foundations—in the way we relate to one another, in the way we see ourselves as separable from one another, in the individualistic values that have become the water in which we swim. The first-mountain culture has proven insufficient, as it always does.

Our society has become a conspiracy against joy. It has put too much emphasis on the individuating part of our consciousness—individual reason—and too little emphasis on the bonding parts of our consciousness, the heart and soul. We've seen a shocking rise of mental illness, suicide, and distrust. We have become too cognitive when we should be more emotional; too utilitarian when we should be using a moral lens; too individualistic when we should be more communal.

So we as people and as a society have to find our second mountain. This doesn't mean rejecting the things we achieved on the first mountain—the nice job, the nice home, the pleasures of a comfortable life. We all need daily ego boosts throughout our lives. But it does require a shift in culture—a shift in values and philosophy, a renegotiation of the structure of power in our society. It's about shifting from one mode of thinking toward another. It's about finding an ethos that puts commitment making at the center of things.

The good news is that what we give to our community in pennies, our communities give back to us in dollars. If there is one thing I have learned over the past five years, it is that the world is more enchanted, stranger, more mystical, and more interconnected than anything we could have envisioned when we were on the first mountain.

Most of the time we aim too low. We walk in shoes too small for us. We spend our days shooting for a little burst of approval or some small career victory. But there's a joyful way of being that's not just a little bit better than the way we are currently living; it's a quantum leap better. It's as if we're all competing to get a little closer to a sunlamp. If we get up and live a different way, we can bathe in real sunshine.

When I meet people leading lives of deep commitment, this fact hits me: Joy is real.

JOY

Before I start describing the journey across the two mountains, I want to pause over that last point—the one about joy being real. Our public conversation is muddled about the definition of a good life. Often, we say a good life is a happy life. We live, as it says in our founding document, in pursuit of happiness.

In all forms of happiness we feel good, elated, uplifted. But the word "happiness" can mean a lot of different things. So it's important to make a distinction between happiness and joy.

What's the difference? Happiness involves a victory for the self, an expansion of self. Happiness comes as we move toward our goals, when things go our way. You get a big promotion. You graduate from college. Your team wins the Super Bowl. You have a delicious meal. Happiness often has to do with some success, some new ability, or some heightened sensual pleasure.

Joy tends to involve some transcendence of self. It's when the skin barrier between you and some other person or entity fades away and you feel fused together. Joy is present when mother and baby are gazing adoringly into each other's eyes, when a hiker is overwhelmed by beauty in the woods and feels at one with nature, when a gaggle of friends are dancing deliriously in unison. Joy often involves self-forgetting. Happiness is what we aim for on the first mountain. Joy is a by-product of living on the second mountain.

We can help create happiness, but we are seized by joy. We are pleased by happiness, but we are transformed by joy. When we experience joy we often feel we have glimpsed into a deeper and truer layer of reality. A narcissist can be happy, but a narcissist can never be joyful, because the surrender of self is the precise thing a narcissist can't do. A narcissist can't even conceive of joy. That's one of the problems with being stuck on the first mountain: You can't even see what the second mountain offers.

My core point is that happiness is good, but joy is better. Just as the second mountain is a fuller and richer phase of life after the first mountain, joy is a fuller and richer state beyond happiness. Moreover, while happiness tends to be fickle and fleeting, joy can be fundamental and enduring. The more you are living a committed life well, the more joy will be your steady state, the frame of mind you carry around with you and shine on others. You will become a joyful person. So throughout this book as in life, joy is our north star, our navigating point. If we steer toward joy, we will wind up at the right spot.

THE LEVELS OF JOY

A few years ago, I started collecting joy. Or, more accurately, I started collecting accounts of joy. I collected people's descriptions of what it felt like when life seemed to be at its peak, in those moments when life felt fullest, most meaningful, and most complete.

When I look over my collection now, I realize that there are different layers of joy. First, there is physical joy. There are moments when you are doing some physical activity, often in rhythm with other people, when you experience flow. In *Anna Karenina*, Levin is out cutting grass with the men who work on the farm. At first Levin is clumsy with his scythe, but then he learns the motion and cuts clean, straight rows. "The longer Levin mowed, the more often he felt those moments of oblivion during which it was no longer his arms that swung the scythe, but the scythe itself that lent motion to his whole body, full of life and conscious of itself, and, as if by magic, without a thought of it, the work got rightly and neatly done on its own. These were the most blissful moments."

Flow is especially wonderful when it is collective flow, something you experience with your team or unit. My former history professor William McNeill experienced that after he was drafted into the army in 1941. In boot camp he was taught to march with the other men in his unit. He began to experience strange sensations while marching: "Words are inadequate to describe the emotion aroused by the prolonged movement in unison that drilling involved. A sense of pervasive well-being is what I recall; more specifically, a strange sense of personal enlargement; a sort of swelling out, becoming bigger than life, thanks to participation in collective ritual."

The next layer of joy is collective effervescence, celebratory dance. In almost every culture, stretching back through time, joyous moments are celebrated and enhanced with rhythmic dancing. I write this the morning after attending the wedding of one of my friends, an Orthodox Jew. After the ceremony, we men danced around the groom as the music raced. We were tightly packed, circling around him, and he was in the center of the whirl, jumping up and down with wild abandon. Every few minutes he would call different people—his grandfather, a friend, even me—to come to the white-hot center and bounce with joy with him and swing our arms and roar in laughter.

The writer Zadie Smith once described being in a nightclub in London in 1999. She was wandering about, looking for her friends, wondering where her handbag was, when suddenly a song by A Tribe Called Quest came on. At that point, she wrote,

A rail-thin man with enormous eyes reached across a sea of bodies for my hand. He kept asking me the same thing over and over: *"You feeling it?"* I was. My ridiculous heels were killing me. I was terrified I might die, yet I felt simultaneously overwhelmed with delight that "Can I Kick It?" should happen to be playing at this precise moment in the history of the world, and was now morphing into "Smells Like Teen Spirit." I took the man's hand. The top of my head flew away. We danced and danced. We gave ourselves up to joy.

In this kind of joy, like all joy, the cage of self-consciousness falls away, and people are fused with those around them. This kind of joy is all present tense; people are captured by and fully alive in the moment.

The third layer of joy is what you might call emotional joy. This is the sudden bursting of love that you see, for example, on the face of a mother when she first lays eyes on her infant. Dorothy Day captured it beautifully: "If I had written the greatest book, composed the greatest symphony, painted the most beautiful painting or carved the most exquisite figure, I could not have felt the more exalted creator than I did when they placed my child in my arms. . . . No human creature could receive or contain so vast a flood of love and joy as I felt after the birth of my child. With this came the need to worship, to adore."

This kind of joy is intimate and powerful. I often speak of the time, more than a decade ago now, when I came home from work one summer evening and pulled into the driveway on the side of the house and found my three kids, then twelve, nine, and four, playing with a plastic ball in the backyard. They were kicking it in the air and then racing one another across the grass to catch it. They were giggling and tumbling all over one another and having a deliriously good time. I sat there in the car looking at this tableau of family happiness through the windshield. The summer sun glowed through the trees. My lawn, for some reason, looked perfect. I experienced a sort of liquid joy and overflowing gratitude that seemed to stop time, that made my heart swell. I'm sure all parents have experienced something like this.

Emotional joy can often happen early in a romantic relationship. Fresh lovers glow at each other across a picnic blanket. Or it can happen later. Old couples can feel like they are deeper in each other than they are in themselves. You'll hear people in happy marriages talk this way: When I make love to her, I disappear.

The writer David Whyte makes the core point. "Joy," he writes,

> is the meeting place, of deep intentionality and self-forgetting, the bodily alchemy of what lies inside us in communion with what formally seemed outside, but is now neither, but becomes a living frontier, a voice speaking between us and the world: dance, laughter, affection, skin touching skin, singing in the car, music in the kitchen, the quiet irreplaceable and companionable presence of a daughter: the sheer intoxicating beauty of the world inhabited as an edge between what we previously thought was us and what we thought was other than us.

The fourth layer of joy is spiritual joy. Sometimes joy comes not through movement, not through love, but from an unexpected contact with something that seems boundaryless, pure spirit. Joy comes with a sensation that, as the writer Jerry Root, citing C .S. Lewis, put it, all reality is iconoclastic—the world is enchanted by a mystical force.

One day, while he was living in Prague, the poet Christian Wiman was working in his kitchen when a falcon landed on the windowsill, about three feet from him. The bird scanned the trees below and the building across the street, but didn't yet turn to look at Wiman. Wiman was transfixed. He called out to his girlfriend, who was in the bath, to come see, and she came out, dripping, and stood next to him, staring at the falcon. "Wish for something," she whispered. Then the falcon turned its head and locked his eyes with Wiman's, and Wiman felt some bottom fall out within him. He later wrote a poem about that moment, which includes this stanza:

> *For a long moment I'm still in*
> *I wished and wished and wished*

the moment would not end.
And just like that it vanished.

This kind of spiritual joy often involves mystical attunement. Tolstoy's mother died when he was a young boy, and before the funeral he found himself in a room alone with her open casket. He climbed up on a chair to look down on her and experienced a strange peacefulness. "Somehow as I gazed, an irrepressible, incomprehensible power seemed to compel me," he later wrote. "For a time I lost all sense of existence and experienced a kind of vague blissfulness which though grand and sweet, was also sad." Then a man walked into the room and Tolstoy realized that the man might think him unfeeling if he wore a blissful look on his face, so to keep with social convention, he pretended to burst out crying. "This egotistic consciousness completely annulled any element of sincerity in my woe."

We are climbing now, to higher and higher experiences of joy. The fifth layer of joy is transcendent joy, feeling at one with nature, the universe, or God. In *Backpacking with the Saints*, Belden Lane describes the experience of hiking this way:

Whenever I plunge into wilderness, my body and the environment move in and out of each other in an intimate pattern of exchange. I wade through water and inhale air filled with the scent of honeysuckle. I'm wrapped in cobwebs and pierced by briars. I swallow gnats drawn to the sweat on my body and feel the rocks on the trail through my boots. Where I "end" and everything else "begins" isn't always clear. What seems to be "me" doesn't stop at the fixed boundary of my skin.

Such transcendent moments can last only a few minutes, but they can alter a lifetime. People have a sense that they are seeing into the hidden reality of things, and afterward they can never go back and be content to watch pale shadows dancing on the wall of the cave. Ralph Waldo Emerson built a philosophy off such moments of transcendence. "Standing on the bare ground—my head bathed by the blithe air and uplifted into infinite space—all mean egotism vanishes. I become the transparent eyeball; I am nothing; I see all; the currents of the Universal Being circulate through me."

This kind of joy is a delicious, if painful, longing. It starts with a taste of something eternal and then the joy consists of longing for that taste again. The joy, as C. S. Lewis put it, is not the satisfaction of the longing but the longing itself. Saint Augustine felt God's love as a delicious and fervent hunger: "You called, shouted, broke through my deafness; you flared, blazed, banished my blindness; you lavished your fragrance, I gasped; and now I pant for you; I tasted you, and now I hunger and thirst; you touched me, and I burned for your peace."

Other people, though not explicitly religious, also experience moments when love seems to shine down on them. Jules Evans was skiing at age twenty-four when he fell off a cliff, dropped thirty feet, and broke his leg and back. "As I lay there I felt immersed in love and light. I'd been suffering from emotional problems for six years and feared my ego was permanently damaged. In that moment, I knew that I was OK, I was loved, that there was something in me that could not be damaged, call it 'the soul,' or 'the self,' 'pure consciousness' or what have you."

In 2016, the Gallup organization asked Americans if they had had a mystical experience, a moment when they went beyond their ordinary self and felt connected to some infinity. Eighty-four percent of respondents said they had had such an experience at least once, even as 75 percent said there's a social taboo against speaking about it in public.

MORAL JOY

Here I want to shift now to the highest layer of joy, which I'll call moral joy. I say this is the highest form of joy in part because this is the kind that even the skeptics can't explain away. The skeptics could say that all those other kinds of passing joy are just brain chemicals in some weird formation that happened to have kicked in to produce odd sensations. But moral joy has an extra feature. It can become permanent. Some people live joyfully day by day. Their daily actions are aligned with their ultimate commitments. They have given themselves away, united and wholeheartedly. They are so grateful to have found their place and taken their stand. They have the inner light.

Pope Francis seems to have this, and so, it is said, do Bishop Tutu and Paul Farmer. So do Geoffrey Canada, who founded the Harlem Children's Zone, and the great cellist Yo-Yo Ma. I once was seated with the Dalai Lama at a lunch in Washington. He didn't say anything particularly illuminating or profound during the lunch, but every once in a while he just burst out laughing for no apparent reason. He would laugh, and I wanted to be polite, so I would laugh, too. He laughed. I laughed. He is just a joyful man. Ebullience is his resting state.

This kind of moral joy can start out as a surge of what the social psychologists call "moral elevation." For example, a researcher working for the social psychologist Jonathan Haidt interviewed a woman who volunteered at the Salvation Army one winter's morning with a few other people from her church. One of the other volunteers offered to give a bunch of them a ride home. It had been snowing solidly that morning. As they were driving through a residential neighborhood they saw an older lady standing in her driveway with a snow shovel. At the next intersection one of the guys in the backseat asked to be dropped off there. They let him out of the car, figuring he was close to home.

But instead of going into some nearby house, he walked up to the lady, took her shovel, and started shoveling her driveway. One of the women in the car witnessed this and recalled, "I felt like jumping out of the car and hugging this guy. I felt like singing and running, or skipping and laughing. Just being active. I felt like saying nice things about people. Writing a beautiful poem or love song. Playing in the snow like a child. Telling everybody about his deed. . . . My spirit was lifted even higher than it already was. I was joyous, happy, smiling, energized. I went home and gushed to my suite-mates, who clutched at their hearts." As Haidt notes, powerful moments of moral elevation seem to push a mental reset button, wiping out feelings of cynicism and replacing them with feelings of hope, love, and moral inspiration.

These moments of elevation are energizing. People feel strongly motivated to do something good themselves, to act, to dare, to sacrifice, to help others.

When people make generosity part of their daily routine, they refashion who they are. The interesting thing about your personality, your essence, is that it is not more or less permanent like your leg bone. Your essence is changeable, like your mind. Every action you take, every thought you have, changes you, even if just a little, making you a little more elevated or a little more degraded. If you do a series of good deeds, the habit of other-centeredness becomes gradually engraved into your life. It becomes easier to do good deeds down the line. If you lie or behave callously or cruelly toward someone, your personality degrades, and it is easier for you to do something even worse later on. As the criminologists say, the people who commit murder don't start there. They have to walk through a lot of doors before they get to the point where they can take another human life.

The people who radiate a permanent joy have given themselves over to lives of deep and loving commitment. Giving has become their nature, and little by little they have made their souls incandescent. There's always something flowing out of the interiority of our spirit. For some people it's mostly fear or insecurity. For the people we call joyful, it's mostly gratitude, delight, and kindness.

How do you build your personality to glow in this way? You might think a bright personality would come from an unburdened life—a life of pleasures and constant delights. But if you closely look at joyful people, you notice that very often the people who have the most incandescent souls have taken on the heaviest burdens.

Benjamin Hardy is a writer who described his decision to take on three foster children in *Inc.* magazine. "Before having that personal load to carry, I was somewhat complacent. I lacked the urgency. I didn't have the traction to move forward," he writes. "A life of ease is not the pathway to growth and happiness. On the contrary, a life of ease is how you get stuck and confused in life." Taking on those kids meant knowing more about frustration, anxiety, and fatigue, but also elation, sweetness, and especially caring love. Happiness can be tasted alone. But permanent joy comes out of an enmeshed and embedded life. Happiness happens when a personal desire is fulfilled. Permanent moral joy seems to emerge when desire is turned outward for others.

Gregory Boyle ministers to gang members in Los Angeles and captures the difference between a life lived for self and one lived for others: "Compassion is always, at its most authentic, about a shift from the cramped world of self-preoccupation into a more expansive place of fellowship." It's one of the inescapable truisms of life: You have to lose yourself to find yourself, give yourself away to get everything back.

You might think this kind of life of joyous service is rare. But in the spring of 2018, I began a project called Weave: The Social Fabric Project at the Aspen Institute. The idea is to shine attention on the people who are doing the grassroots work of community building and relationship repair. In the course of that work I've found myself surrounded by incandescent people almost every day.

There is Stephanie Hruzek in Houston, sitting cross-legged on the floor with kids at FamilyPoint, her after-school program, gleefully repeating tongue twisters with them: "Say 'Unique New York' ten times fast!" There is Kate Garvin in Colorado, being greeted by squeals of delight when she comes across a Somali refugee she is helping to integrate into the local school system. There's Don Flow, who owns a chain of car dealerships in North Carolina and who radiates a quiet satisfaction showing the community center he built in Winston-Salem. There's Harlan Crow, a real estate developer whose every moment, it seems, is devoted to helping the people around him be more comfortable.

There is Mack McCarter, founder of Community Renewal International in Shreveport, Louisiana. Mack is in his seventies. He's one of those people when the first time he walks into a coffee shop he learns everybody's first name and has a joke and story for them all. By his third visit he's everybody's old friend. By his fifth, they want him to officiate at their wedding. People just want to be around the guy because he is flowing joy.

I ask these people what brings joy to their daily lives. The answer is always a variation on the same theme—some moment when they brought delight to another. "There is joy in self-forgetfulness," Helen Keller observed. "So I try to make the light in others' eyes my sun, the music in others' ears my symphony, the smile on others' lips my happiness."

Miroslav Volf is a professor at Yale who has made studying joy his specialty. Joy is not a self-standing emotion, he concludes. It is the crown of a well-lived life. "Joy is not merely external to the good life, a mint leaf on the cake's whipped cream. Rather, the good life expresses and manifests itself in joy. Joy is the emotional dimension of life that goes well and that is led well, a positive affective response to life going well and life being led well."

Happiness is the proper goal for people on their first mountain. And happiness is great. But we only get one life, so we might as well use it hunting for big game: to enjoy happiness, but to surpass happiness toward joy.

Happiness tends to be individual; we measure it by asking, "Are you happy?" Joy tends to be self-transcending. Happiness is something you pursue; joy is something that rises up unexpectedly and sweeps over you. Happiness comes from accomplishments; joy comes from offering gifts. Happiness fades; we get used to the things that used to make us happy. Joy doesn't fade. To live with joy is to live with wonder, gratitude, and hope. People who are on the second mountain have been transformed. They are deeply committed. The outpouring of love has become a steady force.

PART I
The Two Mountains

Moral Ecologies

WHEN I WAS A YOUNG TV PUNDIT, I WORKED WITH JIM LEHRER, WHO cofounded a program that is now called the *PBS NewsHour*. When Jim was on the air and delivering the news, his face tended to be warm but stoical, because he did not think he should be the story; the news should be the story. But when the camera was not on him, his face was incredibly expressive. When I was talking on our segment and I said something cheap or crass, I would see his mouth turn down in displeasure. But when I said something that was useful, civil, or amusing, I would see his eyes crinkle with pleasure. For ten years, working with a man I deeply admired, I tried to behave in a way that would produce the eye crinkle and not the mouth downturn.

Lehrer never had to formally tell me how to behave, but in this subtle and wordless way, he trained me to meet the *NewsHour* standards of what is right. And he didn't offer these reactions just to me; he offered them to everyone on staff, show after show, year after year. In this way, he created the *NewsHour* way of being, a moral ecology in which certain values were prioritized, and certain ways of being expected. It's been several years since Lehrer retired, but the culture he instilled still defines the *NewsHour* today.

We all grew up in one moral ecology or another. We all create microcultures around us by the way we lead our lives and the vibes we send out to those around us. One of the greatest legacies a person can leave is a moral ecology—a system of belief and behavior that lives on after they die.

Some moral ecologies are local, in a home or office, but some are vast and define whole eras and civilizations. The classical Greeks and Romans had their honor code with its vision of immortal fame. In the late nineteenth century, Parisian artists invented a bohemian code celebrating individual freedom and wild creativity, while across the Channel, Victorian morality was beginning to form, with its strict codes of propriety and respectability. Moral ecologies subtly guide how you dress, how you talk, what you admire and disdain, and how you define your ultimate purpose.

Moral ecologies are collective responses to the big problems of a specific moment. For example, around the middle third of the twentieth century, people in the Northern Hemisphere faced a great depression and a cataclysmic world war. Big problems required big institutional responses. People joined armies, formed unions, worked at big companies. They bonded tightly together as warring nations. Therefore, a culture developed that emphasized doing your duty, fitting into institutions, conforming to the group, deferring to authority, not trying to stick out or get too big for your britches. This group-oriented moral ecology could be summed up by the phrase "We're All in This Together."

The spirit of this culture was nicely captured in a book by Alan Ehrenhalt called *The Lost City*, about some of the communities around and in Chicago in the 1950s. There wasn't a lot of emphasis put on individual choice back then. If you were a star baseball player like Ernie Banks, you didn't have the option of becoming a free agent. You spent your career as a Chicago Cub. If you had the wrong accent or the wrong skin color or were the wrong gender, you probably couldn't get a job at one of the fancy office buildings downtown. But people back then tended to have steady attachments and a stable connection to place. They did their duty for their institutions.

If you were a man who lived on Chicago's South Side, there's a good chance you followed your father and grandfather into the Nabisco plant, the largest bakery in the world at that time, and joined the union, the Bakery and Confectionery Workers International.

The houses were small, there was no air-conditioning, and TV had not yet penetrated, so when the weather was warm, social life was conducted on the front stoops, in the alleys, and with children running from house to house all day. A young homeowner was enveloped in a series of communal activities that, as Ehrenhalt puts it, "only the most determined loner could escape: barbecues, coffee klatches, volleyball games, baby-sitting co-ops and the constant bartering of household goods."

If you went to the bank you went to the local bank, Talman Federal Savings and Loan. If you bought meat you went to the local butcher, Bertucci's. Sixty-two percent of Americans in those days said they were active church members, and if you lived in that neighborhood in Chicago, you went to St. Nick's Parish, where you listened to the kindly Father Fennessy say mass in Latin. You probably sent your boys to the local parochial school, where they sat in neat rows and quaked under the iron discipline of Father Lynch.

If you went into politics, you probably couldn't win as a freelancer. But you could join Boss Daley's machine and thrive, provided you did what your authority figures told you to do. For example, John Fary served the machine in the Illinois state legislature, and when he was sixty-four he was rewarded with a seat in the U.S. Congress. When asked what he was going to do once elected to Congress, he told the press, "I will go to Washington to help represent Mayor Daley. For twenty-one years, I represented the mayor in the legislature, and he was always right." He did his duty.

The ethos nurtured the sort of rich, community life that many people pine for today. If somebody asked you where you were from, you didn't just say "Chicago," you mentioned the specific intersection your life revolved around: "Fifty-ninth and Pulaski." The city was a collection of villages.

That moral ecology had a lot of virtues. It emphasized humility, reticence, and self-effacement. The message was you're no better than anybody else, but nobody is better than you. It held that self-love—egotism, narcissism—is the root of much evil. If you talked about yourself too much, people would call you conceited, and they would turn up their nose.

Of course, this culture had failings, which ultimately made it intolerable. This moral ecology tolerated a lot of racism and anti-Semitism. Housewives felt trapped and stifled, and professional women faced daunting barriers. In 1963, Betty Friedan described a problem that had no name, which was the flattening, crushing boredom of many female lives. The culture had an emotionally cold definition of masculinity; men had trouble expressing their love for their wives and children. The food was really boring. People felt imprisoned by the pressure of group conformity and tortured by the intolerant tyranny of local opinion. Many played out their assigned social roles, but they were dead inside.

There's a scene in John Steinbeck's 1962 book *Travels with Charley* that captures how this communal code trapped many people in numb, joyless lives. Steinbeck's cross-country journey with his dog has taken him to Chicago, and he needs a hotel room right away, so he can shower and rest. The only room the manager has available has not been cleaned yet, but Steinbeck says he'll take it anyway.

When he opens the door, he sees the detritus of the previous guest's stay. From a leftover dry-cleaning receipt, Steinbeck deduces that the previous resident, whom he calls Lonesome Harry, lives in Westport, Connecticut. On the desk is a letter he had started to his wife on the hotel stationery. "I wish you were hear [*sic*] with me. This is a lonesome town. You forgot to put in my cuff links."

It's a good thing Harry's wife didn't make a surprise visit. Both a highball glass and half the cigarette butts in the ashtray have lipstick on them. The hairpin by the bed reveals that the woman who had been in the room was a brunette; Steinbeck begins to think of her as Lucille. They drank an entire bottle of Jack Daniel's together. The second pillow on the bed had been used but not slept on—no lipstick traces. The woman had let Harry get drunk, but she secretly poured her whiskey into the vase of red roses on the desk.

"I wonder what Harry and Lucille talked about," Steinbeck writes. "I wonder whether she made him less lonesome. Somehow I doubt it. I think both of them were doing what was expected of them." Harry shouldn't have drunk so much. Steinbeck found Tums wrappers in the wastebasket and two foil tubes of Bromo-Seltzer in the bathroom. There was no sign of anything unexpected, Steinbeck wrote, no sign of any real fun, no sign of spontaneous joy. Just loneliness. "I felt sad about Harry," he concluded. This was what happened when your life was lived in a drab manner serving some soulless organization. Not only were you unfulfilled, you lost the capacity to even feel anything.

There was a lot of commentary in those days about the soul-sucking perils of conformity, of being nothing more than an organization man, the man in the gray flannel suit, a numb status seeker. There was a sense that the group had crushed the individual, and that people, reduced to a number, had no sense of an authentic self.

I'M FREE TO BE MYSELF

Steinbeck published *Travels with Charley* at just about the time that people were beginning to rebel against the "We're All in This Together" moral ecology of the postwar years, and put a new one in its place. The parade of moral ecologies is usually a story of progress, a rational response to the obsolescence of what came before. Nonetheless, this progress is a bumpy kind of progress.

Often it happens in what geographer Ruth DeFries calls the "ratchet, hatchet, pivot; ratchet" pattern. People create a moral ecology that helps them solve the problems of their moment. That ecology works, and society ratchets upward. But over time the ecology becomes less relevant to new problems that arise. The old culture grows rigid, and members of a counterculture take a hatchet to it. There's a period of turmoil and competition as the champions of the different moral orders fight to see which new culture will prevail. At these moments—1848, 1917, 1968, today—it's easy to get depressed and to feel that society is coming apart at the seams. There are gigantic and often brutal wars of consecration, battles about what way of life is admired most. Eventually society pivots over and settles on a new moral ecology, a new set of standards of right and wrong. Once that's in place, there is a new ratchet of progress, and the stumble of progress takes another step.

When a culture changes, obviously not everybody changes all at once. This is a big, diverse society. But the average of behavior changes. Some desires and values get prioritized, and others are not. Some formerly admirable things are disdained and formerly marginal things are admired.

I want to emphasize who leads change in these moments, because it is relevant to the moment we find ourselves in today. It's not politicians who lead this kind of change. Instead it's moral activists and cultural pioneers. Those who shape the manners and mores are the true legislators of mankind—they wield the greatest power and influence. It usually starts with a subculture. A small group of creative individuals finds the current moral ecology oppressive and alienating. So they go back in history and update an old moral ecology that seems to provide a better way to live. They create a lifestyle that others find attractive. If you can create a social movement that people want to join, they will bend their energies and ideas to you.

As Joseph Campbell put it in an interview with Bill Moyers, there are two types of deed. There is the physical deed: the hero who performs an act of bravery in war and saves a village. But there is also the spiritual hero, who has found a new and better way of experiencing spiritual life, and then comes back and communicates it to everyone else. Or, in Iris Murdoch's words: "Man is a creature who makes pictures of himself and then comes to resemble the picture."

In the 1960s, small groups of young people on communes and hippie communities went back and borrowed from the bohemian culture—its preference for long hair, youthfulness, rebellion, revolution, and open sexual mores; its rejection of all things bourgeois. They became, over time, Woodstock freaks, rebels, New Age explorers, and eventually bourgeois bohemians. They dressed differently and talked differently than the 1950s Organization Men. They conducted their relationships differently and organized their living arrangements differently.

What had once been respect for authority became rejection of authority. Once reticence was admired, but now expressiveness was admired. Once experience was revered, but now youth was celebrated. Once life was seen as a cycle of generations rooted in place. But now life was seen as a journey on the open road. Once the dominant ethos was about doing your duty, but now life was about doing your own thing. Where once the group had come first, now the individual came first. Once duty was admired most, now it was personal freedom.

That same year *Travels with Charley* was published, 1962, a group of student radicals met in Port Huron, Michigan. Their immediate goal was to fight racism in the north, but they ended up having a much broader impact. They had recently formed the Students for a Democratic Society and wrote the Port Huron Statement, which turned out to be a pretty good indicator of the moral ecology to come.

"The goal of man and society should be human independence," they wrote, "a concern not with image of popularity but with finding a meaning of life that is personally authentic. . . . This kind of independence does not mean egoistic individualism—the object is not to have one's way so much as it is to have a way that is one's own."

Basically, the 1960s counterculture took the expressive individualism that had been rattling around Romantic countercultures for centuries and made it the mainstream mode of modern life.

If "We're All in This Together" was about the group, this new moral ecology was all about freedom, autonomy, authenticity. You might summarize it with the phrase "I'm Free to Be Myself." This individualistic ethos, which has sometimes been called "selfism," was pumped into the boomers with their breast milk, and it will be drained from every cavity by their morticians. It is an emancipation narrative. The idea was to be liberated from dogma, political oppression, social prejudice, and group conformity. This movement had a right-wing variant—the individual should be economically unregulated—and it had a left-wing variant—each person's individually chosen lifestyle should be socially unregulated. But it was all about individual emancipation all the way down.

I don't want to spend too much time describing this culture of individualism, authenticity, autonomy, and isolation because it has been described so masterfully by others: Philip Rieff in *The Triumph of the Therapeutic*, Christopher Lasch in *The Culture of Narcissism*, Gail Sheehy in *Passages*, Alasdair MacIntyre in *After Virtue*, Tom Wolfe in "The 'Me' Decade," Erica Jong in *Fear of Flying*, Charles Taylor in *The Ethics of Authenticity*, Robert Bellah in *Habits of the Heart*, and Robert Putnam in *Bowling Alone*.

I just want to emphasize that the march toward freedom produced many great outcomes. The individualistic culture that emerged in the sixties broke through many of the chains that held down women and oppressed minorities. It loosened the bonds of racism, sexism, anti-Semitism, and homophobia. We could not have had Silicon Valley or the whole information age economy without the rebel individualism and bursts of creativity that were unleashed by this culture. It was an absolutely necessary cultural revolution.

But many ideas become false when taken to the extreme. America has always had a more individualistic culture than other places, which Tocqueville noticed back in the 1830s. But when individualism becomes the absolutely dominant ethos of a civilization—when it is not counterbalanced with any competing ethos—then the individuals within it may have maximum freedom, but the links between the individuals slowly begin to dissolve. The grand narrative of "I'm Free to Be Myself" has been playing out for about fifty years. It has evolved into a culture of hyper-individualism. This moral ecology is built on a series of ideas or assumptions. I'll just list a few:

The buffered self. The autonomous individual is the fundamental unit of society. A community is a collection of individuals who are making their own choices about how to live. The best social arrangement guarantees the widest possible freedom for individual choice. The central social principle is "No Harm, No Foul." Each individual has the right to live in any way he or she pleases as long as they don't interfere with other people's rights to live as they please. The ideal society is one in which people live unencumbered but together, each doing their own thing.

The God within. The goal of life is to climb Maslow's hierarchy of needs and achieve self-actualization and self-fulfillment. As you make your own personal journey, you learn to better express your own unique self. You learn to get in touch with yourself, find yourself, and live in a way that is authentic to who you really are. The ultimate source of authority is found inside, in listening to the authentic voice of the Hidden Oracle within, in staying true to your feelings and by not conforming to the standards of the corrupt society outside.

The privatization of meaning. It's a mistake to simply accept the received ideas of the world around you. You have to come up with your own values, your own worldview. As Justice Anthony Kennedy put it in a famous Supreme Court decision, "At the heart of liberty is the right to define one's own concept of existence, of meaning, of the universe, and of the mystery of human life."

It's not the job of schools or neighborhoods or even parents to create a shared moral order. It's something you do on your own, and who are you to judge if another person's moral order is better or worse than any others?

The dream of total freedom. In other cultures, people are formed by and flourish within institutions that precede individual choice—family, ethnic heritage, faith, nation. But these are precisely the sorts of institutions that the culture of individualism eats away at, because they are unchosen and therefore seen as not quite legitimate. In an individualistic culture, the best life is the freest life. Spiritual formation happens in freedom, not within obligation.

The centrality of accomplishment. In a hyper-individualistic society, people are not measured by how they conform to a shared moral code. They are not measured by how fully they have submerged themselves in thick relationships. They are measured by what they have individually achieved. Status, admiration, and being loved follow personal achievement. Selfishness is accepted, because taking care of and promoting the self is the prime mission. It's okay to be self-oriented because in a properly structured society, private selfishness can be harnessed to produce public goods, such as economic growth. Researchers at the Harvard Graduate School of Education recently asked ten thousand middle and high school students if their parents cared more about personal achievements or whether they were kind. Eighty percent said their parents cared more about achievements—individual success over relational bonds.

You could add other ideas to my list of things that characterize the culture of a hyper-individualistic society: consumerism, a therapeutic mindset, the preference for technology over intimacy. The big fact is that these ideas, spreading for half a century, have made it harder to live bonded, communal lives.

Hyper-individualism is not a new problem. It comes and goes. A few years ago, I was reading Sebastian Junger's book *Tribe*. I came across a phenomenon that has haunted me ever since. In eighteenth-century America, Colonial society and Native American society sat, unhappily, side by side. As time went by, settlers from Europe began defecting to live with the natives. No natives defected to live with the colonials. This bothered the Europeans. They had, they assumed, the superior civilization, and yet people were voting with their feet to live in the other way. The colonials occasionally persuaded natives to come with them, and taught them English, but very quickly the natives returned home. During the wars with the Indians, many European settlers were taken prisoner and held within Indian tribes. They had plenty of chances to escape and return, but did not. When Europeans came to "rescue" them, they fled into the woods to hide from their "rescuers."

The difference was that people in Indian villages had a communal culture and close attachments. They lived in a spiritual culture that saw all creation as a single unity. The Europeans had an individualistic culture and were more separable. When actually given the choice, a lot of people preferred community over self. The story made me think that it's possible for a whole society to get itself into a place where it's fundamentally misordered.

There's always a tension between self and society. If things are too tightly bound, then the urge to rebel is strong. But we've got the opposite problem. In a culture of "I'm Free to Be Myself," individuals are lonely and loosely attached. Community is attenuated, connections are dissolved, and loneliness spreads. This situation makes it difficult to be good—to fulfill the deep human desires for love and connection. It's hard on people of all ages, but it's especially hard on young adults. They are thrown into a world that is unstructured and uncertain, with few authorities or guardrails except those they are expected to build on their own. Among other things, it becomes phenomenally hard to launch yourself into life.

The Instagram Life

EVERY SOCIETY HAS A WAY OF TRANSMITTING ITS VALUES TO THE YOUNG. Some societies do it through religious festivals or military parades. One of the ways we do it is through a secular sermon called the commencement address.

Colleges generally ask a person distinguished by fantastic career success to give a speech in which they claim that career success is not that important. Then these phenomenally accomplished individuals often go on to tell their audiences that you shouldn't be afraid to fail. From this young people learn that failure can be wonderful—if you happen to be J. K. Rowling, Denzel Washington, or Steve Jobs.

But this lesson is not the only advice we in the middle-aged commencement-giving world offer young adults. We use these speeches to pass along the dominant values of our age. We hand them over like some great, awesome presents. And it turns out these presents are great big boxes of nothing.

Many young people are graduating into limbo. Floating and plagued by uncertainty, they want to know what specifically they should do with their lives. So we hand them the great empty box of freedom! The purpose of life is to be free. Freedom leads to happiness! We're not going to impose anything on you or tell you what to do. We give you your liberated self to explore. Enjoy your freedom!

The students in the audience put down that empty box because they are drowning in freedom. What they're looking for is direction. What is freedom for? How do I know which path is my path?

So we hand them another big box of nothing—the big box of possibility! Your future is limitless! You can do anything you set your mind to! The journey is the destination! Take risks! Be audacious! Dream big!

But this mantra doesn't help them, either. If you don't know what your life is for, how does it help to be told that your future is limitless? That just ups the pressure. So they put down that empty box. They are looking for a source of wisdom. Where can I find the answers to my big questions?

So we hand them the empty box of authenticity: Look inside yourself! Find your true inner passion. You are amazing! Awaken the giant within! Live according to your own true way! You do you!

This is useless, too. The "you" we tell them to consult for life's answers is the very thing that hasn't yet formed. So they put down that empty box and ask, What can I devote myself to? What cause will inspire me and give meaning and direction to my life?

At this point we hand them the emptiest box of all—the box of autonomy. You are on your own, we tell them. It's up to you to define your own values. No one else can tell you what's right or wrong for you. Your truth is to be found in your own way through your own story that you tell about yourself. Do what you love!

You will notice that our answers take all the difficulties of living in your twenties and make them worse. The graduates are in limbo, and we give them uncertainty. They want to know why they should do this as opposed to that. And we have nothing to say except, Figure it out yourself based on no criteria outside yourself. They are floundering in a formless desert. Not only do we not give them a compass, we take a bucket of sand and throw it all over their heads!

Kierkegaard once summarized the question that these graduates are really asking: "What I really need to be clear about is *what am I to do*, not about what I must know. . . . It is a question of finding a truth that is truth *for me*, of finding *the idea for which I am willing to live and die*. . . . It is for this my soul thirsts, as the deserts of Africa thirst for water."

How is it that on this biggest question of all, we have nothing to say?

THE BIG SWIM TO NOWHERE

When you're a student, life is station to station. There's always the next assignment, the next test, the next admissions application to structure a student's schedule and energies. Social life has its dramas, but at least it's laid out right there in front of you in the dining hall and the dorm.

Then, from the most structured and supervised childhood in human history, you get spit out after graduation into the least structured young adulthood in human history. Yesterday parents, teachers, coaches, and counselors were all marking your progress and cheering your precious self. Today the approval bath stops. The world doesn't know your name or care who you are. The person on the other side of the desk at every job interview has that distant Kanye attitude—there's a million of you; there's only one of me.

In centuries past, emerging adults took their parents' jobs, faiths, towns, and identities. But in the age of "I'm Free to Be Myself," you are expected to find your own career path, your own social tribe, your own beliefs, values, life partners, gender roles, political viewpoints, and social identities. As a student, your focus was primarily on the short term, but now you need a different set of navigational skills, to the far-horizon goals you will begin to orient your life toward.

The average American has seven jobs over the course of their twenties. A third of recent college graduates are unemployed, underemployed, or making less than $30,000 a year at any given moment. Half feel they have no plan for their life, and nearly half of people in their twenties have had no sexual partner in the last year. These are peak years for alcoholism and drug addiction. People in this life stage move every three years. Forty percent move back in with their parents at least once. They are much less likely to attend religious services or join a political party.

People in their odyssey years tend to be dementedly optimistic about the long-term future. Ninety-six percent of eighteen-to-twenty-four-year-olds agree with the statement "I am very sure that someday I will get to where I want to be in life." But the present is marked by wandering, loneliness, detachment, doubt, underemployment, heartbreaks, and bad bosses, while their parents go slowly insane.

THE AESTHETIC LIFE

Some people graduate from college with the mindset of daring adventurers. This is the time for fun before real life settles in. Marriage and a real job will just arrive in the mail one day when they are thirty-five. In the meantime, they're going to have experiences.

These are the people who at age twenty-three go teach English in Mongolia or lead white-water rafting trips in Colorado. This daring course has real advantages. Your first job out of college is probably going to suck anyway, so, as the impact investor Blair Miller advises, you might as well use this period to widen your horizon of risk. If you do something completely crazy you will know forever after that you can handle a certain amount of craziness, and your approach to life for all the decades hence will be more courageous. Furthermore, you will build what the clinical psychologist Meg Jay calls "identity capital." At every job interview and dinner party for the next three decades, somebody will want to ask you what it was like teaching English in Mongolia, and that will distinguish you from everybody else.

This is an excellent way to begin your twenties. The problem with this kind of life only becomes evident a few years down the road if you haven't settled down into one thing. If you say yes to everything year after year, you end up leading what Kierkegaard lamented as an aesthetic style of life. The person leading the aesthetic life is leading his life as if it were a piece of art, judging it by aesthetic criteria—is it interesting or dull, pretty or ugly, pleasurable or painful?

Such a person schedules a meditation retreat here, a Burning Man visit there, one fellowship one year and another one the next. There's swing dancing one day, SoulCycle twice a week, Krav Maga for a few months, Bikram Yoga for a few months more, and occasionally a cool art gallery on a Sunday afternoon. Your Instagram feed will be amazing, and everybody will think you're the coolest person ever. You tell yourself that relationships really matter to you—scheduling drinks, having lunch—but after you've had twenty social encounters in a week you forget what all those encounters are supposed to build to. You have thousands of conversations and remember none.

The problem is that the person in the aesthetic phase sees life as possibilities to be experienced and not projects to be fulfilled or ideals to be lived out. He will hover above everything but never land. In the aesthetic way of life, each individual day is fun, but it doesn't seem to add up to anything.

The theory behind this life is that you should rack up experiences. But if you live life as a series of serial adventures, you will wander about in the indeterminacy of your own passing feelings and your own changeable heart. Life will be a series of temporary moments, not an accumulating flow of accomplishment. You will lay waste to your powers, scattering them in all directions. You will be plagued by a fear of missing out. Your possibilities are endless, but your decision-making landscape is hopelessly flat.

As Annie Dillard put it, how you spend your days is how you spend your life. If you spend your days merely consuming random experiences, you will begin to feel like a scattered consumer. If you want to sample something from every aisle in the grocery store of life, you turn yourself into a chooser, the sort of self-obsessed person who is always thinking about himself and his choices and is eventually paralyzed by self-consciousness.

Our natural enthusiasm trains us to be people pleasers, to say yes to other people. But if you aren't saying a permanent no to anything, giving anything up, then you probably aren't diving into anything fully. A life of commitment means saying a thousand noes for the sake of a few precious yeses.

When enough people are going through this phase at once, you end up with a society in which everything is in flux. You end up with what the Polish philosopher Zygmunt Bauman calls "liquid modernity." In the age of the smartphone, the friction costs involved in making or breaking any transaction or relationship approach zero. The Internet is commanding you to click on and sample one thing after another. Living online often means living in a state of diversion. When you're living in diversion you're not actually deeply interested in things; you're just bored at a more frenetic pace. Online life is saturated with decommitment devices. If you can't focus your attention for thirty seconds, how on earth are you going to commit for life?

Such is life in the dizziness of freedom. Nobody quite knows where they stand with one another. Everybody is pretty sure that other people are doing life better. Comparison is the robber of joy.

After several years of pursuing open options, it's not so much that you lose the thread of the meaning of your life; you have trouble even staying focused on the question. David Foster Wallace's epic novel *Infinite Jest* is a description of this distracted frame of mind. It's about a movie so "fatally entertaining" that everybody becomes a drooling zombie in its trance. The big questions of life have been replaced by entertainment. The novel itself embodies the mind of the terminally distracted, with sentences stringing along and doubling back on one another, thoughts just popping up here and there. In such a world, everybody is buzzingly entertained but not necessarily progressing.

Wallace thought the way to fight all this was to focus your individual attention—through a sort of iron willpower. "Learning how to think really means learning how to exercise some control over how and what you think," Wallace told Kenyon College graduates in his famous commencement address. "It means being conscious and aware enough to choose what you pay attention to and to choose how you construct meaning from experience. Because if you cannot exercise this kind of choice in adult life, you will be totally hosed."

But Wallace's remedy is unrealistic. When you are in your distraction, untethered to actual commitments, focusing your attention is precisely what you cannot do. Your mind is afloat and at the play of prompts. Do not flatter yourself in thinking that you're brave enough or capable enough to see into the deepest and most important parts of yourself. One of the reasons you are rushing about is because you are running away from yourself.

You know that at some point you should sit down and find some overall direction for your life. But the mind wants to wander from the meaty big questions, which are completely daunting and unanswerable, to the diverting candy right on your phone—the tiny dopamine lift.

All of this points in one direction: into the ditch. The person who graduates from school and pursues an aesthetic pattern of life often ends up in the ditch. It's only then that they realize the truth that somehow nobody told them: Freedom sucks.

Political freedom is great. But personal, social, and emotional freedom—when it becomes an ultimate end—absolutely sucks. It leads to a random, busy life with no discernible direction, no firm foundation, and in which, as Marx put it, all that's solid melts to air. It turns out that freedom isn't an ocean you want to spend your life in. Freedom is a river you want to get across so you can plant yourself on the other side—and fully commit to something.

The Insecure Overachiever

IF ONE GROUP OF YOUNG PEOPLE APPROACH ADULTHOOD AS AN AESTHETIC experience, another group tries to treat adulthood as much as possible like a continuation of school. These students usually went to competitive colleges and tend to come from the upper strata of society. They were good at getting admitted into places, so they apply to companies that have competitive hiring procedures. As students, they enjoyed the borrowed prestige of high-status colleges, so as adults they enjoy the borrowed prestige of high-status companies and service organizations. As students, they were good at winning gold stars, and so they follow a gold-star-winning kind of life when they enter the workforce, and their parents get to brag that they work at Google or Williams & Connolly, or that they go to Harvard Business School.

This group of emerging adults are pragmatists. They are good at solving problems. The problem for a college junior and senior is anticipated ambiguity. Graduation is approaching, and you don't know what comes next. The pragmatists solve this problem by flocking to companies and such that can tell them, even as juniors in college, what they will be doing for at least a few years hence. The uncertainty is over. Plus, now they will have a good answer when adults ask them, as they are prone to do, what they are going to do after graduation. In order to keep the existential anxiety about what to do with their life carefully suppressed underneath the waterline of consciousness, they grab the first job that comes along.

Unfortunately, this pragmatic route doesn't spare you from the ditch, either. Never underestimate the power of the environment you work in to gradually transform who you are. When you choose to work at a certain company, you are turning yourself into the sort of person who works in that company. That's great if the culture of McKinsey or General Mills satisfies your very soul. But if it doesn't, there will be some little piece of yourself that will go unfed and get hungrier and hungrier.

Moreover, living life in a pragmatic, utilitarian manner turns you into a utilitarian pragmatist. The "How do I succeed?" questions quickly eclipse the "Why am I doing this?" questions.

Suddenly your conversation consists mostly of descriptions of how busy you are. Suddenly you're a chilly mortal, going into hyper-people-pleasing mode anytime you're around your boss. You spend much of your time mentor shopping, trying to find some successful older person who will answer all your questions and solve all your problems. It turns out that the people in your workplace don't want you to have a deep, fulfilling life. They give you gold stars of affirmation every time you mold yourself into the shrewd animal the workplace wants you to be. You've read those Marxist analyses of the bosses exploiting the workers. Suddenly it occurs to you that you have become your own boss and your own exploiter. You begin to view yourself not as a soul to be uplifted but as a set of skills to be maximized.

It's fascinating how easy it is to simply let drop those spiritual questions that used to plague you, to let slide those deep books that used to define you, to streamline yourself into a professional person.

Furthermore, workaholism is a surprisingly effective distraction from emotional and spiritual problems. It's surprisingly easy to become emotionally avoidant and morally decoupled, to be less close to and vulnerable with those around you, to wall off the dark jungle deep inside you, to gradually tamp down the highs and lows and simply live in neutral. Have you noticed how many people are more boring and half-hearted at age thirty-five than they were at twenty?

The meritocracy is the most self-confident moral system in the world today. It's so engrossing and seems so natural that we're not even aware of how it encourages a certain economic vocabulary about non-economic things. Words change their meaning. "Character" is no longer a moral quality oriented around love, service, and care, but a set of workplace traits organized around grit, productivity, and self-discipline. The meritocracy defines "community" as a mass of talented individuals competing with one another. It organizes society into an endless set of outer and inner rings, with high achievers at the Davos center and everybody else arrayed across the wider rings toward the edge. While it pretends not to, it subliminally sends the message that those who are smarter and more accomplished are actually worth more than those who are not.

The meritocracy's soul-flattening influence is survivable if you have your own competing moral system that exists in you alongside it, but if you have no competing value system, the meritocracy swallows you whole. You lose your sense of agency, because the rungs of the professional ladder determine your schedule and life course. The meritocracy gives you brands to attach to—your prestigious school, your nice job title—which work well as status markers and seem to replace the urgent need to find out who you are. Work, the poet David Whyte writes, "is a place you can lose yourself more easily perhaps than finding yourself."

Journalist Lisa Miller describes an "ambition collision" she saw in her peers, mostly young women of the professional set. These are the opportunity seizers, she writes, the list makers, the ascendant females weaned on Sheryl Sandberg's *Lean In*, who delayed marriage and children because they were driven to do big things and run big things.

But at a certain age, Miller writes, they've "lost it, like a child losing grasp of a helium balloon. Grief-stricken, they are baffled too." As one woman told Miller, "There's no vision." Or, as another put it, there's "nothing solid." They fantasize about quitting their jobs and moving home to Michigan, or having kids merely as an excuse to drop out of the rat race. "They murmur about purpose, about the concrete satisfactions of baking a loaf of bread or watching a garden grow." They stay put, diligently working, "waiting for something—anything—to reignite them, to convince them that their wanting hasn't abandoned them for good."

Miller portrays this as a female problem, arising from society's screwed-up attitudes about women and work. But I notice many men also have a sensation that they are under-living their lives. Centuries ago there was a common word for what these people are going through: acedia.

This word is used much less frequently today, which is peculiar since the state it describes is so common. Acedia is the quieting of passion. It is a lack of care. It is living a life that doesn't arouse your strong passions and therefore instills a sluggishness of the soul, like an oven set on warm. The person living in acedia may have a job and a family, but he is not entirely grabbed by his own life. His heart is over there, but his life is over here.

Desire makes you adhesive. Desire pushes you to get close—to the person, job, or town you love. But lack of desire makes you detached, and instills in you over time an attitude of emotional avoidance, a phony nonchalance. In short, the meritocracy encourages you to drift into a life that society loves but which you don't. It's impossible to feel wholehearted.

A person who tries to treat life as if it were an extension of school often becomes what the Danish novelist Matias Dalsgaard calls an "insecure overachiever": "Such a person must have no stable or solid foundation to build upon, and yet nonetheless tries to build his way out of his problem. It's an impossible situation. You can't compensate for having a foundation made of quicksand by building a new story on top. But this person takes no notice and hopes that the problem down in the foundation won't be found out if only the construction work on the top keeps going."

The problem with pragmatism, as they say, is that it doesn't work.

The insecure overachiever never fully wills anything and thus is never fully satisfied. His brain is moving and his status is rising, but his heart and soul are never fully engaged.

When you have nothing but your identity and job title to rest on, then you find yourself constantly comparing yourself to others. You are haunted by your conception of yourself. People who live in this way imagine that there are other people who are enjoying career splendor and private joy. That loser in college who did nothing but watch TV is now a big movie producer; that quiet guy in the training program is now a billionaire hedge fund manager. What does it profit a man to sell his own soul if others are selling theirs and getting more for it?

The Valley

LEO TOLSTOY HAD ONE OF THE MOST SUCCESSFUL FIRST MOUNTAINS IN human history. As a young man he joined the army and sowed his wild oats. He had his adventures, his love affairs; he challenged men to duels. Then he tried to make a name for himself as a great intellectual. He gathered with a group of his fellows and together they launched radical magazines, wrote essays, and tried to spread enlightenment. He became a novelist and succeeded beyond anybody's wildest imaginings. The results were *War and Peace* and *Anna Karenina* and much else.

He was not a moral slacker, either. Tolstoy was always giving up things in order to make himself a better person: tobacco, hunting, alcohol, meat. He wrote up rules for himself so he could love people more and treat all others equally and that sort of thing.

His faith in those years, he later recalled, was in perfecting himself:

> I tried to achieve intellectual perfection; I studied everything I could, everything that life gave me a chance to study. I tried to

perfect my will and set up rules for myself that I endeavored to
follow. I strove for physical perfection by doing all the exercises
that develop strength and agility and undergoing all the hard-
ships that discipline the self in endurance and perseverance. I
took all this to be perfection. The starting point of it all was, of
course, moral perfection, but this was soon replaced by a belief
in overall perfection, that is, a desire to be better not in my own
eyes or in the eyes of God, but rather a desire to be better in the
eyes of other people.

Then life hit him with its blows. His brother Nicholas died at age
thirty-seven. He was a good, serious man who never understood why
he lived or why he died. No theories Tolstoy could think of could explain his brother's death.

Then Tolstoy had an experience that persuaded him that there is a
good far greater than his prestige and perfection. It was absolute truth,
something that is not built by human reason but simply exists. Tolstoy
was in Paris when he witnessed an execution.

When I saw how the head was severed from the body and heard
the thud of each part as it fell into the box, I understood, not
with my intellect but with my whole being, that no theories of
the rationality of existence or of progress could justify such an
act; I realized that even if all the people in the world from the
day of creation found this to be necessary according to whatever
theory, I knew that it was not necessary and that it was wrong.
Therefore, my judgments must be based on what is right and
necessary and not on what people say and do.

Tolstoy had thus far bet his life on the enlightenment project, on
reason, progress, intellectuals, public approval, and progress. And now
he lost faith in that project. What was the point of life?

My life came to a stop. I could breathe, eat, drink, and sleep;
indeed, I could not help but breathe, eat, drink, and sleep. But

there was no life in me because I had no desires whose satisfaction I would have found reasonable. If I wanted something, I knew beforehand that it did not matter whether or not I got it.

Life began to feel absurd and useless. He removed all the ropes from his room so he would not hang himself. He kept himself away from his hunting rifles so he would not shoot himself. He began to regard his former writing intellectual life as a form of madness. Who could really care if he got a good review in this or that journal? It now seemed that he and his cronies hadn't been improving the world, just writing to become rich and famous. Tolstoy was sick of life and saw no point in it. He was in the valley.

If this sense of lostness can happen to a Tolstoy, then it can happen to anybody. After all, the rest of us can be haunted by the idea that we haven't accomplished as much as we could. But Tolstoy was one of the greatest writers who ever lived and knew it. Wealth and fame and accomplishment do not spare anybody from the valley.

THE REST OF US

There are people who go through life without ever stumbling into the valley, and more power to them. But most of us have had to endure some season of suffering, some season when we had to ask ourselves the fundamental questions.

Suffering comes in many forms. Some people are busy at work but realize they've lost the thread of their lives. Some people suffer a heartbreak. Some people lose a loved one, which makes them feel as if some bright future is forever lost. Others get knocked sideways by a heart attack, cancer, or stroke. Others experience failure or scandal; they've built their identity on some external performance, and that is now gone.

For some people this feeling is not a dramatic crisis. It's just a creeping malaise, a gradual loss of enthusiasm in what they are doing. The Jungian analyst James Hollis had a patient who explained it this way: "I always sought to win whatever the game was, and only now do I realize how much I have been played by the game." A person may fight ferociously to win success, to be better than everybody else, and then one day find it all seems empty and meaningless. "Unable to value, unable to enjoy," one of Tolstoy's characters says.

In an essay for Oprah.com, writer Ada Calhoun described the way many women even in their thirties and forties feel adrift, like they're misleading their lives. One of her friends, forty-one, told her, "Sometimes, I have these moments of clarity, usually during lengthy conference calls," she said. "This voice in my head suddenly starts shouting: *What are you doing? This is pointless and boring! Why aren't you out there doing something you love?*"

In his book *Excellent Sheep*, William Deresiewicz describes his own descent into young despond. He grew up in a family of engineers and scientists and assumed that science was what he wanted to do with his life. Before a single class in college, before permitting himself to live with a single moment of uncertainty, he decided to double major in biology and psychology. Before stepping foot on campus he'd locked up three-quarters of the courses he would take there. By the time he realized he should have been an English major, it was too late to change, so he graduated with a degree in two subjects he had no desire to pursue professionally.

Lacking a clear goal for his life, he parked himself in a place that would allow him to keep his options open. He applied to law school, and then when it was clear that he had no interest in the law, he applied to journalism school, which he had no interest in either, and then took a job at a nonprofit. "So there I was, a couple of years after college, bitter from the fact that I had thrown away the chance to get an education, working a job that meant nothing to me, my career essentially dead in the water, my self-belief in ruins, with no idea what I wanted to do or where I should go next."

People generally go through a familiar process before they can acknowledge how comprehensive their problem is. First, they deny that there's something wrong with their life. Then they intensify their efforts to follow the old failing plan. Then they try to treat themselves with some new thrill: They have an affair, drink more, or start doing drugs. Only when all this fails do they admit that they need to change the way they think about life.

THE TELOS CRISIS

This is a telos crisis. A telos crisis is defined by the fact that people in it don't know what their purpose is. When this happens, they become fragile. Nietzsche says that he who has a "why" to live for can endure any "how." If you know what your purpose is, you can handle the setbacks. But when you don't know what your purpose is, any setback can lead to total collapse. As Seamus Heaney put it, "You are neither here nor there, / A hurry through which known and strange things pass."

In my experience, a telos crisis comes in two forms, walking and sleeping. In the walking form, the sufferer just keeps trudging along. She has been hit by some blow, or suffers from some deep ennui, but she doesn't know what she wants or how she should change her life, so she just keeps on doing what she was doing—same job, same place, and same life. She is living with the psychological awareness that she is settling. I had a friend named Casey Gerald who was being interviewed for a job. At the end of the interview he turned the tables on the interviewer and asked her a question: "What would you do if you weren't afraid?" The interviewer burst out crying. If she wasn't afraid, she wouldn't be doing HR for that company. That's a walking telos crisis.

The second kind of telos crisis is the sleeping kind. In this version, the sufferer is just laid low, crawls into bed, and watches Netflix. His confidence is shot. He is paralyzed by self-focus. He has this weird and unwarranted conviction that it's too late for him; life has passed him by. Other people's accomplishments begin to bring real pain, as the distance between their (apparent) swift ascent and his pathetic stasis begins to seem hopelessly wide.

David Foster Wallace noticed it in a lot of his friends: "Something that doesn't have very much to do with physical circumstances, or the economy, or any of the stuff that gets talked about in the news. It's more like stomach-level sadness. I see it in myself and my friends in different ways. It manifests itself as a kind of lostness." Beneath the psychological manifestations, Wallace noticed that the fundamental cause was moral directionlessness. "This is a generation that has an inheritance of absolutely nothing as far as meaningful moral values."

And it's hard to know how many people are suffering in this sort of crisis because people have become so good at masking it. As the young writer Veronica Rae Saron put it, "Conversation after conversation, it has become more and more clear: those among us with flashy Instagram accounts, perfectly manufactured LinkedIn profiles, and confident exteriors (yours truly) are probably those who are feeling the most confused, anxious, and stuck when it comes to the future. The millennial 20-something stuck-ness sensation is everywhere, and there is a direct correlation between those who feel it and those who put off a vibe of feeling extremely secure." Eventually there's no escaping the big questions. What's my best life? What do I believe in? Where do I belong?

THE SOCIAL VALLEY

Individuals can fall into the valley, and whole societies can, too. In the early 1960s our culture began to embrace a hyper-individualistic way of life to help it address the problems of that moment. But after a few decades, that culture, taken to the extreme, produced its own crisis.

The grand narrative of individual emancipation left us with what some have called "the great disembedding." Whereas before people tended to be enmeshed in tight communities with prescribed social norms that sometimes seemed stifling, now they are cut loose. Whereas once they served in hierarchical institutions, now they have trouble thinking institutionally at all—how to live within an institution, steward an institution, and reform an institution—so the quality of our social organizations that make up our common life decays.

Most of all, hyper-individualism has led to a society where people live further and further apart from one another—socially, emotionally, even physically. The English philosopher Simon May said that love is "ontological rootedness." Love gives you a feeling of being grounded. Many people, even within families, don't have that. Many people in romantic relationships don't have that. It used to be that people complained that young adults were having sex without love; now they are increasingly not even having sex at all. A half century of emancipation has made individualism, which was the heaven for our grandparents, into our hell. It has produced four interrelated social crises.

1. THE LONELINESS CRISIS

Thirty-five percent of Americans over forty-five are chronically lonely. Only 8 percent of Americans report having important conversations with their neighbors in a given year. In 1950, less than 10 percent of households were single-person households; now nearly 30 percent are. The majority of children born to women under thirty are born into single-parent households. These are symptoms of a general detachment. The fastest growing political group is unaffiliated. The fastest growing religious group is unaffiliated. Researchers in Britain asked pastors to describe the most common issue they have to address with their parishioners. Seventy-six percent said loneliness and mental health. Former surgeon general Vivek Murthy wrote in the *Harvard Business Review*, "During my years caring for patients, the most common pathology I saw was not heart disease or diabetes; it was loneliness."

The psychological, social, and moral toll caused by this detachment is horrific.

Since 1999, the U.S. suicide rate has risen by 30 percent. The plague hit the young hard. Between 2006 and 2016, suicide rates for those between age ten and seventeen rose by 70 percent. Roughly forty-five thousand Americans kill themselves every year, and suicide is largely a proxy for loneliness. Opioids kill an additional seventy-two thousand Americans every year. And opioid addiction is just slow-motion suicide. In 2018, the Centers for Disease Control and Prevention announced that the life span of the average American had declined for the third consecutive year. This is an absolutely stunning trend. In affluent, cohesive societies, life spans get gradually longer as a matter of course. The last time the American life span contracted for this length of time was 1915 to 1918, when the country was enduring a world war and a flu pandemic that killed 675,000 Americans. The reason American lives are shorter today is the increase in the so-called deaths of despair—suicide, drug overdose, liver problems, and so on. And those, in turn, are caused by the social isolation that is all around us.

2. DISTRUST

The second crisis is one of alienation. The great sociologist Robert Nisbet defines alienation as "the state of mind that can find a social order remote, incomprehensible, or fraudulent." That's pretty much the normal state of affairs in America today. People in that earlier generation generally assumed that self-sacrifice made sense, because if you served your organization, it would serve you back. But, as the pollster Daniel Yankelovich pointed out decades ago, faith in that giving-getting compact has broken down. Now it is assumed that if you give, they will take. If you sacrifice, others will take advantage. The reciprocity is gone, and people feel detached from their neighbors and disgusted by the institutions of public life.

In the 1940s and '50s, when the ethos was more "We're All in This Together," roughly 75 percent of Americans said they trusted government to do the right thing most of the time. Now less than 25 percent do. In that earlier age, according to the General Social Survey, roughly 60 percent of Americans said that their neighbors were trustworthy; now only 32 percent do and only 18 percent of millennials. Every age group in America is less trusting than the one before, and, as Robert Putnam of Harvard points out, that's for a very good reason: People are less trustworthy. It's not that perception is getting worse. It's actual behavior. The quality of our relationships is worse. Distrust breeds distrust. When people feel distrustful they conclude that the only person they can rely on is themselves. "What loneliness is more lonely than distrust?" George Eliot wrote in *Middlemarch*.

3. THE CRISIS OF MEANING

The third crisis is a crisis of meaning. It is a stunning fact of our age that, despite all we have learned about the brain, mental health problems, including depression, are rising, not falling. And things seem to be deteriorating quickly. In 2012, 5.9 percent of young people suffered from severe depression. By 2015 it was 8.2 percent.

This is, in part, because of the smartphone, but also because so many people have lost a sense of purpose in their lives. When you take away a common moral order and tell everybody to find their own definition of the mystery of life, most people will come up empty. They will not have a compelling story that explains the meaning of their life in those moments when life gets hard. In a study for his book *The Path to Purpose*, William Damon found that only 20 percent of young adults have a fully realized sense of purpose.

Many people have lost faith in the great causes and institutions that earlier generations relied on to give life a sense of purpose and meaning. They have lost faith in faith. Actual church attendance has declined by almost half since the early 1960s. They have lost faith in country. In 2003, according to the Gallup organization, 70 percent of Americans said they were "extremely proud" to be Americans. By 2016, only 52 percent of Americans said that, and only 34 percent of millennials agree. And this was before the election of Donald Trump. All of these numbers suggest people do not feel they are part of some larger story that they can believe in and dedicate their lives to.

"Man has a horror of aloneness," Balzac writes. "And of all kinds of aloneness, moral aloneness is the most terrible."

4. TRIBALISM

These three crises have given rise to a fourth one, which is not a facet of extreme individualism itself, but our reaction to it. Psychologists say the hardest thing to cure is the patient's attempt to self-cure. People who are left naked and alone by radical individualism do what their genes and the ancient history of their species tell them to do: They revert to tribe. Individualism, taken too far, leads to tribalism.

Hannah Arendt noticed the phenomenon decades ago. When she looked into the lives of people who had become political fanatics, she found two things: loneliness and spiritual emptiness. "Loneliness is the common ground of terror," she wrote in *The Origins of Totalitarianism*.

True loneliness, Nabeelah Jaffer writes, is not only solitude; it is also a sort of spiritual emptiness, the loss of faith in oneself to come up with answers, "the loss of one's own self." It is a feeling of "uprooted-ness and superfluousness." Jaffer posits that many militants join the Islamic State because they have no place where they can experience a sense of belonging, and at least IS gives them that. It gives them a way to be a martyr, a hero.

People who are experiencing existential dread slip into crisis mode: "I'm in danger! I'm threatened; I must strike back!" Their evolutionary response is self-protection, so they fall back on ancient instincts for how to respond to a threat: us versus them. Tribalists seek out easy categories in which some people are good and others are bad. They seek out certainty to conquer their feelings of unbearable doubt. They seek out war—political war or actual war—as a way to give life meaning. They revert to tribe.

Tribalism seems like a way to restore the bonds of community. It certainly does bind people together. But it is actually the dark twin of community. Community is connection based on mutual affection. Tribalism, in the sense I'm using it here, is connection based on mutual hatred. Community is based on common humanity; tribalism on common foe. Tribalism is always erecting boundaries and creating friend/enemy distinctions. The tribal mentality is a warrior mentality based on scarcity: Life is a battle for scarce resources and it's always us versus them, zero-sum. The ends justify the means. Politics is war. Ideas are combat. It's kill or be killed. Mistrust is the tribalist worldview. Tribalism is community for lonely narcissists.

These days, partisanship for many people is not about which political party has the better policies. It's a conflict between the saved and the damned. People often use partisan identity to fill the void left when their other attachments wither away—ethnic, neighborhood, religious, communal, and familial.

This is asking more from politics than politics can deliver. Once politics becomes your ethnic or moral identity, it becomes impossible to compromise, because compromise becomes dishonor. Once politics becomes your identity, then every electoral contest is a struggle for existential survival, and everything is permitted. Tribalism threatens to take the detached individual and turn him into a monster.

SUFFERING

Whether the valley is a personal one or a societal one or both, there's a lot of suffering. You're enduring a season of pain, a season of feeling lost. This can be a period of soul-crushing anguish, but it can also be one of the most precious seasons of your life.

John Keats said that we live in a mansion of many apartments. When we're on the first mountain, we're living in what Keats called the "thoughtless chamber." This is the default chamber; we just unthinkingly absorb the values and ways of life that happen to be around us.

We want to stay in this chamber. It's comfortable, and everybody nods at you with approval. In *The Age of Anxiety*, W. H. Auden wrote,

> *We would rather be ruined than changed*
> *We would rather die in our dread*
> *Than climb the cross of the moment*
> *And let our illusions die.*

Seasons of suffering kick us in the ass. They are the foghorns that blast us out of our complacency and warn us we are heading for the wrong life.

There's nothing intrinsically noble about suffering. Sometimes grief is just grief, to be gotten through. Many bad things happen in life, and it's a mistake to try to sentimentalize these moments away by saying that they must be happening to serve some higher good. But sometimes, when suffering can be connected to a larger narrative of change and redemption, we can suffer our way to wisdom. This is the kind of wisdom you can't learn from books; you have to experience it yourself. Sometimes you experience your first taste of nobility in the way you respond to suffering.

The theologian Paul Tillich wrote that suffering upsets the normal patterns of life and reminds you that you are not who you thought you were. It smashes through the floor of what you thought was the basement of your soul and reveals a cavity below, and then it smashes through that floor and reveals a cavity below that.

Suffering teaches us gratitude. Normally we take love and friendship for granted. But in seasons of suffering we throw ourselves on others and appreciate the gifts that our loved ones offer. Suffering puts you in solidarity with others who suffer. It makes you more sympathetic to those who share this or some other sort of pain. In this way it tenderizes the heart.

Suffering calls for a response. None of us can avoid suffering, but we can all choose how we respond to it. And, interestingly, few people respond to suffering by seeking pleasure. Nobody says, I lost my child, therefore I should go out and party. They say, I lost my child, and therefore I am equipped to help others who have lost their child. People realize that shallow food won't satisfy the deep hunger and fill the deep emptiness that suffering reveals. Only spiritual food will do that. Many people respond to pain by practicing generosity.

Finally, suffering shatters the illusion of self-sufficiency, which is an illusion that has to be shattered if any interdependent life is going to begin. Seasons of pain expose the falseness and vanity of most of our ambitions and illuminate the larger reality of living and dying, caring and being cared for. Pain helps us see the true size of our egotistical desires. Before they seemed gigantic and dominated the whole screen. After seasons of suffering, we see that the desires of the ego are very small desires, and certainly not the ones we should organize our lives around. Climbing out of the valley is not like recovering from a disease. Many people don't come out healed; they come out different. The poet Ted Hughes observed that the things that are the worst to undergo are often the best to remember, because at those low moments the protective shells are taken off, humility is achieved, a problem is clearly presented, and a call to service is clearly received.

The Wilderness

THE NORMAL REACTION TO A SEASON OF SUFFERING IS TO TRY TO GET OUT of it. Address the symptoms. Have a few drinks. Play a few sad records. Move on.

The right thing to do when you are in moments of suffering is to stand erect in the suffering. Wait. See what it has to teach you. Understand that your suffering is a task that, if handled correctly, with the help of others, will lead to enlargement, not diminishment.

The valley is where we shed the old self so the new self can emerge. There are no shortcuts. There's just the same eternal three-step process that the poets have described from time eternal: from suffering to wisdom to service. Dying to the old self, cleansing in the emptiness, resurrecting in the new. From the agony of the valley, to the purgation in the desert, to the insight on the mountaintop.

So how do you start this three-part journey? Fortunately, people have been thinking about this for thousands of years, and they've given us models on how to do it.

Moses, for example, had an inchoate idea of what his life was about. He was growing up in the pharaoh's palace (very nice!), but he had a moral conscience. He hated the oppression of the Jews, and he killed an Egyptian guard who mistreated a slave. But his mini-rebellion backfired because it was random and self-indulgent. He had to flee Egypt a failure, even in the eyes of his fellow Jews. Moses went off to be alone. He took his flock of sheep "far away into the desert."

While he was out there, according to the rabbinic tradition, a little lamb ran away from the flock, and Moses pursued it. Normally, it's easy to catch a stray lamb. They're not the fastest creatures on earth, and they generally don't wander far. But this time something strange happened. The lamb ran like a gazelle. Moses sprinted farther into the wilderness but could not keep pace. The lamb ran out ahead, farther away. Finally, the lamb stopped at a spring to drink, and Moses caught her.

The lamb, of course, is Moses himself. Moses was hidden and unknown even to himself. As the Sufi saying puts it, "I was a hidden treasure." He had to go far off into the wilderness, and then even farther into that empty place in pursuit of a stray lamb, to finally come to himself.

At the moment when you are most confused about what you should do with your life, the smartest bet is to do what millions of men and women have done through history. Pick yourself up and go out alone into the wilderness.

A lot is gained simply by going into a different physical place. You need to taste and touch and feel your way toward a new way of being. And there are huge benefits in leaving the center of things and going off into the margins. "You are living through an unusual time," Henri Nouwen writes.

You see that you are called to go toward solitude, prayer, hiddenness, and great simplicity. You see that, for the time being, you have to be limited in your movements, sparing with phone calls, and careful in letter writing. . . . The thought that you may have to live away from friends, busy work, newspapers, and exciting books no longer scares you. . . . It is clear that something in you is dying and something is being born. You must remain attentive, calm, and obedient to your best intuitions.

In the wilderness, life is stripped of distractions. It is quiet. The topography demands discipline, simplicity, and fierce attention. Solitude in the wilderness makes irrelevant all the people-pleasing habits that have become interwoven into your personality. "What happens when a 'gifted child' finds himself in a wilderness where he's stripped of any way of proving his worth?" asks Belden Lane in *Backpacking with the Saints*. "What does he do when there's nothing he *can* do, when there's no audience to applaud his performance, when he faces a cold, silent indifference, if not hostility? His world falls to pieces. The soul hungry for approval starves in a desert like that. It reduces the compulsive achiever to something little, utterly ordinary. Only then is he able to be loved."

Solitude in the wilderness changes your experience of time. Normal life happens in ordinary time—the commute to work / do the dishes sense of time. But the wilderness marks time in eons; nothing changes quickly. The wilderness lives at the pace of what the Greeks called *kairos* time, which can be slower but is always richer. Synchronous time is moment after moment, but kairos time is qualitative, opportune or not yet ripe, rich or spare, inspired or flat—the crowded hour or the empty moment. When you have been away in the wilderness for weeks, you begin to move at kairos time. The soul communing with itself in the wilderness is at kairos time, too—slow and serene, but thick and strong, like the growing of the redwood.

The leanness of wilderness life prepares you for intimacy with yourself. Sometimes that surfaces the pain. There are the red-hot memories of past failures and past grief. There are all the wounds inflicted by parents and grandparents. There are your own bad actions that flow from these wounds—your tendency to lash out, or your tendency to be hyper-afraid of abandonment, or your tendency to be incommunicative and to withdraw at the first sign of stress.

"Your pain is deep and it won't just go away," Nouwen continues. "It is also uniquely yours, because it is linked to some of your earliest life experiences. Your call is to bring that pain home. As long as your wounded part remains foreign to your adult self, your pain will injure you as well as others." As the saying goes, suffering that is not transformed is transmitted.

LISTENING TO YOUR LIFE

When people are out there in the wilderness, they learn to receive and review their life. "If I were called upon to state in a few words the essence of everything I was trying to say both as a novelist and as a preacher, it would be something like this: Listen to your life," Frederick Buechner wrote. "See it for the fathomless mystery that it is. In the boredom and pain of it no less than in the excitement and gladness: touch, taste, smell your way to the holy and hidden heart of it because in the last analysis all moments are key moments, and life itself is grace."

The teacher Parker Palmer echoes the theme: "As the darkness began to descend on me in my early twenties, I thought I had developed a unique and terminal case of failure. I did not realize that I had merely embarked on a journey toward joining the human race."

The core of that, for Palmer, was listening. "Trying to live someone else's life, or to live by an abstract norm, will invariably fail—and even do great damage." You don't find your vocation through an act of taking charge. "Vocation does not come from willfulness. It comes from listening. I must listen to my life and try to understand what it is truly about—quite apart from what I would like it to be about."

I have a friend named Pete Wehner who is an amazing listener. I'll describe some problem to him, and he'll ask me some questions. There comes a moment in the conversation, after he's asked four or five questions, when I expect him to start offering his opinions and recommendations. But then he surprises me and asks six or eight more questions, before eventually offering counsel or advice. Real listening, whether to others or yourself, involves that unexpected extra round of questions, stretching the asking beyond what feels natural.

Listening to your life means having patience. Many of us confront most of life with a prematurely evaluating attitude. We have a natural tendency to make up our mind instantly, the moment we encounter something. The problem is that once we've filed something away with a judgment—even our very selves—we stop seeing it in all its complexity. The wilderness teaches negative capability, the ability to rest in uncertainty, to not jump to premature conclusions.

Listening to life means asking, What have I done well? What have I done poorly? What do I do when I'm not being paid or rewarded? Were there times when I put on faces that other people wanted me to wear, or that I thought other people wanted me to wear?

When you're in the wilderness, a better version of yourself has a tendency to emerge. "When I venture into wilderness, I'm surprised by how much I enjoy my own company," Belden Lane writes. "The person I travel with there isn't worried about his performance. He sheds the polished persona he tries so often to project to others. Scribbling in my journal under the shade of a pin oak atop Bell Mountain, I'm happy as a lark. I want to *be* the person that I am when I'm alone in wilderness." This is the beginning of an important revelation.

"In the deeps are the violence and terror of which psychology has warned us," Annie Dillard writes in *Teaching a Stone to Talk*. "But if you ride these monsters deeper down, if you drop with them farther over the world's rim, you find what our sciences cannot locate or name, the substrate, the ocean or matrix or ether which buoys the rest, which gives goodness its power for good, and evil its power for evil, the unified field: our complex and inexplicable caring for each other."

This is the pivotal point, maybe of this whole book. On the surface of our lives most of us build the hard shell. It is built to cover fear and insecurity and win approval and success. When you get down to the core of yourself, you find a different, more primeval country, and in it a deep yearning to care and connect. You could call this deep core of yourself the pleroma, or substrate. It is where your heart and soul reside.

After her first daughter was born, a friend of mine, Catherine Bly Cox, told me, "I found I loved her more than evolution required." I've always loved that observation because it points to that deeper layer. There are the things that drive us toward material pleasure, and there are evolutionary forces that drive us to reproduce and pass down our genes. These are the layers of life covered by economics and political science and evolutionary psychology. But those layers don't explain Chartres Cathedral or "Ode to Joy"; they don't explain Nelson Mandela in jail, Abraham Lincoln in the war room, or a mother holding her baby. They don't explain the fierceness and fullness of love, as we all experience it.

This is the layer we're trying to reach in the wilderness. These are the springs that will propel us to our second mountain.

When you have touched these deeper sources, you have begun to make the ego your servant and not your master. Over the years, your ego has found a specific way it wants you to be in order to win the most approval—what Henri Nouwen calls the "ego ideal." The ego wants you to point your life to the role that will make you seem smart, good-looking, and admirable. It's likely you have spent a lot of time so far conforming to the ego ideal.

As the psychologist James Hollis puts it, "Your ego prefers certainty to uncertainty, predictability over surprise, clarity over ambiguity. Your ego always wants to shroud over the barely audible murmurings of the heart." The ego, says Lee Hardy, wants you to choose a job and a life that you can use as a magic wand to impress others.

It's at this deep level that you sense a different life, one your ego cannot even fathom. There's something in you that senses, as C. S. Lewis wrote, "the scent of a flower we have not found, the echo of a tune we have not heard, news from a country we have never yet visited."

We're at the first stage of renunciation—shedding the old self so the new self can emerge. It's at this point you realize you are a much better person than your ego ideal. It's at this point when you really discover the heart and soul.

Heart and Soul

NOT LONG AGO I READ A PASSAGE IN A BOOK ABOUT A GUY WHO BOUGHT A house with a bamboo stand growing near his driveway. He decided to get rid of it, so he cut it down, then took an ax to its roots and smashed them into little pieces. He dug down and removed as much of the root system as he could and then he poured a plant poison over what remained. He filled the hole with several feet of gravel, and then, taking no chances, paved it over with cement. Two years later he noticed something: A little green bamboo shoot pushing up through the cement. That bamboo was unquenchable. It could not stop pushing upward.

We have something like that inside ourselves. It is our desire. We are often taught by our culture that we are primarily thinking beings—*Homo sapiens*. Sometimes our schools and companies treat us as nothing but analytic brains. But when we're in the valley, we get a truer and deeper view of who we really are and what we really need. When we're in the valley our view of what's important in life is transformed. We begin to realize that the reasoning brain is actually the third most important part of our consciousness. The first and most important part is the desiring heart.

As the Augustinian scholar James K. A. Smith writes, "To be human is to be on the move, pursuing something, *after* something. We are like existential sharks: we have to move to live." There is some deep part of ourselves from where desires flow. We're defined by what we desire, not what we know.

Look at kids in a school play—singing with all their might, dancing as best they can, concentrating furiously to get it right. There is something in them that animates them, the dream of being a star, the drive of pleasing a teacher or making a difference in the world or simply being great. The world may do a good job of paving over their desires, but those green bamboo shoots push stubbornly upward. Cruel adults and broken relationships will do their best to break the green shoots, boring schools try to dull them, poverty tries to starve them, but if you look at kids in even the roughest circumstances, nine times out of ten the green shoot is still there, desiring, dreaming, pushing upward.

Our emotions guide us. Our emotions assign value to things and tell us what is worth wanting. The passions are not the opposite of reason; they are the foundation of reason and often contain a wisdom the analytic brain can't reach. The ultimate heart's desire—the love behind all the other loves—is the desire to lose yourself in something or someone. Think about it: Almost every movie you've ever seen is about somebody experiencing this intense sense of merging with something, giving themselves away to something—a mission, a cause, a family, a nation, or a beloved. In the movie *Casablanca*, for example, the hero, Rick, has had his heart covered over. But love reawakens it. By the end he is a whole person again, committed, full of mission and desire.

The ultimate desire is the desire for fusion with a beloved other, for an I–Thou bond, the wholehearted surrender of the whole being, the pure union, the intimacy beyond fear. In his novel *Captain Corelli's Mandolin*, Louis de Bernières described this last best stop on the journey of heart. An old guy is talking to his daughter about his love for his late wife. He tells her, "Love itself is what is left over when being in love has burned away, and this is both an art and a fortunate accident.

Your mother and I had it, we had roots that grew towards each other underground, and when all the pretty blossoms had fallen from our branches we found that we were one tree and not two."

This is the heart fulfilled.

THE SOUL

The other more important part of the consciousness is the soul. Now, I don't ask you to believe in God or not believe in God. I'm a writer, not a missionary. That is not my department. But I do ask you to believe that you have a soul. There is some piece of your consciousness that has no shape, size, weight, or color. This is the piece of you that is of infinite value and dignity. The dignity of this piece doesn't increase or decrease with age; it doesn't get bigger or smaller depending on your size and strength. Rich and successful people don't have more or less of it than poorer or less successful people.

The soul is the piece of your consciousness that has moral worth and bears moral responsibility. A river is not morally responsible for how it flows, and a tiger is not morally responsible for what it eats. But because you have a soul, you are morally responsible for what you do or don't do. Because you have this essence inside of you, as the philosopher Gerald K. Harrison put it, your actions are either praiseworthy or blameworthy. Because you have this moral piece in you, you are judged for being the kind of person you are, for the thoughts you think and the actions you take.

Because each person has a soul, each person is owed a degree of respect and goodwill from others. Because each person has a soul, we are rightly indignant when that dignity is insulted, ignored, or obliterated. Slavery is wrong because it insults the fundamental dignity of a human soul. Rape is not just an assault on a collection of physical molecules; it is an insult to a human soul. It is an obscenity. Obscenity, the philosopher Roger Scruton teaches, is anything that covers up another person's soul.

The soul is the seedbed of your moral consciousness and your ethical sense. As C. S. Lewis observed, there's never been a country where people are admired for running away in battle, or for double-crossing people who were kind to them. We seem to be oriented by these moral sentiments the way other animals are oriented by the magnetic field. They are embedded in our natures. "Two things fill the mind with ever new and increasing admiration and awe, the oftener and the more steadily we reflect on them: the starry heavens above and the moral law within," Immanuel Kant wrote.

Mostly, what the soul does is yearn. If the heart yearns for fusion with another person or a cause, the soul yearns for righteousness, for fusion with the good. Socrates said that the purpose of life is the perfection of our souls—to realize the goodness that the soul longs for. Everyone I've ever met wants to lead a good and meaningful life. People feel bereft when they don't experience purpose and meaning in their lives. Even criminals and sociopaths come up with rationalizations to explain why the bad things they did were actually good or at least excusable because nobody can live with the idea that they are thoroughly bad.

Because we all have souls, we are all involved in a moral drama, of which we might have lower or higher awareness in any given moment. When we do something good we feel elevation, and when we do something bad we start making moral justifications. John Steinbeck put it beautifully in *East of Eden*:

> Humans are caught—in their lives, in their thoughts, in their hungers and ambitions, in their avarice and cruelty, and in their kindness and generosity too—in a net of good and evil. I think this is the only story we have and that it occurs on all levels of feeling and intelligence. Virtue and vice were warp and woof of our first consciousness, and they will be the fabric of our last. . . . A man, after he has brushed off the dust and chips of his life, will have left only the hard clean questions: Was it good or was it evil? Have I done well—or ill?

If you look at world history or current events, you see how often events are driven by our need to feel morally justified, our need to feel righteous and to offer care, and unfortunately our need to assign guilt and feel morally superior. The moral drive explains so much that is good in the world and, when it is twisted by the desire to feel superior, so much that is evil.

The odd thing about the soul is that while it is powerful and resilient, it is also reclusive. You can go years without really feeling the force of its yearning. You are enjoying the pleasures of life, building your career. It's amazing how untroubled you can be, year after year, while your soul is out there somewhere far away.

But eventually it hunts you down. In this way the soul is like a reclusive leopard living high up in the mountain forest somewhere. You may forget about him for long stretches. You are busy with the normal mundane activities of life, and the leopard is up in the mountains. But from time to time out of the corner of your eye, you glimpse the leopard, just off in the distance, trailing you through the tree trunks.

There are spare moments when you vaguely or even urgently feel his presence. This can happen agonizingly, in the middle of one of those sleepless nights, when your thoughts come, as one poet puts it, like a drawer full of knives. There's trouble in your soul, and it keeps you awake.

The leopard can visit during one of those fantastic moments with friends or family—when you look out at the laughing faces of your own children across a picnic table on some perfect summer day, and you are overwhelmed by gratitude. In those moments, you feel called to be worthy of such undeserved happiness, and the soul sort of swells with joy.

And then there are moments, maybe more toward middle or old age, when the leopard comes down out of the hills and just sits there in the middle of your doorframe. He stares at you, inescapably. He demands your justification. What good have you served? For what did you come? What sort of person have you become? There are no excuses at that moment. Everybody has to throw off the mask.

A FORTUNATE FALL

In the valley, if you are fortunate, you learn to see yourself as a whole person. You learn you are not just a brain and a set of talents to impress the world, but a heart and soul—primarily heart and soul. Now everything you do for the rest of your life is likely to be testimony to that reality.

When you ask people what experience made them the person they are, they never say, "I really was a shallow and selfish jerk until I went on that amazing vacation in Hawaii." No, people usually talk about moments of difficulty, struggle. The British journalist Malcolm Muggeridge put it bluntly, maybe a little too bluntly: "I can say with complete truthfulness that everything I have learned in my 75 years in this world, everything that has truly enhanced and enlightened my existence, has been through affliction and not through happiness, whether pursued or attained."

The reason transformation happens in the valley is because something that had hitherto been useful and pleasant needs to die. That thing is the ego self, the impressive rational way of being we constructed for ourselves on the first mountain. People develop this ego self so they can perform the tasks of the first mountain: to bull your way into the world, get a job, make your mark, build an identity. But there is a deeper self underneath that can't be seen unless the ego self falls away.

For Nathaniel Hawthorne it took a serious illness and a confrontation with death to blast him out of his ego ideal. "My fit of illness had been an avenue between two existences," he wrote, "the low-arched and darksome doorway, through which I crept out of a life of old conventionalisms, on my hands and knees, as it were, and gained admittance into the freer region that lay beyond. In this respect, it was like death. And, as with death, too, it was good to have gone through it. No otherwise could I have rid myself of a thousand follies, fripperies, prejudices, habits, and other such worldly dust as inevitably settles upon the crowd along the broad highway."

After the old self is relinquished, the heart and soul have space to take control. Old desires are shed and bigger desires are formed. The movement, clinical psychologist Daphne de Marneffe writes, is "deepening inward and expanding outward." When you go down inside yourself, you find that there are longings in there that are only completed when you are loving and serving others. "And then," says the poet Rilke, "the knowledge comes to me that I have space within me for a second, timeless, larger life."

When this relinquishment of the ego self and emergence of the heart and soul has happened, people are ready to begin the second mountain. Except they don't describe it as another climb. They describe it, often enough, as a fall. They have let go of something, and they are falling through themselves. Most of us need an earthquake to push us into that fortunate fall. Our job now is to be defeated by ever grander things. It is to trust in life and surrender to the callings that will catch us and show us the way.

You don't have to be in control. You don't have to impress the world. You've got the skill you earned on the first mountain and the wisdom you earned in the valley, and now is the time to take the big risk. "The sowing is behind; now is the time to reap," the theologian Karl Barth writes. "The run has been taken; now is the time to leap. Preparation has been made; now is the time for the venture of the work itself."

In 1849, a young Fyodor Dostoyevsky experienced his valley and the beginning of his recovery in a single moment. He had been imprisoned in Saint Petersburg with a group of other revolutionaries and sentenced to die. The men were marched out into a square in their burial shrouds. The firing squad gathered, and the drums sounded. Death was seconds away. Then, at that instant, by prearranged plan, a messenger arrived on horseback. The execution was to be stayed by the clemency of the czar. The original sentences would apply—hard labor.

One man broke down crying, singing out "Long live the czar!" Another went mad. Dostoyevsky was brought back to his cell and suddenly was overcome with joy. "I cannot recall when I was ever as happy as on that day," he later recalled. "I walked up and down my cell . . . and sang the whole time, sang at the top of my voice, so happy at being given back my life!"

He immediately wrote a letter to his brother: "And only then did I know how much I loved you my dear brother!" All the small questions that used to concern him fell away. "When I look back on my past and think how much time I wasted on nothing, how much time has been lost in futilities, errors, laziness, incapacity to live; how little I appreciated it, how many times I sinned against my heart and soul—then my heart bleeds."

His life, he felt, would begin again. "Never has there seethed in me such an abundant and healthy kind of spiritual life as now. . . . Now my life will change, I shall be born again in new form. . . . Life is a gift. Life is happiness, every minute can be an eternity of happiness. . . . Life is everywhere, life is in ourselves, not in the exterior."

Most of us don't get marched in front of a firing squad and then pardoned. Most of us learn the lesson Dostoyevsky learned gradually, over seasons of suffering, often in the wilderness. The lesson is that the things we had thought were most important—achievement, affirmation, intelligence—are actually less important, and the things we had undervalued—heart and soul—are actually most important.

Maybe some of us will learn these lessons while racking up success after success, or just being thoroughly loved, but for most of us the process is different: We have a season when we chase the shallow things in life. We are not fulfilled. Then comes hardship, which exposes the heart and soul. The heart and soul teach us that we cannot give ourselves what we desire most. Fulfillment and joy are on the far side of service. Only then are we really able to love. Only then are we able to begin the second journey.

The Committed Life

THE PERSON BEGINNING THE SECOND MOUNTAIN CLIMB WAGES A SILENT rebellion against the "I'm Free to Be Myself" culture that is still the defining feature of our age. That individualistic culture, you'll remember, was itself a rebellion against the stifling conformity of the 1950s. The second-mountain ethos is a rebellion against that rebellion.

Individualism says, Shoot for personal happiness, but the person on the second mountain says, No, I shoot for meaning and moral joy. That individualism says, Celebrate independence, but the second-mountain hero says, I will celebrate interdependence. I will celebrate the chance to become dependent on those I care for and for them to become dependent on me. Individualism celebrates autonomy; the second mountain celebrates relation. Individualism speaks with an active voice—lecturing, taking charge—and never the passive voice. But the second-mountain rebellion seeks to listen and respond, communicating in the voice of intimate exchange.

Individualism thrives in the prosaic world, the world of career choices and worldly accomplishment. The second-mountain ethos says, No, this is an enchanted world, a moral and emotional drama. Individualism accepts and assumes self-interest. The second-mountain ethos says that a worldview that focuses on self-interest doesn't account for the full amplitude of the human person. We are capable of great acts of love that self-interest cannot fathom, and murderous acts of cruelty that self-interest cannot explain. Individualism says, The main activities of life are buying and selling. But you say, No, the main activity of life is giving. Human beings at their best are givers of gifts.

Individualism says, You have to love yourself first before you can love others. But the second-mountain ethos says, You have to be loved first so you can understand love, and you have to see yourself actively loving others so that you know you are worthy of love. On the first mountain, a person makes individual choices and keeps their options open. The second mountain is a vale of promise making. It is about making commitments, tying oneself down, and giving oneself away. It is about surrendering the self and making the kind of commitment that, in the Bible, Ruth made to Naomi: "Where you go, I will go, and where you stay, I will stay. Your people shall be my people and your God my God. Where you die, I will die and there I will be buried."

As I mentioned in the introduction, most of us make four big commitments over the course of our lives: to a vocation, to a spouse and family, to a philosophy or faith, and to a community. We think of these commitments as different things. Choosing a marriage seems different from choosing a philosophy or a community. Only one of them, the actual marriage, involves a formal ceremony and an explicit exchange of vows. But the process of commitment making is similar across all four realms. All of them require a vow of dedication, an investment of time and effort, a willingness to close off other options, and the daring to leap headlong down a ski run that is steeper and bumpier than it appears.

How does commitment making happen? It begins with some movement of the heart and soul. You fall in love with something—a person or a cause or an idea, and if that love is deep enough, you decide to dedicate a significant chunk of your life to it.

For most of us this love creeps up slowly. It takes time to figure out if the person or cause is worthy of all the faithfulness, care, and passion that a commitment entails. We build gates around our hearts and let people or causes inside one gate at a time. If you retain a lifelong love for your college or your summer camp or your hometown, you probably had to live in it for a time before its roots sunk ineluctably down into you and the love became deep and permanent.

The few times I've fallen in love with a person, it's been after a long period of nonromantic friendship. Maybe for that reason, I'm fascinated with those cases when the hook gets lodged in the mouth all at once. In 1274 in Florence, a young Dante saw the young girl named Beatrice and, in a flash, was overawed. He gives a striking, almost anatomical, description of a person surrendering to love:

> That spirit which lives in the most secret chamber of the heart began to tremble fiercely so that I felt its agony in the least pulsation, and, then, trembling, it said to me: "Behold a god more powerful than I, who, coming, will rule over me." At that moment, my natural spirit, that which lives in the high chamber to which all the spirits of the senses carry their perceptions, began to marvel deeply, and speaking especially to the spirit of sight, spoke these words: "Now your blessedness appears." At that moment the natural spirit, which dwells in the place where all our nourishment is brought, began to weep, and weeping said these words: "Oh misery, how often will I be troubled from this time on!"

Dante saw and was conquered, and knew instantaneously what trouble this new ruling passion would cause him. But he loved on nonetheless. And this can happen with the love of a person, but also with the love of a political cause or an idea or a God. The love will change everything in unexpected and inconvenient ways.

Once the heart has fallen in love and has acknowledged that love, then the soul feels a powerful urge to make a promise to it. Once love strikes, there is an urge to say, "I will always love you." That's because the very essence of love is dedication. As Dietrich and Alice von Hildebrand once wrote, "A man who would say: 'I love you now, but how long it will last I cannot tell,' does not truly love; he does not even suspect the very nature of love. Faithfulness is so essentially one with love, that everyone, at least as long as he loves, must consider his devotion an undying devotion. This holds good for every love, for parental love and filial love, for friendship and for spousal love. The deeper a love, the more it is pervaded by fidelity."

A commitment is a promise made from love. A commitment is making a promise to something without expecting a return—out of sheer lovingness. There may be a psychic return on a good marriage, or from a commitment to a political cause, or from making music, but that is not why one makes it or why one does it. If a couple is actually in love, and you pull them aside and tell them that this love probably doesn't make sense and they should forsake it, you will almost certainly not persuade them. They'd rather be in turmoil with each other than in tranquility alone.

There is something that feels almost involuntary about a deep commitment. It happens when some person or cause or field of research has become part of your very identity. You have reached the point of the double negative. "I can't not do this." Somewhere along the way you realized, I'm a musician. I'm a Jew. I'm a scientist. I'm a Marine. I'm an American. I love her. I am his beloved.

In this way, a commitment is different from a contract. A person making a contract is weighing pros and cons. A person entering into a contract doesn't really change. She just finds some arrangement that will suit her current interests. A commitment, on the other hand, changes who you are, or rather embeds who you are into a new relationship. You are not just man or woman. You are husband and wife. You are not just an adult; you are a teacher or a nurse. Rabbi Jonathan Sacks clarifies the difference: "A contract is a *transaction*. A covenant is a *relationship*. Or to put it slightly differently: a contract is about interests. A covenant is about identity. It is about you and me coming together to form an 'us.' That is why contracts *benefit*, but covenants *transform*."

A committed person is giving her word and placing a piece of herself in another person's keeping. The word "commitment" derives from the Latin *mittere*, which means "to send." She is sending herself out and giving another person a claim. She is creating a higher entity. When you enter a marriage, your property is still yours, but it is no longer only yours. It belongs to your spouse, too, or, more properly, it belongs to the union you have both created—this new higher-level thing.

This fervent, love-drenched, identity-changing definition of a commitment is true, but not the whole truth. A commitment isn't just love and a promise, of course. It is love and promise put under law. In living out a commitment, each party understands the fickleness of feelings, so they bind their future selves to specific obligations. Spouses love each other, but they bind themselves down with a legal, public, and often religious marriage commitment, to limit their future choices for those times when they get on each other's nerves. Curious people may read books, but they also enroll in universities to make sure they follow a supervised course of study for at least a few years into the future. Spiritual people may experience transcendence, but understand that for most people spirituality lasts and deepens only if it is lived out within that maddening community called institutionalized religion. Religions embed the love of God in holidays, stories, practices, and rituals, and make them solid and enduring. As Rabbi David Wolpe once wrote, "Spirituality is an emotion. Religion is an obligation. Spirituality soothes. Religion mobilizes. Spirituality is satisfied with itself. Religion is dissatisfied with the world."

Thus, the most complete definition of a commitment is this: falling in love with something and then building a structure of behavior around it for those moments when love falters. Orthodox Jews love their God, but they keep kosher just in case. But let's not be too stern about this. The yoke committed people place on themselves is not a painful yoke. Most of the time it is a delicious yoke. When I had my first child, a friend emailed me, "Welcome to the world of unavoidable reality." You can be late with a work assignment and you can postpone a social occasion, but if your kid needs feeding or has to be met at the bus stop, you're in an unavoidable reality. Parents groan under the burdens they took on with the commitment of parenthood, but how often have you met a parent who wished they hadn't done it? A thick life is defined by commitments and obligations. The life well lived is a journey from open options to sweet compulsions.

WHAT COMMITMENTS GIVE US

Though commitments are made in a spirit of giving, they produce many benefits. Let me spell out a few:

Our commitments give us our identity. They are how we introduce ourselves to strangers. They are the subjects that make our eyes shine in conversation. They are what give our lives constancy and coherence. As Hannah Arendt put it, "Without being bound to the fulfillment of promises, we would never be able to achieve the amount of identity and continuity which together produce a 'person' about whom a story can be told; each of us would be condemned to wander helplessly and without direction in the darkness of his own lonely heart, caught in its ever-changing moods, contradictions, and equivocalities." Identity is not formed alone. Identity is always formed by joining a dyad with something else.

Our commitments give us a sense of purpose. In 2007, the Gallup organization asked people around the world whether they felt they were leading meaningful lives. It turns out that Liberia was the country where the most people felt a sense of meaning and purpose, while the Netherlands was the place where the lowest percentage of people did. This is not because life was necessarily sweeter in Liberia. On the contrary. But Liberians possessed what Paul Froese calls "existential urgency." In the turmoil of their lives, they were compelled to make fierce commitments to one another merely to survive. They were willing to risk their lives for one another. And these fierce commitments gave their lives a sense of meaning. That's the paradox of privilege. When we are well-off we chase the temporary pleasures that actually draw us apart. We use our wealth to buy big houses with big yards that separate us and make us lonely. But in crisis we are compelled to hold closely to one another in ways that actually meet our deepest needs.

Our commitments allow us to move to a higher level of freedom. In our culture we think of freedom as the absence of restraint. That's freedom *from*. But there is another and higher kind of freedom. That is freedom *to*. This is the freedom as fullness of capacity, and it often involves restriction and restraint. You have to chain yourself to the piano and practice for year after year if you want to have the freedom to really play. You have to chain yourself to a certain set of virtuous habits so you don't become slave to your destructive desires—the desire for alcohol, the desire for approval, the desire to lie in bed all day.

As the theologian Tim Keller puts it, real freedom "is not so much the absence of restrictions as finding the right ones." So much of our lives are determined by the definition of freedom we carry around unconsciously in our heads. On the second mountain it is your chains that set you free.

Our commitments build our moral character. When my older son was born, the delivery was difficult and he came out bruised and blue, with a low Apgar score. He was whisked away to intensive care. It was a harrowing time. In the middle of that first night, I recall thinking, If he should live for only thirty minutes, will it have been worth a lifetime of grief for his mother and me? Before having a kid, I might have thought, Of course not. How could thirty minutes of life for a being who is not even aware of itself be worth a lifetime of grief for two adults? Where's the cost-benefit in that? But every parent will know that it makes perfect sense. After his birth, the logic is different. Instantly it became clear that the life of the child has infinite dignity. Of course it is worth the grief, even if the candle is only lit for such a short time. Once a kid is born you've been seized by a commitment, the strength of which you couldn't even have imagined beforehand. It brings you to the doorstep of disciplined service.

When a parent falls in love with a child, the love arouses amazing energy levels; we lose sleep caring for the infant. The love impels us to make vows to the thing we love; parents vow to always be there for their kid. Fulfilling those vows requires us to perform specific self-sacrificial practices; we push the baby in a stroller when maybe we'd rather go out alone for a run. Over time those practices become habits, and those habits engrave a certain disposition; by the time the kid is three, the habit of putting the child's needs first has become second nature to most parents.

Slowly, slowly, by steady dedication, you've transformed a central part of yourself into something a little more giving, more in harmony with others and more in harmony with what is good than it was before. Gradually the big loves overshadow the little ones: Why would I spend my weekends playing golf when I could spend my weekends playing ball with my children? In my experience, people repress bad desires only when they are able to turn their attention to a better desire. When you're deep in a commitment, the distinction between altruism and selfishness begins to fade away. When you serve your child it feels like you are serving a piece of yourself. That disposition to do good is what having good character is all about.

In this way, moral formation is not individual; it is relational. Character is not something you build sitting in a room thinking about the difference between right and wrong and about your own willpower. Character emerges from our commitments. If you want to inculcate character in someone else, teach them how to form commitments—temporary ones in childhood, provisional ones in youth, permanent ones in adulthood. Commitments are the school for moral formation.

When your life is defined by fervent commitments, you are on the second mountain.

The Second Mountain

KATHY FLETCHER AND DAVID SIMPSON HAVE A SON NAMED SANTI WHO went to public school in Washington, D.C. Santi had a friend named James who sometimes went to bed hungry, so Santi invited him to occasionally sleep over at his house. James had a friend and that kid had a friend and so on. Now if you go to Kathy and David's house on any given Thursday night there will be about twenty-six kids sitting around the dinner table. There are generally four or five living with Kathy and David or with other families nearby. Every summer Kathy and David round up a caravan and take about forty kids out of the city for a vacation on Cape Cod. Simply by responding to the needs around them, Kathy and David are now at the center of a sprawling extended family.

I started going to dinner at Kathy and David's house sometime early in 2014, invited by a mutual friend. I walked in the door and was greeted by a tall, charismatic man named Edd, who had dreadlocks dripping over soulful eyes. I held out my hand to shake his and Edd said, "We don't shake hands here. We hug here." I'm not naturally a huggy guy, but so began what has been so far five years of hugging.

We nominally gather around the table on Thursdays to eat, but, in reality, we gather to feed a deeper hunger. The meal is always the same, spicy chicken and black rice. Cellphones are banned ("Be in the now," Kathy says). About a third of the way through the meal, we go around the table and each person says something they are grateful for, something nobody knows about them, or some other piece of information about their life at that moment. There are frequent celebrations—somebody passed the GED exam, got a job, or graduated from barber school. People also throw more complicated things on the table, too. A seventeen-year-old girl is dealing with a pregnancy. Another young woman has a failing kidney, and Medicaid refuses to pay the cost for a new one. A young man announces he's bisexual, and another admits he is depressed. One day a new arrival sat at the table and told us that though she was now twenty-one, she hadn't sat at a dinner table since she was eleven.

Most of our conversations are pure affirmation; people have had enough crap in their lives and need to hear how valuable they are, how much they are loved and needed. Often, we just tell jokes and laugh. The kids sing in their chairs. I brought my daughter one day and as she walked out she told me, "That's the warmest place I've ever been in my life."

After the meal we head over to the piano, and somebody will play an Adele song and people will sing. But the dinner table is the key technology of social intimacy here. It is the tool we use to bond, connect, and commit to one another. I've learned to never underestimate the power of a dinner table. It's the stage on which we turn toward one another for love like flowers seeking the sun. "Thank you for seeing the light in me," one young woman said to Kathy one night. The adults come from the emotionally avoidant world of Washington, D.C., and get to shed their armor. The kids come from the streets and call Kathy and David "Mom" and "Dad," their chosen parents.

The kids around the table have been through the normal traumas of poverty in America—some have been homeless, some have traveled through the foster care system. The theme of male cruelty runs through their histories—some father or other male figure abused them, abandoned them, or misled them. But they are enmeshed now. Bill Millikan, who founded the organization Communities in Schools, came to the table one night. He's in his seventies now. "I've been working in this field for fifty years," he says, "and I've never seen a program turn around a life. Only relationships turn around lives."

That's what's happening around the table. You wouldn't know it if you were white and over thirty-five, but Washington, D.C., is a fantastic place to be if you are an artist, black, and under twenty-five. The kids who come to dinner are connected to this underground arts scene—as poets, painters, DJs, singers, or something else. We adults in the group provide them an audience in front of which they can realize their talents. Their gift to us is a complete intolerance of social distance.

Emotional combustion happens in the most mysterious ways. No one can really trace the chemical processes by which love bursts into flame in one community and not another. But it is here in this community, and all of us have been transformed in surprising ways. David gave up his job and now works with the kids full-time. Kathy organizes arts programs across America but comes home and has another full-time vocation waiting.

For years, the adults told the kids they could go to college, so when they began coming of age, they took Kathy and David up on the offer, and now we all have to find a way to pay for it. Kathy and David set up a nonprofit called AOK, which stands for All Our Kids. We are all deeply embedded now, giving each other helping hands. And it is because Kathy and David responded simply to need. Kathy grew up in a large Catholic family, so she's used to having a large loving mess of people around. When she's asked how she could possibly host that many young people, she looks out uncomprehendingly. "How is it you don't?"

Kathy and David are exhausted a lot of the time, as you can imagine. Maybe you are a parent trying to look after two or three kids; imagine what a day is like intertwined with forty. One of the kids has just lost a cellphone or smashed his bike. Sometimes real crises hit. In 2018, Kathy and David had to race against time after Medicaid refused to pay for a kidney transplant for one of the young women. Everybody mobilized to get Medicaid to reverse their decision, which it did. Fortunately, we had a donor. David gave one of his kidneys to Madeline.

The exhaustion comes with its compensations. Kathy and David are now enmeshed in dozens of loving relationships. They sometimes ask themselves if there is a better way to do the work they do, but they don't have to ask themselves if they are doing anything valuable with their lives. They know. After you have fallen in love with Kesari or James or Koleco, Taruq and Thalya, it's not even a question. These are young people of infinite depth and promise. The chance to be with them is just what you do.

To me, AOK is what the second-mountain life looks like. It is a life of love, care, and commitment. It is the antidote to much that is wrong in our culture.

THE WEAVERS

I now get to spend a lot of time around people like Kathy and David, thanks to my Aspen Institute program, Weave: The Social Fabric Project. The first idea behind the effort was that social isolation is a core problem that underlies a lot of other social problems. The second idea was that across the nation there are people who are building healthy communities. We have a lot to learn from such people.

We travel around the country and meet people who are restoring social capital and healing lives. These people are everywhere. We are a nation of healers. We at Weave drop into a small town, and it is not a problem to find thirty-five people who completely fit the mold.

There's Jade Bock in Albuquerque, who lost her dad when she was young and now helps children process grief. There's Stephanie Hruzek in Houston, who runs an after-school kids' program and who plays with them hour after hour—a fervent believer that an hour spent in play with a child is the most important purposeless hour you will ever spend. "I am broken," Stephanie says. "I need other people to survive." There's Sam Jones, who has run an amateur boxing ring in southeastern Ohio, where, for no fee, he coaches young men, nominally in boxing but really about life.

Over the course of 2018, I probably met between five hundred and one thousand of these people. Almost without exception, they have what Kathy and David have: vocational certitude. They are poorly paid and often feel ignored; their small acts of care often go unrewarded by the larger status systems of our society. But they find joy in the light they bring others, and they know why they have been put on this earth. "This is not a job I'll retire from," says Sharon Murphy, who runs Mary House, a refugee-housing organization in Washington. "I love what I do. This kind of work is a way of being."

They can seem very altruistic. But it's worth remembering, as Alasdair MacIntyre has pointed out, that the concept of altruism was invented only in the eighteenth century. Once people decided that human nature is essentially egoist and selfish, then it was necessary to invent a word for when people weren't driven by selfish desires. But before that, what we call altruism—living for relationships—was just how people lived. It wasn't heroic or special.

There are many kinds of second-mountain people—men and women whose lives are defined by deep commitments. There are such people in business, in teaching, the arts, the military. But, because of my work with Weave, I've gotten to know the ones in the nonprofit world best. They are standing athwart the culture of individualism and isolation. Their daily activities are in contact with their ultimate ends.

Spending time around such people has been an education. I'd like to describe them for a bit to give a sense of what the second-mountain life looks like and what values people on that mountain tend to share. I'll put the key commonalities in italics.

THEIR VALLEYS

Most of the people I've met through Weave have had some sort of valley in their lives, sometimes in the form of a hard childhood. Or the valley took the form of a *walkout experience*. They worked in a normal place of employment, but it just rubbed against the grain of their moral nature, and they walked out. A man in North Carolina had a good job at IBM, but he felt called to keep alive the culture of his Appalachian small town, so he opened up a moonshine distillery and a store where people could gather. "I worked at an agency that was clearly a racist agency," a government worker in South Carolina said. "But I called them on what were [their] practices." So she walked out of her former life into a new one that felt right.

Some of the valleys these people have suffered are shocking. Cara Brook from Ohio finished college in three years and was immediately diagnosed with a rare form of cancer—fewer than ten people get it each year in the United States. She spent a year in chemo, and when she emerged, she says, it was like she was shot out of a cannon. She was determined to make a difference in whatever time she had left, and now raises money to revitalize Appalachian Ohio. When Darius Baxter of Washington was nine, his father had an affair with a stripper who arranged his murder. Now, having played football at Georgetown, Darius runs football camps for boys in his neighborhood so that there will be adult men in their lives.

Sarah Adkins is a pharmacist in Ohio. She raised two small boys, Samson and Solomon, with her husband, Troy. But over the years Troy suffered increasing bouts of depression and anxiety. He stopped working and became angry and obsessive. Sarah and Troy struggled to cope and sought therapy. For a time, it seemed to be working.

Then, one fall weekend in 2010, when the boys were eight and six, Sarah went on a long-planned antiquing trip with her mother and sister. Troy said he'd take the boys to a friend's house on a lake. She called a few times on Saturday but got no answer, so she figured they were out boating or something. She returned home Sunday around five and was surprised that the mail was still outside the front door, including some toys she'd ordered for her children. She entered the door and cried out "Mommy's home!" but got no response. Then she noticed that a mattress had been pushed up against the door going down to the basement. She figured the boys were playing hide and seek with her, so she went downstairs smiling. At the bottom of the stairs, she saw Troy slumped over against a cabinet. Then she saw one boy, Samson, on the couch, which appeared to be covered in chocolate. She couldn't process what she was seeing. Then she touched Samson's forehead and realized he was cold. A vision of gold flashed across her brain, like a blast of sunshine, and she had a vision of Samson up with God. The vision lasted only a second. She ran upstairs to find Solomon. He was in his bed. She pulled back the covers and to this day cannot describe what she saw. He, too, had been shot and was cold.

She called 911. "He killed my babies! My beautiful babies. They're dead!" she cried into the phone. The operator asked her to perform CPR, but Sarah explained that they were already cold. Troy had left a note: "I will shield S&S from a life filled with confusion, questioned allegiances, guilt, hopelessness, co-dependence and insecurity. This cycle of misery ends with me."

Thousands of people rallied around Sarah. She stayed with her parents for the next three months and slept in their bed. Meals were brought to her daily for six months. It has taken years to recover. She jokes that she's still living on the edge. Her mind wanders. When you spend time with her you notice radically different moods passing across her face. She has a slightly manic quality, like everything is hyper-charged, a bit out of control.

Her house was declared a biohazard zone, and it cost $35,000 to clean. Sarah realized that poor women can't afford funerals and other costs when their own boys are shot, or when there is violence in their homes. They have to cut the blood from their own carpets. She started a foundation to help pay for funerals and cleanup. She teaches at Ohio University and Ohio State. She works at a free healthcare clinic and is working to open a new one. She is an example of someone who has suffered the worst life can throw at you and is permanently affected by it. But she has come out with a ferocious desire to serve.

"I grew from this experience because I was angry," she says. "I was going to fight back against what he tried to do to me by making a difference in the world. See, he didn't kill me. My response to him is whatever you meant to do to me, fuck you, you're not going to do it to me." Her motivation is part defiance against her husband, part love for the people in front of her.

MORAL MOTIVATION

That is the thing you notice about second-mountain people. There's been *a motivational shift*. Their desires have been transformed. If you wanted to generalize a bit, you could say there are six layers of desire:

1. Material pleasure. Having nice food, a nice car, a nice house.
2. Ego pleasure. Becoming well-known or rich and successful. Winning victories and recognition.
3. Intellectual pleasure. Learning about things. Understanding the world around us.
4. Generativity. The pleasure we get in giving back to others and serving our communities.
5. Fulfilled love. Receiving and giving love. The rapturous union of souls.
6. Transcendence. The feeling we get when living in accordance with some ideal.

Social science and much of our modern thinking tends to emphasize the first two desires. We often assume that self-interest—defined as material gain and status recognition—are the main desires of life and that service to others is the icing on the cake. And that's because for centuries most of our social thinking has been shaped by men, who went out and competed in the world while women largely stayed home and did the caring. These men didn't even see the activity that undergirded the political and economic systems they spent their lives studying. But when you actually look around the world—parents looking after their kids, neighbors forming associations, colleagues helping one another, people meeting and encountering each other in coffee shops—you see that loving care is not on the fringe of society. It's the foundation of society.

These community builders are primarily driven by desires four through six—by *emotional, spiritual, and moral motivations*: a desire to live in intimate relation with others, to make a difference in the world, to feel right with oneself. They are driven by a desire for belonging and generosity.

They exhibit *bright sadness*. I get the phrase from the Franciscan friar Richard Rohr and his great book *Falling Upward*, which is about finding meaning in middle age and beyond. When you are serving those in need you see pain and injustice close up. The closer you get to wisdom, Rohr continues, the more of your own shadow you see, and the more of other people's shadow, and the more you realize how much we need each other. Hope gets infused with realistic awareness. "There is a gravitas in the second half of life," Rohr writes, "but it is now held up by a much deeper lightness, or 'okayness.' Our mature years are characterized by a bright sadness and a sober happiness, if that makes any sense."

I once asked my *New York Times* readers whether they had found purpose in their lives. Thousands wrote back to describe their experiences. One in particular sticks out and illustrates Rohr's concept of bright sadness and okayness. Greg Sunter from Brisbane, Australia, wrote:

> Four years ago, my wife of 21 years passed away as the result of a brain tumor. Her passage from diagnosis to death was less than 6 months. As shocking as that time was, almost as shocking was the sense of personal growth and awakened understanding that has come from the experience for me through reflection and inner work—to a point that I feel almost guilty about how significant my own growth has been as a result of my wife's death.
>
> In his book *A Hidden Wholeness*, Parker Palmer writes about the two ways in which our hearts can be broken: the first imagining the heart as shattered and scattered; the second imagining the heart broken open into new capacity, holding more of both our own and the world's suffering and joy, despair and hope. The image of the heart broken open has become the driving force of my life in the years since my wife's death. It has become the purpose to my life.

My friend Kennedy Odede grew up in Kenya. When he was three, his cherished grandmother died after she was bitten by a rabid dog. His drunken stepfather beat him. His best friend died at eight of malaria. He joined a street gang, sniffed glue and petrol, committed crimes, and was nearly killed several times. He was rescued by a Catholic priest who sexually abused him. Yet, he is now one of the most joyful people I know.

I once asked him how he could have turned out so joyful amid the struggles. Well, he replied, when she could, his mother poured unconditional love into him. Kennedy has also poured unconditional love onto others. He founded SHOFCO (Shining Hope for Communities), an organization that combats urban poverty and provides a school for girls, in the Nairobi slum of Kibera. "SHOFCO saved my life," he told me, "and helped me remain positive even when the worst happened. It made me feel not like a passive victim, but like I had agency and power to change what was happening in my community. I think starting SHOFCO also gave me a sense of the power of 'ubuntu,' feeling connected to universal humanity." In the cruelty of slum life, there is still brightness shining forth.

These people are *somewheres, not anywheres*, localists not cosmopolitans. They are attached to a particular place, a spot of ground. Sarah Hemminger founded a mentoring program in Baltimore. There is a pendant depicting a map of the city of Baltimore on the necklace she wears to work every day, because that is where her devotion lies. Phil Good of Youngstown, Ohio, began his career by standing in the town square and holding up a sign that read DEFEND YOUNGSTOWN, and is spending his life helping that town recover from deindustrialization. An educator in Houston told us, "When I came back to Houston I made a commitment to this place that I knew growing up but which I got disconnected from because of globalization."

They tend to be *hedgehogs, not foxes*. In the famous formulation, the fox knows many things and can see the world with an opposable mind, from many points of view. But the hedgehog knows one thing, has one big idea around which his or her life revolves. This is the mentality that committed community weavers tend to have.

They *assume responsibility*. Somebody in their background planted an ideal of what a responsible life looks like, of what you are supposed to do. Some people walk down the street and see passing forms. But these community builders see persons and their needs. Responding comes naturally to them. These people wouldn't recognize themselves if they didn't act in this way. As a woman who works with battered women in D.C. told us, "I do the work because I don't consider it work. I do it because my mother and grandmother have taught me it is a responsibility to respond." They do their work in the matter-of-fact way other people do the dishes. There are dishes in the sink so of course they have to be done. "What I do is as simple and common as the laughter of a child," Mother Teresa once said.

They often use the phrase *"radical hospitality"* to describe their philosophy of life, because their goal is that nobody should ever be shut out from their welcome. As one young man who works at a youth center in Washington told us, "Once you realize that these are lives, you must risk life and limb for a life. You can't turn from a life."

And so they get gripped. Like Kathy and David, they rarely went out looking for the people they serve and the problem they spend their lives addressing. These things sort of just came into their path. "I didn't choose this job. It chose me," says Franklin Peralta, who works at the Latin American Youth Center, echoing a refrain we heard constantly.

It is a paradox that when people are finding themselves they often have a sensation that they are letting go and surrendering themselves. You meet a person in need. At first you just commit to help them a little. An hour a week. It's no big deal. But then you get to know and care about the person, and the hooks of commitment are set. Now you'll do what needs to be done. At this point you just *let go of the wheel*. You stop asking, What do I want? and start asking, What is life asking of me? You respond.

"A person's life can be meaningful only if she cares fairly deeply about some things, only if she is gripped, excited, interested, engaged," writes the philosopher Susan Wolf. Notice the verbs Wolf uses: "gripped," "excited," "engaged." They describe response at some deep level, not a self-initiated conscious choice. These are the verbs our community builders use.

Anne Colby and William Damon of Stanford studied these kinds of community weavers for their book *Some Do Care*. There's *not a lot of moral reflection* that goes into the choice to give yourself away, they found. There's not a lot of internal battles, or adding up the costs and benefits. "Instead, we saw an unhesitating will to act, a disavowal of fear and doubt, and a simplicity of moral response. Risks were ignored and consequences went unweighed."

A few years ago, Barbara Goodson from Houston started giving free haircuts to the homeless. At first it was just a few cuts a month. But then she started giving haircuts to people coming out of prison and battered women. What started as a few haircuts a month turned into hundreds. "What motivated me?" she asks. "Enhancing the dignity of every client."

Recently a friend told me about a crossing guard he met in Florida. Standing there on the corner, he asked her if she did any volunteer work in the community. She said no, she didn't have time. But then he learned she was in fact volunteering at that second as a crossing guard outside the elementary school so the children would be safe. Then, a few minutes later, he learned that she was going to take some meals to sick neighbors later in the day. The longer she talked, the more he learned about the ways she was giving to others. But she didn't consider any of it volunteer work. It was just what you do.

We think of giving as something we do on rare occasions, on Christmas and birthdays. But the German theologian Dietrich Bonhoeffer argued that *giving is the primary relationship between one person and another*, not the secondary one. It is family member to family member. Friend to friend. Colleague to colleague. People to community. It is the elemental desire to transform isolation and self-centeredness into connectedness and caring. A personality awakens itself by how it gives.

I hear the word "abide" a lot when I'm out with community builders. They use it to suggest a kind of giving that is not heroic or cinematic. It's just being present with other people year after year, serving in both routine ways and large ones. This kind of giving creates stability in life, a continuity of the self as the circumstances of life ebb and flow. In *Some Do Care*, Ann Colby and William Damon quote an anti-poverty activist who expresses this perfectly: "I also know that I am part of a struggle. I am not the struggle. I am not leading the struggle. I am there. And I have been there for a long time, and I'm going to be there for the rest of my life. So I have no unrealistic expectations. Therefore, I am not going to get fatigued."

DEEP RELATIONALITY

The weavers I've met are *extremely relational.* They are driven to seek deep relations with others, both to feed their hunger for connection and because they believe that change happens through deepening relationships.

When they are working with the homeless or the poor or the traumatized, they are laboring alongside big welfare systems that offer services but not care. These systems treat people as "cases" or "clients." They are necessary to give people financial stability and support, but they can't do transformational change. As Peter Block, one of the leading experts on community, puts it, "Talk to any poor person or vulnerable person and they can give you a long list of the services they have received. They are well serviced, but you often have to ask what in their life has fundamentally changed."

Relationship is the driver of change. Think of who made you who you are. It was probably a parent, a teacher, or a mentor. It wasn't some organization that was seeking a specific and measurable outcome that can be reduced to metrics. It wasn't a person looking to create a system of change that could scale. It was just a person doing something intrinsically good—making you feel known, cared for, trusted, unconditionally loved—without presuming to know how that relationship would alter the trajectory of your life.

In her book, *The Fabric of Character*, my wife, Anne Snyder, writes about the Other Side Academy in Salt Lake City. The organization takes hardened criminals and gives them a chance to get out of jail and turn their lives around by living in a group home and working for a moving company. The whole group meets at sessions—called "games"—where the men and women call one another out for even the slightest moral infraction. Connection happens at the nexus of truth and love, the founders say. Truth without love is harshness. Love without truth is sentimentality. But if you can be completely honest with somebody in the context of loving support, then you have a trusting relationship. Norms are enforced as people hold one another accountable for violating them. Community is woven through *love-drenched accountability*.

The weavers talk a lot about how important it is to act and not just talk about things. They often describe themselves as GSD types—Get Shit Done. They publish the books of their lives with their actions. But they also put *tremendous emphasis on listening* and conversation. A lot of what they do is to create spaces where deep conversations can happen. One day at Stephanie Hruzek's after-school program in Houston, FamilyPoint, a ten-year-old-boy came up to her with a note he claimed he had found on the floor. It was an obscenity-laced tirade. Words like "bitch," "asshole," and "fuck you" leapt out from the page. Stephanie asked him who had written such an angry note. He said he didn't know.

That night, the staff watched the security tapes and discovered that the boy who brought up the note was also the one who'd actually written it. The next day they confronted him with the evidence. He denied it at first, and their natural impulse would have been to punish him for the hate-filled document. But instead of acting quickly they sat with him for a while and talked. Eventually he began to cry and said, "I wrote that note to a man who hurt me."

It turned out that two men with guns had recently broken into his house and had threatened to kill him. His neighbors heeded frantic calls from his mother and interrupted the break-in, pounding on the door until the police arrived and interrupted it, but the boy and his mother were both traumatized. The note was just a disorganized attempt to deal with what he was feeling. Stephanie wonders what would have happened if they had just gone ahead and punished him—punished him for in effect crying for help. What lesson would he have learned and what trajectory would that have set him off on? The lesson is that you have to stay in the conversation long enough; you have to listen patiently enough.

Community builders believe in *radical mutuality*. They utterly reject the notion that some people have everything in order, and others are screwups. In their view, we are all stumblers. As W. H. Auden put it, the task in life is to "love your crooked neighbor with all your crooked heart."

"Charity" is the ultimate dirty word. We are all equal, and we all need one another. Sarah Hemminger even banned the word "mentor" from her organization because it implies the adults are higher and ministering down to the young. It always comes back to the dignity of the person in front of you.

The single phrase I heard most often from their lips was *"the whole person."* Over the past few decades, our institutions have tended to divide human beings into slices. Schools treat children as brains on a stick and pump information into them. Hospitals treat patients as a collection of organs to be repaired; doctors don't really know the people they are operating on. But community builders talk about the need to take a whole-person approach. When a child enters school, she doesn't leave behind her healthcare issues, her safety issues, her emotional traumas, her nutritional needs, her need for purpose and meaning. Whatever sector one is working in, you have to be aware and connect to the whole person all at once.

And over it all is the spirit of loving-kindness. Speaking with the weavers, I was often reminded of a quote somebody passed to me from John E. Biersdorf's book *Healing of Purpose*:

> Compassion is expressed in gentleness. When I think of persons I know who model for me the depths of spiritual life, I am struck by their gentleness. Their eyes communicate the residue of solitary battles with angels, the costs of caring for others, the deaths of ambition and ego, and the peace that comes from having very little left to lose in this life. They are gentle because

they have honestly faced the struggles given to them and have learned the hard way that personal survival is not the point. Their care is gentle because their self-aggrandizement is no longer at stake. There is nothing in it for them. Their vulnerability has been stretched to clear-eyed sensitivity to others and truly selfless love.

ETTY HILLESUM

I'd like to conclude this glimpse at second-mountain people with one more short portrait. It's of a woman who, because of the freakish circumstances of her life, moved from her first to second mountain with dramatic speed. And because she kept a journal, we get a glimpse of what the shift from egocentric immaturity to selfless maturity looks like from the inside.

Her name was Etty Hillesum. She was born on January 15, 1914, and spent her teenage years in Deventer, a midsize city in eastern Holland. Her father was a shy, bookish man who worked as a principal of a local school but generally abstracted himself from the world and existed in the realm of lofty but vague ideas. Her mother, biographer Patrick Woodhouse writes, was needy: "chaotic, extravert and noisy, she was given to sudden emotional outbursts."

Etty and her two brilliant but unstable brothers grew up in a home that was melodramatic, disorganized, and emotionally exhausting. In her diary, she describes her upbringing as a mixture of high culture and emotional barbarism:

> I think my parents always felt out of their depth and as life became more and more difficult they were gradually so overwhelmed that they became quite incapable of making up their minds about anything. They gave us children too much freedom of action, and offered us nothing to cling to. That was because they never established a foothold for themselves. And the reason why they did so little to guard our steps was they themselves had lost the way.

Hillesum grew into an insecure and directionless young woman. In her late twenties, she would describe herself in her diaries as "a weakling and a nonentity adrift and tossed by the waves." She felt "fragmented . . . depressed . . . a mass of uncertainties . . . Lack of self-confidence. Aversion. Panic."

She had no structure to stabilize her life. She was nominally Jewish but not observant in any way. Nor did she have any intellectual sense of fixed truth or solid convictions. "My capable brain tells me that there are no absolutes, that everything is relative, endlessly diverse and in eternal motion." She dreamed that some man would come along and give direction to her life. As she put it in her diary, "What I really want is a man for life. And to build something together with him. And all the adventures and transient relationships I have had have made me utterly miserable, tearing me apart."

When Hillesum was twenty-six, the Nazis invaded Holland. In her early journal entries, the occupation appeared as the backdrop, something that never pierced the wall of her narcissism. She wrote almost exclusively about her own internal dramas. At about this time Hillesum began to see a therapist named Julius Spier. Spier was some combination of wise and creepy. He had studied under Carl Jung. But he also specialized in palm reading and believed that it was not enough for a therapist to talk with a patient; since the mind and the body are one, he also insisted on physically wrestling with his patients. Most of them were young women.

The first time they wrestled, Hillesum dumped Spier on his back. "All my inner tensions, the bottled-up forces, broke free," she wrote, "and there he lay, physically and also mentally, as he told me later, thrown. No one had ever been able to do that to him before."

Hillesum fell in love with him, and a strange relationship developed, one that was intellectual, sexual, and therapeutic. "You are my beloved . . . priceless, private psychological university," she wrote to him. "I have so much to discuss with you again and so much to learn from you."

For all his flaws and perversities, Spier at least offered her a coherent worldview and an introduction to contemporary psychology. She could accept his views or reject them, but at least there were handholds to grab on to or push off from. Spier urged her to keep a diary and to cultivate her spiritual nature. When he died of cancer in the fall of 1942, Hillesum remembered him as the man "who attended at the birth of my soul."

Around the time of Spier's death, Hillesum's tone in the diary changes. There's less obsessive self-analysis. She's more inclined to look outward and to experience the world in a more direct way. "Thinking gets you nowhere," she wrote in her diary. "It may be a fine and noble aid in academic studies, but you can't think your way out of emotional difficulties. That takes something altogether different. You have to make yourself passive then, and just listen. Re-establish contact with a slice of eternity."

One day she was sitting in the sun on her family's stony terrace, gazing at a chestnut tree while listening to the birds. Her first instinct was to capture the scene in words, to explain the sensations of delight she was experiencing.

In other words, I wanted to subject nature, everything to myself. I felt obliged to interpret it. And the quite simple fact is that now I just let it happen to me. . . . As I sat there like that in the sun, I bowed my head unconsciously, as if to take in even more of that new feeling for life. Suddenly I knew deep down how someone can sink impetuously to his knees and find peace there, his face hidden in his folded hands.

For most of her life, she wrote, she had lived in anticipation, as if she were not living her real life, but just some preparation for it. But something shifted inside. She now felt some urgency to be seized by some great ideal she might devote herself to. "Oh God," she prayed, "take me into Your great hands and turn me into Your instrument."

She was not religious in any formal sense, but she began to pray. At first, she called herself a "kneeler in training," because the act of praying felt so vulnerable and uncomfortable. But after a while it seemed as if her body was made for prayer. "Sometimes, in moments of deep gratitude, kneeling down becomes an overwhelming urge. . . . When I write these things down I still feel a little ashamed, as if I were writing about the most intimate of intimate matters."

In prayer, she wrote, it is

> No longer: I want this or that, but: Life is great and good and fascinating and eternal, and if you dwell so much on yourself and flounder and fluff about, you miss the mighty eternal current that is life. It is in these moments—and I am so grateful for them— that all personal ambition drops away from me, and that my thirst for knowledge and understanding comes to rest, and a small piece of eternity descends on me with a sweeping wingbeat.

In April 1942, the Nazis began their first major roundups of Jews, forcing them to wear the yellow Star of David. Each morning brought more news of arrests, of Jewish families being rounded up and shipped off, of men expelled from their jobs and life shutting down, of rumors about concentration camps and gas chambers. For a time Hillesum simply sought shelter from the storm.

She would walk around her neighborhood and count the casualties. From this house, a father had been taken. From another, two sons. People were being shipped eastward, but none were ever coming back. "The threat grows ever greater, and terror increases from day to day," she wrote. "I draw prayer round me like a dark protective wall, withdraw inside it as one might into a convent cell."

But gradually she began to feel called to take some active role in saving her people. "What is at stake is our impending destruction and annihilation," she acknowledged on July 3, 1942. "We can have no more illusions about that. They are out to destroy us completely, we must accept that and go from there."

The brutality of Nazism seems to demand a brutal response, and many of us look back and wish there had been more Jewish resistance, more angry determination to go down, if one must go down, fighting. But as the genocide spread, Hillesum did not have that reaction. "I no longer believe that we can change anything in the world until we have first changed ourselves. And that seems to me the only lesson to be learned from this war."

If the Nazis were trying to extinguish love from the world, she would stand as a force for it. As the world grew heartless, she felt called to enlarge her own heart.

That meant doing what she could to care for her own people, to help the teenage girls who were now being rounded up. She was determined not to hate her oppressors, not to relieve her fear through hatred. She lectured herself to never hate the wickedness of others but to first hate the evil within herself.

For the dying, there are no trivial pleasures. As the Nazis tightened their grip on her neighborhood, Hillesum began to appreciate every lovely blouse, every scented bar of soap. She confronted death directly and assumed her own destruction was imminent, and found that by dropping her evasive attitude toward death, by admitting it into her life, that she could enlarge and enrich her life.

Hillesum could have led her family into hiding. Of the twenty-five thousand Dutch Jews who did, roughly eighteen thousand survived the war. (Anne Frank was an obvious exception.) But she resisted pleas to do that. Her biographer, Patrick Woodhouse, argues that there were three reasons for this. First was her sense of solidarity. She belonged to the whole Jewish people and felt she should live a life of connection with her people. If others had to go to the camps, she was not interested in saving herself. Second, she associated hiding with fear and did not want to live a life of fear. Third, she began to feel a sense of commitment, of vocation. She had come to understand her gifts, and to feel that her gifts could be used in service of the Jews of her country as they waited for deportation.

She went to work at the Jewish Council. This was an organization set up under the Nazis to look after the Jewish population. The Nazis gave the orders, and the council, staffed by Jews, decided how to fulfill them. The Jews who founded it worked under the misapprehension that they could mitigate the worst of the genocide.

In June 1943, Etty volunteered to work at Westerbork, a transit camp where one hundred thousand Dutch Jews were held before being shipped east to Auschwitz and other extermination centers. The writings we have from her at this stage are in the form of letters home, not diaries, so the tone is a bit less personal. But that's also because she had begun to transcend herself. "It is just as if everything that happens here and that is still to happen were somehow discounted inside me. As if I had been through it already and was now helping to build a new and different society."

Much of her letter writing consists of descriptions of the people she is caring for in the camp, the old who come bewildered and lost, the children who don't understand. She felt especially sad for those who were formerly rich and famous: "Their armor of position, esteem and property has collapsed, and now they stand in the last shreds of their humanity."

Sometimes she worked in the punishment barracks serving as messenger between those who had been sentenced to hard labor and their family members in the rest of the camp. Otherwise, her job was to walk around the camp and do whatever it was that needed doing, caring for the sick, helping people send telegrams back home. She was given free access to the four hospital barracks and spent her days moving from bed to bed. The other inmates in the camp describe her, in their own letters home, as radiant and full of warmth. By this point there was a calm and solidity to her writing that was entirely absent before she had taken up her great moral task. Some go to pieces in the face of calamity, or turn desperate, but Hillesum became more mature and deeper. "There are many miracles in a human life," she wrote to one friend. "My own is one long sequence of inner miracles."

The rhythm of life in the camp was governed by the train schedule. Each week a train would arrive to take a certain number of prisoners to their deaths, and just prior to its arrival a list would be published of those condemned to go. Hillesum's letters are filled with descriptions of those sentenced to get on the train. She writes of "the ash-grey freckled face of a colleague. She is squatting beside the bed of a dying woman who has swallowed some poison and who happens to be her mother."

Her letters at this point often contain bursts of an inner hopefulness.

> The misery here is quite terrible; and yet, late at night when the
> day has slunk away into the depths behind me, I often walk with
> a spring in my step along the barbed wire. . . . I can't help it,
> that's just the way it is, like some elementary force—the feeling
> that life is glorious and magnificent and that one day we shall be
> building a whole new world.

On September 6, 1943, Hillesum was shocked to see her own name
on the transport list, along with her parents and brother Mischa. Her
mother had written to the head of the German SS asking that her son
be spared. The letter seems to have backfired, and they were all sentenced to die.

A friend, Jopie Vleeschhouwer, later reported that Hillesum was at
first devastated by the news. But after an hour, she recovered her spirit.
She began scrounging what provisions she could find for the journey.
Vleeschhouwer then described her departure. "Talking gaily, smiling,
a kind word for everyone she met on the way, full of sparkling good
humor, perhaps just a touch of sadness, but every inch the Etty you all
know so well."

Once inside the train she wrote a postcard to a friend, which she
tossed through a crack in the boarded-up carriage. It was picked up by
some farmers and sent back to Amsterdam. "Christine," it begins,
"opening the Bible at random I find this: 'The Lord is my high tower.'
I am sitting on my rucksack in the middle of a full freight car. Father,
mother and Mischa are a few cars away. . . . We left the camp singing,
Father and mother firmly and calmly, Mischa too."

She died in Auschwitz on November 30, 1943.

INTEGRATION

Few of us are going to experience a personal transformation as complete as the one Hillesum experienced. Few of us are going to live as
selflessly as the community weavers. But their lives serve as models.
They are models for many reasons, but in part because they illustrate

a core point: One task in life is synthesis. It is to collect all the fragmented pieces of a self and bring them to a state of unity, so that you move coherently toward a single vision.

Some people never get themselves together; they live scattered lives. Some get themselves together but at a low level. Their lives are oriented around the lesser desires. Hillesum got herself together at a very high level. As the external conditions of her life became more miserable, her internal state became more tranquil.

And the way she achieved unity was not through an endless inner process of self-excavation. It was through an outer process of giving her whole self away. "Happiness," Dr. William H. Sheldon wrote, "is essentially a state of going somewhere, wholeheartedly, one-directionally, without reservation or regret."

The practical way we do that is through commitments—through making maximal commitments to things we really care about and then serving them in a wholehearted way. The core challenges of the second-mountain life are found in the questions, How do I choose my commitments? How do I decide what is the right commitment for me? How do I serve my commitments once they have been chosen? How do I blend my commitments so that together they merge into a coherent, focused, and joyful life?

These are the sorts of question the next section of the book is designed to address. It aims to be a practical (and yet spiritual!) guidebook to the committed life, to the life lived in service of a vocation, a marriage, a creed, and a community. The second-mountain life is a spiritual adventure, but it is lived out very practically day by day.

The Four
Commitments

PART II
Vocation

What Vocation Looks Like

In 1946, George Orwell published a brilliant essay called "Why I Write" about his vocation as a novelist and essayist. In it, he tries to puncture a lot of the pious and pretentious writing about writing. With the sense of guilt that is never far from the surface in his work, Orwell wants to expose and maybe shock you with his own low and selfish motives.

He writes, he says, for four basic reasons. First, sheer egoism. The desire to seem clever and to get talked about. Second, aesthetic enthusiasm. The pleasure he gets from playing with sentences and words. But Orwell is nothing if not honest. And he has to admit that there are higher motives as well. Third, then, is the "historic impulse," the desire for understanding. The desire to see things as they are and find out true facts. Fourth, his political purpose. The desire to push the world in a certain direction, and to alter people's ideas of what sort of society they should strive for.

Orwell was one of those people who had an inkling, early on, of what he should do with his life, but drifted away from it. Early on, he wanted to be a writer. But after school he moved to India and worked for the British Empire as a policeman. Then he came home and lay about. But, as he was avoiding writing, he "did so with the consciousness that I was outraging my true nature and that sooner or later I should have to settle down and write books."

Finally, at age twenty-five, he succumbed to his destiny. He decided that if he was going to be a writer he needed to do three things. First, he needed to live among the poor. He was a man of the left, but believed that the problem with his fellow socialists was that they didn't have much direct contact with the poor people they were allegedly liberating. So at the start of his writing career he went tramping. Homeless people in those days were forbidden by the Vagrancy Act to beg or erect permanent camps. Many tramped from one village to the next, all across England, staying in one charity hotel one night and then another in a nearby town the next. After that experience, Orwell worked as a dishwasher in a French hotel and restaurant, thirteen hours a day. These experiences gave him firsthand knowledge of the working class, and increased his natural hatred of authority.

Next, he needed to invent a new way of writing. He would turn nonfiction writing into a literary form. He became a master at using parable to make a political point—how shooting an elephant symbolized all that was wrong with British imperialism. He did not get intrinsic joy out of the writing process. "Writing a book is a horrible, exhausting struggle, like a long bout of some painful illness," he wrote. "One would never undertake such a thing if one were not driven on by some demon whom one can neither resist nor understand." But the pain was purifying. Like T. S. Eliot, Orwell believed that good writing involves a continual extinction of personality. One struggles, Orwell wrote, "to efface one's own personality. Good prose is like a windowpane." The act of writing well involved self-suppression, putting the reader in direct contact with the thing described.

Finally, Orwell decided that in order to fulfill his calling he had to be ruthlessly honest, even about the people on his own side. In the 1930s, with the fascists fighting the communists in the Spanish Civil War, he went to fight with the anarchists, taking the hopeless side in that conflict. He learned to see reality without illusion. He learned, as

Albert Camus put it, "that one can be right and yet be beaten, that force can vanquish spirit, that there are times when courage is not its own recompense."

But he did not become a cynic. Totalitarianism, in Spain, Germany, and the Soviet Union, presented Orwell with the moral challenge that controlled the rest of his life. He wrote, from then on, because he wanted to expose a lie or draw attention to some fact. "Every line of serious work that I have written since 1936 has been written, directly or indirectly, *against* totalitarianism and *for* democratic Socialism."

When Orwell returned from Spain he was transformed. He had experienced his call within a call, that purifying moment when you know why you were put on this earth and you are ruthless about pursuing this mission. A friend remarked, "It was almost as if there'd been a kind of fire smoldering in him all his life which suddenly broke into flame." He became angry at any injustice and coolly passionate. He was outraged by lies, but kindly toward people. He was fully engaged in fighting fascism, but always detached enough to be able to face the unpleasant truths about his own side.

He wasn't always a joyful man to be around. He was wintry, bleak, prickly, independent, fierce, both shy and assertive. But by the end of his life, when he was deathly ill and writing *1984*, his vocation had given him a purity of desire and a unity of purpose. As George Bernard Shaw once wrote in another context, Orwell's vocation took "a mob of appetites and organized them into an army of purposes and principles." People began to recognize him as some sort of saint of the age.

I mention Orwell's experience because I think it illustrates a few common features of the process of finding a vocation.

The thing everybody knows about finding a vocation is that it's quite different from finding a career. When you have a career mentality, the frontal cortex is very much in charge. You take an inventory of your talents. What are you good at? What talent has value in the marketplace? Then you invest in your abilities by getting a good education. You hone your professional skills. Then you survey the job market to see what opportunities are out there. You follow the incentives to get the highest return on your investment of time and effort. You strategize the right route to climb upward toward success. You reap the rewards of success: respect, self-esteem, and financial security.

In the vocation mentality, you're not living on the ego level of your consciousness—working because the job pays well or makes life convenient. You're down in the substrate. Some activity or some injustice has called to the deepest level of your nature and demanded an active response. Carl Jung called a vocation "an irrational factor that destines a man to emancipate himself from the herd and from its well-worn paths. . . . Anyone with a vocation hears the voice of the inner man: He is *called*."

At first the summons is often aesthetic. Annie Dillard once asked a friend how he knew he was meant to become a painter. "I like the smell of paint," he replied. It wasn't some grandiose sense of fate. It was the aroma that came out of putting paint on canvas. Some people just like working on cars or fiddling around with numbers or making pastry or speaking in front of crowds.

For still others, the call can come from our historical circumstances. All of us are stationed at a certain place in a certain moment, and the circumstances throw concrete problems before us that demand to be answered. Václav Havel found himself living under the tyranny of communism. Gloria Steinem found herself living under the weight of a male-dominated society. These are just a few of the famous examples, but millions of people have found their vocation in fighting collectivism, racism, sexism, and other wrongs.

When the psychoanalyst Viktor Frankl was about thirteen, a teacher of his declared that all of life is nothing but a process of material combustion. Frankl leapt up and declared, "Sir, if this is so, what then can be the meaning of life?" Intensely preoccupied with this question at a young age, he struck up a correspondence with Sigmund Freud. As a young therapist, he set up suicide prevention centers around Vienna, and invented methods to give people on the verge of self-destruction a way to find meaning in their lives.

Then came World War II and the Nazi occupation. Frankl found himself thrown into a concentration camp. He realized that the career questions—What do I want from life? What can I do to make myself happy?—are not the proper questions. The real question is, What is life asking of me? Frankl realized that a psychiatrist in a concentration camp has a responsibility to study suffering and reduce suffering. "It did not really matter what we expected from life, but rather what life expected from us," he realized. "We needed to stop asking about the meaning of life, and instead to think of ourselves as those who were being questioned by life—daily and hourly. Our answer must consist not in talk and meditation, but in right action and in right conduct. Life ultimately means taking responsibility to find the right answer to its problems and to fulfill the tasks which life constantly sets for each individual." The sense of calling comes from the question, What is my responsibility here? Frankl went on to work as a psychotherapist in the camp, reminding despairing prisoners that the world still expected things of them. They still had responsibilities and purposes to pursue.

Vocations invariably have testing periods—periods when the costs outweigh the benefits—which a person must go through to reach another level of intensity. At these moments, if you were driven by a career mentality you would quit. You're putting more into this thing than you are getting out. But a person who has found a vocation doesn't feel she has a choice. It would be a violation of her own nature. So she pushes through when it doesn't seem to make sense. As Stanford professors Anne Colby and William Damon write, "When an issue is less central to one's identity, it's possible to feel, for example, 'I really should do more to help those in need, but it's just too hard' or 'I just can't find the time.' But when the issue lies at the very heart of who one is, it becomes unthinkable to turn away."

The second thing you notice about the Orwell story is that he had a presentiment of his vocation when he was young. But then he walked away from it. Maybe he forgot about it. Maybe he couldn't figure out how to make a living. He had to go through a period of wandering before he settled back into the vocation that called him all along. This, too, is not uncommon. Often people feel a call but don't really understand it, or they forget the call or just wander off. It's only later that they make up a neat linear narrative of their life to describe how they took the road less traveled.

People who write about vocation often cite a poem by William Wordsworth that makes vocation finding sound straightforward and delightful. Early one morning, when he was in college, Wordsworth was walking back to his home in Hawkshead, England, after a summer night's dance. Two miles into his hike, dawn broke. He found himself greeted by a morning "more glorious than I had ever beheld." The sea, he wrote, seemed to be laughing in the distance. The mountains were bright as clouds. All of creation was pure delight: "Dews, vapors, and the melody of birds, / And Laborers going forth into the fields." He was overwhelmed by beauty. It touched him at the level of heart and soul. Suddenly a switch flipped inside:

My heart was full; I made no vows, but vows
Were then made for me; bond unknown to me
Was given, that I should be, else sinning greatly,
A dedicated Spirit. On I walked
In thankful blessedness, which even yet remains.

His heart was full. He himself didn't make a promise, but somehow "vows were made for me." He was destined, he realized at that moment, to become a poet, a dedicated spirit, to spend his life capturing what he then felt. If he didn't fulfill those vows, he would, he realized, be "sinning greatly." He'd be denying his own nature and his own destiny.

What the tellers of that tale usually don't mention is that this account is semi-mythical. Wordsworth recounted this clear moment when he was older and looking back on his life, but it wasn't so clear at the time. Drifting into his midtwenties, Wordsworth was trying to find something to do with his life. He slid through university, despising most of it, writing very little poetry. He tried joining the clergy while doing a fair share of drinking and dancing. He thought about becoming a lawyer, and spent four months bumming around London doing very little. He fathered a child while touring around France, observed the French Revolution, abandoned the mother of his child, imagined starting a magazine, thought of becoming a political reporter, tried to get a job as a tutor in Ireland. Wordsworth, in other words, had to endure a period of drift while waiting to settle into his groove in life, the way most of us do.

Wordsworth's life came into focus only after two strokes of good fortune he couldn't have imagined beforehand. A casual acquaintance of his named Raisley Calvert saw a spark of genius in him, when almost no one else did. Calvert readjusted his will so that Wordsworth would get £900 on the event of his death. Calvert serves as the patron saint of a rare sort of social type: the person who can see a gift in others, push that person toward their vocation, and provide practical assistance to make it happen.

Calvert performed one more service. At age twenty-one, he died, giving Wordsworth a financial cushion. Shortly thereafter, another friend offered Wordsworth and his sister the use of their country home in exchange for tutoring their sons. In two strokes, Wordsworth had money and a rent-free residence of a grand estate. The rest is history.

The summons to vocation is a very holy thing. It feels mystical, like a call from deep to deep. But then the messy way it happens in actual lives doesn't feel holy at all; just confusing and screwed up. Over the next few chapters I'll try to describe how vocations are found and grow.

The Annunciation Moment

WHEN E. O. WILSON WAS SEVEN, HIS PARENTS ANNOUNCED THEY WERE getting a divorce. They sent him away over the summer to stay with a family he didn't know in Paradise Beach, in northern Florida. Every morning, Wilson would have breakfast with the family, then wander alone in search of treasures on the beach until lunch. Then after lunch he'd head back to the water to wander until dinner.

The creatures he found cast a spell on him. He saw crabs and needlefish in the water, toadfish and porpoises. One day he saw his first jellyfish. "The creature is astonishing. It existed outside my previous imagination," he would write decades later. Another day he was sitting on a dock with his feet dangling in the water, when a gigantic ray, much bigger than anything else he'd seen, glided silently under his feet. "I was thunderstruck. And immediately seized with a need to see this behemoth again, to capture it if I could and to examine it close up."

To a child everything looks bigger. "I estimate that when I was seven years old I saw animals at about twice the size I see them now,"

Wilson later wrote. He was transfixed by these silent creatures but glimpsed something more—a hidden new world under the surface of the waters to venture into and explore. His family life was falling apart a few hundred miles away, but here he felt a curiosity and a sense of belonging, one that would last all his life. That summer, a naturalist was born.

"A child comes to the edge of deep water with a mind prepared for wonder," Wilson observed decades later in *Naturalist*, his memoir. "Hands-on experience at the critical time, not systematic knowledge, is what counts in the making of a naturalist. . . . Better to spend long stretches of time just searching and dreaming."

This was what you might call Wilson's annunciation moment. That's the moment when something sparks an interest, or casts a spell, and arouses a desire that somehow prefigures much of what comes after in a life, both the delights and the challenges. Most days pass in an unmemorable flow, but, every once in a while, a new passion is silently conceived. Something delights you and you are forever after entranced by that fascinating thing. Wilson found nature at age seven and has spent the ensuing seven decades studying it, becoming one of the most prominent scientists in the world.

When you hear adults talk about their annunciation moments, they often tell stories of something lost and something found. Wilson was losing his parental home, and found in nature a home where he would always be welcome. I know a man whose father drank too much, and the family was always desperately short of money. This man fell in love with shopkeeping and business and eventually made himself into a multibillionaire. The writer Andrew Solomon heard about the Holocaust when he was a boy and thought about how awful it was that the European Jews had nowhere to go when trouble came. "I decided that I would always have someplace to go," he declared in one book talk, and so was born a life of travel and travel writing. As my friend April Lawson puts it, we were all missing something as children, and as adults we're willing to put up with a lot in order to get it.

The other interesting thing about annunciation moments is how aesthetic they are. Often, they happen when a child finds something that just seems sublime. They are going about their life in its normal course, and then suddenly beauty strikes. Some sight or experience renders them dumb with wonder—a stingray gliding beneath one's feet.

To feel wonder in the face of beauty is to be grandly astonished. A person entranced by wonder is pulled out of the normal voice-in-your-head self-absorption and finds herself awed by something greater than herself. There's a feeling of radical openness, curiosity, and reverence. There's an instant freshness of perception, a desire to approach and affiliate.

The ocean for Wilson was an entire captivating world to explore. "A beautiful thing, though simple in its immediate presence," Frederick Turner observes, "always gives us a sense of depth below depth, almost an innocent wild vertigo as one falls through its levels."

I have a son who as a five-year-old glimpsed the beauty of a baseball field and of the players on it; before long he was obsessed and entranced by baseball. Baseball became the way he processed the world. It was the way he organized geography, learned math. Baseball became the language we used to speak to each other, father and son. My daughter, at about the same age, found herself at home around hockey rinks, and teaches hockey to this day. My other son found beauty in philosophy, at a very early age. While the rest of the world is a vast, buzzing confusion, this is the realm they can master and understand. "Some of our most wonderful memories are beautiful places where we felt immediately at home," John O'Donohue writes.

The Greek word for "beauty" was *kalon*, which is related to the word for "call." Beauty incites a desire to explore something and live within it. Children put posters of their obsessions on the wall. They draw images of them in art class and on the covers of their notebooks. "I am seeking. I am striving. I am in it with all my heart," Vincent van Gogh wrote, in the middle of a life obsessed with beauty.

One day, when he was four or five, Albert Einstein had to stay home sick. His father brought him a compass. The sight of it, with the magnetic needle swinging about under the influence of a hidden force field, made him tremble. "I can still remember—at least I believe I can remember—that this experience made a deep and lasting impression on me. Something deeply hidden had to be behind things," he later wrote.

He became obsessed with hidden forces, magnetic fields, gravity, inertia, acceleration. As one biographer put it, "Music, Nature and God became intermingled in him in a complex of feeling, a moral unity, the trace of which never vanished."

That metaphysical curiosity drove him his entire life. "Only those who realize the immense efforts and, above all, the devotion without which pioneering work in theoretical science cannot be achieved are able to grasp the strength of the emotion out of which alone such work, remote as it is from the immediate realities of life, can issue," Einstein wrote. "The scientist's religious feeling takes the form of a rapturous amazement at the harmony of natural law."

I am obviously no Wilson, van Gogh, or Einstein, but I also had my annunciation moment at age seven. I was reading a book about Paddington Bear and realized (or at least think I realized) that I wanted to be a writer. It's easy now in retrospect to see how all the pieces fit together. My parents were academics, so books and writing were valued around the house. My grandfather was a beautiful letter writer who dreamed of getting his letters to the editor published in *The New York Times*. As the Paddington story opens, the little bear has traveled from Peru to London. He is alone and stranded at a train station until a loving family takes him in and cares for him. I guess as little children we all, at some level, feel that we are alone, and know we need a family to take us in.

In the fifty years since I read that opening scene of *A Bear Called Paddington*, there probably haven't been two hundred days when I didn't write something or at least prepare to write something. Recently I bought a Fitbit. It kept telling me that I was falling asleep between eight and eleven in the morning. But I wasn't asleep; I was writing. Apparently writing is the time when my heartbeat is truly at rest; when I feel right with myself.

THE LAW OF YOUR VERY SELF

In this chapter, I've described childhood annunciation moments, but of course they don't just happen in childhood. We've all known people who have had them, or had them again, at age thirty or fifty or eighty. But often when they happen in adulthood they can still be traced back to some grandparent, some ancient seed that first blossomed when we were young. In his essay "Schopenhauer as Educator," Nietzsche wrote that the way to discover what you were put on earth for is to go back into your past, list the times you felt most fulfilled, and then see if you can draw a line through them.

He writes, "Let the young soul survey its own life with a view to the following question: 'What have you truly loved thus far? What has ever uplifted your soul, what has dominated and delighted it at the same time?' Assemble these revered objects in a row before you and perhaps they will reveal a law by their nature and their order: the fundamental law of your very self."

In fact, the tricky part of an annunciation moment is not having it, but *realizing* you're having it. The world is full of beautiful things and moments of wonder. But sometimes they pass by without us realizing their importance. Often, we're not aware of our annunciation moments except in retrospect. You look back and realize, "Okay, that's when this all started. . . . That was the freakishly unlikely circumstance that set things off on this wonderful course."

The best thing about an annunciation moment is that it gives you an early hint of where your purpose lies. The next best thing is it rules out a bunch of other things. "Lucky is the man who does not secretly believe that every possibility is open to him," Walker Percy observes.

Ed Wilson's annunciation moment involved an additional step, which was also, in the long run, a stroke of good fortune. One day that summer on Paradise Beach he was fishing. He caught a pinfish but got careless when yanking it from the water. It flew up and flopped in his face, with one of the spines on its dorsal fins piercing the pupil of Wilson's right eye. The pain was excruciating, but Wilson didn't want to stop fishing, so he stayed out there in his pain all day. That night he told the host family what had happened, but by then the pain had dulled and they didn't take him to a doctor. His eye clouded over several months later and then, after a botched procedure, he lost sight in that eye altogether.

Wilson was going to be a naturalist, but he was never going to study something like birds, which required stereoscopy to see properly. He was going to have to study something small, something he could pick up with his fingers and bring close for inspection with his good left eye. Fortunately, that same year he happened to be walking down Palafox Street in Pensacola, Florida, when he came across some lion ants swarming out of their nest. He stood there with the same feeling he'd had by the ocean. Here was another hidden and entrancing world. He would study ants and go on to scientific greatness.

Forty years later, Wilson happened to be on the same street in Pensacola. He saw the descendants of those first ants scurrying about. Fascinated, he got down on his hands and knees, peering once again at the lion ants. An elderly man, passing by, was alarmed to see a grown man crawling on all fours on the sidewalk, and asked if he needed any help. But of course, Wilson was just returning to his childhood love and continuing his lifelong call.

What Mentors Do

WILSON DIDN'T BUILD HIS CAREER BY HIMSELF. HE HAD MENTORS. THE first was a professor at the University of Alabama named Bert Williams. Williams took him on field trips, lent him a dissecting microscope, welcomed him into his home, and generally provided Wilson with a practical sense of what life as a natural scientist might look like.

Williams seems to have done the things that good mentors do. Good mentors coach you through the various decisions of life, such as where to go to graduate school or what jobs to take. Good mentors teach you the tacit wisdom embedded in any craft.

Any book or lecture can tell you how to do a thing. But in any craft, whether it is cooking or carpentry or science or leadership, there are certain forms of knowledge that can't be put into rules or recipes—practical forms of knowledge that only mentors can teach. The philosopher Michael Oakeshott tried to capture the ineffable quality of this practical knowledge by telling the story of a Chinese wheelwright who was making a wheel at the lower end of a great chamber while his duke, Duke Huan of Ch'i, was reading a book at the upper end. Putting aside his mallet and chisel, the wheelwright called out to the duke and asked him what he was reading.

"A book that records the words of the sages," the duke answered.

"Are those sages alive?" the wheelwright asked.

"They are dead," the duke replied.

"In that case, what you are reading can be nothing but the lees and scum of bygone men."

The duke was outraged. How dare the wheelwright dismiss such a book and such sages? "If you can explain your statement, I shall let it pass. If you cannot, you shall die!" the duke thundered.

"Speaking as a wheelwright," the craftsman began, "I look at the matter this way: When I am making a wheel, if my stroke is too slow, then it bites deep but is not steady; if my stroke is too fast, then it is steady, but does not go deep. The right pace, neither slow nor fast, cannot get into the hand unless it comes from the heart. It is a thing that cannot be put into words."

Technical, book knowledge, Oakeshott writes, consists of "formulated rules which are, or may be, deliberately learned." Practical knowledge, on the other hand, cannot be taught or learned but only imparted and acquired. It exists only in practice. When we talk about practical knowledge, we tend to use bodily metaphors. We say that somebody has a *touch* for doing some activity—an ability to hit the right piano key with just enough force and pace. We say that somebody has a *feel* for the game, an intuition for how events are going to unfold, an awareness of when you should plow ahead with a problem and when you should put it aside before coming back to it. We say that somebody has *taste*, an aesthetic sense of what product or presentation is excellent, and which ones are slightly off.

When the expert is using her practical knowledge, she isn't thinking more; she is thinking less. She has built up a repertoire of skills through habit and has thereby extended the number of tasks she can perform without conscious awareness. This sort of knowledge is built up through experience, and it is passed along through shared experience. It is passed along by a mentor who lets you come alongside and participate in a thousand situations. This kind of pedagogy is personal, friendly, shared, conversational—more caught than taught. A textbook can teach you the principles of biology, but a mentor shows you how to think like a biologist. This kind of habitual practice re-wires who you are inside. "The great thing in all education," William James wrote, "is to *make our nervous system our ally instead of our enemy.*"

These are the things good mentors do. But E. O. Wilson was fortunate to have an extra and extraordinary mentor, a man who took his craft and therefore his mentorship to another level.

After the University of Alabama, Wilson went to graduate school at Harvard, where he met Philip Darlington, who studied beetles and was a scholar of the geographic distribution of animals. Darlington gave Wilson practical advice on how to collect his samples: "Don't stay on the trails when you collect insects," he told him. "You should walk in a straight line through the forest. Try to go over any barrier you meet. It's hard, but it's the best way to collect."

More fundamentally, Darlington showed Wilson what a true vocation looked like. As a young man, Darlington had climbed the Sierra Nevada de Santa Marta, collecting bugs along the way. In Haiti, he hacked through one thousand meters of virgin forest to reach the summit of that nation's highest peak. When he was thirty-nine, Darlington floated himself on a log into a stagnant jungle pool in South America to collect a water sample that would help in his research. A giant crocodile emerged from the water, grabbed Darlington in its jaws, spun him over and over, and dragged him down to the bottom of the pool. Darlington kicked and fought and managed to swim free. He scrambled onto the bank of the pool, and the crocodile attacked again. Darlington was dragged back into the water and then broke free again. The crocodile's teeth had pierced both his hands. The muscles and ligaments on both of his arms were shredded. The bones in his right arm were crushed. As he hauled himself back toward civilization, he became aware of how weak he had become from loss of blood.

Escaping death by crocodile is not proof of character, Wilson would later wryly observe. But what happened next was, and that is what left a mark in Wilson. Darlington was stuck in a cast for several months. So he devised a method to collect his samples with his functioning left hand, tying his specimen jars onto sticks that he jammed into the ground and then dropping the bugs in one-handed.

"The teacher, that professional amateur," the critic Leslie Fiedler once wrote, "teaches not so much the subject as himself." Through his behavior, Darlington taught Wilson that the naturalist's life was not an easy life but an arduous one. He taught that the search for knowledge about our world is an important mission, that those who do it are part of a long procession, stretching back through time. He taught him what it looks like to fiercely love science. As Wordsworth writes in *The Prelude*, "What we have loved, others will love, and we will teach them how."

And that is something that most young people, and maybe all of us, want to be taught. What most people seek in life, especially when young, is not happiness but an intensity that reaches into the core. We want to be involved in some important pursuit that involves hardship and is worthy of that hardship. The mentors who really lodge in the mind are the ones who were hard on us—or at least were hard on themselves and set the right example—not the ones who were easy on us. They are the ones who balanced unstinting love with high standards and relentless demands on behalf of something they took seriously. We think we want ease and comfort, and of course we do from time to time, but there is something inside us that longs for some calling that requires dedication and sacrifice.

In this way, a lot of what mentors do is to teach us what excellence looks like, day by day. As Alfred North Whitehead wrote, "Moral education is impossible without the habitual vision of greatness." Or, as Sir Richard Livingstone put it, "The most indispensable viaticum for the journey of life is a store of adequate ideals, and these are acquired in a very simple way, by living with the best things in the world—the best pictures, the best buildings, the best social or political orders, the best human beings. The way to acquire a good taste in anything, from pictures to architecture, from literature to character, from wine to cigars, is always the same—be familiar with the best specimens of each."

By thrusting us face-to-face with excellence, mentors also induce a certain humility. They teach us how to humbly submit to the task. The natural tendency is to put oneself at the center of any activity. To ask, How am I doing? That question is fine to ask once. But it becomes paralyzing if you ask it all the time. A pitcher who is thinking about how he is pitching cannot pitch well. His focus is on self, not the task. "In any hard discipline, whether it be gardening, structural engineering, or Russian," the philosopher and motorcycle mechanic Matthew Crawford writes, "one submits to things that have their own intractable ways."

He illustrates the point by citing Iris Murdoch: "If I am learning, for instance, Russian, I am confronted by an authoritative structure which commands my respect. The task is difficult and the goal is distant and perhaps never entirely attainable. My work is a progressive revelation of something which exists independently of me. Attention is rewarded by a knowledge of reality. Love of Russian leads me away from myself towards something alien to me, something which my consciousness cannot take over, swallow up, deny or make unreal."

Mentors also teach how to deal with error. As you get more experienced, you get a lot better at recognizing your mistakes and understanding, through experience, how to fix them. Mentors give us a sense for how to do the second and fourth and tenth drafts, and, in the process, they give us the freedom to not fear our failures, but to proceed with a confidence that invites them, knowing they can be rectified later on. One of the things good writing mentors do, for example, is to teach you not to be afraid to write badly. Get the first draft out even if it's awful. Your ego is not at stake.

Finally, mentors teach how to embrace the struggle—that the struggle is the good part.

William James once visited Chautauqua, which, then as now, was a wonderful village in upstate New York built around a summer ideas and music festival. It has the sort of a calm, elevated atmosphere that has been described as the PBS audience at prayer. At first, he was utterly pleased by it. "I went in curiosity for a day. I stayed for a week," James recalled, "held spell-bound by the charm and ease of everything, by the middle-class paradise, without a sin, without a victim, without a blot, without a tear." And yet when he left the village and returned to the real world, he felt a great sense of relief. The order within Chautauqua, he wrote, was "too tame, this culture too second-rate, this goodness too uninspiring."

James concluded that there is something in us that seems to require difficulty and the overcoming of difficulty, the presence of both light and darkness, danger and deliverance. "But what our human emotions seem to require," he wrote, "is the sight of struggle going on. The moment the fruits are being merely eaten, things become ignoble. Sweat and effort, human nature strained to its uttermost and on the rack, yet getting through it alive, and then turning its back on its success to pursue another [challenge] more rare and arduous still—this is the sort of thing the presence of which inspires us."

At their highest, James argued, human beings are ideal-forming animals. And their lives go best when they are lived in service to an ideal. As he climactically put it, "The solid meaning of life is always the same eternal thing, the marriage, namely, of some unhabitual ideal, however special, with some fidelity, courage, and endurance; with some man's or woman's pains."

The last thing a mentor does, of course, is send you out into the world and, in some sense, cut you off. My mentor early in my career was William F. Buckley, Jr. I worked for him at his magazine for eighteen months, and during this period he taught me what excellence looked like. Then he sent me off, and I never really was close to him again. Some people who held the same job I did and went through this process were hurt by it. I missed him in the years that followed, but I still think Buckley did the right thing. At some point you have to let adult protégés, and children, go.

Eventually everybody gets cut adrift; you are faced with the big decisions on your own. Maybe you had the clearest annunciation moment. Maybe you had the best mentor. But there will still be big, baffling decisions you have to make. Do I take this job or that job? Do I use my talents this way or that way? Do I move to this city or that city?

How do you make the big, transformational decisions of life? It is to that problem we now turn.

Vampire Problems

LET'S SAY YOU HAD THE CHANCE TO BECOME A VAMPIRE. WITH ONE magical bite you would gain immortality, superhuman strength, and a life of glamorous intensity. You'd have all sorts of new skills. You could fly around at night. You wouldn't even have to drink human blood; you could get some donated cow's blood. Friends who have undergone the experience say it is incredible. They claim that as vampires they experience the world in new ways they couldn't have even have imagined back when they were human.

Would you do it? Would you consent to receive that life-altering bite, knowing that once changed you could never go back?

The difficulty of the choice is that you have to use your human self to try to guess if you would enjoy being a vampire self. Becoming a vampire is what the philosopher L. A. Paul calls a "transformative choice." This is the sort of choice that changes who you are.

Life is filled with vampire problems. Marriage turns you into a different person. Having kids changes who you are and what you want. So does emigrating to a new country, converting to a different religion, going to med school, joining the Marines, changing careers, and deciding on where to live. Every time you make a commitment to something big, you are making a transformational choice.

All decisions involve a large measure of uncertainty about the future. What makes transformational choices especially tough is that you don't know what your transformed self will be like or will want, after the vagaries of life begin to have their effects. Things that seem sweet now may seem disgusting to the new you. New sorts of misery and joy, none of which you've experienced so far, may be the meat and potatoes of your future existence. It's really hard to know your current self, but it's pretty well impossible to know what your future transformed self will be like. You can't rationally think through this problem, because you have no data about the desires of the transformed you.

Furthermore, you're aware that this is the kind of choice that will cast a lingering shadow. Every choice is a renunciation, or an infinity of renunciations. You will be forever after aware of the road not taken, what might have been if you'd gone another way. You could be opening yourself up to a lifetime of regret.

You look around and you see people facing these sorts of transformational decisions and screwing it up big-time. More than a third of all marriages end in divorce. We all know people who waste years following career paths that don't satisfy them. Eighty-three percent of all corporate mergers fail to create any value for shareholders, and these mergers are only made after months and years of analysis. When making the big choices in life, as L. A. Paul puts it, "You shouldn't fool yourself—*you have no idea what you are getting into.*"

No wonder so many people have commitment phobia. No wonder some people are so paralyzed by the big choices that they just sort of sleepwalk through them. The paradox of life is that people seem to deliberate more carefully over the little choices than the big ones. Before buying a car, they read all the ratings, check out resale values on the Internet, and so on. But when it comes to choosing a vocation, they just sort of slide rather than decide. They slide incrementally into a career because someone gave them a job. They marry the person whom they happen to be living with. For many, the big choices in life often aren't really choices; they are quicksand. You just sink into the place you happen to be standing.

"It is remarkable that I am never quite clear about the motives for any of my decisions," the German theologian Dietrich Bonhoeffer once admitted. Daniel Kahneman and Amos Tversky, two of the greatest psychologists of all time, spent their entire careers studying decision-making. But if you asked them about the decision that got them into psychology in the first place, they could barely tell you. "It's hard to know how people select a course in life," Tversky once said. "The big choices we make are practically random."

So how do you make these big decisions? How do you decide what career to go into, what person to marry, where to live, how to spend your retirement?

Some people rely on the "You Just Know" model. When the right thing comes along, you get a feeling and you just know. T. D. Jakes says life is like having a big ring of keys, and there's a single lock that is your best life. You try some of the keys and eventually you get to one that feels different. As soon as you put it in the keyhole, before you even turn it, you feel a *whoosh* and you know it's right.

There's some wisdom in this method. There are some situations in which people make better decisions when they have less time to think. But there's not *enough* wisdom here. Are you really going to bet your life on a momentary feeling? On an intuition?

For one thing, intuitions are unstable. Feelings are usually fleeting and sometimes inexplicable in the days or even minutes after you feel them. I was recently up for a job, and during the competition to get it I invented all sorts of reasons why I would enjoy the job, which was mostly fundraising and administration. Then, when I didn't get the job, I felt a huge surge of relief: What was I thinking? I'm a middle-aged man and apparently I have no clue about who I really am.

Second, our intuitions frequently lead us astray. Kahneman and Tversky, along with many other behavioral economists, have filled books and books with all the ways our intuitions can betray us—loss aversion, priming effects, the halo effect, the optimism bias, and so forth. I have friends who have gone six months thinking that such and such a person is the love of their life and then the next four decades thinking that person was an absolute disaster. As George Eliot once put it, "Men and women make sad mistakes about their own symptoms, [mistaking] their vague uneasy longings, sometimes for genius, sometimes for religion, and oftener still for a mighty love."

Finally, intuition is reliable only in certain sorts of decisions. "Intuition" is a fancy word for pattern recognition. It can be trusted only in domains in which you have a lot of experience, in which the mind has time to master the various patterns. But when you are making a transformational choice, you are leaping into an unknown territory. You don't know the patterns there. Intuition can't tell you. It's just guessing.

THE RATIONAL FABLE

The seemingly better method, especially in our culture, is to step back and make the decision "rationally." Put your emotions off to one side and adopt a detached, scientific point of view. Find an engineering method, a design model, or some technique that will allow you to self-distance. Grab a legal pad. Write out a list of costs and benefits down either side.

By approaching the decision rationally, scientifically, you can break the decision-making down into clear stages. Decision-making experts fill books with clear decision stages: preparation (identify the problem; determine your objectives), search (assemble a list of the possible jobs or people that will help you meet your objectives), evaluation (make a chart and rate the options on a ten-point scale according to various features), confrontation (ask disconfirming questions; create constructive disagreement to challenge existing premises), selection (tally up the scores; build a consequences table that will help you envision the future outcome of each choice).

If you follow this kind of formal methodology, you will certainly be able to apply some useful frameworks. For example, when you are considering quitting your job, apply the 10-10-10 rule. How will this decision feel in 10 minutes, 10 months, and 10 years? That will help you put the short-term emotional pain of any decision in the context of long-term consequences.

When buying a house, look at eighteen houses on the market without making a decision about any of them. Then make an offer on the next home that is better than the first eighteen. That will ensure that you have a fair sample of what's out there before making any choice.

Rational techniques are all designed to counteract our cognitive biases. For example, people tend to "narrow frame." As the management experts Chip and Dan Heath argue, they try to turn every open-ended question into a "whether or not" question, or an "either-or" question. People unconsciously think of decisions as a choice between two options. Should I take this job or not? Should I break up with Sue or not? In most key decision moments, there are actually many more options that are being filtered out by that point of view. Every time you find yourself saying "whether or not," the Heaths argue, it's a good idea to step back and find more options. Maybe the question is not breaking up with Sue or not; it's finding a new way to improve your relationship.

YOUR DAEMON

The rational process seems so foolproof. Unfortunately, when it comes to making the big-commitment decisions in life, it, too, is insufficient. The first problem is the one described at the start of this chapter. You can have no data on what your transformed self will want, so you can't rationally think it through by tallying up the evidence. The second problem is that when you're making a decision about a big commitment, you are making a decision about the ultimate moral purpose and meaning of your life.

Logic can't help much with these ultimate questions. Logic is really good when the ends of a decision are clear, when you are playing a game with a defined set of rules. When you buy a toaster, you want a machine that will heat up bread. But commitment decisions are not like that. When making a commitment decision, defining the purpose of your life is the biggest part of the problem. That's a matter of the ultimate horizon. The question What is my ultimate good? is a different kind of question than How can I win at Monopoly?

If you go to the career-advice gurus to find your vocation, the question many will put at the center of your search is "What is my talent?" One of the central preoccupations in the career-advice world is helping people identify strengths and then helping them figure out how to exploit them. One of the implications here is that in selecting a career path, talent should trump interest. If you are really interested in art but you're not actually that good at it, you'll wind up at some boring design job for a company you don't care about at the bottom of the profession. When making a vocational choice ask, What am I talented at?

That may be fine if you're willing to settle for something meager like a career. But if you are trying to discern your vocation, the right question is not What am I good at? It's the harder questions: What am I motivated to do? What activity do I love so much that I'm going to keep getting better at it for the next many decades? What do I desire so much that it captures me at the depth of my being? In choosing a vocation, it's precisely wrong to say that talent should trump interest. Interest multiplies talent and is in most cases more important than talent. The crucial terrain to be explored in any vocation search is the terrain of your heart and soul, your long-term motivation. Knowledge is plentiful; motivation is scarce.

Robert Greene gets at the core truth in his book *Mastery*: "Your emotional commitment to what you are doing will be translated directly into your work. If you go at your work with half a heart, it will show in the lackluster results and in the laggard way in which you reach the end."

The Greeks had a concept, later seized by Goethe, called the daemonic. A daemon is a calling, an obsession, a source of lasting and sometimes manic energy. Daemons are mysterious clusters of energy deep in the unconscious that were charged by some mysterious event in childhood that we imperfectly comprehend—or by some experience of trauma, or by some great love or joy or longing that we spend the rest of our lives trying to recapture. The daemon identifies itself as an obsessive interest, a feeling of being at home at a certain sort of place, doing a certain activity—standing in front of classroom, helping a sick person out of bed, offering hospitality at a hotel.

When you see an individual at the peak of her powers, it's because she has come into contact with her daemon, that wound, that yearning, that core irresolvable tension. This is especially obvious in writers and academics. There's often some core issue that obsesses them and they scratch at it for their entire lives. For example, W. Thomas Boyce is an eminent scholar of child psychiatry. He's most famous for his theory of the orchid and the dandelion. Some kids are highly reactive (orchids) and either soar to extraordinary heights or plunge to depths, depending on their contexts. Other are less reactive (dandelions); even bad circumstances don't bring them down.

This academic interest was no accident, he writes in his book *The Orchid and the Dandelion*. He had a sister named Mary, who was brilliant and beautiful and charismatic. As a kid she was always doing audacious things. One naptime she managed to hilariously shove an entire small box of raisins up her nose one by one. (This resulted in a trip to the doctor's office.) But as she got older the effects of her disrupted childhood began to be more obvious. She managed to get a college degree from Stanford and a graduate degree from Harvard, but her mental health problems grew more and more severe and finally she ended her life just before her fifty-third birthday. Boyce spent his life worrying about his sister, obsessed with that core contrast: two children, the same family, the same context. One highly and tragically reactive and the other not. It is that emotionally intense center that drives much of his work.

When you see a city in the midst of an artistic renaissance, such as Florence in the fifteenth and sixteenth centuries, it's because the people in it are haunted by some fervent clash of values deep in their culture, and they struggle—usually fruitlessly—to resolve the tension. In the Florentine case, the clash between the classical moral ecology and the Christian one sparked off enormous energy. In a thousand different ways, the Florentines tried to square that unsquarable circle.

When a person or a community touches its peculiar daemon, when it confronts some unresolvable tension, the creativity can be amazing, like some kind of nuclear explosion. When a person or culture is outside its daemon, then everything becomes derivative and sentimental.

A person or culture that has lost touch with its daemon has lost touch with life. Look at Florentine art just a century later.

THE BIG SHAGGY

When you are looking for a vocation, you are looking for a daemon. You are trying to enact the same fall that is the core theme of this book—to fall through the egocentric desires and plunge down into the substrate to where your desires are mysteriously formed. You are trying to find that tension or problem that arouses great waves of moral, spiritual, and relational energy. That means you are looking into the unconscious regions of heart and soul that reason cannot penetrate. You are trying to touch something down there in the Big Shaggy, that messy thicket that sits somewhere below awareness.

By one calculation the mind can take in eleven million bits of information a second, of which the conscious mind is aware of forty. The rest is in the Big Shaggy. As Timothy Wilson of the University of Virginia put it, consciousness is like a snowball sitting on an iceberg. In other words, most of what guides us is not our conscious rationalization; it's our unconscious realm. Matthew Arnold, without the advantage of modern cognitive science, put it best:

Below the surface-stream, shallow and light
Of what we say we feel—below the stream,
As light, of what we think we feel—there flows
With noiseless current strong, obscure and deep,
The central stream of what we feel indeed.

When you raise children, you notice that their daemons are wide-awake a lot of the time. They have direct access to these deep realms. Moral consciousness is our first consciousness. But as adults we have a tendency to cover over the substrate, to lose touch with the daemon and let it drift asleep. Sometimes we do this by being excessively analytic about everything. I grew up loving movies. In my sophomore year of college, I went to see a classic old movie almost every night.

Then, as an adult, I became a movie critic. I would sit in the screening room with my notebook in hand. I was no longer watching movies, I was analyzing movies. The notebook became a wall between me and the story I was supposed to be experiencing. I had lost the ability to discern what I liked and what I didn't. By being so analytical I had lost the ability to have an authentic response.

Sometimes we lose touch with the daemon by adopting an excessively economic view of life. It is an interesting phenomenon that when you see life exclusively through an economic lens, that tends to replace the moral lens. For example, a few years ago, six day care centers in Haifa, Israel, realized they had a problem. Parents kept arriving late at pick-up time, so the teachers had to hang around an extra hour or so until the kids were gone. To address the issue, the day care centers began imposing fines on parents who were late. The plan backfired. The share of parents who arrived late doubled. Before, picking up your kids on time was an act of consideration toward the teachers—a moral responsibility. Afterward, it became an economic transaction; you perform the service of looking after my kid and I pay you for it. In the former, people are thinking in terms of right and wrong, being considerate or inconsiderate. In the latter, a cost-benefit calculation kicks in. What's best for me? People who spend their lives thinking exclusively in economic terms tend to cover over their access to the Big Shaggy and to the daemons found there. Whatever is materialistic is taken to be real, and anything that's not does not exist.

Sometimes it's the whole totality of bourgeois life that covers over the deep regions. We're just going about life, doing our normal prosaic things like shopping and commuting, and a film of dead thought and clichéd emotion covers everything. Ultimately, you get used to the buffer you've built around yourself, and you feel safer leading a bland life than a yearning one. The result is not pretty, and was best described in a famous passage by C. S. Lewis:

There is no safe investment. To love at all is to be vulnerable. Love anything, and your heart will certainly be wrung and possibly be broken. If you want to make sure of keeping it intact, you must give your heart to no one, not even to an animal. Wrap it carefully round with hobbies and little luxuries; avoid all entanglements; lock it up safe in the casket or coffin of your selfishness. But in that casket—safe, dark, motionless, airless—it will change. It will not be broken; it will become unbreakable, impenetrable, irredeemable. The alternative to tragedy, or at least the risk of tragedy, is damnation. The only place outside Heaven where you can be perfectly safe from all the dangers and perturbations of love is Hell.

Nobody makes a conscious decision to entomb the heart and to anesthetize the daemon; it just sort of happens after a few decades of prudent and professional living. Ultimately, people become strangers to their own desires. José Ortega y Gasset believed that most people devote themselves to avoiding that genuine self, to silencing the daemon and refusing to hear it. We bury the faint crackling of our inner fire underneath other, safer noises, and settle for a false life.

REAWAKENING THE SOUL

If you really want to make a wise vocation decision, you have to lead the kind of life that keeps your heart and soul awake every day. There are some activities that cover over the heart and soul—the ones that are too analytic, economic, prudently professional, and comfortably bourgeois. There are some that awaken the heart and engage the soul—music, drama, art, friendship, being around children, being around beauty, and, paradoxically, being around injustice. The people who make the wisest vocation decisions are the people who live their lives every day with their desires awake and alive. They get out of boring offices and take jobs where the problems are. They are the ones who see their desires, confront their desires, and understand what they truly yearn for.

Sometimes an artist can awaken the heart and soul. James Mill raised his son John Stuart to be a thinking machine. He taught him Greek at age two. Between the ages of eight and twelve, he read all of Herodotus, Homer, and Xenophon; six Platonic dialogues; and Virgil and Ovid (in Latin), while learning physics, chemistry, astronomy, and mathematics. He was given no holidays off. It all worked wonderfully—John Stuart Mill was an astounding prodigy—until he turned twenty and went into a deep depression.

Mill realized what constant study of data and nonfiction had done to him. He realized that "the habit of analysis has a tendency to wear away the feelings." But then something pulled him out. It wasn't an epiphany, some new burst of insight. It was poetry. William Wordsworth's poetry: "What made Wordsworth's poems medicine for my state of mind, was they expressed, not mere outward beauty, but states of feeling, and of thought colored by feeling, under the excitement of beauty. . . . In them I seemed to draw from a source of inward joy, of sympathetic and imaginative pleasure, which could be shared by all human beings; which had no connection with struggle or imperfection, but would be made richer by every improvement in the physical or social condition of mankind."

Mill got depressed when he felt his desires go lukewarm. He pulled out of it when he discovered the existence of infinite desires, which are spiritual and moral, and not worldly desires. Henceforth, he wrote, "the cultivation of the feelings became one of the cardinal points in my ethical and philosophical creed."

Sometimes it's simple glee that awakens the soul and helps us find our daemon. Shortly after Tom Clancy published *The Hunt for Red October*, I was invited to a dinner with Clancy. He had just come back from a tour of some battleship, courtesy of the U.S. Navy, where he had seen some sort of new weapons system. His face was aglow; his eyes glistened. He spent the first half of the meal gleefully describing that new system, practically bouncing in his chair with childish delight, going through each part of the technology in, to me, numbing detail. I remember thinking: Oh, that's what it takes. You can't write military bestsellers unless you genuinely feel what you're writing about is the coolest thing on earth. It won't work unless the boyish enthusiasm flows genuinely from your very heart. You can't fake it.

Sometimes you see someone you really admire, and it arouses a fervent desire to be like that. In Mary Catherine Bateson's book *Composing a Life*, she describes a woman named Joan who was studying to be a gym teacher. She liked dancing but never thought of herself as a dancer because she was husky, while dancers were petite. Then a dance teacher came into her school, as husky and as tall as Joan, but light on her feet. "I watched her move around, and I thought, well, you're no bigger than she is, maybe you've got what it takes," Joan recalled. "So I began really taking my dancing seriously, and after a while I began to be commended, I mean I was doing good. I think it was toward the end of that year when I really latched on and I said, Boy! That's it. That's what I am. I'm a dancer. I just knew it like that. And after that, everything was just sheer bliss that I had to do."

Sometimes it's tragedy that shocks us out of false desires and helps us see our real ones. In her book, *The Power of Meaning*, Emily Esfahani Smith describes a woman named Christine who grew up very close to her mother. One day, when she was a junior at the University of Michigan studying engineering and planning on a career as an engineer, her mother was hit by a truck as she crossed the street and was killed. "She was killed by an idiot. Someone who was being irresponsible and stupid," Christine said. "I just felt so hopeless after; nothing made sense. She was gone now. How? And I'm torn between this anger and this part of me that wants to let go and live my life. Move forward. . . . I hate humans so much. At the same time, you have to live your life."

Eventually Christine abandoned engineering and became a pastry chef. "After an event like that, you think about your life and who you are and what you want to do. Ninety-five percent of the decisions I make are now influenced by the fact that she died. So, yeah, pastry."

Sometimes it's a problem that burns at your conscience. If you work in a normal office doing some sort of organizational job, you're probably not going to be thrust face to face with gigantic social problems. But if you get a job as a teacher in a school on an Indian reservation, you will see injustice face to face. Your soul will burn with a yearning to make things right. Your course in life will be clear.

I know a man named Fred Wertheimer who has spent his life try-ing to reform the way political campaigns are financed. Fred hates the way money corrupts politics, but he loves his problem. Every day I get mass emails from him linking to some news story on campaign fi-nance reform. I want to unsubscribe from his email list, because it's clogging up my in-box, but I don't want to hurt his feelings because telling him I don't care that much about his problem would be like telling him I don't care that much about his child.

"One's mind has to be a searching mind," Thomas Bernhard writes of the person looking for a calling. "A mind searching for mistakes, for the mistakes of humanity, a mind searching for failure."

Over time, a commitment to addressing a problem often eclipses the love of the activity that led someone to tackle the problem in the first place. For example, there comes a time in many careers when people face a choice between helping a small number of people a lot or helping a large number of people a little. A woman may have gone into education because she loved teaching. But then midway through her career she is asked if she'd be willing to be a principal or an adminis-trator, a position that would take her away from her treasured class-room and involve a lot of boring administrative and difficult personnel tasks that she doesn't love.

Some people turn down this "promotion." They decide they'd rather be line workers than managers, teachers rather than principals, writers rather than editors. The thing other people call "impact," or working "at scale," is overrated. But in most of the cases I've been around, people take the promotion. Their new job as a principal (or editor, or manager, or what have you) will be a lot less fun, but it will be more rewarding. They went into their vocation for the immediate aesthetic pleasure of some activity, but over time, they realize they are most fulfilled when they are instruments for serving an institution that helps address a problem. They have found their vocation.

At that point a feeling of certainty clicks in. When that happens, you aren't asking, "What should I do with my life?" Instead, one day you wake up and realize the question has gone away.

MOMENTS OF OBLIGATION

The best advice I've heard for people in search of a vocation is to say yes to everything. Say yes to every opportunity that comes along, because you never know what will lead to what. Have a bias toward action. Think of yourself as a fish that is hoping to get caught. Go out there among the fishhooks.

Simple questions help you locate your delight. What do I enjoy talking about? If it's motorcycles, maybe your work is mechanics. When have I felt most needed? If it was protecting your country as a soldier, maybe your vocation is in law enforcement. What pains am I willing to tolerate? If you're willing to tolerate the misery of rejection, you must have sufficient love of theater to go into acting. Or there's Casey Gerald's question: What would you do if you weren't afraid? Fear is a pretty good GPS system; it tells you where you true desires are, even if they are on the far side of social disapproval.

I have a friend named Fred Swaniker who was born in Ghana in 1976, the son of a lawyer and magistrate, and lived in four different African countries as a boy. His father died while he was a teenager, and his mother opened a school in Botswana, at first with just five students. She made her son the headmaster.

After high school, Swaniker won a scholarship to attend Macalester College in Minnesota. Then he got a job at McKinsey and a degree at Stanford Business School. Throughout all this, he was haunted by the fact that he had been given these opportunities while hundreds of millions of young Africans just like him never would be.

He thought about returning to Africa and opening a chain of healthcare clinics. But at the crucial moment of his life, he came to the conclusion that the biggest impediment to progress in Africa was the lack of a well-trained leadership class. So he raised some money from friends in Silicon Valley and went back to South Africa to launch the African Leadership Academy, with the goal of training six thousand leaders over a fifty-year period. ALA now takes some of the most talented students from across the continent, offers them a free education, and sends them to universities abroad so long as they promise to return to Africa to lead their lives.

In 2006, Swaniker was nominated to receive an Echoing Green Fellowship, which at that time was given annually to sixteen of the most promising social entrepreneurs in the world. During the interview process, Swaniker was asked to describe his "moment of obligation," the moment when he realized he had to quit his job and pursue this calling. As Swaniker later wrote on Medium, "being asked that question helped me to crystallize why I had been put on this earth."

Swaniker believes that we are defined by these moments of obligation, which are "usually caused by a sense of outrage about some injustice, wrong-doing or unfairness we see in society." But he goes on to argue that "you should ignore 99% of these moments of obligation," no matter how guilty it makes you feel. The world is full of problems, but very few are the problems you are meant to address.

When you feel the tug of such a moment, Swaniker advises, ask three big questions:

First, Is it big enough? Those who have been fortunate to receive a good education, who are healthy, and have had great work experiences should not be solving small problems. If you were born lucky, you should solve big problems.

Second, "Am I uniquely positioned . . . to make this happen?" Look back on the experiences you have had. Have they prepared you for this specific mission?

Third, "Am I truly passionate?" Does the issue generate obsessive thinking? Does it keep you up at night?

If your answer to each question is not a resounding yes, Swaniker advises, you should ignore that idea. Swaniker's life fits his own formula. He grew up across Africa, so had a pan-African perspective. He was raised by a teacher and had seen his own life transformed by a scholarship, so was fit to focus on education. He picked an audaciously big problem—educating the cream of students from across the continent—something that could occupy a lifetime.

But Swaniker's really impressive moment came later in life. He'd already launched ALA, the school. He'd launched something called the African Leadership Network, an association of about two thousand promising young professionals from across the continent. But in his thirties, he saw a new big problem: Africa has a university shortage. Someone should create an African Leadership University, he thought, with the goal of building a network of twenty-five new universities across the continent. Each campus would have ten thousand students. Over fifty years it would produce three million leaders.

He urged his friends to start building universities. None would. But he could not let the idea rest. It was a big problem, it was something he cared about passionately, and it was something he was uniquely prepared to do. How many people had been a headmaster at eighteen and developed a feeder system of five thousand high schools and a leadership network of young entrepreneurs across the continent? "As I connected the dots, I realized that the last 15 years had been preparing me with the expertise, know-how and relationships to pull off this much bigger feat. Raising $100 million had been the 'training wheels' I needed to raise $5 billion."

ALU opened its first college in Mauritius and its second in Rwanda; its third will open soon in Nigeria. ALU received six thousand applications on its first day for 180 slots. It will take twenty-five to thirty years to build all of the universities Swaniker thinks need to be built.

Swaniker's story is epic, and the institutions he is building are on a vaster scale than anything most of us will do. But he is still a good example of someone who listened to his life, who plumbed his desires, who asked, What problems are around me? What has my life given me as preparation? How can the two go together?

His story illustrates two final features of the vocation decision. First, it's not about creating a career path. It's asking, What will touch my deepest desire? What activity gives me my deepest satisfaction? Second, it's about fit. A vocation decision is not about finding the biggest or most glamorous problem in the world. Instead, it's about finding a match between a delicious activity and a social need. It's the same inward journey we've seen before: the plunge inward and then the expansion outward. Find that place in the self that is driven to connect with others, that spot where, as the novelist Frederick Buechner famously put it, your deep gladness meets the world's deep hunger.

THIRTEEN

Mastery

After William Least Heat-Moon lost his teaching job at the University of Missouri, he decided to take time off and travel around the United States, taking the small back roads that are marked in blue on the Rand McNally maps. Near the town of Hat Creek, California, he met an old man who was taking his dog for a walk.

"A man's never out of work if he's worth a damn," the old man reflected. "It's just sometimes he doesn't get paid. I've gone unpaid my share and I've pulled my share of pay. But that's got nothing to do with working. A man's work is doing what he's supposed to do, and that's why he needs a catastrophe now and again to show him a bad turn isn't the end, because a bad stroke never stops a good man's work."

That's a useful distinction. A job is a way of making a living, but work is a particular way of being needed, of fulfilling the responsibility that life has placed before you. Martin Luther King, Jr., once advised that your work should have length—something you get better at over a lifetime. It should have breadth—it should touch many other people. And it should have height—it should put you in service to some ideal and satisfy the soul's yearning for righteousness.

We all know people whose real work is hospitality, but they practice hospitality over the span of many different kinds of jobs. Belden Lane's work is trying to write down and describe the spiritual transcendence he sometimes experiences in nature. But he can't just tell people at dinner parties he's a guy who wanders around in the woods seeking transcendence. "My own particular cover is that of a university professor," he writes. "It's a way of looking responsible while attending to much more important things." As a professor, he appears to be "engaged in reputable endeavors, locked into acceptable categories. I manage to satisfy my employer, meet society's expectations, sign checks." But his real work is up in the mountains, stalking that eternity that is seen in not being seen.

DIGGING THE DAMN DITCH

A person who has found his vocation has been released from the anxiety of uncertainty, but there is still the difficulty of the work itself. All vocational work, no matter how deeply it touches you, involves those moments when you are confronted by the laborious task. Sometimes, if you are going to be a professional, you just have to dig the damn ditch.

All real work has testing thresholds, moments when the world and fate roll stones in your path. All real work requires discipline. "If one is courteous but does it without ritual, then one dissipates one's energies," Confucius wrote. "If one is cautious but does it without ritual, one becomes timid; if one is bold but does it without ritual, then one becomes reckless; if one is forthright but does it without ritual, then one becomes rude."

All real work requires a dedication to engage in deliberate practice, the willingness to do the boring things over and over again, just to master a skill. To teach himself to write, Benjamin Franklin took the essays in *The Spectator*, the leading magazine of his day, and translated them into poetry. Then he took his poems and translated them back into prose. Then he analyzed how his final work was inferior to the original *Spectator* essays.

When he was teaching himself to play basketball, Bill Bradley set himself a schedule. Three and a half hours of practice every day after school and on Sundays. Eight hours on Saturdays. He wore ten-pound weights on his ankles to strengthen them. His great weakness was dribbling, so he taped pieces of cardboard to the bottom of his glasses so he could not see the ball as he dribbled it. When his family took a trip to Europe by boat, Bradley found two long, narrow corridors belowdecks where he could dribble his basketball at a sprint, hour upon hour, day after day.

Deliberate practice slows the automatizing process. As we learn a skill, the brain stores the new knowledge in the unconscious layers (think of learning to ride a bike). But the brain is satisfied with good enough. If you want to achieve the level of mastery, you have to learn the skill so deliberately that when the knowledge is stored down below, it is perfect.

Some music academies teach pianists to practice their pieces so slowly that if you can recognize the tune you're playing too fast. Some golf academies slow down their pupils so it takes ninety seconds to finish a single swing (try it sometime). Martha Graham covered the mirrors in her dance studies with burlap. If the dancers wanted to check out how they were doing, they would have to feel it by concentrating on the movement of their own bodies.

The more creative the activity is, the more structured the work routine should probably be. When she was writing, Maya Angelou would get up every morning at 5:30 and have coffee. At 6:30 she would go off to a hotel room she kept—a modest room with nothing in it but a bed, a desk, a Bible, a dictionary, a deck of cards, and a bottle of sherry. She would arrive at 7:00 A.M. and write every day until 12:30 P.M.

John Cheever would get up, put on his only suit, and ride the elevator in his apartment building down to a storage room in the basement. Then he'd take off his suit and sit in his boxers and write until noon. Then he would put his suit back on and ride the escalator upstairs to lunch.

Anthony Trollope, an extreme case, would sit down at his writing table at 5:30 each morning. A servant would bring a cup of coffee at the same time. He would write 250 words every fifteen minutes for two and a half hours every day. His daily total was exactly 2,500 words, and if he finished a novel without writing that allotment, he would immediately start a new novel to hit the mark.

H. A. Dorfman is one of the great baseball psychologists. In his masterpiece, *The Mental ABC's of Pitching*, Dorfman says that this kind of structured discipline is necessary if you want to escape the tyranny of the scattered mind. "Self-discipline is a form of freedom," he writes. "Freedom from laziness and lethargy, freedom from expectations and the demands of others, freedom from weakness and fear—and doubt."

Dorfman advises pitchers to adopt the same pregame rituals, game after game. Walk from the locker room to the same spot on the bench, put your water bottle in the exact same spot, stretch in the same way. He tells pitchers to structure the geography of their workplace. There are two locales in a pitcher's universe—on the mound and off the mound. When a pitcher is on the mound he should be thinking about only two things, pitch selection and pitch location. If he finds himself thinking about something else, he should get off the mound.

The mind is focused when it is going forward in a straight line, he argues. The discipline is to put the task at the center. The pitcher's personality isn't at the center. His talent and anxiety aren't at the center. The task is at the center. The master has the ability to self-distance from what he is doing. He's able to be cool about the thing he feels most passionate about.

If you do this long enough, you begin to understand your own strengths and limitations, and you develop your own individual method. A few years into writing, I came to see how bad my memory is, and how hard it is to organize my thoughts sequentially. Ideas occur to me in some sort of random order, when I'm least expecting them. So I took to carrying around little notebooks in my back pocket, where I can put my jottings. When I research a piece, I collect hundreds of pages of printed documents. If a read a book, I photocopy all the important pages.

It turns out I think geographically. I need to see all my notes and pages physically laid out before me if I'm to get a sense of what I have.

So I invented a system that works for me. I separate all my relevant papers into piles on the carpet of my study or living room. Each pile is a paragraph in my column or my book. My newspaper column is only 850 words, but it may require fourteen piles on the floor. The writing process is not sitting at the keyboard typing. It is crawling around on the carpet laying out my piles. Once that's done, I pick up each pile from the floor and bring it to the big table on which I write, and I separate the paragraph piles into sentence piles. And then after I've typed the ideas on my keyboard, I throw out the pile and move to the next pile. Writing is really about structure and traffic management. If you don't have the structure right, nothing else will happen. For me, crawling about on the floor working on my piles are the best moments of my job.

THE VOCATION MAKES THE PERSON

Work is the way we make ourselves useful to our fellows. "There may be no better way to love your neighbor," Tim Keller put it, "whether you are writing parking tickets or software or books, than to simply do your work. But only skillful, competent work will do."

Vocation can be a cure for self-centeredness, because to do the work well you have to pay attention to the task itself.

Vocation can be a cure for restlessness. Mastering a vocation is more like digging a well. You do the same damn thing day after day, and gradually, gradually, you get deeper and better. "In silence, in steadiness, in severe abstraction, let him hold by himself," Emerson wrote, "add observation to observation, patient of neglect, patient of reproach; and bide his own time, happy enough if he can truly satisfy himself alone, that this day he has seen something truly."

Emerson underlines one of the key elements of the commitment decision. At the beginning it involves a choice—choosing this or that vocation. But 99.9 percent of the time it means choosing what one has already chosen. Just as all writing is really rewriting, all commitment is really recommitment. It's saying yes to the thing you've already said yes to.

Mike Beebe grew up in a tar shack, the son of a teenage single mom. He graduated from high school in Arkansas, got a college degree from Arkansas State, and a law degree from the University of Arkansas. In 1982, he was elected to the state legislature, and in 2007 he became governor. He became one of the most popular governors in state history, and in the nation. In 2010, Republicans were beating Democrats all around the nation, but in Arkansas Beebe swept all seventy-five counties on his way to reelection.

What was his secret? One key factor was that he had no national ambitions. Arkansas was his home and Arkansas was where he would focus all his energy. A Unitarian pastor in New York, Galen Guengerich, read about Beebe and drew the proper conclusion. Sometimes it's right to move on and try something new, Guengerich observed,

> but we also need to learn the virtue of staying put and staying true, of choosing again what we chose before. In my view that's one of the main reasons we come to church.
>
> We're here not so much to make spiritual progress each week, though that's wonderful when it happens. Rather, we mostly come for the consistency—for what remains the same from week to week: the comfort of the liturgy, the solace of the music, the reassuring sight of familiar faces, the enduring presence of ancient rites and timeless symbols. We're here to remind ourselves of values that unite us and commitments that keep us heading in the right direction. We're here to choose again what we chose before.

If you watch people over the course of long careers, you notice that people get better at some mental tasks and worse at others. They say the brain peaks early in life, in the twenties. After that, brain cells die, memory deteriorates. But the lessons of experience compensate. We get much better at recognizing patterns and can make decisions with much less effort. The neuropsychologist Elkhonon Goldberg studies the patterns of the brain. Late in his career he wrote this about his own abilities: "Something rather intriguing has happened in my mind that did not happen in the past. Frequently, when I am faced with what would appear from the outside to be a challenging problem, the grinding mental computation is somehow circumvented, rendered, as if by magic, unnecessary. The solution comes effortlessly, seamlessly, seemingly by itself. What I have lost with age in my capacity for hard mental work, I seem to have gained in my capacity for instantaneous, almost unfairly easy insight."

People who have achieved mastery no longer just see the individual chess pieces; they see the whole. They perceive the fields of forces that are actually driving the match. Musicians talk about seeing the entire architecture of a piece of music, not just the notes.

BECOMING THE BOSS

Bruce Springsteen's life neatly traces the path from inexperience to mastery, and illustrates what happens to a person when he has given himself to his vocation. Springsteen had his annunciation moment when he was seven. He was watching *The Ed Sullivan Show*, and suddenly Elvis Presley appeared. It was astounding, as Springsteen put it in his memoir, "a new kind of man, of modern human, blurring racial lines and gender lines and having . . . FUN! . . . FUN! . . . the real kind. The life-blessing, wall-destroying, heart-changing, mind-opening bliss of a freer, more liberated existence."

Little Bruce Springsteen looked at Elvis and had a visceral sense that that's what he wanted to be. "All relationships begin in projection," James Hollis observes. Springsteen dragged his mother to the music store and, with almost no money to spend, rented a guitar. He took it home, practiced on it for a few weeks, and promptly quit. It was too hard.

Springsteen came from the sort of house that seems to regularly produce childhood misery, a lifetime of analysis, and phenomenal success. That is, he had a loving and doting mother and a cold and distant father. They were so poor their house was literally falling apart. They had to carry hot water from the kitchen to the bathtub. As a child he was nicknamed "Blinky" because he had a nervous tic of blinking hundreds of times a minute. He was a shy, awkward teenager.

But then lightning struck again. In 1964, the Beatles appeared on

The Ed Sullivan Show. Springsteen felt the same call he'd felt with Elvis, the same devouring curiosity. He went to the local five-and-ten-cent store, made his way to the small record section in the back, and found what he later called "the greatest album cover of all time." All it said was *Meet the Beatles!* and all it showed was four half-shadowed faces. "That was exactly what I wanted to do."

When we talk about these moments afterward, we tend to emphasize the low ambitions in them and get shy when talking about the high ones, because we don't want to sound pretentious. When you ask musicians why they went into music, they invariably say that they did it to get girls or be loved or make money, but those low motivations are often tales they tell because they don't want to appear earnest about their high and powerful idealism—the need to express some emotion in themselves, to explore some experience.

One of the best pieces of advice for young people is, Get to yourself quickly. If you know what you want to do, start doing it. Don't delay because you think this job or that degree would be good preparation for doing what you eventually want to do. Just start doing it. Springsteen, with no plan B options and no distractions, got to himself quickly.

He bought a beat-up old guitar and tried to teach himself to play. Five months later, his fingers were callused and hard. He joined a band, played a gig at his own high school, was completely terrible, and got kicked out of the band.

That night, he pulled out a Rolling Stones album, heard a Keith Richards guitar solo, and stayed up all night trying to copy it. Springsteen spent every weekend at YMCA or high school dances. He did no dancing. He just stood off to the side studying the lead guitarist. Then he'd rush home alone to his room and play everything he'd seen. As Oswald Chambers once noted, "Drudgery is the touchstone of character."

Springsteen joined more bands, and by the time he was twenty, he'd played in every conceivable small venue—YMCAs, pizza parlors, gas station openings, weddings, bar mitzvahs, firemen's conventions, the Marlboro Psychiatric Hospital. He began, slowly, to get good. He knew no one in Asbury Park, New Jersey, but there was a bar there with a set of speakers. Musicians could just sign up for a half-hour slot, plug in, and play. Springsteen walked into the room, where no one knew him, and let loose. As he wrote in his memoir, *Born to Run*, "I watched people sit up, move closer, and begin to pay serious attention." What followed, he recalled, was "thirty scorching minutes of guitar Armageddon, then I walked off." A new gunslinger had come to town.

Springsteen gathered the best musicians he could find—others who had also closed off all the other options. They toured Jersey relentlessly. They went to Greenwich Village in New York, ninety minutes and a world away, and were hit by the hard truth that most of the bands there were better than they were. There are (at least) two kinds of failure. In the first kind you are good, but other people can't grasp how good you are. Melville's *Moby-Dick* sold only 2,300 copies in its first eighteen months and only 5,500 copies in its first fifty years. It was savaged by reviewers. Some artists have to create the taste by which they will be judged. In the second kind, you fail because you're not as good as you thought you were, and other people see it.

We all want to imagine that our failures are of the first kind, but one suspects that something like 95 percent of failures are of the second kind. One of the character tests on the road to mastery involves recognizing that fact.

You can be knowledgeable with other men's knowledge, but you can't be wise with other men's wisdom. Springsteen's early struggles taught him to pay attention to the parts of the job that are not the fun parts, but are the stuff you have to take care of to make the thing work. He spent more and more time thinking about how to craft a band. He fired a manager. He fired a drummer who was occasionally brilliant but often inconsistent. He thought about management structures. The band would not be a democracy. He would run it.

We like to think that rock stars, of all people, work hard and party hard. But the master almost never lives in the same body as the swinger. Mastery takes too much discipline and usually involves some form of asceticism. Bruce Springsteen worked in bars throughout his early career, but he never had a drink. He sang about factories all his life, but he never actually set foot in a working factory. He sang song after song about cars, but as a young man he didn't know how to drive. Rock and roll is about wildness and pleasure, but after his concerts Springsteen has a ritual. He's in his hotel room alone—with fried chicken, french fries, a book, TV, and bed.

Art is, as Springsteen says, a bit of a con job. It's about projecting an image of the rock star, even if you don't really live it.

Some people achieve flow socially. They are out with a bunch of friends at dinner or at a party, or dancing with a gang, and self-consciousness fades away. But many artists have trouble disappearing naturally into their lives. They feel separate from others and want to be connected somehow. It's precisely the lack of social and emotional flow that can propel creativity. As the poet Christian Wiman puts it, "An artist is conscious of always standing apart from life, and one of the results of this can be that you begin to feel most intensely what you have failed to feel: a certain emotional reserve in one's life becomes a source of great power in one's work."

In 1972, at age twenty-two, Springsteen was finally discovered. His first two records were not commercially successful, so the fate of his career hung on the third. It turned out to be *Born to Run*. Springsteen was on the cover of both *Time* and *Newsweek* in the same week, back when that meant something.

He was suddenly a star. The next obvious step was to take it up a notch, to broaden his appeal even more. This, of course, is what the record company and everybody around him wanted. It's the natural progression. If you're a beginner, you become a star. If you're a star you become a superstar.

What followed was the crucial moment in Springsteen's climb to mastery. Instead of going outward and national, he went down and local. His next album would be a deeper dive into his own people, the people on the margins of small towns in central New Jersey. He would pare back the music to make it reflect the solitary characters he was writing about. There's a moment in many successful careers when the prospect of success tries to drag you away from your source, away from the daemon that incited your work in the first place. It is an act of raw moral courage to reject the voices all around and to choose what you have chosen before. It looks like you are throwing away your chance at stardom, but you are actually staying in touch with what got you there.

"Here was where I wanted to make my stand musically and search for my own questions and answers," Springsteen writes. "I didn't want out. I wanted in. I didn't want to erase, escape, forget or reject. I wanted to understand. What were the social forces that held my parents' lives in check? Why was it so hard?"

Here was the paradox: Springsteen grew up in the height of the "I'm Free to Be Myself" era. Rock music was the classic expression of that ethos. Springsteen himself sang about escaping and running away to total freedom. But personally, he never fell for that false lure. He went back deeper into his roots, deeper into his unchosen responsibilities, and to this day lives ten minutes from where he grew up.

"I sensed there was a great difference between unfettered personal license and real freedom. Many of the groups that had come before us, many of my heroes, had mistaken one for the other and it'd ended in poor form. I felt personal license was to freedom as masturbation was to sex. It's not bad, but it's not the real deal." Springsteen felt accountable to the people he'd grown up with, few of whom had been to college, most of whom were struggling, and so he went back and planted himself in that ground.

A few decades later, I watched him perform to sixty-five thousand screaming young fans in Madrid. Their T-shirts celebrated all the local central Jersey places that pop up in Springsteen songs and lore— Highway 9, the Stone Pony, Greasy Lake. It turns out he didn't really have to go out and find his fans. If he built a landscape about his own particular home, they would come to him. It makes you appreciate the tremendous power of the particular. If your identity is formed by hard boundaries, if you come from a specific place, if you embody a distinct tradition, if your concerns are expressed through a specific imaginative landscape, you are going to have more depth and definition than you are if you grew up on the far-flung networks of eclecticism, surfing from one spot to the next, sampling one style then the next, your identity formed by soft commitments or none at all.

One of my students, Jon Endean, once told me about a college professor he had at Rice University named Michael Emerson. Emerson, who is white, is a sociologist who taught about racial justice. To demonstrate the power of identity, he invented a label for each student in the class: "Kentucky Guy," "Fried Pickles Gal," and the like. He called himself "A Common Guy" or just "Common." He walked them through a series of exercises to show how labels shape lives. For example, they created black and white online dating profiles so they could observe the differences in how people reacted. Endean told me that Common was one of the best teachers he ever had, and his work, on the role of race, religion, and urban life, is prominent in the field.

Common not only taught about racial justice, every house he and his wife, Joni, have ever bought was in a black neighborhood. As a result, every one of those houses lost value over the time of his residence. Common and Joni also sent their children to nearly all-black schools. When they were five or six, they self-identified as black. For them racial identity was not a skin tone; it was who all their friends were.

Rice's sociology department has a fund of money for research that it splits up equally among the faculty each year. Common, who already had a tenured chair, gave his money to junior faculty, figuring they would need it more in order to get tenure. He eventually left his chair at Rice to go to work at North Park University in Chicago. He gave up a prestigious job at a prestigious school for a job at an obscure school because he thought the students at North Park could be served in different ways than the students at Rice.

Endean told me about Common several years ago, but he stays in the mind, a vision of a person who has found a total commitment, and an example of the way a vocation, when lived out to the fullest, connects all things, comes together in one coherent package, overshadows the self, and serves some central good.

PART III

Marriage

The Maximum Marriage

JACK GILBERT WAS BORN IN PITTSBURGH IN 1925. HE FAILED OUT OF high school, worked manual jobs, and bummed around Europe before establishing himself as a poet and teacher. Much of his writing was about love, and especially his love for his wife, Michiko Nogami, twenty-one years his junior. Michiko died of cancer at thirty-six. Shortly after her death he wrote a poem called "Married":

> *I came back from the funeral and crawled*
> *around the apartment, crying hard,*
> *searching for my wife's hair.*
> *For two months got them from the drain,*
> *from the vacuum cleaner, under the refrigerator,*
> *and off the clothes in the closet.*
> *But after other Japanese women came,*
> *there was no way to be sure which were*
> *hers, and I stopped. A year later,*
> *repotting Michiko's avocado, I find*
> *a long black hair tangled in the dirt.*

I begin a chapter on marriage with a poem about death because marriage defies anecdote and sometimes is felt most powerfully after it has gone. A beautiful marriage is not dramatic. It is hard to depict in novel and song because the acts that define it are so small, constant, and particular. Marriage is knowing she likes to get to the airport early. Marriage is taking the time to make the bed even though you know that if you didn't do it she probably would. At the grand level, marriage means offering love, respect, and safety, but day to day, there are never-ending small gestures of tact and consideration, in which you show you understand her moods, you cherish his presence, that this other person is the center of your world. At the end of the day there is the brutal grinding effort of surrendering the ego to the altar of marriage, giving up part of yourself, the desires you have, for the larger union.

Marriage is the ups and downs. There are private jokes, retelling the stories about the sacred places where love was born, hearing his familiar anecdotes at dinner parties, and, inevitably, endless planning.

That passage from Corinthians that everybody reads at weddings really does define marital love: "Love is patient, love is kind. It does not envy, it does not boast, it is not proud. It does not dishonor others, it is not self-seeking, it is not easily angered, it keeps no record of wrongs. Love does not delight in evil but rejoices with the truth. It always protects, always trusts, always hopes, always perseveres."

Who you marry is the most important decision you will ever make. Marriage colors your life and everything in it. George Washington had a rather interesting life, but still concluded, "I have always considered marriage as the most interesting event of one's life, the foundation of happiness or misery."

I have a friend who married a beautiful and talented woman about his own age. Seven years later, after a season of infertility troubles, they had a child, but something went wrong in the delivery room. His wife had an amniotic fluid embolism and lost an immense amount of blood. At the height of the crisis, the doctors told him she might well die—50 to 80 percent of mothers with the condition do. If she lived, it was extremely likely that she would have severe and permanent brain damage. My friend sat there in the waiting room coming to terms with the fact that the rest of his life might be spent caring for a woman who no longer recognized him. "That's when you realize what you've committed to with your marriage vows," he said a few years after the event, sitting beside her, and their daughter, after their full and miraculous recoveries.

Marriage comes as a revolution. To have lived as a one and then suddenly become a two—that is an invasion. And yet there is a prize. People in long, happy marriages have won the lottery of life. They are the happy ones, the blessed ones. And that is the dream of marital union that lures us on. "What greater thing is there for two human souls," George Eliot wrote in *Adam Bede*, "than to feel that they are joined for life—to strengthen each other in all labor, to rest on each other in all sorrow, to minister to each other in all pain, to be one with each other in silent unspeakable memories at the moment of last parting?"

Passion peaks among the young, but marriage is the thing that peaks in old age. What really defines the happy marriage is the completeness of a couple who have been together for decades. Gabriel García Márquez captured it when describing an old couple in *Love in the Time of Cholera*:

> In the end they knew each other so well that by the time they had been married for thirty years they were like a single divided being, and they felt uncomfortable at the frequency with which they guessed each other's thoughts. . . . It was the time when they loved each other best, without hurry or excess, when both were most conscious of and grateful for their incredible victories over adversity. Life would still present them with other mortal trials, of course, but that no longer mattered: they were on the other shore.

We've all met couples like that, who have come to look alike, smile alike. I know a couple, Jim and Deb Fallows, who are famous in our circle for having the happiest marriage. They radiate a single intelligence and a sincere goodness. Another writer had lunch with them one day, saw what a joyous marriage looked like, and immediately decided to propose to his girlfriend.

In their book *The Good Marriage*, Judith Wallerstein and Sandra Blakeslee estimate that in about 15 percent of marriages the passion never wanes. The women in these marriages, they write, tended to come from families where the father was the more nurturing parent and the mother somewhat cold. The women transferred their idealization of their father onto their husband. The men in these marriages often had lonely childhoods and had suffered losses. "These men came to adulthood with intense, long-postponed needs for love and closeness."

One of the couples they studied was Matt and Sara Turner. "It's always felt magical, and it continues to feel that way, thirty-two years later," Sara said. "We both felt the magic within the first hour we met. We talked about it then, and we still talk about it."

Another was Fred and Marie Fellini. "I was trying to think of the worst fight we ever had," Fred said, "and I can't remember it. But we really did fight. I just can't remember what we fought about. One of us would flare up at the other and get over it. None of that is important now."

This is what the maximal marriage looks like. Marriage is a decades-long commitment. It is two people who have become one flesh.

THE ASSAULT OF MAXIMUM MARRIAGE

When you look at the contemporary writing on marriage, you see a general effort to scale it back and shrink it down to manageable (and supposedly more realistic) size. Passion is temporary, the current thinking runs, so don't trust it. A soul mate is an illusion; don't think you're going to find the One True Love. Alain de Botton wrote a popular and eloquent essay for *The New York Times* called "Why You Will Marry the Wrong Person" in which he downplayed the idea that we should find the person who takes us on a magic carpet ride. "We need to swap the Romantic view for a tragic (and at points comedic) awareness that every human will frustrate, anger, annoy, madden and disappoint us. . . . There can be no end to our sense of emptiness and incompleteness."

Many modern books pick up the realist/anti-romantic theme. Laura Kipnis wrote *Against Love: A Polemic.* In 2013, Pascal Bruckner wrote the provocative *Has Marriage for Love Failed?* In 2008, Lori Gottlieb wrote a much-discussed piece in *The Atlantic* that became a book called "Marry Him!: The Case for Settling for Mr. Good Enough." Don't worry about passion and deep connection, she advised. "Based on my observations, in fact, settling will probably make you happier in the long run, since many of those who marry with great expectations become more disillusioned with each passing year."

The assault on maximal marriage comes from three directions. First, in a culture where divorce is common, and the effects often severe, many people adopt a safety-first attitude. Don't put your eggs in the marriage basket. Don't reach for the stars; just build something sensible that won't fall apart. Many people who have been hurt by divorce prioritize self-protection over complete vulnerability.

Second, many people find themselves in marriages that aren't that great, and they embrace a definition of marriage that allows them to make do. They are, in Wallerstein and Blakeslee's words, "companionate marriages." The couple gets along. They parent together. But the passion has faded. They may or may not have sex, and if they do, it is rare. Work and parenting become the most important part of the spouses' lives, and the marriage comes in third, or fourth, or fifth. An academic friend of mine observed over lunch recently, "I don't really know of many happy marriages. I know a lot of marriages where parents love their kids." In such a marriage, you learn to live in an arrangement that really doesn't occupy your interest or your energies.

Some people prefer this low-drama kind of marriage. Wallerstein and Blakeslee quote one woman who reported, "I think what was so refreshing was that the relationship didn't have to suck up all my energy in life—which all my previous relationships did. I had more free time with friends, and more fun."

Third, the culture of individualism undermines the maximal definition of marriage. We live in the culture, Northwestern sociologist Eli Finkel observes, in which the needs of the self take priority over all other needs. The purpose of life is to self-actualize, to express your own autonomy and individuality, to climb Maslow's hierarchy of needs. As Finkel writes, "Expressive individualism is characterized by a strong belief in individual specialness; voyages of self-discovery are viewed as ennobling." In an individualistic culture, marriage is not fusion; it is alliance. The psychologist Otto Rank redefined relationship as a social connection in which *one individual is helping the other to develop and grow*, without infringing too much on the other's personality."

Since around 1965, Finkel writes, "we have been living in the era of the self-expressive marriage. Americans now look to marriage increasingly for self-discovery, self-esteem, and personal growth." A spouse becomes, in the famed psychologist Carl Rogers's words, "my companion in our separate but intertwined pathways of growth."

If the maximum definition of marriage is to be flesh of my flesh, then the individualist definition of love is autonomy but support. If a covenantal view of marriage is putting the needs of the relationship above the needs of each individual, then the individualist view of marriage puts the needs of the individual above the relationship.

When she was young, Polina Aronson moved from Russia to the United States and found she had entered a romantic regime based on individual choice. She read the American magazines and found they celebrated "the savvy, sovereign chooser who is well aware of his needs and acts on the basis of self-interest." Perhaps the greatest problem with this regime of choice, she continues, "stems from its misconception of maturity as absolute self-sufficiency. Attachment is infantilized. The desire for recognition is rendered as 'neediness.' Intimacy must never challenge 'personal boundaries.'"

People overwhelmingly still want to get married. But sociologists observe that marriage is more commonly seen as a capstone, not a keystone. It used to be that people got married and the marriage formed them into the sort of self-disciplined, ordered person who was capable of building a good career. Now more people seek to establish themselves first, then get married. The social script has flipped.

IN PRAISE OF MAXIMAL MARRIAGE

One problem with the individualistic view, as always, is that it traps people in the small prison of the self. If you go into marriage seeking self-actualization, you will always feel frustrated because marriage, and especially parenting, will constantly be dragging you away from the goals of self.

Another problem with the individualistic view is that it doesn't give us a script to fulfill the deepest yearnings. The heart yearns to fuse with others. This can be done only through an act of joint surrender, not through joint autonomy. The soul desires to chase some ideal, to pursue joy. This can happen only by transcending the self in order to serve the marriage.

In the committed life, a maximal marriage is viewed the way the scholar of myth Joseph Campbell viewed it, as a heroic quest in which the ego is sacrificed for the sake of a relationship. In the ethos of commitment, marriage is a moral microcosm of life, in which each person freely chooses to take on responsibility for others, and become dependent on others in order to do something larger. In this understanding of marriage, people don't become lovely by loving themselves; they become lovely by loving others, by making vows to others, by taking on the load of others and fulfilling those vows and carrying that load. All the dignity and gravity of life is in this surrender.

The maximal marriage is something you hurl yourself into, burning the boats behind you. "We must return to an attitude of total abandonment," Mike Mason writes in *The Mystery of Marriage*, "of throwing all our natural caution and defensiveness to the winds and putting ourselves entirely in the hands of love by an act of will. Instead of falling into love, we may now have to march into it."

People talk about "settling down." But, in fact, marriage is a hopeful revolution two people undertake together, without any real idea of what's on the other side. It involves a set of far-reaching personal reforms, so that you might become the sort of person with whom it is possible to live. It is a dangerous thing not to be aware of the crisis-like nature of marriage, Mason continues. "Whether it turns out to be a healthy, challenging, and constructive crisis or a disastrous nightmare, depends largely upon how willing the partners are to be changed."

MARRIAGE IS THE ULTIMATE MORAL EDUCATION

Marriage is, as Lord Shaftesbury once put it, like a gem tumbler. It throws two people together and bumps them up against each other day after day so they are constantly chipping away at one another, in a series of "amicable collisions," until they are bright. It creates all the situations in which you are more or less compelled to be a less selfish person than you were before.

In *The Meaning of Marriage,* Tim and Kathy Keller describe how the process of improvement and elevation happens. First, you marry a person who seems completely wonderful and mostly perfect. Then, after a little while—maybe a month or two, maybe a year or two—you realize that the person you thought was so wonderful is actually imperfect, selfish, and flawed in many ways. As you are discovering this about your spouse, your spouse is making the exact same discovery about you.

The natural tendency in this situation is to acknowledge that of course you are a little selfish and flawed, but in fact it is your spouse's selfishness that is the main problem here. Both spouses will also come to this conclusion at about the same time.

Then comes a fork in the road. Some couples will decide that they don't want all the stress and conflict that will come from addressing the truths they have discovered about each other and themselves. They'll make a truce, the Kellers says. Some subjects will not be talked about. You agree to not mention some of your spouse's shortcomings so long as she agrees not to mention some of yours. The result is a truce-marriage, which is static, at least over the short term, but which gradually deteriorates over the long one.

"The alternative to this truce-marriage is to determine to see your own selfishness as a fundamental problem and to treat it more seriously than you do your spouse's. Why? Only you have complete access to your own selfishness, and only you have complete responsibility for it," the Kellers write. "If two spouses *each* say, 'I'm going to treat my self-centeredness as the main problem in the marriage,' you have the prospect of a truly great marriage."

Before you are married, as Alain de Botton notes, you can live under the illusion that you are easy to live with. But to be married is to volunteer for the most thorough surveillance program known to humankind. The person who is married is watched, more or less all the time. Worse, the awareness that you are being watched compels you to watch yourself. This new self-consciousness introduces you to yourself, to all the stupid things you do, from leaving the cupboards open, to the way you are silent and grumpy in the morning, to the way you avoid any difficult conversation or play passive-aggressive when you are feeling hurt, as if life were some elaborate game of victimhood in which if you can make your spouse feel guilty for hurting you you will get a slice of cherry cake at the end.

Marriage involves fighting and recovery, small and large acts of betrayal, and apology. "And there's the great problem of marriage," the Kellers write. "The one person in the whole world who holds your heart in your hand, whose approval and affirmation you most long for and need, is the one who is hurt more deeply by your sins than anyone else on the planet."

Things get even harder when your spouse, who loves you so much, wants to help you become a better person. Your spouse wants to give you service. But we don't want to receive service! We want to be independent and take care of our own lives. Back when we were single nobody gave us gifts, at least not the kind that required a humiliating acknowledgment of our dependence on another person. But in marriage the big humiliation is that you need help from somebody else.

Receiving and giving gifts is the daily business of marriage. For the marriage to work, you've got to know your spouse well enough to love her in the way that will bring out her loveliness. A successful marriage demands and draws out types of love that were not even conceived of by people before marriage. "We can break through marriage into marriage," the poet Jack Gilbert writes. "We find out the heart only by dismantling what the heart knows."

Great marriages are measured by how much the spouses are able to take joy in each other's victories. They are also measured by how gently they correct each other's vices. "I should never like scolding anyone else so well; and that is a point to be thought of in a husband," George Eliot wrote. There's this constant internal struggle when you're having a fight, a friend of mine observes. The ego wants you to say the mean thing that will take the fight up a notch. The heart wants you to say, "I love you, honey." The ego responds, "Screw It. I'm angry. Say it!" You have to decide.

And that is why marriage works best when it is maximal. It demands nearly everything and gives nearly everything. Kierkegaard wrote about fighting under the victorious banner of love. "I secretly wear on my breast the ribbon of my order, love's necklace of roses. Believe me, its roses do not wither. Even if they change with the years, they still do not fade; even if the rose is not as red, it is because it has become a white rose—it did not fade. . . . What I am through her she is through me, and neither of us is anything by oneself, but we are what we are in union."

Marriage is the sort of thing where it's safer to go all in, and it's dangerous to go in half-hearted. At the far end, when done well, you see people enjoying the deepest steady joy you can find on this earth.

The Stages of Intimacy I

THE GLANCE

How do two strangers get to the point where they want to marry? Well, they follow the stages of intimacy. It's never the same in any two cases, but we can observe some general patterns. In the next few chapters I'll be describing how couples go through the various stages of intimacy. I want to do it not only to explain how marriage happens, but to show how intimacy develops across realms.

It starts with a glance. You take a little look at a person—like any of the million little glances you take each day—but, this time, unexpectedly, a spark is struck, a flame is lit, an interest is aroused. Some kindling that was already somewhere inside you gets lit in a surprising way. The person you're looking at seems thrillingly new, but also feels familiar. Love begins with seeing. Love is a quality of attention. In some cases, maybe when the glimpser is a little older, there's also a premonition in that glance that is a mixture of "Behold! My joy appears!" and "Uh-oh. Here comes trouble."

Most of the times, that first look leads to nothing. But sometimes it leads to a great deal. We all know couples who met at a bar or a party.

One person heard a laugh across the room. One person pulls the other in with the three-second look, that most powerful of all social gestures. You lock a stranger's eyes, and then you hold them, by simply staring, for three seconds. Then there's a smile. Some little flicker of mutual recognition is sent and received.

You never know when the heart will open. Two decades ago, there was a concert pianist living in Houston who was about to move to be with her fiancé in San Francisco. Just before she was scheduled to leave, she thought she would get her hair done. She went to a salon she'd never been to before called Etudes de Paris, walked in the door, and saw a man cutting someone else's hair. A certainty formed within her.

She went back into the dressing room, draped her gown around her, and called her mother. "I've just seen the man I'm actually going to marry," she said. She went out, got her shampoo, and was eventually sitting before the man she'd noticed, whose name, it turned out, was David—pronounced in the French way, *Daveed*. They chatted about this and that, and eventually David asked her story. She mentioned she was a pianist, about to move out to join her fiancé in San Francisco. "But," the woman added, "I won't go if you'll marry me."

There was a pause.

David looked down at his scissors, and, as he later recalled, "I never felt more free in my entire life." He responded: "It's a deal."

They got engaged at that moment and then got to know each other and eventually wed.

"It is always astonishing how love can strike," John O'Donohue writes in his book *Beauty*. "No context is love-proof, no convention or commitment impervious. Even a lifestyle which is perfectly insulated, where the personality is controlled, all the days ordered and all actions in sequence, can to its own dismay find that an unexpected spark has landed; it begins to smoulder until it is finally unquenchable. The force of Eros always brings disturbance; in the concealed terrain of the human heart Eros remains a light sleeper."

I don't know about you, but for me the pregnant glance never comes with the first look. It's usually something like the millionth look. For some reason, I have to know someone well in nonromantic circumstances before any meaningful spark can happen. I met a girl in eighth grade and we hung out casually as part of the same circle for the next five years. Then one evening, just before high school graduation, a bunch of us were sitting around a campfire. She and I exchanged a new kind of glance, her hand slipped into mine, a little fire was lit. Within three months it turned into the raging firestorm of full-blown adolescent love.

Love starts as a focusing of attention. The opposite of love is not hate; it's indifference.

CURIOSITY

The second stage of intimacy is curiosity, the desire to know. Your energy is up. Your mind is moving toward something. You hope this person is as great as she seems to be.

Think of the facets of curiosity: They are all comparable to the stages of early intimacy and early love. There is *joyous exploration*, the desire to learn more about the person. There is *absorption*, seeing only this person and not anyone else in the room. There is *stretching*, the willingness to be in new situations if you get the chance to be with him. There is what some psychologists call *deprivation sensitivity*, the feeling of emptiness when you are not with the person.

There is what the experts call *intrusive thinking*: She's on your mind all the time. When you look at a crowd in a train station, you think you see her in the throng, when it's really someone who looks only vaguely like her. You have imaginary conversations with her as you run—bold conversations, the way the thoughts you have while exercising are always bold.

If you're in school, you study together. You may not even talk that much. You just want the other person around. As C. S. Lewis notes, at this stage you may not even be sexually attracted to each other, you're just overwhelmed by this curiosity: "A man in this state really hasn't leisure to think of sex. He is too busy thinking of a person. The fact that she is a woman is far less important than the fact that she is herself. He is full of desire, but the desire may not be sexually toned. If you asked him what he wanted, the true reply would often be, 'To go on thinking of her.'"

DIALOGUE

You talk. Dialogue is the third state of intimacy. It is the dance of mutual unveiling. When couples get together for dinner or a date, they are on their best behavior, hoping that something comes of this. As they talk, their breathing begins to synchronize, the words come out at a similar speed. They are unconsciously taking in each other's pheromones. (Smell is a surprisingly powerful way of knowing.) Before long they are smiling. People are unconsciously good at discerning sincere smiles from fake, I'm-just-being-polite smiles. The so-called Duchenne-Smile involves the lift of an eyebrow muscle that we can't control consciously. So when a person gives you a D-Smile it feels like heaven. Then they are laughing together. We think of laughter as the way we respond to jokes, but only about 15 percent of the comments that trigger laughter are funny in any way. Instead, laughter is a language that people use to bond. It is what bubbles up when some social incongruity has been resolved or when people find themselves reacting in the same way to some emotionally positive circumstance. Laughter is the reward for shared understanding.

At the early stages of dialogue, couples are looking for similarity. When intimacy is happening, couples find commonalities that feel like destiny. You don't like foie gras? Neither do I! It's a miracle! You find those six-dollar cupcakes ridiculous? So do I! We're soul mates! Their constant delicious refrain is, You, too? I thought I was the only one! We Are the Same! WATS!

One key ground for similarity is in your senses of humor; you better laugh at the same things. As time goes by, the dialogue goes deeper. The couple starts flirting, little inside jokes and sly sideways glances. Then, people start sharing their life goals. They begin subtly feeling out the other person's conception of marriage and how they feel about kids. People begin looking for vulnerability, the process of the slow, step-by-step unveiling. This is part of the inevitable effort to get to know the person's fragile places. But it's also the phase of moral testing. You want to know, If I unveil, will you protect? If I proceed cautiously, will you understand me and match my pace? If I pause, will you respect my pause and wait for me? If I reveal the scariest of my dark monsters, will you hold me? Will you reveal yours? Politeness is at the core of morality.

We've all been in restaurants where just one table over, an atrocious date is under way. Most of the time the woman is making conversational volleys to establish intimacy and similarity, but the guy is intent on establishing dominance. He's barreling forth with all his supposed knowledge, with the stories he tells in which he's his own hero. Her eyes glaze over, but his torrent never stops. You want to take your fork and stab it in the guy's neck and cry out, "For the love of God! Ask her a question!"

The biggest problem in the dialogue phase is fear. Intimacy happens when somebody shares something emotionally meaningful, and the other person receives it and shares back. One obvious fear is that you'll expose your tender flesh and the other person will trample it and then leave. Another obvious fear is that you'll discover that the other person seeks a future you cannot provide. The deeper and more potent fear is that in exposing yourself to others you will actually understand yourself.

"Those of us who wish to pride ourselves on autonomy, on the self-made life, on freedom of choice, are often humbled by the recognition that archaic patterns are playing through us. Who is in charge of our lives if we are not?" James Hollis writes. Down in the unconscious layer of our minds, there are complexes and wounds that lead us to act in the same self-destructive ways again and again. Your personality is the hidden history of the places where love entered your life or was withdrawn from your life. It is shaped by the ways your parents loved you, the ways they did not love you. All of us have certain attachment patterns lodged deep in our minds. Some people provoke a crisis because they are scared of intimacy. Some withdraw at exactly the moment things are getting close.

Most of the time the dance of mutual unveiling stops at a certain shallow level. Some people feel a tendency to skate through a hundred relationships that don't involve intimacy. They haven't yet come to themselves and don't want to. They are estranged from their inner lives. "My friends tell me I have an intimacy problem, but they don't really know me," Garry Shandling used to joke.

About a fifth of adults in Western cultures are afraid of intimacy, afraid of commitment. They expect abandonment to happen and take actions to ensure that what is familiar will indeed come to pass. You can spot the people who fear intimacy because they suddenly disappear for a time, just when you thought you were getting close. They dislike the words "boyfriend" or "girlfriend" or any other term that suggests an official relationship. They tend to hide behind a wall of questions; they turn conversations to you in order to avoid exposing anything about themselves. They tend to express strong opinions or lewd jokes as a tactic for driving people away. They are always positive, always the cheerful one that others turn to, but never vulnerable themselves.

But every once in a while, to everyone's great surprise, the dialogue continues, deeper and deeper. You keep expecting it to stop where all the other conversations used to stop, but no, she's still with you, he's still with you. The gates keep opening, so you keep walking through. The only cure for fear is direct action. You push open the next gate.

PUSHING OPEN THE GATES

A dialogue between two people takes the form of a tennis rally. One partner takes a deep breath and provides a small display of, This is what I like. She shares her favorite movies. He volleys back with his own. She shares the playlists on her phone, and he volleys back with his own. He sends some favorite video late at night, and she sends one back.

Then comes, These are the important moments of my life: the stories, ever deepening, from childhood to adulthood, and gradually, bravely, past relationships and losses.

Phase by phase, the risks become bigger and bolder. Love is possible only if two people eventually reveal the center of their existences. If the love is to bloom, they have to get to, This is how I'm crazy. As Alain de Botton notes, we are all crazy in some way. The crucial question at the depth of any relationship is not Is he crazy? It is What are the ways you are crazy? What parts of your life have been blocked by fear? How exactly do you self-destruct? In what ways have you not been loved?

My wife and I really got to know each other over email. The steps of self-disclosure were so gradual, the progress would have been like watching a lake evaporate to any outsider. But each successive email was carefully considered to not push things too far. I'd hit SEND and wait with a dread that I had crossed some forbidden line. I once sent her an email about some completely innocent topic, some minor step forward of mutual knowing, and then got on a cross-country flight with no Wi-Fi service. I spent the entire flight in an anxiety of uncertainty, wondering if the tone had been too familiar. I can still remember the great relief I felt upon landing and finding that my volley had been returned. In any courtship, you show your trustworthiness by the safe steadiness of your advance.

And with the sensitivity of your ear. People are judged as much by their listening as by what they say, because when you think you are passively listening to others, you are actually teaching them about yourself.

"Good people will mirror goodness in us, which is why we love them so much," Richard Rohr writes. "Not-so-mature people will mirror their own unlived and confused life onto us." Thus, a meeting of the minds is not always gentle. When the poet Ted Hughes first met Sylvia Plath, he made a bold advance to kiss her on the neck. She reached up and bit his cheek so hard that she broke through his skin. She was saying, I understand you. I am your match.

When you choose to marry someone, you had better choose someone you'll enjoy talking with for the rest of your life. It doesn't work unless two people can fall into a state of fluid conversational flow. The phone calls can last hours. They can spend a fourteen-hour day together and the words don't stop. Everything can eventually be said, and every topic can be discussed. This is what Martin Buber called "pure relation," when I–It becomes I–Thou. This is what it feels like to be known.

The Stages of Intimacy II

George Washington was not an outwardly romantic man, but in 1795 he wrote a letter to his step-granddaughter, observing, "In the composition of the human frame there is a good deal of inflammable matter, however dormant it may lie for a time, and . . . when the torch is put to it, that which is within you must burst into a blaze."

This is combustion. It's like when you refract light onto a tissue through a magnifying glass. The tissue gets warmer and warmer. It begins to brown, and then suddenly it bursts into flame. It's in an altered state.

And in that state there is a kiss. Embedded within that kiss is the first promise, I will protect. The next stage of intimacy has begun: combustion. We are not at full-bore love yet. We are at the sunniest and most carefree stage of intimacy, the bright springtime when delight is at its peak without any of the urgent stakes that will come later.

Now they are doing activities together, biking, hiking, maybe a game of basketball. People go to movies on dates because arousal is sloppy and contagious. If the heart starts palpitating during an action movie or the romance of *Moulin Rouge*, the energy gets transferred onto your date as you walk out of the theater. You go kayaking together and inexplicably you feel closer.

At this stage, the couple begins a lifetime of debriefing. After a party or a movie or a dinner, they retreat to a bar or a coffee shop and compare their reactions to what they have just experienced. They meet each other's thoughts simply and guilelessly, the way a child meets reality. One makes an observation, and the other agrees and builds on it. There's a sense of sheer relief in being able to talk so freely without fear of being misunderstood. J. B Priestley once observed that there is probably no talk quite so delightful as the talk between two people who are not yet in love, but who might fall in love, and are aware that each has hidden reserves waiting to be explored.

People are on their best behavior in this phase. Partners at this phase are looking to see how the other nurtures, how the other might parent. In Rousseau's *Emile*, the hero, Emile, is enchanted by a young woman, Sophie. At first, they don't speak but just eye each other across a family dinner table. Their courtship, Allan Bloom writes, "is divided into a series of stages in which the ever-eager Emile passes between the ecstasy of apparent acceptance by Sophie and the agony of an apparent rejection."

Emile and a friend visit Sophie and her family at their home from time to time. One evening they are invited and expected, but do not arrive. At first, Sophie is desolate. Why has Emile not arrived? Perhaps he is dead. The next morning, Emile and his friend arrive. Her anguish turns into rage. There's nothing wrong with him. He stood her up. "She would rather not be loved than be loved moderately. She has that noble pride based on merit which is conscious of itself, esteems itself, and wants to be honored as it honors itself."

The young men then tell her what happened. On the way to the visit, they came upon a peasant who had fallen off his horse and broken his leg. Rather than leave him there on the ground, they had carried him back to his home. Sophie's aspect changes. She wants to visit the family to see what she can do for them. When they arrive at the shabby home, she flies into action. "One would say that she guesses everything which hurts them. This extremely delicate girl is rebuffed neither by the dirtiness nor the bad smell and knows how to make both disappear without ordering anyone about and without the sick being tormented." She turns the man over and changes his clothes and bandages without scruple. "Wife and husband together bless the lovable girl who serves them, who pities them, who consoles them."

Combustion is also the phase of peak idealization. In his great book *On Love*, Stendhal once described a salt mine near Salzburg, Austria. The miners would stick small, leafless branches down into the salt mines and leave them there for a time. When they would retrieve them, the branches would be covered with a shining layer of diamond-like crystals that shimmered in the light. Stendhal said that enchanted lovers crystallize each other in this way, their adoring eyes scattering diamonds on every virtue of the beloved.

The more they idealize each other at this phase, the more lasting their marriage is likely to be in the decades to come. Love relies a bit on generous idealizations. Judith Wallerstein, the marriage counselor, observes, "Many of the divorced couples I've seen appear to have never idealized each other. I've learned to ask myself about a divorcing couple (obviously I can't ask it directly), was there ever a marriage here? Was there ever love, joy, hope, or idealization in this relationship? Often, I'm hard put to find it. Divorce does not always represent an erosion of love or high expectations; in many cases the expectations weren't high enough. Idealization of the other is part of every happy marriage."

The combustion eventually reorients everything.

"There is a lovely disarray that comes with attraction," John O'Donohue writes.

When you find yourself deeply attracted to someone, you gradually begin to lose your grip on the frames that order your life. Indeed, much of your life becomes blurred as that countenance comes into clearer focus. A relentless magnet draws all your thoughts toward it. Wherever you are, you find yourself thinking about the one who has become the horizon of your longing. When you are together, time becomes unmercifully swift. It always ends too soon. No sooner have you parted than you are already imagining your next meeting, counting the hours. The magnetic draw of that presence renders you delightfully helpless. A stranger you never knew until recently has invaded your mind; every fibre of your being longs to be closer.

Combustion is the phase when you finally see the other person at full depth. Not the way others see, but the way only you can see. He is just sitting at the table, paying the family bills, and you pause with your loving eyes and you see him tenderly, with all his goodness. She is just coming into the living room, home from work, her hair a little frazzled, juggling a dozen bags and things, and she looks up in the doorway, outlined by the light behind her, her mouth half open expectantly, and you just think—*I saw you. I saw all the way through.*

THE LEAP

At some point in any serious journey toward intimacy, somebody has to take the leap. The act of faith was beautifully captured by W. H. Auden:

> *The sense of danger must not disappear:*
> *The way is certainly both short and steep,*
> *However gradual it looks from here;*
> *Look if you like, but you will have to leap.*
> . . . .
> *A solitude ten thousand fathoms deep*
> *Sustains the bed on which we lie, my dear:*
> *Although I love you, you will have to leap;*
> *Our dream of safety has to disappear.*

Eventually you take a look at the other person in front of you, you consider the possibility of being without that person, and you take a leap. You declare your love. You have the relationship-defining talk. You two are now in the deep water.

Lots of big and small decisions that were once "I" decisions become "we" decisions—even the smallish ones—what movie to see, how to spend your weekends. Independence is replaced by dependence.

You are also adopting a role—boyfriend, girlfriend, partner, whatever you want to call it—that comes with responsibilities. The chief responsibility is to care for the other above yourself. This layer of intimacy is not about warm feelings; it's about unselfish actions. When the American writer Sheldon Vanauken fell in love with Davy, the woman who would become his wife, they adopted a mutual code of courtesy. "Courtesy" is a word that has lost its meaning, especially as the daily currency of love, but for the Vanaukens it meant that whatever one person asked of the other, the other would do. "Thus one might wake the other in the night and ask for a cup of water; and the other would peacefully (and sleepily) fetch it. We, in fact, defined courtesy as 'a cup of water in the night.' And we considered it a very great courtesy to ask for the cup as well as to fetch it."

CRISIS

Obviously, this is now the time to have a fight.

This phase of intimacy is the perfect moment for a gigantic crisis. You have been around each other long enough to reveal your natural selves. The first projections have begun to fade away.

Most of all, a consuming desire has been born. You want something worse than you've ever wanted anything before—the other person's love—and the slightest perturbation can provoke the most extreme emotional reaction. You have not only opened your heart to joy and togetherness; you have opened your heart to jealousy, insecurity, fear of loss, and betrayal. You are not a stable system at this point.

"All love stories are frustration stories," Adam Phillips writes in *Missing Out*. "To fall in love is to be reminded of a frustration that you didn't know you had." You were merrily going on with your life not really aware that you were missing something, and then suddenly this other person shows up and now the thought of living without them seems like absolute hell.

Sometimes the crisis comes from an act of pure selfishness. Sometimes it comes from confusion over who assumes the power role when.

In each sphere of life, one member of the couple is going to take the lead and the other member is going to be the partner. But it takes time to figure out and negotiate who is going to lead in what sphere.

Sometimes the fight comes with the surfacing of the central disagreement. Every relationship has a central disagreement, which will never go away and which both people are just going to have to live with. But couples don't realize what their central disagreement is until they are in it. Sometimes the disagreements are deep and moral or philosophical. But some of the most troublesome ones can be superficial but devastating. Sometimes it is time (he's prompt, she's late), or money (she's thrifty, he's profligate), or neatness (she's neat, he's sloppy), or sex (he likes it every day, she likes it every week), or communication (he's a bottler, she's a spiller), but it's going to surface, and when it does, blood will flow.

It's interesting, when you're in the crisis, how romantic pain feels so much like physical pain. When you are in a fight with your beloved, when you are missing the thing that you want the most, it feels like an ache or burning in your torso. You want to go running or do something strenuous to ease the physical torment. A powerful description of this pain is from an anonymous Kwakiutl Indian poem, transcribed from native tongue in 1896: "Fires run through my body—the pain of loving you. Pain runs through my body with the fires of my love for you. Sickness wanders my body with my love for you. Pain like a boil about to burst with my love for you. Consumed by fire with my love for you. I remember what you said to me. I am thinking of your love for me. I am torn by your love for me. Pain and more pain."

There are some people so lug-headed that you have to break up with them before they realize how much they need you. There are some people so attachment averse they have to taste abandonment to get over their fear of engulfment.

FORGIVENESS

After the fight comes forgiveness. Forgiveness is often spoken of in sentimental terms—as gushy absolution. But real forgiveness is rigorous. It balances accountability with mercy and compassion.

The process of rigorous forgiveness begins with a gesture by the one who has been wronged. Martin Luther King, Jr., argued that forgiveness isn't an act; it's an attitude. We are all sinners. So the person with a forgiving attitude expects sin, empathizes with sin, and is slow to think him- or herself superior to the one who has done the sinning.

The forgiving person is strong enough to display anger and resentment toward the person who has wronged her, but she is also strong enough to put away that anger and resentment. She is strong enough to make the first move, even before the offender has asked. She resists the natural urge for vengeance and instead offers the offender a welcoming context in which the offender can confess. "He who is devoid of the power to forgive is devoid of the power to love," King wrote.

Once the victim has created the context for forgiveness, the offender is obliged to get out in front of the process. To confess. To show penitence. At this stage, total honesty is the hardest course; we all want to rationalize our wrong. My tendency is to let my sins dribble out in a gradual way, so they won't seem so wrong and they won't scare off the other person. But the act involves probing down to the root of the error, offering a confession more complete than expected. It involves an act of pure submission.

Then it is the moment for judgment. A wrong is an occasion to reevaluate. What is the character of the person in question? Should a moment of stupidity eclipse an overall record of decency? Or is this a permanent character trait? Both partners ask these questions together—and then bend toward each other.

As King said, trust doesn't return immediately. The sin doesn't have to be ignored. But the wrong act is no longer a barrier to a relationship. The offender endures his season of shame and is better for it. The offended, when she offers grace, is freed from emotions such as vengeance and is uplifted. The relationship is made stronger by reunion.

"Suffering makes immature love grow into mature love," Walter Trobisch writes. "Immature unlearned love is egotistic. It's the kind of love children have, demanding and wanting—and wanting instantaneously." But the love that comes after forgiveness is marked by empathy, compassion, understanding, and inexplicable care. As Thornton Wilder once put it, "In love's service only the wounded soldiers can serve."

FUSION

We now come to the thing itself. To "love" full-bore, the climactic phase on the path to intimacy. We've seen so many movies about love and heard so many songs, sometimes we forget how strange a phenomenon it is. It is both a selfish desire and a selfless gift. It fills us up and reminds us of our own incompleteness. Love plows open the hard crust of our personality and exposes the fertile soil below. Love decenters the self. It teaches us that our riches are in another. It teaches us that we can't give ourselves what we truly need, which is somebody else's love. It smashes the walls of ego and leaves a pile of jagged stones.

At the end of his book *Love & Friendship*, Allan Bloom has a beautiful paragraph on the paradoxical nature of love—it is everything and its opposite. Love, Bloom writes,

> is a self-forgetting that makes man self-aware, an unreason that is the condition of his reasoning about himself. The pain it produces is linked to the most ecstatic of pleasures, and it provides the primary experiences of beauty and of life's sweetness. It contains powerful elements of illusion, it may be thought to be entirely illusion, but its effects are not illusory. Love can produce the most prodigious deeds in the most immediate way, without guidance by principle or command of duty. The lover knows the value of beauty and also knows that he cannot live well, or perhaps at all, alone. He knows that he is not self-sufficient. The lover is the clearest expression of man's natural imperfection and his quest for perfection.

When love strikes, it becomes clear that under the influence of our own egos we have been sleepwalking through life. Love wakes us up. It exposes the fact that the chasms within us cannot be filled by the food the ego hungers for. "The unrelated human being lacks whole-ness," Carl Jung wrote, "for he can achieve wholeness only through the soul, and the soul cannot exist without its other side, which is al-ways found in a 'you.'" Every lover in the throes of love knows this.

Passionate love is the only force strong enough to overthrow the ego. People describe it as a madness, a fever, a flood or a fire or a strong emotion. In fact, it is not an emotion, though it contains a lot of emo-tions. It is actually a drive, an extreme motivational state. It is a fervent longing for eternal union with someone else. It pushes people to do ridiculous things, to drive five hundred miles so you can have dinner with her, to get the car washed before every time you pick her up be-cause you want her to feel special, to alter your running route so you can go by her building and gaze at her window.

Once, while I was engaged, I found myself around a conference table with about fifteen people, including my fiancée. We'd been through many of the phases of intimacy by that point, the furtive get-ting to know each other, the crises, and the forgiving. I sat at that table marveling at the fact that of all the people around it, only she was special to me. Why should that be? Everybody else seemed bright and kind, too. They all had heads and torsos, arms and legs. And yet I was connected by magical life-altering chords to just this one, magical chords that no one else in the room could see but which shaped the whole room and made it revolve around her.

They say love is blind, but, as G. K. Chesterton noted, love is def-initely not blind. Love is the opposite of blind. It is supremely atten-tive. You probably can't know a person down to the core of his soul unless you love that person.

All those passionate stares over each other's laptop in the coffee shop where you are inconveniently working together because you can't bear to be apart, all that giddy rolling around in and falling out of hammocks. Lovers spend a lot of the time laughing at each other, C. S. Lewis notices, until they have a baby, which gives them some-thing new to laugh at. "People who are sensible about love are inca-pable of it," the poet Donald Yates writes. Dignity is not part of love's equation; in fact, dignity is probably a thing that could kill love.

People who have made it to this stage feel like they are flying. In the first place, the love is always changing. Sheldon Vanauken fell in love with Davy in the wintertime. "We said, 'If we aren't more in love in lilactime, we shall be finished.' But we were more in love: for love must grow or die. Every year on our anniversary we said, 'If we are not more deeply in love next year, we shall have failed.' But we were: a deeper inloveness, more close, more dear."

Love is hunting for bigger game than happiness. Love is a union of souls. When one member of a couple suffers from Alzheimer's, the other doesn't just go away. Instead, as Lewis puts it, love says, "Better this than parting. Better to be miserable with her than happy without her. Let our hearts break provided they break together."

Wuthering Heights is perhaps the most famous rendering of what happens when somebody squelches such a love. It's a kind of homicide. When they part, Heathcliff cries out, "Kiss me again; and don't let me see your eyes! I forgive what you have done to me. I love *my* murderer— but *yours*! How can I?" They hold each other tight, as if in the face of death, "their faces hid against each other, and washed by each other's tears."

The tragedy in that scene is not only in the sorrow but in the hiding, the inability of two people who are destroying love to even look into each other's eyes.

Montaigne captured this fusion in his description of his friendship with La Boétie, a friendship so deep it can only be called love: "Our souls mingle and blend with each other so completely that they efface the seam that joined them, and cannot find it again. If you press me to tell why I loved him, I feel that this cannot be expressed, except by answering: Because it was he, because it was I."

The ego has been defeated. You find yourself in more pain when your partner is suffering than when you are suffering, more angry when the one you love has been insulted than when you are insulted. You notice it in lovers who are slowly dying from cancer or some lingering illness. The dying are strong while their partners fall apart. It seems to be weirdly easier to be the victim of the disease than the one who has to watch the beloved suffer.

The poets have had a field day with this condition. Milton's Adam to Eve in *Paradise Lost*: "We are one / One flesh; to lose thee were to lose myself." Iain Thomas: "This is my skin and it's thick. This is not your skin, yet you are under it." Roman poet Paulus Silentiarius, 1,500 years ago: "And there lay the lovers, lip-locked / delirious, infinitely thirsting / each wanting to go completely inside the other." Mallarmé: "In the wave, you become / Your naked ecstasy."

The Marriage Decision

LOVE WANTS TO BE FOREVER, OF COURSE. THEREFORE, WE MUST MARRY. IN this way the heart demands resoluteness. You've been flying in circles for long enough. The aircraft carrier is below. It's time to stick the landing.

But this is the time to step back again, to make an appraisal. This is a moment to give reason its due. I've put a lot of emphasis on the heart and soul in this book, but in any commitment decision the rational brain is an equal partner. This is the time to say, as an acquaintance of mine did: I am going to make a good decision here. We may marry or we may part, but this is my life. I am responsible for my choices. I'm perfectly capable of deciding well.

The obvious reason to step back and appraise, even at this late juncture, is that you're not the first person on earth to feel this way. Presumably most of the couples that went on to get married walked through most of the same stages of intimacy you did; they felt the same rush of love, the same sense of fusion and destiny—and then they married and then they got divorced. Love and passion are not enough. You're setting a higher bar.

You do this deeper appraisal because when making a marriage decision you are making a leap against the odds. In the United States, nearly 40 percent of marriages end in divorce. Another 10 or 15 percent of couples separate and do not divorce, and another 7 percent or so stay together but are chronically unhappy. In other words, more than half of the people who decide to marry, presumably driven by passionate love, wind up unhappy. The odds are worse for couples that marry before age twenty-five.

And there are very few things worse than a bad marriage. Being in a bad marriage will increase your chance of getting sick by 35 percent and shorten your life span by an average of four years. There is no loneliness so lonely as the loneliness you feel when you are lying there loveless in bed with another. People go into marriages imagining they are going to sail the open seas together, but when you are in a bad marriage, as George Eliot put it, you are trapped in an enclosed basin.

You step back and appraise because you are aware that to some inevitable degree, you have no idea what you are doing. You will never know what you are doing, but you still want to have the best shot possible. "What is fascinating and almost existentially mischievous about marriage," David Whyte writes, "is that whatever one side of the partnership wants will not occur; whatever the other side of the partnership desires will not occur, and the whatever that does occur is the combined life that emerges from first, the collision, and then the conversation between the two: a conversation that may seem foreign to both to begin with; something they might not recognize or even think they want."

So how do you make this appraisal? Since this is the most important decision of your life, you would think society would have prepared you for this moment. You would think that the schools would have provided you with course after course on the marriage decision, on the psychology of marriage, the neuroscience of marriage, the literature of marriage. But no, society is a massive conspiracy to distract you from the important choices of life in order to help you fixate on the unimportant ones.

THE THREE LENSES

This is the moment to ask hard questions about yourself. Everybody spends too much time appraising the other person when making marriage decisions, but the person who can really screw things up is you. These are questions such as:

Have you got to the place where you can really do this? D. H. Lawrence once wrote, "You can't worship love and individuality in the same breath." The ultimate question for yourself is whether you are ready to lose control and be overwhelmed by marriage, come what may.

Do I like the person I am when I'm around him? We all have multiple personalities we project into the world, depending on whom we are around. Does this person bring out your crass, social-climbing self, or your kind, serving self?

What's my core issue, and does this person fill it? We tend to marry the person who fills our greatest unresolved psychic problem. Maybe you yearn for emotional reliability, and this person is your steady hand. Maybe you yearn for emotional intensity, and this person is your fountain of love.

How high is my bar? Some people say, Never settle: You had better feel insanely lucky to have this person. Others say, Be more realistic: You're never going to find the perfect person, and it's better to be in a decent relationship than alone. Jane Austen thought it was "wicked" to settle, and I'm with her. If you marry without total admiration and rapture, you will not have enough passion to fuse you together in the early days, and you will split apart when times get hard. Moreover, settling is immoral because there is another person involved. The other person is not going to want to be the fourth best option in your life. Are you going into the relationship telling the person that you're "settling" in being with them? If you're honest and tell him that, you're introducing a fatal inequality into your relationship right away. If you don't tell him that, you are lying to the person you are supposedly closest to in the whole world. Settling seems realistic, but only a love built on rapturous devotion is pragmatic in the end.

The rest of the questions are about the other person and the relationship itself. The most important consideration is this: Marriage is a fifty-year conversation. The most important factor in when you think about marrying someone is, *Would I enjoy talking with this person for the rest of my life?*

If the answer to that question is yes, there are three lenses that people apply when making the rest of the marriage decision: the psychological lens, the emotional lens, and the moral lens.

The first is the psychological lens. Characters in Jane Austen and George Eliot novels spend a lot of time evaluating each other's temperament, or what we call personality traits. There's a good reason for that. Personality traits are pretty steady across adulthood. As Ty Tashiro puts it in *The Science of Happily After*, "If you choose some dreamy partner who is bright, funny, self-confident, kind and good-looking, and loves his or her mother, then the good news is that when you reassess your romantic situation after twenty-five years of marriage, that partner, compared to others in your same age cohort, will probably still be bright, funny, self-confident, kind and good-looking, and a good son or daughter."

So how do you discern a person's permanent personality traits? In 1938, the researcher Lewis Terman argued that you should look at a person's relational background. He ranked the things to look for:

1. Superior happiness of parents
2. Childhood happiness
3. Lack of conflict with mother
4. Home discipline that was firm, not harsh
5. Strong attachment to mother
6. Strong attachment to father
7. Lack of conflict with father
8. Parental frankness about matters of sex
9. Infrequency and mildness of childhood punishment
10. Premarital attitude toward sex that was free from disgust or aversion

Others say the most telling thing to look for is attachment style. People who were securely attached to one caregiver as early as eighteen months (about 60 percent of all people) have a model in their heads for how to build and maintain secure relationships. When such people are in the presence of someone they love, their heart rate declines and their respiration slows. They relax because it feels normal to them.

People who experienced anxious attachment patterns when they were infants are more likely to have trouble relaxing when they are in loving relationships. The model in their head tells them that the person they love is about to leave. Their heart rates and respiratory patterns speed up. People who had avoidant attachment patterns when they were young (they sent signals to their caregivers, but nothing came back), have preemptively shut down. Their model says, If I don't get close then the nonresponse won't hurt.

According to one authoritative longitudinal study, 90 percent of securely attached people marry, and of those 21 percent get divorced. Seventy percent of avoidantly attached people marry, and of those 50 percent get divorced. For people with anxious attachments, the divorce rates are even higher.

You'd think that everybody would try to marry securely attached people. But that's not how it works out. People disproportionately marry people with their own attachment style. Secure with secure, avoidant with avoidant, and anxious with anxious. Early childhood attachment patterns are not destiny; people can change, but if you see the markers of avoidant or anxious attachment styles in your partner, it's worth making a mental note.

Still others say that the best way to understand another person's psychology is by applying the Big Five personality traits matrix. The Big Five are openness to experience, conscientiousness, extraversion, agreeableness, and neuroticism. When it comes to a relationship partner, the last two traits are the most important. Basically, Ty Tashiro argues, you want to seek agreeableness and avoid neuroticism.

Agreeableness—being a nice guy—doesn't sound like the sexiest or most romantic possible trait. The agreeable person is kind, affectionate, friendly, compliant, understanding, warm, sensitive, and trusting. People often say an agreeable man is masculine but with a feminine touch.

Neuroticism, Tashiro continues, is what you want to avoid. It seems exciting and dramatic at first, but neurotic people are tense, moody, prone to sadness. Neuroticism is the tendency to experience negative emotions such as anger and anxiety with great force. "Neurotic individuals tend to have a history of turbulent and unstable relationships with others, including family and friends. They also tend to be prone to what looks like bad luck, but with time, one often sees that there are ways that their neuroticism evokes unfortunate events from their environment," he writes. "I cannot stress enough how important it is to dispel any wishful thinking that neuroticism will simply go away because there are remarkably consistent findings about the tendency of neuroticism to remain constant across the life span."

The second lens to apply when making a marriage decision is the emotional lens. This means asking questions about the nature of your love for each other. The Greeks distinguished between three types of love: *philia* (friendship), *eros* (passion), and *agape* (selfless giving). You can sometimes feel eros toward a person, without philia or agape, in which case all you have is an infatuation. Or you can have agape without philia and eros, in which case all you have is admiration. Or, more likely, you may just be experiencing philia with a little eros but without agape. The person makes you happy. But somehow the explosive burst of selfless love never erupts. This is a wonderful friendship, but not the basis of a lifelong devotion. If an enchantment is going to be one of your life-defining commitments, it will already have elements of all three: intimacy, desire, and self-sacrificial love.

Some relationships simply stop at the level of beautiful friends. Both people really admire each other but somehow they never quite touch each other at the depths of their soul, and they can't figure out why, because the relationship makes so much sense. They may tell each other that they love each other, they may feel real love for each other, but somehow it's not the kind of love that makes it painful to be away from the person, the kind of love that stirs up turmoils of fear that the other person might go away, the kind of love that produces enchantment and deep happiness when the two of you are just next to each other doing nothing, the kind of love that calls forth the everyday service and constant solicitude that marriage requires.

Medium-depth relationships are the hardest to break off, because friendship and admiration are there, but for whatever reason they do not exist at the depth of heart and soul, and in marriage there will be untapped layers that will feel like loneliness and separation.

Finally, there is the moral lens. This is an important lens, because admiration of the other person will carry you through times when the emotional well goes dry; admiration will carry you through the times when you get a little annoyed at the other person's personality quirks. Good character will endure through those times things are going badly. So the essential questions are: *Is this person honest? Does she have integrity?*

Disagreement is inevitable, and marriages survive it, but contempt is deadly and always kills a marital bond. So a crucial question is, *Do I deeply admire this person?* When you are making a marital commitment, you are making a vow, a promise. So another crucial question is, *Does this person keep his or her promises?* When you are choosing a spouse, you are choosing the mother or father to your children. So the question is, *Does this person have the qualities you would want passed down to your precious kids?* Sooner or later in any marriage, sickness or ill fortune or something else will strip you down to your essentials. So the question is, *What is at the core of this person, after you take away the education, the skills, the accomplishments, and the brands?* Marriage involves a thousand decisions as you navigate your way. So the question is, *Do I often second-guess his or her judgment?* Marriage is lived out in the day-to-day realities of life. So the question becomes, *Does this person ever brag about behavior that he should be ashamed of—cheating other people to get ahead, being cruel to underlings to establish dominance, manipulating other people to get what he wants?* The other person isn't going to be perfect, obviously. Everybody is selfish at some level, and so you ask yourself, *Is this person's form of selfishness the kind I can live with?*

COMPLETION

It's too bad *Jerry Maguire* monopolized the line, but marital love really does feel like a completion. It feels like the old story from Plato's *Symposium*, of the two separated halves finding together that they form a completed soul. It's only together that they can really take their full journey. They are ready for a life bigger than anything they could have considered alone.

Dostoyevsky was a man who struggled with his own nature. Through gambling or the sheer chaos of his own nature, he would fall into debt and have to write himself out of debt. One day, with a deadline approaching and faced with the crush of writing an entire novel in a month, he met a stenographer named Anna Grigoryevna. They worked together on *The Gambler*. Anna later recalled: "Each day, chatting with me like a friend, he would lay bare some unhappy scene from his past. I could not help being deeply touched at his accounts of the difficulties from which he had never extricated himself, and indeed could not."

Dostoyevsky finished the novel, paid her the equivalent of $1,500 for her stenography, and they parted ways. She found she missed him. "I had grown so accustomed to that merry rush of work, the joyful meeting and lively conversation with Dostoyevsky, that they had become a necessity to me. All my old activities had lost their interest and seemed empty and futile."

They stayed in touch, and one day in the course of a conversation that was supposed to be a theoretical discussion of the nature of marriage, they had a disagreement over whether it was wise to marry a writer or an artist. Dostoyevsky believed that only a fool would marry such a person. No sane person would accept a proposal from such an unstable type. "Imagine that this artist is me," he said by way of example, "that I have confessed my love to you and asked you to be my wife. Tell me, what would you answer?"

Anna realized that this was no longer just a theoretical conversation. "I would answer that I love you and will love you all my life," she responded.

She later reflected, "I won't try to convey the words full of tenderness and love that he said to me then; they are sacred to me. I was stunned, almost crushed by the immensity of my happiness and for a long time I couldn't believe it."

They tasted tragedy in marriage. They lost two children. But it turned out gloriously. Anna managed his career, basically opened a publishing house for him, and turned him into a financial and literary success. He never lost his deep respect for what he saw in her soul. "Throughout my life," she wrote, after his death, "it has always seemed a kind of mystery to me that my good husband not only loved and respected me as many husbands love and respect their wives, but almost worshipped me, as though I were some special being created just for him. And that was true not only at the beginning of our marriage but through all the remaining years of it, up to his very death."

Marriage: The School You Build Together

MARRIAGE STARTS AS A JOY AND ENDS UP AN EDUCATION. IT STARTS AS A joy because at first you get to spend every day with the person you care about most in the world, the one who makes you happiest just to be around. But then it turns into something else. When you agree to marry, you are agreeing to be completely known, a scary prospect. Living as a "we" instead of an "I" is a transformation of the routines of daily life. The thing you love about the person is connected to the exact thing that will come to drive you the most crazy. Her caustic wit can sometimes feel like cynicism. His emotional sensitivity can feel like neediness. The only way to thrive in marriage is to become a better person—more patient, wise, compassionate, persevering, communicative, and humble. When we make a commitment, we put ourselves into a pickle that we have to be more selfless to get out of.

Marriage educates by throwing a series of difficult tasks in your path. Judith Wallerstein and Sandra Blakeslee list some of the most important ones:

- To separate emotionally from the family of one's childhood
- To build intimacy combined with some autonomy
- To embrace the role of parents and absorb the impact of "Her Majesty, the Baby's" arrival
- To confront the inevitable crises of life
- To establish a rich sexual life
- To create a safe haven for the expression of difference
- To keep alive the early idealized images of each other

A marriage survives when both partners admit their individual inadequacy to the challenges before them. A marriage survives when the partners agree to take lifelong courses together—in subjects like empathy, communication, and recommitment. The good news is you don't have to get an A+ in any of them. If you get a solid B you're doing pretty well.

EMPATHETIC WISDOM

When marriages break down, it's because one or both partners feels unknown and misunderstood. When people feel unknown or misunderstood, they minimize and excuse their own failings: "Okay, I'm screwed up, but you don't see and understand me!" They shift the blame onto the other person and reinforce their own worst traits.

Marital love is a seeing love. John Gottman, the dean of marriage scholars, grasped the essence: "Happy marriages are based on a deep friendship. By this I mean mutual respect for and enjoyment of each other's company. These couples tend to know each other intimately— they are well versed in each other's likes, dislikes, personality quirks, hopes, and dreams. They have an abiding regard for each other and express this fondness not just in big ways but in little ways day in and day out."

Marital love is understanding the other person's patterns. In *Things I Wish I'd Known Before We Got Married*, Gary Chapman describes a variety of different personality types that can coexist in marriage. There are painters and pointers. In conversation, painters describe an elaborately detailed picture of an event. Pointers just get to the nub. There are organizers and free spirits. The organizer sweats the details. The free spirit figures the details will take care of themselves. There are engineers and dancers. The engineers want to logically think through every decision. The dancers will go with their heart. These differences can be conflicts or complementarities, depending on how well each partner understands the other and accommodates.

Marital love is being aware of how the past is present in the marriage. Psychologists joke that a marriage is a battleground in which two families send their best warriors to determine which family's culture will direct the couple's lives.

Before you were together, the influence of these lineages was largely unconscious; it was just the way you did things. But in the first few months of marriage, your way of doing things comes into contact with another way of doing things. This new awareness usually is not a gradual, scholarly awareness in which you calmly stroke your chin and say, "Hmmm. Interesting." It often comes in the form of an unexpected eruption. You completely overreact to some small thing your partner has done, and in the middle of your overreaction you are silently asking yourself, "What the hell is going on?!"

"We too often act from scripts generated by crises of long ago that we've all but consciously forgotten," Alain de Botton writes. "We behave according to an archaic logic which now escapes us." For example, people who were raised with conditional or critical love may hear "I wish you hadn't done that" as "I'm about to leave you!" They may have trouble understanding that anger doesn't threaten the relationship.

Couples who possess an empathetic understanding step back and understand how each member responds to stress. One of the most common forms of marital breakdown is the demand-withdraw cycle. One partner makes a request of the other—clean the house, show up on time—but there's a hint of blame within the request. The other partner hears the request as nagging or complaining. Instead of fully engaging, this partner just withdraws. This prompts the person doing the requesting to repeat the request with a more explicit assignment of blame and to up the criticism. This causes the withdrawing partner to withdraw more. If the withdrawing partner occasionally gives in, this reinforces the message to the demanding partner that blame and criticism work. More blame follows until the withdrawing partner goes into complete withdrawal and disassociation mode. The more one lashes out, the more the other withdraws.

Healthy couples step back from the cycle and help each other grow out of it. "The magic of a couple's relationship is that, when two people fall in love, whatever they need to do for themselves to grow emotionally is most often the very thing that the partner needs from them," Ayala Malach Pines writes in *Falling in Love*. "Instead of turning into a rejected little girl that needed to pound on doors to be heard, she needed to learn to stay an adult and ask for what she wanted in a way that would increase the likelihood of getting it."

In the end, people in an enduring marriage achieve *metis*. That's the Greek word for a kind of practical wisdom, an intuitive awareness of how things are, how things go together, and how things will never go together.

A teacher with *metis* can feel when the classroom is just beginning to get out of control. A mechanic with *metis* has a feel for what's wrong with the engine based on some semi-consciously heard rumble or sound. A marriage partner with *metis* knows when to give space and when to intrude, when to offer the surprise gift and when not to tell the teasing joke. The university of marriage, at its best, teaches this form of emotional awareness, which can't be reduced to rules or communicated in books, and which emerges as a sort of loving nimbleness.

COMMUNICATION

Words are the fuel of marriage. "Everything else is transitory," Nietzsche writes, "but most of the time you are together will be devoted to conversation."

The quality of the conversation is the quality of the marriage. Good conversation creates warmth and peace, and bad conversation creates frigidity and stasis. Conversation is how marriage partners rub off on each other.

Most of the conversation, of course, is mundane—about dinner, paint colors, or the baby's digestive system. There was a time when the whole idea of manners went out of style, when politeness came to seem hopelessly bourgeois. But manners are the morality of everyday life. As Edmund Burke put it, "Manners are what vex or soothe, corrupt or purify, exalt or debase, barbarize or refine us, by a constant, steady, uniform, insensible operation, like that of the air we breathe in. They give their whole form and color to our lives. According to their quality, they aid morals, they supply them, or they totally destroy them."

A well-mannered conversation is shaped by what John Gottman calls the pattern of bids and volleys. Let's say you are reading the paper at the dining room table and your partner comes up and says, "Look at the beautiful blue jay on the tree outside the window." That's a conversational bid. You might look up and exclaim, "Wow, that *is* beautiful. Thanks for pointing it out." That's a "toward bid." With your remark, you are moving toward your partner. Or you could respond, "I was reading the paper; would you please let me finish?" That would be an "against bid." Or you could just grunt and ignore the remark or change the subject with a non sequitur. The would be a "turning-away bid."

In marriages that succeed, Gottman has found, the couple experiences five toward bids for every one against or turning-away bid. The people Gottman calls "relationship masters" go out of their way to store up chits in their emotional bank account. "There's a habit of mind that the masters have, which is this: they are scanning the social environment for things they can appreciate and say thank you for. . . . Disasters are scanning the social environment for partners' mistakes," Gottman said in an interview with Emily Esfahani Smith for *The Atlantic*.

Divorce doesn't generally happen when the number of conflicts increases; it happens when the number of positive things decreases. Julie Gottman, John's wife, points out that masters of relationship are on alert for what their partner is doing right, and they are quick to compliment. According to the Gottmans, there are four kinds of unkindness that drive couples apart: contempt, criticism, defensiveness, and stonewalling. The rule of their research is pretty simple: If you're tired and your partner makes a bid, turn toward in kindness. If you're distracted, turn toward in kindness. If you're stressed, turn toward in kindness.

Relationship masters also learn how to communicate well in times of triumph and conflict. Moments of triumph would seem to be the easy part of a relationship. But Shelly Gable, a psychologist at UC Santa Barbara, found that those are the moments that often drive people apart. One spouse comes home reporting some promotion at work, but the other person can't simply join in the happiness because he is too focused on self, so he a) changes the subject to some triumph of his own; b) acknowledges the triumph with a grunt and then gets back to his own business; or c) belittles the triumph by asking, "Are you sure you'll be able to handle this new job?"

Masters also learn never to sulk. Sulking consists of feeling angry about something but determined not to communicate about it. "The sulker," Alain de Botton writes, "both desperately needs the other person to understand and yet remains utterly committed to doing nothing to help them do so. The very need to explain forms the kernel of the insult: if the partner requires an explanation, he or she is clearly not worthy of one." The sulker is returning to childhood, and dreams of finding a mother who understands what he wants without words or explanation.

Nobody becomes more reasonable when they are blamed and attacked. Nobody becomes mature because their spouse, in the middle of an argument, screams at them to "Grow up!" The advice books offer a better formula, even if it is hard to follow while angry. First, try to state the problem in neutral terms. Then, stroke, stand, and contract. Remind the person that you hear and understand them (stroke); state your positions clearly (stand); find a way to meet in the middle (contract).

THE ART OF RECOMMITMENT

There are two classic crisis periods in marriage—just after the children are born and in the doldrums of middle age. In the former, the temptation is to replace the complicated and difficult relationship you have with your spouse for the joyous and captivating love you have with your children. In the latter crisis, people in middle age are haunted by a feeling of generalized sadness and incompleteness. There's a sense that life is slipping away, and a tendency to see the spouse, with all of their flaws and negativity, nagging and unhappiness, as the real problem, the real anchor that is holding you back from your fullness.

During these crisis moments, there's a tendency to recoil, to distance yourself from your partner. You begin to dissociate and withdraw. You construct parallel lives with outside interests and separate friend groups. You get used to marriage without intimacy—the marriage bed, as they say, where the spouses are a centimeter apart and a million miles away. You use drugs, booze, work, or the care of your children to occupy the psychic space formerly filled by the marriage.

In a study at Cameron University in Oklahoma, Joanni L. Sailor interviewed people who had fallen out of love. The quotes she collected are a searing testimony of how horrible it is to be in a relationship after the fire has died: "During sex there was no kissing. I remember just craving to be kissed, but not by him." "The pain is so overwhelming." "I think I cried for a year." "Yes, it was the depression caused by profound loneliness." "My love is disappearing; my heart feels like he is stepping all over it, and he does not seem to care." "My personality had been rejected. . . . It changed me permanently. . . . I spent several years with no personality at all."

After dissociation, you come to that terrifying time when the love in a marriage seems to dry up. Sometimes marriages truly are dead. Neither partner can hurt the other any longer, because neither really cares. In that case, divorce happens. But in other cases the embers are still warm, and the marriage just needs an act of courageous recommitment. And that is the next course in the curriculum of marriage: the art of recommitment.

During these low moments, it is helpful to remember that marriage is not just a relationship; it is a covenant. It's a moral promise to hold fast through thick and thin. Both people have vowed to create this project or cause, the marriage, that is more important than each person's emotional weather. Of course, there are times when divorce is the right and only course, but there are other times when the sentiment that guides Parker Palmer comes in handy: "If you can't get out of it, get into it!" If you can't easily walk away from something, then the only way forward is to double down.

When the well of love dries up, it takes an act of will to dig a little deeper. "It is a deliberate choosing of closeness over distance, of companionship over detachment, of relationship over isolation, of love over apathy, of life over death," Mike Mason writes.

That's not the natural inclination. Believe me. I know what it's like to fail here. Recommitment involves going against yourself. But life is defined by the moments we're asked to go against ourselves. Marriage, like all commitments, isn't there to make you happy; it is there to make you grow. As Mason puts it, "A marriage lives, paradoxically, upon those almost impossible times when it is perfectly clear to the two partners that nothing else but pure sacrificial love can hold them together."

In a weird way, one model of marital recommitment can be found in Abraham Lincoln's second inaugural address. He gave the speech at a time of great national brokenness. It was clear by that point that the North was going to win the Civil War. Lincoln could have used this moment as a chance for great chest-thumping: We prevailed in a righteous cause. We fought for good; you fought for evil. We were right; you were wrong. We are vindicated, and you Southerners, who have so much of our blood on your hands, are disgraced.

Lincoln's love of union—the whole nation—was stronger than his love for his own side. In the second inaugural, the key words are unifying words: "we," "all," "both." "All thoughts were anxiously directed to an impending civil war. All dreaded it, all sought to avert it. . . . Both parties deprecated war." He puts North and South on the same humble footing.

Lincoln does not say slavery was a Southern institution. He says it was an American institution. The scourge of war, which purges this sin, falls rightly on both sides. Lincoln puts us all in the same category of culpability and fallenness. He realistically acknowledges the divisions and disappointments that plague the nation. But he does not accept the inevitability of a house divided, and calls for a radical turning of the heart: "With malice toward none, with charity for all."

Healing a broken marriage is not all that different from healing a broken nation. There are always differences and disagreements in relationships, but most of the time that's not what destroys them. It's the way we turn disagreement into a quest for superiority. It's not I'm right / you're wrong; it's I'm better / you're lesser, I'm righteous / you're deplorable, I'm good / you're contemptible. It's the tendency to be quick to take offense in a way that declares your own moral superiority. Marshall McLuhan was harsh but not wrong when he observed, "Moral indignation is a technique used to endow the idiot with dignity."

Recommitment often means putting your own sins on the table. Forbearance means acknowledging the wrongs that have been committed, and even the anger that they have created, but it puts anger in the context of love. Loyalty just repeats "I love you." It is astonishing how often that sentence "I love you" needs to be said, and how powerful it can be in a moment of disagreement and crisis.

The experts are aligned when it comes to how to recommit: Don't expect some ultimate solution to the big disagreement in your marriage. Overwhelm the negative by increasing the positive. Swamp negative interactions with the five love languages: words of affirmation, acts of service, gifts, quality time, and personal touch.

Recommitment is the time for "Can we take a walk this afternoon?" and "You relax. I'll vacuum." This is the time for what Abraham Joshua Heschel called "an ecstasy of deeds." You do a mitzvah, a good deed, and then you do another, and each one creates "luminous moments in which we are raised by overpowering deeds above our own will, moments filled with outgoing joy, with intense delight." It is an immemorial law of human nature that behavior change precedes and causes attitudinal change. If you behave kindly toward a person, you will become kind and you will cherish them. Sex heals a lot of wounds in marriage, or at least provides a start to their healing. There is an ancient wisdom in the Jewish belief that a marriage without sex is not a marriage. "The ethic of marriage is hedonistic, not monastic," writes Rabbi Joseph Soloveitchik; it is dangerous to be too spiritual about it.

A few years ago, Lydia Netzer wrote a blog post called "15 Ways to Stay Married for 15 Years," which gave some good, realistic advice on sailing through the hazards of life together:

Go to bed mad. Everybody says you shouldn't let the sun go down on your wrath. Sometimes that's just stupid. You're tired. Go to bed. Get some sleep. Wake up the next morning and make pancakes. See if the fight looks so serious then.

Be proud and brag. Boast about your spouse's accomplishments in public and let him overhear your boasting.

Bitch to his mother, not to yours. If you complain about him to his mother, she'll forgive him; your own mother never will.

Trust the person you married. Let the other person help you. Trust them to know what's right.

Be loyal. "You and your spouse are a team of two," Netzer writes. "No one else is allowed on the team, and no one else will ever understand the team's rules. . . . Sometimes she's in the spotlight, sometimes you. Ups and downs, ultimately, don't matter because the team endures."

Netzer's advice captures one of the other paradoxes of marriage—that it's a sacred institution built out of crooked timber. There's no room for perfectionism when you're dealing with something as broken as real human beings, only bemused affection. Marriage starts in rhapsodies and ends up in carpools.

THE SECOND LOVE

The first love is champagne. But after you've been married and you've had scores of fights and scores of recoveries, you find you've entered into your second love, which is less passionate but more enduring. Second love is the kind of love people have for each other after they've seen each other at their worst, after they've forgiven a few times and been forgiven, after they can take some pride in having survived together and some comfort in the knowledge that they will survive. This is the person you will be with. This is your life. Second love is second-mountain love—after the thrill of the first mountain, the valley of suffering, and now up on the heights of your larger and more selfless life together.

You've probably met older couples who have come to look like each other, react like each other, talk like each other. "You're 82 years old," the philosopher André Gorz once wrote in a letter to his wife. "You've shrunk six centimetres, you only weigh 45 kilos yet you're still beautiful, graceful and desirable. We've lived together now for 58 years and I love you more than ever. I once more feel a gnawing emptiness in the hollow of my chest that is only filled when your body is pressed against mine."

This love endures after death. Viktor Frankl had an elderly patient who could not overcome the grief he felt over the loss of his wife. It had been two years since her passing, and the pain was still acute. Eventually Frankl asked what would have happened if he had died first. What would his wife have experienced?

"For her this would have been terrible; how she would have suffered!" the man replied.

"You see," Frankl replied, "such a suffering has been spared her, and it was you who have spared her this suffering—to be sure, at the price that now you have to survive and mourn her." The man picked up his hat, shook Frankl's hand, and left the office.

Couples who have reached this final harmony haven't only achieved contentment; they've achieved catharsis, which is a moral state as well as an emotional one. Catharsis comes after the long ups and downs. It comes when you look back and realize that it's more accurate to say that you've really had five or six different marriages, that you were married to five or six different people who happened to inhabit, over the years, the same body. It comes after the episodes of comedy and tragedy, the exposure of sin and joy. It's like the end of the play when the characters have been exposed and forgiven, tears have been shed, and everyone is laughing together.

In catharsis, needy love has morphed into giving love. Each partner has leapt into the absurd for the other, made sacrifices that made no earthly sense. They have arrived at a peaceful glen, after all the sick children, the college anxieties, the flight delays on the way to vacation, and on and on. We applaud people for having a fiftieth wedding anniversary because we know it is an achievement, even though to them it just feels like a delight. They are not done living, but they can pause on a winter's evening, lean their heads together, and stare into the fire.

PART IV
Philosophy and Faith

Intellectual Commitments

WHEN I WAS A YOUNG MAN I DREAMED OF REVOLUTION. PHYSICALLY, I was living in the 1980s, the age of Reagan, but intellectually I was back in 1917 in Greenwich Village. I would sit in the stacks of my college library reading copies of an old magazine called *The New Masses*. It was a gorgeously designed, beautifully written journal for Marxist radicals who were inspired by the Russian Revolution, who believed that a new world was being born from the ashes of the old, and that it was bliss to be alive.

Left-wing intellectuals of the time felt swept up in the rush of history, fully committed to a paradise that seemed close at hand. Karl Marx and Friedrich Engels had revealed the deep historical currents. The revolutionary vanguard led the way. John Reed, Harvard class of 1910, went to Russia, joined the revolution, and wrote *Ten Days That Shook the World*. A few decades later, young Jewish radicals at the City College of New York would blow off their classes, hang around the student cafeteria, and argue about the future of communism in America. The Trotskyites sat in alcove one and the Stalinists sat in alcove two, and their arguments could last for six or eight hours at a time. The arguments consumed them. When the revolution came it would matter which interpretation of Marxism had the upper hand.

I don't know if I was really committed to Marxism—I called myself a Democratic Socialist back then—but I was committed to this kind of life: passionate intellectual engagement for the sake of justice and world historical change.

Then, in my second year of college, I was assigned a book called *Reflections on the Revolution in France*, by Edmund Burke. Burke argued against everything I believed in, or thought I believed in. He argued that revolutionary change is rash—you never know what sort of unintentional effects it is going to set off—that the power of reason is inadequate to understand the complexity of the world, and that we should respect the "just prejudice" of our culture, the traditions that have stood the test of time. He defended the decent drapery of life, the etiquette, manners, and chivalry, which, he said, give life its softness and society its glory.

I can't tell you how much I loathed that book. I wrote paper after paper pouring scorn on it. But, even then, I was vaguely aware that Burke had gotten under my skin.

In my senior year, William F. Buckley, Jr., came to campus. I was a humor columnist at the school paper, and I wrote a savage parody of Buckley, basically accusing him of being a name-dropping blowhard. A professor named Nathan Tarcov handed the parody to Buckley, and apparently he thought it was funny, because at the end of his address to the student body he said, "David Brooks, if you're in the audience I want to give you a job."

I wasn't in the audience. I had been selected to appear on a PBS show to debate the great economist Milton Friedman, and so I was out in Palo Alto, where Friedman was working at the Hoover Institution. The conceit of the show was Friedman talking to the young. It was my first TV appearance, and you can find it on YouTube—me with big hair and round glasses that are roughly the circumference of the moon. On the show, I would make a point that I regurgitated from some left-wing book, then Friedman would destroy my point and then the camera would linger on my face for what felt like several hours as I tried to think of something to say.

It took a week to tape all the episodes of that show. In the evenings, Friedman and his wife, Rose, would take us out to dinner and talk to us about economics. I had never seen a real live libertarian before, so this was a new world for me. I had also never encountered, face-to-face, a couple who had so totally given themselves over to ideas and, through them, to each other. My mind was opened. I was and remain inspired by their life of shared intellectual mission.

A few years later, I was working as a reporter on the south and west side of Chicago, covering, in part, some awful housing projects that had become basically unlivable. It occurred to me that these projects had been designed by sociologists who'd had the best of intentions—to raze the old tenements and replace them with something shiny and new. They didn't realize that when they tore down the old tenements, they were also tearing down the invisible webs of support that people had built to make their lives bearable. The builders had made the neighborhoods materially better, for a time, but socially worse. They lacked epistemological modesty.

It occurred to me that this was exactly what Burke warned about. I went back and read *Reflections* and was transfixed by it. I didn't buy everything Burke was selling, but I now began to see some wisdom in this thing called conservatism.

I reached out to Buckley and asked him if the job offer was still on the table. It was. Before long I was working at *National Review*. Suddenly I was enveloped within a movement of people that was as committed to ideas and revolutionary change as the Marxists I had read about in college. In fact, many of them were the same exact people. The modern conservative movement was largely started by former Marxists who had been mugged by reality—Whittaker Chambers, James Burnham, Irving Kristol, Max Eastman, and on and on.

They carried the residue of their earlier stance. As Kristol, citing Trotsky, put it in his book *Neoconservatism*, "Joining a radical movement when one is young is very much like falling in love when one is young. The girl may turn out to be rotten, but the experience of love is so valuable it can never be entirely undone by the ultimate disenchantment."

It took me a few decades to find out what kind of conservative I was, but eventually I realized that I'm a Burkean conservative. The core of what I think is true is contained in Burke's *Reflections*. I don't doubt the power of ideas because that book changed my life. By naming a philosophy, it called into being some knowledge that was latent within me. It has become a foundation for how I view the world. Ideas have consequences.

When they were old and near death, I asked both Friedman and Buckley if they felt content. They had each changed history in ways more profound than they could have expected when they set out. Did they feel they could rest now and be at peace? Neither man even understood what I was talking about. There was so much for them left to do. Until the day they died, they pushed ideas, lived for ideas, and tried to bend the world a little in the direction of their ideas. They were examples of what intellectual commitment looks like.

How radical they were, at least when they started out. There was almost no one in America who agreed with them at the time. But hundreds of millions would eventually. There is something beautiful about somebody who stands against the tides on behalf of some idea and yells *Change!*

I think back to my college years and am so grateful for a university—the University of Chicago—that gave me the open stacks where I could find *The New Masses*, and had the gall to force me to read a book that at the time I truly hated. A school can transform a life.

THE HUMANISTIC IDEAL

American higher education has evolved over the decades. For the last half of the nineteenth century and the first half of the twentieth, most universities believed in something Anthony Kronman of Yale Law School calls the "humanistic ideal." This ideal held that a university's purpose was teleological—to help answer the ultimate questions of life. To put it more bluntly, the purpose of a school was to shape the students' souls.

"Character is the main object of education," said Mary Woolley, president of Mount Holyoke a century ago. When J. F. Roxburgh, the headmaster of the Stowe School in Vermont, was asked in the 1920s about the purpose of his institution, he said it was to turn out young men who were "acceptable at a dance, invaluable in a shipwreck."

It did that by exposing students to excellence. "One is apt to think of moral failure as due to weakness of character," the British educator Sir Richard Livingstone wrote. "More often it is due to an inadequate ideal." So one job of a teacher was, in this educational model, to hold up exemplars. "I make honorable things pleasant to children," a Spartan educator put it. When the students emerged from school they would have had at least some contact with the best things human beings have thought and done.

Since then, of course, universities have become more diverse and pluralistic. We've realized there can be no single ideal for how to live. The pace-setting universities gradually dropped the humanistic ideal and adopted what Kronman calls the "research ideal." Bodies of knowledge such as biology, literature, and history were divided up into specialties and smaller and smaller subspecialties, and scholars worked away in their specialties trying to advance the frontiers of knowledge.

A lot was discovered by this method, especially in the sciences, but, as Kronman argues, this emphasis on specialization "draws our attention away from the whole of our lives and requires that we focus on some small aspect of them instead." The idea that one could survey the main forms of living, or ask big, vague questions like "What makes life worth living?" began to seem not only unrealistic but irresponsible and pernicious. "For it made the question of the meaning of life appear unprofessional—a question that no responsible teacher of the humanities could henceforth take seriously," Kronman writes. The research ideal offers little way for the university to engage the student as a whole person, an entity that has longings and a hunger for meaning. It subtly says, Ignore the soul behind the curtain.

It's not that moral education was actively expelled from the universities, but the whole enterprise just became awkward, and people more or less let it drop. Moral development is tremendously important, everybody acknowledged, but it's something you sort of do on your own. Steven Pinker of Harvard summarized the research ethos of the modern university: "I have no idea how to get my students to build a self or become a soul. It isn't taught in graduate school, and in the hundreds of faculty appointments and promotions I have participated in, we've never evaluated a candidate on how well he or she could accomplish it."

Students are taught to engage in critical thinking, to doubt, distance, and take things apart, but they are given almost no instruction on how to attach to things, how to admire, to swear loyalty to, to copy and serve. The universities, like the rest of society, are information rich and meaning poor.

Fortunately, I went to one of those institutions that has one foot inside the research ideal and one foot still stubbornly planted in the humanistic ideal, the University of Chicago. When I attended, the study of the Great Books occupied at least the first two years of study, and often beyond. Our professors didn't just teach the books, they proselytized them. Some of the old German refugees from World War II were still around then, and they held the belief, with a religious fervor, that the magic keys to the kingdom were in these books. The mysteries of life and how to live well were there for the seizing for those who read well and thought deeply.

When I was a student, a legendary professor named Karl Weintraub was teaching Western Civilization. He epitomized the commitment and zeal that many put into the teaching of these books. Years later, when he was nearing death, he wrote to my classmate Carol Quillen about the difficulties of teaching Western Civ: "Sometimes when I have spent an hour or more, pouring all my enthusiasm and sensitivities into an effort to tell these stories in the fullness in which I see and experience them, I feel drained and exhausted. I think it works on the student, but I do not really know."

It is a tragedy of teaching that sometimes the professors pour more into the class than the students are able at their ages to receive. And in that way good teaching is like planting. Those teachers like Weintraub were inserting seeds that would burst in us years or decades later when the realities of adult life called them forth. I don't know about you, but I felt more formed by my college education twenty-five years out than I did on the day I graduated.

There is an old saying that if you catch on fire with enthusiasm people will come for miles to watch you burn. Part of my education was just watching my professors burn. The essayist Joseph Epstein, who went to Chicago a quarter century before me, remembers the same tone of extensive erudition: "From the deep abyss of my late-adolescent ignorance," Epstein remembers, "I never for a moment thought I could hope to emulate such men and women. I nevertheless somehow sensed that there was something immensely impressive about them. I mostly remember getting caught up in an immense admiration for these professors and these authors." As the philosopher Eva Brann put it, there is a feeling of delightful humility in knowing that you are lesser, but are bound by love to something greater, that you recognize superiority and are inspired by it.

Many say that Western Civ and this kind of Great Books education is an elitist enterprise dominated by dead white males. But Western Civ was and remains radicalism—a subversive, revolutionary counterculture that makes it impossible to remain fat and happy within the status quo. Western Civ is Socrates, a man so dangerous, his city couldn't tolerate him living within it. Western Civ offers ways to step out of the cave and see reality in its true colors, not just as the shadows that ideologues are content to see. Western Civ took me outside the assumption of my time, outside the values of the modern meritocracy and America's worship of success. Western Civ inspired me to spend my life pursuing a philosophy—to spend decades trying to find a worldview that could handle the complexity of reality, but also offer a coherent vision that could frame my responses to events and guide me through the vicissitudes of life. Western Civ is the rebel base I return to when I want to recharge my dissatisfactions with the current world. Once you've had a glimpse of the highest peaks of the human experience, it's hard to live permanently in the flatlands down below. It's a little hard to be shallow later in life, no matter how inclined in that direction you might be.

THE INTELLECTUAL VIRTUES

The Chicago professors, like all initiators, did at least six things. First, they welcomed us into the tradition of scholars, the long line of men and women who have dedicated themselves to reading, thinking, agitating, and living more fully. They gave us entry into a long conversation, which, as the philosopher Michael Oakeshott wrote, is "an endless unrehearsed intellectual adventure in which, in imagination, we enter a variety of modes of understanding the world and ourselves and are not disconcerted by the differences or dismayed by the inconclusiveness of it all." We were just novices in this eternal procession, but still we were part of it.

Second, they introduced us to a range of history's moral ecologies. All of us require a constructive philosophy of life, a set of criteria to determine what is more valuable than what. Fortunately, over the centuries human beings at different times and different places have come up with distinct systems of values and ways of finding meaning in the world. There is, for example, the Greek tradition, emphasizing honor and glory; the Hebraic tradition, emphasizing obedience to law and strictness of conscious; the Christian tradition, emphasizing humility, surrender, and grace; the Enlightenment project, based on reason, individual liberty, and personal freedom. Our professors threw these and other moral ecologies before us: Stoicism, German romanticism, Gnosticism, Buddhism, Confucianism, African animism, Marxism, feminism, deconstructionism. They didn't tell us which moral ecology to live by, but offered us the chance to try on different ones and to see which one fit.

Third, our professors taught us how to see. Seeing reality seems like a straightforward thing. You just look out and see the world. But anybody who is around politics knows how many of us see the world through the distorting lens of partisanship, how many of us see only what we want to see, and how many of us see through the filter of our fear, insecurity, or narcissism.

Seeing well is not natural. It is an act of humility. It means getting your own self—your own needs and wishes—out of the way, so that you can see the thing you're looking at as itself, and not just as a mirror of your own interests. Seeing well is a skill you learn from others who see reality clearly: Leonardo da Vinci, George Eliot, George Orwell, Jane Jacobs, James Baldwin, Leo Tolstoy.

John Ruskin once wrote, "The greatest thing a human soul ever does in this world is to *see* something, and tell what it *saw* in a plain way. Hundreds of people can talk for one who can think, but thousands can think for one who can see."

The fourth thing our professors did was teach us intellectual courage. There is no such thing as thinking for yourself or thinking alone. All thinking is communication, and all the concepts in your head are inherited from a procession of thinkers stretching back thousands of years. We are social animals, and a lot of our thinking is in pursuit of bonding, not truth seeking. A lot of our thinking is trying to have the opinion that will help you win social approval and admittance into the right social circles. The hard part of intellectual life is separating what is true from what will get you liked.

Fifth, they gave us emotional knowledge. To read Whitman as he exults in joy, to be with Antigone as she struggles to bury her brother, to travel with Galileo as he follows his discoveries wherever they may take him, to be with the mathematician Pascal as he feels the direct presence of God, or to travel with Sylvia Plath into the depths of madness is not necessarily to learn a new fact, but it is to have a new experience.

Emotional knowledge, Roger Scruton argues, is knowing what to feel in certain situations—so that you can be properly disgusted by injustice, properly reverent before an act of self-sacrifice, properly sympathetic in friendship, and properly forbearing when wronged. This emotional knowledge is a skill that has to be acquired like any other. We are all born with certain basic emotions, but we have to be taught what it feels like to be in circumstances we haven't directly experienced—the sense of dehumanizing invisibility that Ralph Ellison experiences in the face of racism, the feeling of guilt that haunts a Holocaust survivor. We have to be taught the refined emotions: the tragic sadness that is appropriate when a good man is undone by his own flaw, the stubborn courage of Joan of Arc in the face of the fire, the disciplined joy that Mozart puts into his "Jupiter" symphony.

Sixth, Chicago gave us new things to love. All men and women are born with a desire to know. Children will stare at wheels and levers, driven by a passion to understand. We all get a little thrill when we come across a passage in a book that puts into words something we had vaguely intuited. When a poet captures an emotion perfectly, it doesn't just seem true; it seems beautiful.

Plato advised teachers to take advantage of this natural longing for beauty. Present more and more beautiful objects to students, and so form their imaginations in such a way that as they age they will desire more and more serious things. Start by presenting a student with a beautiful face. Once he has appreciated physical beauty, he will be grasped by a higher beauty, which is the beauty of lovely personality and a good person's lovely heart. And when he has understood that, he will grasp at an even higher beauty, which is the beauty of a just society. And when he has seen that, he will hunger for a higher beauty still, which is the search for truth and wisdom, and when he has seen that, he will feel a longing for the ultimate form of beauty, which is beauty itself, the everlasting form of all-encompassing transcendent beauty, which neither flowers nor fades, to which nothing can be added and from which nothing can be subtracted—which for Plato was divinity itself.

The teachers at Chicago aroused this hunger for higher beauties simply by putting some great masterworks in front of us, and by creating what can only be described as an erotic atmosphere around them. One evening, for example, I was doing my homework in the basement of the school's main library, which is possibly the ugliest level of the ugliest building on God's green earth. I was assigned to read a passage of Nietzsche's *The Birth of Tragedy*. I sat down at around seven o'clock and started reading. Sometime around ten-thirty I looked up, startled and shocked, and realized where I was. What happened in those intervening hours I can't really tell you. I guess I was in a sort of trance. Maybe it was Nietzsche's wicked brilliance, the soaring incantations of his prose, or his subject, the primitive Dionysian dances that thousands of years ago drove the birth of drama. All I can tell you is the rest of the world slipped away; time slipped away. I was in the book, not in myself.

Once you've had this kind of experience, you really want to have it again. None of us are as deep as the poet Rilke, but we can sort of understand what he was getting at: "I am learning to see. I don't know why it is, but everything penetrates more deeply into me and does not stop at the place where until now it always used to finish. I have an inner self of which I was ignorant. Everything goes thither now. What happens there I do not know."

We walk into a college, most of us, with a certain set of normal desires, most of them having to do with being well thought of. But if the college does its job, it reveals the inner self, or at least the possibility of the inner self. "Man is a metaphysical being," Jacques Maritain once wrote, "an animal that nourishes its life on transcendence." By dragging you to that level, a university awakens a new set of desires—to understand this realm, to understand something about the eternal.

The old desires don't go away. You still want to be popular and good-looking and have fun. But it becomes obvious that there's a hierarchy of desires. A sublime artistic experience is more worth wanting than a Snickers bar. The central message is to be watchful over what you love, because you become what you desire.

David Foster Wallace grasped the importance of wanting well in his famous commencement address at Kenyon College:

In the day-to-day trenches of adult life, there is actually no such thing as atheism. There is no such thing as not worshipping. Everybody worships. The only choice we get is *what* to worship. And an outstanding reason for choosing some sort of god or spiritual-type thing to worship—be it J.C. or Allah, be it Yahweh or the Wiccan mother-goddess or the Four Noble Truths or some infrangible set of ethical principles—is that pretty much anything else you worship will eat you alive. If you worship money and things—if they are where you tap real meaning in life—then you will never have enough. Never feel you have enough. It's the truth. Worship your own body and beauty and sexual allure and you will always feel ugly, and when time and age start showing, you will die a million deaths before they finally plant you. . . . Worship power—you will feel weak and afraid, and you will need ever more power over others to keep the fear at bay. Worship your intellect, being seen as smart— you will end up feeling stupid, a fraud, always on the verge of being found out.

The people and institutions who leave a mark provide you with better things to love, a new field of knowledge or a new form of carpentry or auto repair, or a new vision of social change. Leadership, Peter Drucker wrote, "is lifting a person's vision to higher sights, raising of a person's performance to a higher standard, of building a personality beyond its normal limitations."

Chicago, when I went there, had some problems. Many of us left school completely uneducated in the realm of jobs and career. While we were passionate about ideas, we tended to be estranged from other human beings. In those days, the institutional culture attracted the socially awkward and encouraged an interpersonal diffidence and aloofness that has taken me years to overcome, and I never really have. But the place did put us in ardent contact with ideal visions of the human condition. It made us all aware of what people are capable of. It offered us the true wine, and made it harder later in life to be satisfied with the cheap stuff. Everyone says that a university like Chicago is a heady and brainy place. But that was actually the opposite of my experience. What Chicago did most excellently was train the heart.

When I go back and think about our classroom discussions, the topics of our papers, and the rambling dining hall and bar-stool conversations, they were really about trying to figure out what was worth wanting, what desire was better than the others, what longings were to be embraced and which ones were to be subordinated or renounced.

One of the nicest compliments I ever got from one of my own students, at Yale, came on the last day of class: "This class has made me sadder," one outstanding man reflected. He meant it in a good way, and I took it as that. Once you've been introduced to some of history's greatest lovers, and seen what kind of love is possible, it's hard to feel completely satisfied because you have an A average. You'll always be plagued by a sort of dissatisfaction. Moreover, that dissatisfaction will never go away, because the more progress you make toward your ideals, the more they seem to recede into the distance. As artists get better at their craft, their vision of what they are capable of dashes out even further ahead.

But ultimately joy is found not in satisfying your desires but in changing your desires so you have the best desires. The educated life is a journey toward higher and higher love.

TWENTY

Religious Commitment

WENDELL BERRY'S NOVEL *JAYBER CROW* IS ABOUT A YOUNG MAN WHO has had a series of failures at school and work that leave him at loose ends and unattached. So, in the depths of the Great Depression, he packed his things into a cardboard box and started to walk toward his ancestral home in Port William, Kentucky.

As he walked, a great torrential rain began to fall, swelling the Kentucky River and sweeping away bridges and houses. Trudging through the stormy night, he found one bridge still standing and recklessly crossed it. From out there on the crest of that bridge, he said, the river

> was like a living element. It was like a big crowd shouting. And above or within the uproar of the water, I could hear the sleet hissing down. I could feel the river throbbing in the bridge. I can't say that I was not afraid, but it seemed the fear was not in me but in the air, like the sound of the river. It seemed to be something I had gone into and could not expect to get out of easily or very soon.

He could see barrels, logs, whole trees, and pieces of houses being swept along by the currents, and a Bible passage popped into his head: "The earth was without form, and void; and darkness was upon the face of the deep. And the Spirit of God moved upon the face of the waters." It was as if Crow were traveling back in time to some primal awareness:

> I'm not sure that I can tell you what was happening to me then, or that I know even now. At the time I surely wasn't trying to tell myself. But after all my years of reading in that book and hearing it read and believing and disbelieving it, I seemed to have wandered my way back to the beginning—not just of the book, but of the world—and all the rest that was yet to come. I felt knowledge crawl over my skin.

He marched onward, trying to make his way to Port William, but constantly taking wrong turns and getting lost, his teeth chattering in the cold and hunger stabbing at his stomach. He finally came to a town where refugees from the flood were stumbling into the town hall, looking for food and shelter. Crow joined the drenched lost souls and was met by love—caring volunteers from somewhere who were buzzing around and offering food and coffee.

He watched the parents around the hall tenderly put their kids to bed in the makeshift shelter. He was bone-tired and closed his eyes but didn't fall asleep. In his mind's eye he saw the river again. But this time, inwardly, he saw the whole river, its entire length, with the currents picking up logs and a barn and maybe an entire house itself. The world seemed to be cast adrift and tossed about on the currents.

> And I knew that the Spirit that had gone forth to shape the world and make it live was still alive in it. I just had no doubt. I could see that I lived in the created world, and it was still being created. I would be part of it forever. There was no escape. The Spirit that made it was in it, shaping it and reshaping it, sometimes lying at rest, sometimes standing up and shaking itself, like a muddy horse, and letting the pieces fly.

Crow broke through to a deeper awareness that night. A spiritual knowledge crawled, as he put it, over his skin.

Just as earlier in this book I mentioned that I collect people's accounts of joy, so do I also collect people's accounts of mystical experiences. These are moments when the shell of normal reality cracks, and people perceive some light from someplace beyond shining though.

Many of these experiences, unsurprisingly, happen in nature. In *The Varieties of Religious Experience*, William James quotes a man who had such a moment as bold as a thunderclap:

> I remember the night, and almost the very spot on the hill-top, where my soul opened out, as it were, into the Infinite, and there was a rushing together of the two worlds, the inner and the outer. It was deep calling unto deep—the deep that my own struggle had opened up within being answered by the unfathomable deep without, reaching beyond the stars. I stood alone with Him who had made me, and all the beauty of the world, and love, and sorrow, and even temptation. I did not seek Him, but felt the perfect unison of my spirit with His.

A surprising number of history's great figures have had mystical experiences while in prison. The experience of being imprisoned takes away everything else—material striving, external freedom, their busy schedules. For at least a few people, inner experience and spiritual states become all that they have. The realization dawns upon them that these inner states are actually the essential experience in life, and everything else is secondary.

Anwar Sadat was imprisoned during World War II for plotting against British imperialism. In his memoir, *In Search of Identity*, he recalled that in prison, "I was able to transcend the confines of time and place. Spatially, I did not live in a four-walled cell but in the entire universe." With material things taken away, he felt somehow larger. "I felt I had stepped into a vaster and more beautiful world and my capacity for endurance redoubled. I felt I could stand the pressure, whatever the magnitude of a given problem." His emotional stance altered. "When my individual entity merged into the vaster entity of all existence, my point of departure became love of home (Egypt), love of all being, love of God."

Václav Havel grew up in communist Czechoslovakia. The Marxist doctrine spewed out by the state was based on material determinism, the belief that the work a person does and the physical conditions of life determine who he is and how he thinks. When Havel was thrown into prison in 1977 for his dissident activity, he discovered that this was not the case. Material reality is not the fundamental driving force in human history, he concluded; spiritual reality is.

"The specific experience I'm talking about has given me one certainty," Havel wrote.

Consciousness precedes being, and not the other way around, as Marxists claim. For this reason, the salvation of this human world lies nowhere else than in the human heart, in the human power to reflect, in human modesty, in human responsibility. Without a global revolution in the sphere of human consciousness, nothing will change for the better.

Havel grew quite ill in prison and nearly died. One day, while looking through the prison fence, he saw the top of a tree. As he gazed at the tree, he was, as he wrote to his wife, Olga,

overcome by a sensation that is difficult to describe: all at once I seemed to rise above all the coordinates of my momentary existence in the world into a kind of state outside time in which all the beautiful things I had ever seen and experienced existed in a total "co-present"; I felt a sense of reconciliation, indeed of an almost gentle assent to the inevitable course of events as revealed to me now, and this combined with a carefree determination to face what had to be faced.

A profound amazement at the sovereignty of Being became a

dizzying sensation of tumbling endlessly into the abyss of its mystery; an unbounded joy at being alive, at having been given the chance to live through all I have lived through, and at the fact that everything has a deep and obvious meaning—this joy formed a strange alliance in me with a vague horror at the inapprehensibility and unattainability of everything I was so close to in that moment, standing at the very "edge of the infinite"; I was flooded with a sense of ultimate happiness and harmony with the world and with myself, with that moment, with all the moments I could call up, and with everything invisible that lies behind it and which has meaning. I would even say that I was somehow "struck by love," though I don't know precisely for whom or what.

Viktor Frankl experienced life in the Nazi concentration camps as a constant assault on a person's dignity. He found that he couldn't control his life, but he could control his response to what was imposed upon him. He could exercise an "inner hold," which meant enduring suffering in a dignified way. Life became not only a physical struggle but a spiritual one, a struggle to protect his own humanity from the dehumanizing conditions that surrounded him. "In reality there was an opportunity and a challenge," he wrote.

> One could make a victory of those experiences, turning life into an inner triumph, or one could ignore the challenge and simply vegetate.
>   The way in which a man accepts his fate and all the suffering it entails, the way in which he takes up his cross, gives him ample opportunity—even under the most difficult circumstances—to add a deeper meaning to his life.

Frankl discovered that while the body grows according to what it consumes, the soul grows by the measure of love it pours out.

> We who lived in concentration camps can remember the men who walked through the huts comforting others, giving away

their last piece of bread. They may have been few in number, but they offer sufficient proof that everything can be taken from a man but one thing—the last of the human freedoms—to choose one's attitude in any given circumstances, to choose one's own way.

One winter morning, Frankl was with a group of other prisoners digging a trench in icy ground. The sky was gray, the rags they wore were gray, their faces were gray. He began conversing, silently, in his head, with his beloved wife, even though she was somewhere outside the camp and might have already been dead. He scratched at the ground for hours while internally declaring his love for his wife. Suddenly a strange feeling came over him:

> I sensed my spirit piercing through the enveloping gloom. I felt it transcend that hopeless meaningless world, and from somewhere I heard a victorious "Yes" in answer to my question of the existence of an ultimate purpose.

At that moment, a light went on in a distant farmhouse.

> The guard passed by, insulting me, and once again I communed with my beloved. More and more I felt that she was present, that she was with me; I had the feeling that I was able to touch her, able to stretch out my hand and grasp hers. The feeling was very strong; she was there.

A bird flew down silently and perched in front of him. They gazed at one another.

> For the first time in my life I saw the truth as it is set into song by so many poets, proclaimed as the final wisdom by so many thinkers. The truth—that love is the ultimate and highest goal to which man can aspire. Then I grasped the meaning of the greatest secret that human poetry and human thought and be-

lief have to impart: *The salvation of man is through love and in love.* I understand how a man who has nothing left in this world may still know bliss, be it only for a brief moment, in the contemplation of his beloved.

Frankl said that this was the first time he understood the words "The angels are lost in perpetual contemplation of infinite glory." He spent the rest of his long life arguing that human beings' primary motive is not for money or even happiness, but for meaning. We are driven above all to understand the purpose of our lives. Once that is understood even the most miserable conditions cannot upend inner peace.

Frankl came to realize that it didn't even matter if his beloved was gone from this world. It was the pouring forth of love that was salvific. He found, in the course of his research in the camp, that the prisoners who died quickly of disease or some breakdown were those who had nothing outside the camp that they were committed to. But those who survived had some external commitment that they desired and pushed toward, whether it was a book they felt called to write or a wife they were compelled to come back to.

One day in the concentration camp, he met a young woman, ill and dying in the infirmary. "I am grateful that fate has hit me so hard," she told him. "In my former life I was spoiled and did not take spiritual accomplishments seriously."

She was lonely in her deathbed, but, she told him, she had befriended the only living creature she could see, a chestnut tree just outside her window. "This tree is the only friend I have in my loneliness," she told Frankl. She said she often talked to the tree. Startled, Frankl didn't know how to respond, but eventually asked if the tree talked back to her. She said that it did. It said: "I am here—I am here—I am life, eternal life." That transcendent connection with eternal life explained the young woman's tranquility and good cheer in the face of death.

"Bless you, prison," the Soviet dissident Aleksandr Solzhenitsyn wrote in *The Gulag Archipelago*. "Bless you for being in my life. For there, lying upon the rotting prison straw, I came to realize that the object of life is not prosperity as we are made to believe, but the maturity of the human soul."

In the course of his imprisonment, Solzhenitsyn looked at the guard who treated him most cruelly. He realized that if fate had made him a prison guard instead of a prisoner, perhaps he would have been cruel, too. He came to realize that the line between good and evil passes not between tribes or nations but straight through every human heart. Prison, and the tyranny it represented, gave Solzhenitsyn a sense of participation in a larger story: "It makes me happier, more secure, to think that I do not have to plan and manage everything for myself, that I am only a sword made sharp to smite the unclean forces, an enchanted sword to cleave and disperse them. Grant, O Lord, that I may not break as I strike! Let me not fall from Thy hand!"

Many people look at these spiritual experiences with blinking disbelief: What on earth are you talking about? Many people have never had such experiences and so understandably have trouble believing in these supposedly hidden dimensions of existence you can't actually provide any evidence of. And, frankly, there are good reasons to mistrust these experiences. Maybe they are just the product of some cocktail of brain chemicals, some hallucination, an altered state caused by weariness or stress. In that case they are certainly not something to base your life around.

Believers, on the other hand, look at atheists with the same blinking disbelief. As Christian Wiman writes in *My Bright Abyss*,

Really? You have never felt overwhelmed by, and in some way inadequate to, an experience in your life, have never felt something in yourself staking a claim beyond your self, some wordless mystery straining through words to reach you? *Never?* Religion is not made of these moments; religion is the means of making these moments part of your life rather than merely radical intrusions so foreign and perhaps even fearsome that you can't even acknowledge their existence afterward. Religion is what you *do* with these moments of over-mastery in your life.

The universe is alive and connected, these moments tell us. There are dimensions of existence you never could have imagined before. Quantum particles inexplicably flip together, even though they are separated by vast differences of time and space. Somehow the world is alive and communicating with itself. There is some interconnecting animating force, and we are awash in that force, which we with our paltry vocabulary call love.

The odd thing about these moments is that, as Wiman continues, "it is not only as if we were suddenly perceiving something in reality we had not perceived before, but as if we ourselves were being perceived."

A Most Unexpected Turn of Events

SOME PEOPLE HAVE DRAMATIC STORIES OF HOW THEY CAME TO FAITH. A blinding light appeared! A voice called forth! The trumpets blared! I don't have that. I am telling you the story of my journey to faith because even though every leap of faith is mystical and absurd by any normal logic, I want to illustrate how normal it can be. It can happen to the most spiritually average person. But you wind up in an astonishing place, believing that God is, in Paul Tillich's phrase, the ground of being.

I first heard the biblical stories as a kid—Noah and the ark, David and Goliath, Esther and Haman, Abraham and Isaac. These tales were just part of the architecture of my childhood. In my life, and even in Hebrew school, they were myth, performing the functions of myth—helping me understand right and wrong, helping me to grapple with my emotions, helping me to understand heroism and all the rest of that Bruno Bettelheim stuff. They also helped me understand my group, the Jewish people. Those stories, starting with biblical stories and then blending up through historical stories of Hanukkah and the Holocaust, were the stories of our people and our identity. They helped me understand the consistency of my group across the vast horizon of time.

Then, in college and early adulthood, I began to use them as wisdom literature, as tools for understanding and solving the problems of life. The characters in the Bible are normal, mottled human beings who are confronted with moral challenges. The key question is whether they respond to the challenge with the right inner posture—whether they express charity when it is called for, forgiveness when it is necessary, and great humility before goodness. David shows us what bravery looks like in the face of Goliath. Solomon illustrates wisdom before the women and the baby. Boaz exemplifies loving-kindness toward Ruth. During this phase I held these stories at arm's length, to see what useful information they might have. I was big, and the stories were small, just an old book in my hands to be used by me in leading my life.

Over the decades things began to change imperceptibly. Life happened and, as Wiman puts it, "My old ideas were not adequate for the extremes of joy and grief I experienced." These stories kept coming back, but they changed, as if re-formed by the alchemy of time. They grew bigger and deeper, more fantastical and more astonishing. Wait, God asked Abraham to kill his own son?

I suppose this happens to most of us as we age: We get smaller, and our dependencies get bigger. We become less fascinating to ourselves, less inclined to think of ourselves as the author of all that we are, and at the same time we realize how we have been the ones shaped—by history, by family, by forces beyond awareness. And I think what changed, in the most incremental, boring way possible, is that at some point I had the sensation that these stories are not fabricated tales happening to other, possibly fictional, people: They are the underlying shape of reality. They are renditions of the recurring patterns of life. They are the scripts we repeat.

Adam and Eve experienced temptation and a fall from grace, and we experience temptation and a fall from grace. Moses led his people from bondage meanderingly toward a promised land, and we take a similar spiritual journey. The psalmist looked into himself and asked,

"Soul, why are you so downcast?" and we still do that. The prodigal son returned, and his father, infused by grace and love, ran out to meet him. Sometimes we, too, are outrageously forgiven. These stories are not just about common things that happen to people. They are representations of ongoing moral life. We are alive in the natural world, and we use science to understand that layer of aliveness. We are also alive in another dimension, the dimension of spirit and meaning. We use the biblical stories to understand that dimension of aliveness.

"I can only answer the question 'What am I to do?'" Alasdair MacIntyre wrote, "if I can answer the prior question 'Of what story or stories do I find myself a part?'" If there are no overarching stories, then life is meaningless. Life does not feel meaningless. These stories provide, in their simple yet endlessly complex ways, a living script. They provide the horizon of meaning in which we live our lives—not just our individual lives, but our lives together. These stories describe a great moral drama, which is not an individual drama but a shared drama. We are still a part of this drama, as Jayber Crow put it, created and being created still.

A PILGRIMAGE TOWARD FAITH

A pilgrimage is a journey undertaken in response to a story. I was raised in a Jewish home, which means I was raised within the Exodus myth. The amazing thing about Exodus is that, as the great Torah scholar Avivah Gottlieb Zornberg observes, it was a story that happened in order to be told. God commands Moses to tell the story of the liberation before He actually performs the liberation.

As a young man, I didn't know if there ever was a man named Moses or if Jews were ever enslaved in Egypt. I tended to doubt it. There'd be more archeological evidence, I figured.

But Jews have been telling this story to one another for thousands of years, and in the telling it has become true. In the telling and passing down, Exodus has become the shaping reality of Jewish life, how Jews understand and fashion their lives. It's how Jews understood exile. It's why, year after year, Jews continue to dream: Next year in Jerusalem! The Jewish migration to America was the ultimate Exodus story.

So was the return home, to the state of Israel. In all of these cases, Exodus was reenacted. The story was the landscape, the living creation, on which Jews lived out their lives.

Rabbi Abraham Isaac Kook put it clearly: "With a penetrating consciousness, we come to realize that the essential event of the Exodus is one that *never ceases at all*. The public and manifest revelation of God's hand in world history is an explosion of light of the divine soul which lives and acts throughout the world."

Exodus is a journey of spiritual formation. Slaves in Egypt, the Jews are not capable of running their own lives. They were not even capable of being saved by others. They are described as hopeless, dejected, passive, apathetic, and in despair. Fear has caused them to close in on themselves, to become secretive, inert, and weak. Reduced to a childlike state by oppression, they are unable to accept responsibility for themselves.

God must build a people capable of upholding His covenant, capable of exercising agency and accepting responsibility for their own lives. He yanks them out of Egypt, and He keeps them moving even when they want to crawl back into slavery. He forces Moses to take on the mantle of leadership, even though Moses tries to evade this responsibility. He forces the diverse tribes into relationship with one another and compels them to overcome the normal human fear of being judged and rejected. He sends His people into the wasteland. Difficulty, as Rabbi Nachman of Breslov notes, can have a paradoxical effect. It doesn't always make a people more passive; it sometimes arouses a desire to fight back. Obstacles can arouse desire. Slowly the Israelites begin to show signs of life.

The trek through the wilderness is not only an ordeal that gives them strength. They are living out a narrative that gives them identity. Before long, they are singing. They are crossing the Red Sea, and Miriam and the other women are leading them in song. Soon, they are able to trust again. People who have been betrayed and oppressed cannot trust and therefore cannot have faith. But eventually the Jews, even with all their constant kvetching and whining, do learn that sometimes promises are kept, that God abides. They become a people capable of faith, capable of receiving law, obeying law, and upholding their end of the covenant.

It's interesting that Moses descended from Sinai at the exact moment his people were worshipping the golden calf. He was bringing them the law that would make them an adult people at the exact moment they were behaving like children.

That's a reminder that the passage into adulthood, and a leap of faith, doesn't happen when you are ready to make it. It happens, Zornberg says, when you are not quite ready. The leap is made by one who is hurried, troubled, a little nervous but still ecstatic and energetic. Exodus is not just describing a ragtag group of people wandering around in the desert. It is describing how resilient people are made. It's an eternal story of spiritual and moral formation that happens again and again and again.

My ancestors also lived in a state of fear, a state of hiddenness, cowering from the terror brought by the thundering Cossacks, the mob violence of the pogrom. They, too, had to be awakened by a journey across the wilderness and the rough arrival in the new land. They, too, arrived with an aroused desire. My maternal great-grandfather opened a kosher butcher shop on the Lower East Side of Manhattan, married a German Jew, and began the great climb upward. The shop flourished, and that freed my grandfather, Bernard Levy, to go to City College, the free university where young Jews went to make it in America.

My grandfather then went to Columbia Law School, took the middle name "Justinian" to distinguish himself from the other Levys, and got a job in a Jewish law firm in the Woolworth Building, at one point the tallest building in the world. Another step up the ladder. He spent much of his time writing briefs and some of it trying to get his letters to the editor published in *The New York Times*.

He did not live to see me become a columnist there, but he set me on the path. He showed me the route upward, the long trek that our people must take from the cramped apartments of Brooklyn, the Bronx, and the Lower East Side up to the glimmering vistas of Madison Avenue, Fifth Avenue, the promised land. He wrote me beautiful letters telling the family stories—his mother's hard-boiled sayings, his own tricks for getting ahead (always buy the nicest shoes you can afford). He delighted in my writing and showed me that you could write your way up. We didn't make that Exodus with our feet in my generation but with our wits. He and his daughter, my mother, subtly communicated that immigrant mentality—the feeling of being an outsider, yet just a bit cleverer and more hardworking than those insiders. The culture of immigrant Jews instilled a burning hunger to make it. The hunger, once implanted, stays as you age, but the food it seeks changes. Success is no longer enough.

We only said the Shema on the High Holy Days, but we recited the "Did you know _____ is a Jew?" every day. All the geniuses turned out to be Jews: Einstein, Freud, Marx, Lionel Trilling. All the entertainers turned out to be Jews: the Gershwins, the Marx Brothers, Lauren Bacall and Kirk Douglas, Sandy Koufax and Woody Allen. All the writers, all the playwrights, and, yes, even the surprising Jews: Marilyn Monroe, Bob Dylan, and Sammy Davis, Jr. Exodus was the journey from obscurity to accomplishment. It was a journey from oblivion to excellence. We had exchanged the robes of the righteous for the dream of the Nobel Prize. Israel wasn't so much the Holy Land; it was the tiny David that beat Goliath and won the Six-Day War. In the modern Exodus, every little Ralph Lifshitz could rise up to be Ralph Lauren.

I had a fantastically happy childhood. My parents gave me support, attention, conversation, and love, though it was never actually expressed in words or in hugs. I knew what it meant to be loved, but I didn't know how to express it. For example, when I was about twenty-two, I visited my grandfather in the hospital. His room was stifling hot, and he sat in a chair in a robe. The doctors did not give him long to live.

"I'm a dead duck," he told me as I walked in. We talked about this and that for the next few hours, and then when I got up to leave he let out a sob and said to me, "Oh God, I love you so." My family had always shown and presumed love, but we didn't talk about it. I froze, unpracticed, not knowing what to say. It was constipation of the heart, I guess. I acknowledged his love but I was too inhibited to tell him I loved him back, and he died without ever hearing those words from me.

This was the Jewish ethos of my childhood. Imagine a better future; build a better future. Don't let them destroy us. Make it in the promised land. It was a worldly ethos, but it grew out of a deeper and more eternal one. We are commanded to co-create the world. We are commanded to finish what God has begun. Our common salvation comes through works and good deeds. Salvation through work. Survival through intelligence. Righteousness is something you achieve together, collectively as a people. And then you argue about it over a dinner table. If I had to capture the core of my Jewish experience, it would be this: Eighteen people sitting around a Shabbat dinner table, all of them talking at once, all of them following all eighteen conversations that are simultaneously crossing the table, all of them correcting the eighteen wrong things that other people have just said.

GRACE

The other odd thing about my Exodus story is that it led to church. One of the ways New York Jews assimilated in the middle of the twentieth century was by embracing Anglophilia. The genteel, elegant, stiff-upper-lip English aristocracy seemed like the farthest point possible from the squabbling mobs of the Ukrainian shtetl, the past that American Jews were running away from.

A certain sort of Jew became an Anglophile. The slogan was, "Think Yiddish, Act British." Jews such as Isaiah Berlin, Gertrude Himmelfarb, and Lionel Trilling glommed on to Dickens, Shakespeare, Burke, and Jane Austen. Jewish parents began giving their children English names in the hopes that nobody would think their boys were Jewish: Norman, Irving, Milton, Sidney, and Lionel. (It didn't work; now everybody thinks of those names as Jewish names.)

My parents studied Victorian literature and Victorian history. My turtles growing up were named Disraeli and Gladstone, after the two Victorian prime ministers. The poetry in our house was Auden. I wound up spending my childhood with the Episcopalians. My nursery school was called St. George's. My elementary school was Grace Church School, on lower Broadway in Manhattan. My summer camp, which I attended for fifteen years and was the center of my childhood, was Incarnation Camp, sponsored by the Church of the Incarnation on Madison Avenue.

We can never know how the precious moments of early childhood shape a life. Influences come in and are buried so deep it's hard to see the mechanism by which they wield their power. But I do remember sitting there at the chapel services each morning at Grace Church School, singing the hymns and reciting the prayers and, most of all, staring up at the soaring gothic arches of the apse. I loved the songs, but it was the architecture that communicated a sense of loftiness— the complex weave of columns, the biblical heroes looking down from the stained glass, the dark wood pews. I was living in a fairy tale, a land of timeless figures, hidden forces, chivalry, and infinite depth.

The first glimmerings of faith came to me architecturally—during those mornings at Grace, and then years later at Chartres. Grace Church is at Tenth and Broadway, near the Strand bookstore. It is in a normal, crowded part of Manhattan, and in fact Broadway bends to accommodate it. But to leave the sidewalk and enter the church is to walk into a deeper story. The Kingdom of Heaven is announced on the façade; you sink into a hushed reverence inside the door as the world falls away; you take the slow journey down the aisle and glimpse the heroes of the faith in the chapels and windows on either side. There's the moment of illumination in the transept, as light floods in from all directions, and then, turning around, the glory of the rose windows. Grace isn't a big church, but it seemed infinite to me.

I learned the Lord's Prayer at Grace, the hymns and the liturgies, and of course I became acquainted with the story of Jesus. I sort of knew he was on the other team. There were lots of Jews at Grace then, and we didn't sing his name when it came up in the hymns. In my memory the whole volume in the church would drop.

In its outline, the Jesus story is a pretty familiar myth, which probably recurs in all cultures: The city is riven by fractures, by cycles of vengeance and counter-vengeance. The only way to purge the hatred and division is by piling the sins of the community onto a scapegoat. It is by casting out the scapegoat that the sins of the society can be external-ized and expurgated. It is by killing the scapegoat that unity is achieved.

Jesus is the classic scapegoat, the innocent outsider that all the groups could rally around in their bloodlust, and dump their hatreds on. The only thing that is different about the Jesus story—and it is a big difference—is that in this story Jesus came to earth precisely to be the scapegoat. He volunteered for this job, forgave those who executed him, and willingly carried the sins of the world on his shoulders. He came precisely to bow down, to suffer, and to redeem the world. He came not to be the awesome conquering Messiah that most of us would want, but to be the lamb, to submit, to love his enemies. He came not to be the victim of sin but the solution. His strength was self-sacrificial, and his weapon love so that we might live.

That's a clever plot twist.

AMPHIBIAN

In my semi-secular world of Jewish New York, we put peoplehood before faith. We were living in the shadow of the Holocaust, so sur-vival was not taken for granted. We celebrated effort, work, smarts, discipline, accomplishment, achievement. In the rabbinic tradition, the Messiah was associated with poverty, righteousness associated with the poor and the miserable. But that is not how Judaism is lived out in American culture. We were pointing toward accomplishment.

But the Jesus story was not about worldly accomplishment. It was nearly about its opposite. Jesus bowed down in order to rise up; he died so others might live. Christians are not saved by works but by faith. In fact, you can't earn the prize of salvation, because it has already been given to you by grace.

In the Christian story, the poor are closer to God, not the accom-plished; the children, not the prominent. The meek are the blessed ones—the leper, the wounded, and those who bear pain. Jesus was blandly uninterested in the rich and the powerful, who could have done him a lot of good and around which everything in the outside world revolved. He gravitated downward—to the prostitute, the outcast, and the widow.

In the story of my childhood, the pushy are blessed for they getteth shit done. But the Christian way is the little way—small acts of radical kindness done with great love. In my world, you take possession of your life, exercising agency. But in the Christian one, you are not even the owner of yourself. Your talents merely flow through you; you give yourself to the one who made you.

In my childhood world, you delivered yourself from the slavery of other men's oppression. Jesus also offers delivery from slavery, but it is a different kind of slavery—the slavery to pride, to ego, to self. In my world, wisdom was revered, but in the Christian world God chose what is foolish in the world to confound the wise, and he chose the weak to shame the strong. The meek shall inherit the earth.

I was and remain an amphibian, living half in water and half on land. I wish I could remember being confused by the two different stories that were rattling around in my head. But the truth is, I don't really remember that. I was just raised in a dualism.

Judaism came to me through the precious lineage of my family and our people, especially all those great-uncles and -aunts with their Yiddish, their strange names (Aggie and Fagel), their matzo balls, the way they could feud and scream at one another for hours around the kitchen table. Christianity came to me as an arm draped around my shoulder, a hug, the sweaty contact of a basketball game.

Starting at age six, I spent my summers at Incarnation Camp, two months a year that overshadowed the other ten. The camp was Episcopalian in that progressive mainline sort of way—we sang "Puff, the Magic Dragon" and "If I Had a Hammer" along with "Lord of the Dance." We were always rising and shining and giving God our glory, glory. The only explicitly religious people were the God Squadders, Christian hippies who played guitars, smoked weed, and expressed their love of Jesus through their hairstyles. But everybody else was implicitly Christian. There were tons of PKs—preachers' kids—who had grown up with the Gospel and, a lot of the time, exemplified it.

There was no success or failure at Incarnation, not even much status or lack of status. There was love, free flowing and unabashed.

We lived in tents, cooked meals over an open fire, swam and sailed in a mile-long lake, and had intimacy forced upon us. Incarnation is the most successfully integrated community I've ever experienced. Half the campers were from Westchester or fancy private schools in Manhattan, and the other half from the poorest areas of Brooklyn and the Bronx. We learned courage—to cliff-dive into the lake, to shoot the rapids on a canoe trip, to sneak across the camp at midnight to be with your girlfriend. Every significant rite of adolescent passage happened at Incarnation—weed, first drinks, kissing, second base, third. Every early metaphysical sensation happened there, too—the feeling on a canoe trip of seeing a mountain at dawn, the way a simple rock can be coated with enchantment when it was the place you sat during the first raptures of teenage love. I have few friends left over from high school or college, but I have about forty or fifty lifelong friends from camp, and for decades they did not even realize that Brooksie had a first name.

There were many people who left a mark at Incarnation, but I'll pick out just one, a counselor and unit director named Wes Wubbenhorst. He was a big, athletic, goofy man-child. His conversation was all overflowing enthusiasm, interspersed with whistles, pops, weird exclamations, sudden laughter, and good cheer. He was always interrupting himself mid-sentence as another thing that delighted him sprang into consciousness. He lived to be over sixty and walked through the darkest parts of the world, but I don't think he ever learned to talk in that serious way adults do. Some piece of him always remained a Holy Child.

I've come to recognize people who were formed by a camp, and they often had what Wes had: bubbling enthusiasm, a radiance, a wardrobe mostly of old sneakers, tattered shorts, and ripped T-shirts. Wes later became an Episcopal priest. He ministered to the poor in Honduras, comforted victims of domestic violence. His God was a God of love, and his life at camp was training for his mission of selfless love. He was, as the saying goes, a man for others: enthusiastically waking you up in the morning and singing you to bed each night, the best passer on the basketball court I've ever encountered. When someone did something extraordinarily stupid, he would just smile and sigh in wonder at the wackiness of life.

When I was a seventeen-year-old counselor and he was maybe twenty-five, we were walking across a playing field and he told me that one day I would be famous. I took it as a compliment then. But decades later, I visited him in Annapolis on the day of his death. Wes was not speaking anymore, just gesticulating and making unformed noises. I couldn't really tell if he understood anything I said to him, about my meandering walk of faith, the loves in my life, but as I drove away it occurred to me that maybe there was a warning embedded in his early forecast of my life. Wes was coming from a radical vantage point I didn't understand back then.

Religion doesn't produce as many truly good people, like Wes, as you'd think it would. Religious people talk so much about holiness and goodness and love, you'd think they would be more virtuous than atheists and agnostics. In my experience they are not, and some religious people, like the Catholic priests who prey on young children, live very religious lives that are also very bad.

But I do think religions point people toward certain visions of goodness. Growing up, I experienced a stereotypically Jewish kind of goodness. It is *chessed*, loving-kindness. It is the smiling eyes of a wise rabbi gleaming at you through his beard; it is the warmth of Bubbe giving you seconds on a Shabbat meal; it is the good of a community dropping everything for a shivah, the goofy kindness of a mensch, a whole people turning like a beacon when a Jew is murdered. It is an earthy goodness, a folk goodness, and the rich, enveloping goodness of a family gathering together for a holiday meal.

The kind of good Wes was, was a different kind of good, and I associate it as a Christian flavor of goodness. It is simple, sincere, cheerful, pure, overflowing joy, and an erasure of self in the gift of love. Wes was just not thinking of himself all that much. Maybe because I grew up with it, Jewish good makes sense to me. Christian good has the power to shock. As Dorothy Day once said, Christians are commanded to live in a way that doesn't make sense unless God exists.

Sometimes Christian good is hard to be around. It's not of this world, and the juxtaposition jars. For example, Jean Vanier spent seven years in the British navy, starting in 1942. Later in life he noticed the way people with mental disabilities were mistreated and discarded by society into miserable asylums. He visited the asylums and noticed that nobody in them was crying. "When they realize that nobody cares, that nobody will answer them, children no longer cry. It takes too much energy. We cry out only when there is hope that someone may hear us." He bought a little house near Paris and started a community for the mentally disabled. Before long there were 134 such communities in thirty-five countries.

Vanier exemplifies a selflessness that is almost spooky. He thinks and cares so little of himself. He lives as almost pure gift. People who meet him report that this can have an unnerving effect. Vanier walked out of a society that celebrates the successful and the strong to devote his life purely to those who are weak. He did it because he understands his own weakness. "We human beings are all fundamentally the same," he wrote. "We all belong to a common, broken humanity. We all have wounded, vulnerable hearts. Each one of us needs to feel appreciated and understood; we all need help."

He also understands the beauty of weakness. "Weakness carries within it a secret power. The care and the trust that flow from weakness can open up the heart. The one who is weaker can call forth powers of love in the one who is stronger."

One of the people influenced by Vanier was Henri Nouwen, who left teaching posts at Harvard and Yale so he could live in one of Vanier's L'Arche communities, serving people so mentally disabled that some of them were unable to even thank him.

When Nouwen left the L'Arche community to speak, he often brought patients from the community with him on the trip. Once, on a trip to Washington, he brought a man named Bill. When Nouwen mounted the stage to deliver his remarks, Bill mounted the stage as well.

When Nouwen repeated a familiar trope from his speeches, Bill announced to the audience, "I have heard that before!" When Nouwen finished, to a standing ovation, Bill announced that he, too, would like to give a speech. A hint of panic crept across Nouwen's mind. What on earth would Bill say? He might ramble on and create an embarrassment. But Nouwen realized that it was presumptuous to think that Bill would have nothing important to say and led him to the microphone.

Bill said, "Last time, when Henri went to Boston, he took John Smeltzer with him. This time he wanted me to come with him to Washington, and I am very glad to be here with you. Thank you very much." That was it. The audience rose. Bill got a standing ovation, too.

Afterward, Bill went from person to person, saying hello. The next morning at breakfast, he went from table to table saying goodbye to the people he had met. On the flight home he asked Nouwen if he liked the trip. "Oh, yes," Nouwen answered. "It was a wonderful trip and I am so glad you came with me."

"And we did it together, didn't we?"

Then Nouwen thought of Jesus's words "Where two or three meet in my name, I am among them."

ADULTHOOD

I seem to live my life as what my friend Mako Fujimori calls a "border stalker," perpetually on the line between different worlds. Politically, I am not quite left and not quite right. Professionally, I am not quite an academic and not quite a journalist. Temperamentally, I am not quite a rationalist but not quite a romantic.

Somebody should scream at me: Make up your damn mind about something! And sometimes I wonder if it comes from spending my childhood in the crossroads between two great moral ecologies. I realize that, in theory, both Judaism and Christianity contain both the majestic and the humble, the yearning glory and holy submission. But I didn't grow up in a theology book; I grew up in the late-twentieth-century American version of Judaism, and the late-twentieth-century version of Christianity. I grew up either the most Christiany Jew on earth or the most Jewy Christian, a plight made survivable by the fact that I was certain God did not exist, so the whole matter was of only theoretical importance.

I won't bore you with a description of my decades of atheism. They say that religion is the opiate of the masses, but I found the atheist life surprisingly untroubling. I was in the presence of religion, of course. Almost all my close friends were Jewish. It was irony at first sight. We spoke the same language and told the same jokes. But the Christians had their magnetic pull: the writings of Reinhold Niebuhr, the paintings of Fra Angelico, my mentor William F. Buckley, that scene near the end of *Brideshead Revisited*, when the patriarch of the family accepts Christ on his deathbed and the fabric of the universe is rent in two.

In college I met and later married a strong, intelligent woman. We were married in a Unitarian Church, but a few years later she converted to Judaism, went to work at our synagogue, and decided she wanted us to keep a kosher home and send our children to Jewish schools. I'd been on a trajectory away from Judaism, but now I was back in. We settled into the Halachic life: the life of kosher rules, strange prohibitions, rich community, and the cycle of Jewish holidays.

Her commitment to Judaism is deep and impressive and has deepened with each passing year. We don't communicate often about these matters, but when we do there is a great wisdom and learnedness to her. Now her life is a commitment of study of and service to the Torah, Judaism, her friends, and her community.

My attitude toward the kosher rules oscillated between ferocious resentment and profound respect. I resented a practice that can descend into dry and pedantic legalism. But I respected how Judaism has a ritual for every occasion. The idea is that behavior change precedes and causes internal change (a belief well supported by experimental psychology). "When halakhic man approaches reality," Joseph Soloveitchik writes, "he comes with his Torah, given to him from Sinai, in hand. He orients himself to a world by means of fixed statutes and firm principles. An entire corpus of precepts and laws guides him along the path leading to existence. When he looks to the horizon and sees the rising or the setting of the sun, he knows that each occasion comes with commandments to be performed, the morning Shema, the laying on of tefillin, and so forth. When he comes across a spring, he knows what uses the water can be put to: immersion, expiation of sin, drinking. He has blessings for each occasion and prayers for each action."

These rituals and blessings root the earthly life. Judaism, Soloveitchik continues, is a "concrete religion, a religion of the life of the senses, in which there is sight, smell, and touch, a religion which a man of flesh and blood can feel with all his senses, sinews, and organs, with his entire being." At the same time these commandments also point upward to an ideal. They hold up an ideal standard and describe the relationship between our concrete reality and divinity. "Transcendence becomes embodied in man's deeds," Soloveitchik continues, "deeds that are shaped by the lawful physical order of which man is a part."

The Jew does not experience faith primarily in solitude. He or she experiences it primarily in community, in what one does with others. The synagogue is not the locus of Jewish life. The Shabbat dinner table is. My general rule is that most church services are more spiritual than synagogue services, but a Shabbat dinner can be more spiritual than any church service.

The Jew is not looking for some eternal and purified existence in some other world on the other side of death. "Better is one hour of Torah and good deeds in this world than the whole life of the world to come," an ancient scholar declared. In Judaism this world is the stage upon which holiness can be achieved. The Jew is looking to fulfill the 613 commandments that govern life on this earth. Very few of these commandments have to do with religious belief, and fewer than 5 percent have to with the things a person should say, such as prayer and vows. Sixty percent of them, the American philosopher Abraham Kaplan points out, have to do with physical ritual, the lighting of candles, the ritual bath, or using palm branches in a certain way—they have to do with doing stuff.

These rituals and good deeds are a kind of language, Kaplan argues, and in performing them we are acting out the rules of grammar and syntax of a language that is too deep for words. After a while, the rituals don't feel like acts that some book has told you to perform; they seem to emerge from the center of your very being.

Judaism demands creative action. "Holiness is created by man, by flesh and blood," Soloveitchik writes. Many Jews have sort of a mental block when thinking about the afterlife. The first problem with the next world is that it's already perfect, so there's no need to build and repair it. So how could it be so great?

Occasionally Christianity would make a visit into my life. For example, at a cocktail party in 2004, somebody mentioned an unfamiliar name, John Stott. I called a friend, Michael Cromartie, who told me that if evangelicals had a pope, Stott would be it. He was arguably the most influential active evangelical. I did a little research and found that with one exception, in 1956, his name had never appeared in *The New York Times*. So I decided to learn about him and write a column called "Who Is John Stott?"

To anybody who lives in the secular culture, one's first encounter with a joyful intelligent Christian comes as something of a shock. We're used to looking down on the Franklin Graham / Pat Robertson types, but it's unnerving to encounter a Christian you would, on balance, very much like to be. Stott's voice, I wrote, "is friendly, courteous and natural. It is humble and self-critical, but also confident, joyful and optimistic. Stott's mission is to pierce through all the encrustations and share direct contact with Jesus. Stott says that the central message of the Gospel is not the teachings of Jesus, but Jesus himself, the human/divine figure. He is always bringing people back to the concrete reality of Jesus' life and sacrifice." It's about putting on the mind of Christ.

In Stott I met someone entirely confident in his faith, yet drawn to its paradoxes. Jesus teaches humility, so why does he always talk about himself? What does it mean to gain power through weakness, or freedom through obedience? In Stott I found a more unapologetic and direct version of Christianity. "Every time we look at the cross, Christ seems to be saying to us, 'I am here because of you,'" Stott wrote. "'It is your sin I am bearing, your curse I am suffering, your debt I am paying, your death I am dying.' Nothing in history or in the universe cuts us down to size like the cross. All of us have inflated views of ourselves, especially in self-righteousness, until we visit a place called Calvary. It is there, at the foot of the cross, that we shrink to our true size."

When Stott came to Washington, he asked me to lunch. I learned many years later, after Stott had died, that he had spent some time pondering, praying, and talking to others about how to handle his lunch with me. He told his friends that he sensed some quaver in the way I wrote that column, some movement or premonition of faith. At lunch we chatted for a bit, and then he questioned me directly and hard: What did I believe? Where was I on my faith journey? What did I think of the Gospel? What did I think of Judaism? He told me he sensed something in me, some motion toward God. I thought we were there to talk about him, but he was interested only in me.

I was unnerved. If the hound of heaven was nipping at my heels, that was either something I did not feel or a truth I did not want to face. I must have known unconsciously how much disruption to my life that would lead to. I shut the door and blocked out the light.

But other cracks began to appear—from time to time at first, and then in a steady pour. Moments of spiritual transcendence came to me as mesmerizing beauty. Chartres Cathedral casts a spell every time I visit, like a point of contact between our world and some other unseen one. I wrote a book in which I profiled amazing individuals. About two-thirds were secular, but Dorothy Day was among them, one of the most emotionally rich and spiritually deep people I have ever encountered. Day discovered faith at the birth of her child—she felt such joy that she needed something to worship, thank, and adore. She turned over her life to faith, embracing poverty, serving the poor, living with the destitute.

Near the end of Day's life, Robert Coles asked her if she had any plans to write a memoir. She was a gorgeous and prolific writer, so it was a natural question to ask. She told Coles that she had once thought of doing that, and had pulled out a piece of paper and wrote "A Life Remembered." Then, "I just sat there and thought of our Lord, and his visit to us all those centuries ago, and I said to myself that my great luck was to have had Him on my mind for so long in my life." She felt no need to write anything.

What must such peace and tranquility feel like?

Another character in the book was Saint Augustine, a man of breathtaking brilliance. Augustine's conversion scene is famous, his prayers less so. I was gripped by them. My favorite is a prayer called "What Do I Love When I Love My God?"

> It is not physical beauty nor temporal glory nor the brightness of light dear to earthly eyes, nor the sweet melodies of all kinds of songs, nor the gentle odor of flowers, and ointments and perfumes, nor manna or honey, nor limbs welcoming the embraces of the flesh; it is not these I love when I love my God. Yet there is a light I love, and a food, and a kind of embrace when I love my God—a light, voice, odor, food, embrace of my inner man, where my soul is floodlit by light which space cannot contain, where there is sound that time cannot seize, where there is a perfume which no breeze disperses, where there is a taste for food no amount of eating can lessen, where there is a bond of union that no satiety can part. That is what I love when I love my God.

Reading about Day and Augustine, I was encountering a sensation that millions of people would later encounter as they observed Pope Francis. Even if you have no faith at all, there is something moving about seeing a person who acts like Jesus. My heart and soul were clenched, but occasionally moral beauty loosened the grip.

I would say that in those days I was a friendly supporter of faith but had none. I was one of those people who endorsed religion in theory and thought it a good influence on other people, but I didn't believe in it myself. At most, I experienced religion as a useful collection of self-help hacks. For example, my first six months as a columnist for *The*

New York Times were the hardest months of my professional life. I had never been hated on a mass scale. The core theme of my email in-box was Paul Krugman is great. You suck. My critics were not only hostile but *effectively* hostile, hitting exactly those tender spots that made me feel insecure, floundering, and worthless. The only proper attitude, I discovered, is, Love your enemies. Treat them as people who are in their own strange way bringing you gifts. Any other attitude—hatred toward them or fear of them—is emotional suicide.

THE QUICKENING

Then came the events of the summer of 2013 and the suffering that entailed. My divorce happened. I was lonely, humiliated, adrift. I had a constant physical sensation of burning in my stomach and gut. I saw the world as if through some sort of muddy, distorted funhouse mirror—through the prism of my own pain and humiliation.

In seasons of suffering, you have a tendency to grip the steering wheel tighter, trying to redirect life, but sometimes you get defeated and just let go of the wheel. Strange things begin happening. "Healing means moving from *your* pain to *the* pain," Nouwen writes. "When you keep focusing on the specific circumstances of your pain, you easily become angry, resentful, and even vindictive. . . . But real healing comes from realizing that your own particular pain is a share of humanity's pain. . . . Every time you can shift your attention away from the external situation that caused your pain and focus on the pain of humanity in which you participate, your suffering becomes easier to bear."

The knowledge that we acquire through suffering can be articulated, but it can't really be understood by someone who did not endure the path it took to get there. I will say I did not come out of that pit with empty hands. Life had to beat me up a bit before I was tender enough to be touched. It had to break me a bit before I could be broken open. Suffering opened up the deepest sources of the self and exposed fresh soil for new growth.

And that's when it happened. I was sitting in my apartment one day when Jesus Christ floated through the wall, turned my water into wine, and commanded me to come follow him.

No, I'm kidding. Nothing like that happened at all. Though that sort of thing does seem to happen to other people, and I don't make light of it. But my experiences have all been more prosaic and less convincing. They came as stray moments of porousness. I was going about my normal day-to-day life when suddenly, for reasons I don't understand, some mystical intrusion pierced through, hinting at a deeper reality.

One morning, for example, I was getting off the subway in Penn Station in New York at rush hour. I was surrounded as always by thousands of people, silent, sullen, trudging to work in long lines. Normally in those circumstances you feel like just another ant leading a meaningless life in a meaningless universe. Normally the routineness of life dulls your capacity for wonder. But this time everything flipped, and I saw souls in all of them. It was like suddenly everything was illuminated, and I became aware of an infinite depth in each of these thousands of people. They were living souls. Suddenly it seemed like the most vivid part of reality was this: Souls waking up in the morning. Souls riding the train to work. Souls yearning for goodness. Souls wounded by earlier traumas. Souls in each and every person, illuminating them from the inside, haunting them, and occasionally enraptured within them, souls alive or numb in them; and with that came a feeling that I was connected by radio waves to all of them—some underlying soul of which we were all a piece.

I suddenly regarded the whole crowd with a kind of awe, a reverence, not from the depth of a particular morning but from the depth of centuries. If you think about that for a bit, you are confronted by the possibility that we are connected not just with the souls living now, but with the souls of all the people who have ever lived, from generation to generation, who are still present today because this underlying animating spirit is still and always omnipresent. And if there are souls, it's a short leap to the belief that there is something that breathed souls into us through an act of care and love. I remember that as quite a wonderful thought.

Rabbi Heschel says that awe is not an emotion; it is a way of under-standing. "Awe is itself an act of insight into a meaning greater than ourselves." And I find that these days I can't see people except as en-souled creatures. I can't do my job as a journalist unless I start with the premise that all people I write about have souls, and all the people I meet do, too. Events don't make sense without this fact. Behavior can't be explained unless you see people as yearning souls, hungry or full depending on the year, hour, or day.

That summer, I took my annual walk up to American Lake, which is at the top of a mountain near Aspen, Colorado. I was in a spiritual frame of mind that morning, and on the hike up the mountain I com-posed a list of all the things I would have to give up to God if He actu-ally existed: my work, my reputation, my friendships, my life, my loves, my family, my vices, my bank accounts.

I reached the lake, sat on a rock, and pulled out a book of Puritan prayers that I'd brought. Most of them are grim affairs, about human depravity and all that. Then I came upon one called "The Valley of Vision." The first line is "Lord, high and holy, meek and lowly." I looked at the spare and majestic mountain peaks in front of me. Just then a little brown creature who looked like a badger waddled up to the lake, not noticing me. He came within two feet of my sneaker before looking up, startled, and scrambling away. High and holy, meek and lowly.

The next sentence is "Thou hast brought me to the valley of vi-sion." Well, there I was in the bowl formed around that lake. "Where I live in the depths but see Thee in the heights." I was in all sorts of depths but could see mountaintops. "Hemmed in by mountains of sin I behold Thy glory." The rest of the text summarizes the whole inverse logic of faith: The broken heart is the healed heart. The contrite spirit is the rejoicing spirit. The repenting soul is the victorious soul. Life in my death. Joy in my sorrow. Grace in my sin. Riches in my poverty. Glory in my valley.

I had a sensation of things clicking into place, like the sound of a really nice car door gently closing. It was a sensation of deep harmony and membership, the kind Jayber Crow described on that bridge: that creation is a living thing, a good thing, that we are still being created and we are accepted in it. Knowledge crept across my skin. I didn't so much feel at one with nature. I had a sensation that there is an animating spirit underlying all creation. The universe bends toward our goodness.

I'd always heard that phrase "God is the ground of being"—that he's not a big guy in the sky with a beard but a caring moral presence that pervades all reality, a flowing love that gives life its warmth, existence its meaning. By the lake, I had the sensation that life is not just a random collection of molecules that happen to have come together in space. Our lives play out within a certain moral order. I sat there for a while and looked at the sloping hillsides surrounding the lake leading up to the mountain peaks. I imagined little moral dramas and clashes of armies—*Lord of the Rings* style—the forces of love and selfishness playing themselves out within this mountaintop basin. And all of it is held in the cupped hands of God. I wrote an account that day: "God really does tailor himself to you. For those of us with a sense of not belonging, of being sojourners, He gives membership, acceptance and participation." The hike down took about an hour and half and was marked by giddiness.

This was not a religious conversion. It wasn't moving from one thing to another. It felt more like deeper understanding. I understand those who cannot relate to this experience or who just see it as an emotional response to nature. I can report only how it felt and feels. It was and is a sensation of opening my eyes to see what was always there, seeing the presence of the sacred in the realities of the everyday. Like there's a play you've been watching all your life, and suddenly you realize that the play you are seeing onstage is not the only play that's going on. There's an underplay, with the same characters, but at a different level, with different logic and forces at work, and greater stakes. There's a worldly story to follow, as people move closer or further from their worldly ambitions. But there's also a sacred story to follow, as souls move closer or further from their home, which is God.

It's easy to not be aware of the underplay, but once you see it, it's hard to see the other play about worldly ambitions as the ultimate reality. The main story is the soul story.

Jonathan Haidt is a secular Jewish academic who studies moral sentiments. Early in his career he went to India to study. When he got there, he found that people experienced everyday reality in not just the normal dimensions, but also in a spiritual dimension. This other axis was a vertical axis. Everything you do can take you up toward purity or down toward pollution. Everything people in India ate, everything they said, everything they thought, and everything they did could move them up toward consecration or down toward degradation on this spiritual axis.

When Haidt returned to the United States, he missed being surrounded by people who felt the vertical spiritual dimension in everyday life. He began to think of the United States as "Flatland," a thinner realm. He found that he was still carrying around the Indian mentality, even though he was back home in Flatland. He felt disgust at the thought of wearing the shoes that he'd been marching around in all day in the sanctity of his own home, even into his very bedroom. He noticed a sudden shame in bringing certain books into the bathroom. He became more aware of his subtle feelings upon witnessing sleazy behavior, an awareness that people were somehow bringing themselves down, toward pollution and away from holiness. He was still seeing reality through all these gradations of purity and pollution.

After my hike up to American Lake, I realized I was a religious person. I became aware of this supernatural presence, which is God, permeating the physical world. Jews have a concept of *tzimtzum*, or contraction, to describe the way spiritual essences infuse the material world. Christians have a concept of incarnation: when divinity became incarnate on earth in the man. Through Jesus, Christians believe, the world of eternity stepped into time.

To be religious, as I understand it, is to perceive reality through a sacred lens, to feel that there are spiritual realities in physical, imminent things. Thomas Merton once wrote that "trying to solve the problem of God is like trying to see your own eyeballs." God is what you see and feel with and through.

Most of us carry this kind of proto-religious consciousness around with us as we go about our lives, even if we are not religious. We are

morally repulsed when terrorists decapitate a prisoner, not only because there has been a death, but because something sacred has been
insulted. A human body is not just a piece of meat; it is also a temple
with some ghost of the transcendent infused within it. Even when a
person is dead, the body still carries the residue of this spiritual presence and deserves dignified handling. This is why we feel elevated by
the Jewish ritual of taharah, when members of a synagogue tenderly
wash the body of a congregant who has died earlier that day.

The month after my American Lake hike, I was in Ireland, the
guest of a friend who had rented a large house, where he'd invited a
bunch of us to come stay. Our host and his friend, both elderly, spent
much of their days discussing politics and economics and monetary
policy. The host's wife was quiet, because she was suffering from Alzheimer's and her memory was going. One night, when we were in the
midst of our political discussion, she seemed particularly confused.
Her husband turned to look at me, and there were tears in his eyes. We
exchanged a long, powerful look that pierced down to something
deeper than just empathy and care. I suddenly saw whole dimensions
of experience deep in his eyes.

At one level we were a bunch of people talking monetary policy,
but at a deep, silent level, it was the whole underplay again: the immortal chords of love, bodies living and dying, souls seeking deep
gladness and spiritual peace, the whole thing animated by some mysterious life force, the patterns of life formed by and re-creating the
eternal stories.

"Wonder or radical amazement is the chief characteristic of the
religious man's attitude toward history and nature," Rabbi Heschel
writes in *God in Search of Man*. "One attitude is alien to his spirit: taking things for granted." There are holy sparks in every occasion and a
cosmic universe in every person.

I did not go on this spiritual journey alone. I consulted dozens of
people, seeking, in a rather pathetic and needy way, advice and counsel. The Jews, by and large, didn't know how to talk to me. Judaism
doesn't really have much of a tradition of entrance and exit. You are
born a member of the tribe and there's not an evangelical tradition.

Some of my inquiring emails to my Jewish friends went unanswered. I took my rabbi to lunch and told him of my joint Christian and Jewish background. He said he understood the beauty of the Christian story and was captivated by it himself. "Think of it!" he exulted. "The Lord Jesus Christ dying for our sins!" Thanks, Rabbi.

The Christians were all over me. Word of my spiritual wanderings spread, and before long dozens were praying for me. Loving friends flew in from Chicago and elsewhere to talk and minister. One friend began praying for me and my family and has sent me an encouraging text every Friday ever since. Some Christians crudely sought to woo me over as a sort of win for their team, and they were a destructive force. Most gave me books. I received about three hundred books about faith in those months, only one hundred of which were different copies of C. S. Lewis's *Mere Christianity*.

I had a few steady companions, including Stuart and Celia McAlpine, who lead a local church, and Jerry Root, a C. S. Lewis scholar. Then there was Anne Snyder, my researcher and colleague at the *Times*. I actually first gave Anne a job interview because she had gone from Andover, the prep school, to a Christian college, Wheaton. That struck me as an unusual step that probably required some courage. Then, as now, I try to hire people who have some progression on their résumé that doesn't make sense by the conventional logic of the meritocracy. I want to see that they believe in something bigger than the conventional definition of success.

Anne and I had worked together for three years, and I valued her work tremendously but barely noticed her as a person. We never went to lunch or had coffee, and I recall maybe one perfunctory performance review. I was an inept and absent colleague.

Anne was one of the researchers I worked with on my last book, *The Road to Character*, especially on the chapter on Dorothy Day. Around this time, we exchanged a series of memos on different chapters of the book, and through them I began to see how radically different the religious consciousness is from the secular one, how big and absurd the leap of faith really is. I was describing Day's spiritual journey as an effort to achieve superior goodness and understanding; Anne corrected me and argued that it is a willingness to surrender to a truth that is outside yourself. I was always writing as if Day were the prime mover. Anne helped me to see that in Day's eyes, God is the mover and Day is the one moved upon.

The core of that book was Rabbi Soloveitchik's distinction between the two sides of our nature, which he called "Adam the first" and "Adam the second," and which I called the résumé virtues and the eulogy virtues. I said that Adam I was about majesty and career, and Adam II, the spiritual side, was about the search for goodness and purpose. Anne would send me memos saying that my rendition of Adam II was too New Age, or too drenched in contemporary secular categories. Anne pointed out that Day didn't serve the poor because she wanted to find some purpose in her life so she could rest contentedly and be happy with herself. What Adam II really sought, she wrote, was devotion and obedience to "absolute truth, objective truth."

In these memos, Anne tried to usher me into a deeper understanding of Soloveitchik's worldview. She wrote: "By becoming aware of an external reality that demands one's loyalties and lays out a specific bounded path, Adam II ultimately does find fulfillment, but the goal is not to rest at the place of self-satisfaction. There is so much more, and beyond oneself. There is a truth to stake a life on. And the grasp of this truth will permeate everything. Staking a claim on it will cost."

In the early months of Day's conversion to Catholicism, she met some Catholic women who had agreed to hold off on sex until marriage. Day admired them lavishly, for their sacrifice and the dignity in that withholding. I was flummoxed. In my world, prohibitions on premarital sex had gone away with the Victorians. I was old-fashioned enough to believe that you should have sex only with someone you love, but sex is a form of communication, and it is appropriate to have sex with someone you are committed to, as a way of deepening and exploring that bond, and having fun.

Anne explained the orthodox Christian view. Day was not puritanical. She was an intensely sensual person who did not regard sex as something dirty. But, ultimately, she saw marriage as a sacred covenantal bond, a one-flesh creation, a mutual obedience to and movement toward God. Sex, too, is not just a physical coupling but a spiritual union, a way of giving your entire person entirely to another, a "whole life entrustment," an act of total and naked honesty, the consummation of two people's loving journey to become one.

Its place is thus within the covenant of marriage. In Day's view—and in Anne's as well—to have sex outside and before marriage is to cheapen and isolate it, to diminish the ultimate gift implied by the act. To reserve sex for marriage, that one-flesh creation, is to preserve the loftiness and true beauty of sex, to keep it from being dragged into the materialistic shallowness of the world.

I had been around orthodox believers, Jewish and Christian, at different times of my life, but I was not the sort of person who invited vulnerable conversations about faith, or much of anything else. So I didn't know what orthodox faith really involved, how much surrender to the vertical axis required, and how much it reoriented an entire life. I eventually learned that Anne was sensitive to all sorts of sins that I had never even considered, including impenitence, the failure to seek proper penance for your sins. She felt spiritually tarnished by things I took for granted—such as the consumerism of a luxury mall. I later came to see that she experiences different states of the soul at different times of the day, or at different times of her life. Sometimes, depending on what she is doing and what the circumstances are, she feels close to God, but other times far away.

As we worked on the book, I would sit in my little apartment and write these memos. Anne would write me back, and the correspondence became much of the spine for *The Road to Character*, especially the chapters on Day and Saint Augustine. The mesmerizing subject I kept dragging her back to was agency and grace. I am a product of the meritocratic culture. In that culture, you take control of your life by working hard and producing results. At some instinctive level I treated my journey to faith as a homework assignment: If I did all the reading and wrote the final papers, certainty would come. I sort of knew this was ridiculous, but it was how I was wired.

As work on the book progressed, I was captivated by Day and Augustine, and really wanted to understand faith as they experienced it.

Anne had suggested I read a book called *A Severe Mercy*, by Sheldon Vanauken, about a couple coming to faith in Oxford. I wrote a memo with fifteen questions about the book and faith generally. Anne answered each question as best she could. She never led me. She never intervened or tried to direct the process. She hung back. If I asked her a question she would answer it, but she would never get out in front of me. She demonstrated faith by letting God be in charge. And this is a crucial lesson for anybody in the middle of any sort of intellectual or spiritual journey: Don't try to lead or influence. Let them be led by that which is summoning them.

I was struggling with the concept of surrender and grace. I didn't like Martin Luther's idea that you can't be saved by works, but only by faith. I wanted to stake out a middle ground, which I called "participatory grace." You'd do some good things for your fellow human, and God would sort of meet you halfway.

Anne was having none of it:

> I want to reiterate that yes, grace is the central thing Christ offers, but that is the doorway. And it is to know him. I see lots of emphasis on striving in your note, and I appreciate its antidote to cheap grace. But the foundational fact is you cannot earn your way into a state of grace—this denies grace's power, and subverts its very definition. Grace must reach out to the broken and undeserving. It must reach out to those recognizing plainly, vulnerably, their own need and emptiness. It can only find welcome in those sitting still.

The name of my condition was pride. I was proud of who I had become. I had earned a certain identity and conception of myself by working hard and being pretty good at what I did. I found it easier to work all the time than to face the emptiness that was at the heart of my loneliness.

Pride of self comes in many forms. Among them is the pride of power, the illusion that you can gain enough worldly power to make yourself secure. This is the pride suffered by those who seek to control others or to dominate other nations. There is also intellectual pride, the pride suffered by those who try to organize life into one all-explaining ideology that allegedly explains away all mystery. Every form of fanaticism, Niebuhr says, is an attempt to cover over existential insecurity. Then there is moral pride, the ego's desire to escape moral insecurity by thinking it is better than other people, that it has earned its own salvation. In the grip of moral pride, we judge ourselves by a lax standard, which we surpass, and judge others by a strict standard and find them wanting. There is also religious pride. This is the pride that afflicts people who think religion involves following the moral codes and who think highly of themselves because they follow those codes. Such a person may pray every day, but his real concern is self. Is God listening to my prayers? Is God answering my requests? Is God granting me peace? Is everyone seeing my goodness, and am I being rewarded for my righteousness?

All pride is competitive. All pride contains a hint of malice. All pride is bloated and fragile, because the ego's attempts to establish security through power, money, status, intellect, and self-righteousness are never quite successful.

In the regular world, pride is often rewarded, but in the underplay of which I was becoming slowly aware, pride is the great tormentor and humility the great comfort. In *Crime and Punishment*, the protagonist, Raskolnikov, suffers from pride. He is seeking to master knowledge and morality. A character named Sonia stands for holiness. She is a young woman who lives with her father and stepmother in poverty. Her sisters and brothers were starving, and the family had nothing to sell. So Sonia sold her body. She became a prostitute to prevent her family members from starving. She became a social outcast and did things that were morally wrong.

If holiness was just following the rules, Sonia certainly broke the rules. But as Jaroslav Pelikan put it, "In Dostoyevsky's novel, this prostitute was a heroine, yes, a kind of saint. Raskolnikov knelt before her in recognition of the fact that she represented the suffering of all humanity. Sonia was a holy person, in spite of the fact—or perhaps because of the fact—that she was an immoral person." Those who see reality with a sacred lens see a great moral drama, a great true myth, and in this true myth the normal rules don't apply. In fact, they are reversed. The weak and the outcast are often closer to God than the great and the wise, because they are further from pride and self-sufficiency.

It was relatively easy to perceive God's presence up at American Lake. It was going to be a lot harder to actually practice a faith. I was always proud, striving, taking control. They don't make the eyes of needles big enough.

Anne was hanging back, for professional, moral, and spiritual reasons. She really did believe that Aslan was on the march, not her or me. I'd had many friends who were Christian, but now I was asking them a bit more about how they lived. I learned about the spiritual disciplines and concepts that formed their daily and annual routine—prayer journals, fasting, tithing, silent retreats, Bible study, accountability groups, healing prayer, constant direct contact with the poor, discussions of spiritual warfare, the presence or absence of God, genuine rage at God for those long stretches of absence. To me, corporate life meant working for a big company. For them, it meant worship in community.

Many people, as I say, sent me books. But the wisest sent me back to the story. If you want to have babies, make love. If you want to explore faith, read the Bible and pray. Religion is not theology, despite the tendency of bookish people to want to make it so. It is not sensation, despite the tendency of mystical people to want to make it so. It is betting your life that a myth is true. Billions of Jews, Muslims, Christians, and others have bet their whole lives—organized their lives and often surrendered their lives—on a supposition that a certain myth is true. It was necessary to return, again and again, to the biblical story.

So I kept going back to the stories, wondering if they were true, or, more precisely, letting the stories gradually sink into this deeper layer inside that was suddenly accessible. Walker Percy says that good fiction tells us what we know but don't quite know that we know. The Bible is like that, too.

Anne was not around for a lot of the journey. The first several months of my wandering were what Anne calls "the golden period." We exchanged memos and learned about each other. But there was not even a thought of romance. My private life was on its own separate track, which she knew little or nothing about. She had her beaus, whom she would vaguely mention and whom I referred to collectively as the Fellowship of Christian Athletes. Something much bigger was going on, and it was all engrossing. Our conversations were about cathedrals, not courtship.

As you can probably anticipate, the golden period did not last. By the fall of 2013, strong emotional feelings existed between us. I was in a tumultuous period of life, living alone in an apartment, desperately lonely, so the emotions hit me with force.

Two thoughts occurred simultaneously: We cared for each other deeply. And any possible relationship between us was doomed.

Anne is twenty-three years younger than me, a daunting age gap. Moreover, she had been my researcher for years when I was still in my first marriage. Though we knew there had been nothing romantic or wrong between us during this period, it didn't take a cynic to see how outsiders could tell our story. I'm a semi-public person, and it didn't take a communications genius to understand what that version of the story would do to her reputation. Nonetheless, by the fall of 2013, I was getting to the emotional place where I was ready to start dating again, and I wanted to try dating Anne. She balked, and asked friends and clergy for advice. She instituted a series of clean breaks—periods when we had no contact at all so she could step back and understand what was happening. Then, in late December, she moved away to Houston to take a job writing about the immigrant experience there. I moved my social life to New York, found a wonderful group of new friends, and eventually entered into a serious relationship with a deeply thoughtful woman there.

HANGING ON THE LIP

There is a Muslim saying, Whatever you think God is, He is not that. Some cosmologists say there are an infinite number of universes, and in one of them there's a person just like you sitting in a place just like the place you are sitting. That's a weird idea, but even that idea is not as weird and incomprehensible as God.

The hard part of faith, Kierkegaard wrote, is that it requires infinite surrender to something that is absurd. This requires infinite resignation. Kierkegaard used the story of Abraham and Isaac to illustrate the immensity of what God is asking. He asked Abraham to murder his own son. Abraham has to have so much faith in God that he's willing to disobey the logic of the world. You have to be willing to lose yourself, Kierkegaard emphasizes, denude yourself and renounce all the power you have earned over the course of your life.

Again and again, Kierkegaard describes what it feels like to hang on the lip of faith without being able to take this absurd leap. "For my part, I can very well describe the movements of faith, but I cannot make them. If one wants to learn how to swim, one can let oneself be suspended in a sling from the ceiling and very well go through the motions, but one is not swimming."

He continues: "I cannot make the movement of faith, I cannot shut my eyes and plunge confidently into the absurd; that is for me an impossibility, but I do not praise myself for it. I am convinced that God is love; this thought has for me a primordial lyrical validity. When it is present to me I am unspeakably happy; when it is absent I long for it more intensely than the lover for the object of his love. But I do not believe; this courage I lack."

Somehow, Kierkegaard argues, the room must be crossed, the leap into the absurd must be taken. Only the knight of infinite resignation captures the beloved. You can only find yourself by losing yourself. You have to surrender what you love in order to get it back better and more joyfully than before.

In his memoir, *A Severe Mercy*, Sheldon Vanauken describes how his wife, Davy, came to faith. All her adult life she had felt that religion was ridiculous. Then she encountered sin, fell in with Christian friends, read all sorts of Christian books, and faith "fell into her soul as the water of life." One day, she wrote in her journal, "Today, crossing from one side of the room to the other, I lumped together all that

I am, all I fear, hate, love, hope; and, well, Did it. I committed my ways to God in Christ."

A few nights later, Sheldon was sitting by the fire, staring into the coals, when he became aware of Davy on her knees praying beside him. She whispered to him: "Oh, my dearest—please believe!"

Moved almost to tears, he whispered back, "Oh, I believe." He was, he writes, "shaken by the affirmation that swept over him." But it didn't last. It was his love for his wife that made him say those words, not real belief. In fact, he came to resent the special goodness that came over Davy after she believed, even her goodness toward him. He wanted the old Davy back.

Sheldon's coming to faith was different. It didn't come as a sudden conviction and surrender. It was more intellectual. Instead of a full vision, he was eventually persuaded by arguments that God must exist. In these arguments, he perceived glimpses of the divine, but he would have to make a choice, without certainty. A deliberate conscious choice. "One can only choose a side. So I—I now choose my side; I choose beauty; I choose what I love. But choosing to believe *is* believing," he claimed. "It's all I can do: choose. I confess my doubts and ask my Lord Christ to enter my life. . . . I do but say: Lord, I believe—help Thou mine unbelief."

A religious commitment—like other commitments—is more like responding to a summons than it is like choosing which can of soup to buy in the supermarket. It's something you sort of control and sort of don't control. Nobody catches faith simply by running after it, but nobody catches faith without running after it in some way. I know a lot of people who would prefer to have religious faith, but they just don't. And I know others, no better and no worse, who do have faith, and perhaps sometimes wish they didn't.

I like Christian Wiman's description of coming to faith as assenting to a truth that was already latent within him. I like C. S. Lewis's description of faith as a loss of inhibition, an unshackling:

Without words and (I think) almost without images, a fact about myself was somehow presented to me. I became aware that I was holding something at bay, or shutting something out. Or, if you like, that I was wearing some stiff clothing, like corsets, or even a suit of armor, as if I were a lobster. I felt myself being, there and then, given a free choice. I could open the door or keep it shut; I could unbuckle the armor or keep it on. . . . The choice appeared to be momentous but it was also strangely unemotional. . . . I say, "I chose," yet it did not really seem possible to do the opposite. . . .

Then came the repercussion on the imaginative level. I felt as if I were a man of snow at long last beginning to melt. The melting was starting in my back—drip-drip and presently trickle-trickle. I rather disliked the feeling.

The best way I've heard to describe my own moment of decision is this: Imagine you are riding in a train. You're in your seat, reading a book or staring at your phone. There are people around you doing all the normal things. On the surface everything seems the same. But all the while you have been traveling across miles of country. Suddenly it occurs to you, with no great surprise but simply an obvious recognition, that you are very far from the station where you started. There's a lot of ground behind you. Moreover, at some point in the journey you crossed over a border. There was no customs officer and no great fanfare. You realize that while God is still a big mystery, you don't not believe in him. You're not an atheist. You're not even an agnostic. You're not going to live without the biblical metaphysic. You've crossed into a different country, and the myths feel true.

It's fair to ask, Did I convert? Did I leave Judaism and become a Christian? The first thing to say is that while these categories are very much opposites in the world, in history, and in the minds of pretty much everybody I know, they have never been big opposites in my life. I've had both stories running through my life since I was four, and nothing is different now. I feel more Jewish than ever before. I was always and will always be culturally Jewish, but now I feel religiously Jewish. God's covenant with the Jewish people is a real thing. When

I'm at Jewish events, as I often am, my heart swells and I feel at home. I love the faith more now than before. If Jews don't want me as a Jew, they're going to have to kick me out.

On the other hand, I can't unread Matthew. The beatitudes are the moral sublime, the source of awe, the moral purity that takes your breath away and toward which everything points. In the beatitudes we see the ultimate road map for our lives. There are a lot of miracles in the Bible, but the most astounding one is the existence of that short sermon.

As Cynthia Bourgeault summarizes it: "Our only truly essential human task here, Jesus teaches, is to grow beyond the survival in-stincts of the animal brain and the egoic operating system into the kenotic joy and generosity of full human personhood. His mission was to show us how to do this."

Jesus is the person who shows us what giving yourself away looks like. He did not show mercy; he is mercy. He did not offer perfect love; he is perfect love. As the Catholic intellectual Romano Guardini writes, "In the Beatitudes something of the celestial grandeur breaks through. They are no mere formulas for superior ethics, but tidings of sacred and supreme reality's entry into the world." Those accounts do feel like a completion to me. Which brings me to the crucial question: Do I believe in the resurrection of Jesus Christ? Do I believe his body was gone from the tomb three days after the crucifixion? The simple, brutally honest answer is, It comes and goes. The border stalker in me is still strong.

The fuller answer is that the way I experience faith is not a block of concrete. Faith is change. Faith is here one moment gone the next, a stream that evaporates. At least for me. The novelist Frederick Buechner once observed that if he were asked what faith is, "it's exactly the journey through space and time I'd talk about, the ups and downs over the years, the dreams, the odd moment, the intuitions. . . . Faith is homesickness. Faith is a lump in the throat. Faith is less a position on than a movement toward, less a sure thing than a hunch. Faith is waiting."

I have to confess I don't really resonate with most religious people I meet. I don't want to use my doubts as a badge of honor to make me seem more reasonable or sophisticated before the world. I fully acknowledge that these doubts probably grow out of my own insufficiency, the years of living life on the upper level of the play. I will just say I don't experience faith the way some people do, for whom God is as real as the table in front of you. For them, faith is wholehearted. They are in it with all their soul. In *Varieties of Religious Experience*, William James quotes a woman who can't imagine dallying with doubt and all this head scratching. "The very instant I heard my Father's cry calling unto me, my heart bounded in recognition. I ran, I stretched forth my arms, I cried aloud, 'Here, here I am, my Father.'" There's something beautiful in that singleness of heart.

But I come at faith from a different angle, based on a different journey, in ways that are undoubtedly connected to my makeup and personality. I connect more with a smaller group of people who struggle with faith, who wrestle with all the ridiculous unlikelihood of faith. I experienced grace before I experienced God, and sometimes I still have trouble getting back to the source. But I find that as long as there are five or ten people in your life whose faith seems gritty and real and like your own, that keeps the whole thing compelling. All you need is a minion of Christians and Jews.

RELIGIOUS REALISM

For these religious realists, there is the struggle to be faithful to faith itself. For these people, faith comes as an expansion of consciousness that doesn't last. You become aware of an extra dimension of existence, that, once experienced, feels like home, and then it's gone. As the poet Richard Wilbur put it:

> *Joy's trick is to supply*
> *Dry lips with what can cool and slake,*
> *Leaving them dumbstruck also with an ache*
> *Nothing can satisfy.*

Faith is not so much living constantly in that extra dimension of depth as much as it is glimpsing it and then longing for it. People in this camp describe faith not as a steady understanding but as a kind of desire, or maybe as a kind of hunch. It is not so much knowing God in all his particulars but a constant motion toward something that half the time you don't even feel.

In this kind of faith, the mystery is always out front. "Lord, I can approach you only by means of my consciousness, but consciousness can only approach you as an object, which you are not," Wiman writes. "I have no hope of experiencing you as I experience the world—directly, immediately—yet I want nothing more. Indeed, so great is my hunger for you—or is this evidence of your hunger for me?—that I seem to see you in the black flower mourners make beside a grave I do not know . . . in the bare abundance of a winter tree whose every limb is lit and fraught with snow. Lord, Lord, how bright the abyss inside that 'seem.'"

Water metaphors abound in religious talk because there is so much thirsting. God is said to be the stream of living water for which we pant, the way a deer pants for water in a brook. Faith is said to be a sip that arouses a thirst.

If you read the accounts of faith by even the most profound believers, you see there are dry spells, agonies, and moments of profound challenge. Rabbi Joseph Soloveitchik notes that "Religion is not, at the outset, a refuge of grace and mercy for the despondent and desperate, an enchanted stream for crushed spirits, but a raging, clamorous torrent of man's consciousness with all its crises, pangs and torments." It is precisely the journey down these rocky rapids that purges faith of its superficiality, Soloveitchik argues. It's not easy and comforting. As Wiman puts it, if God is supposed to be a salve to heal psychic wounds or an escape from the pains of life, "then I have to admit: *it is not working for me.*"

Mother Teresa had an intense experience of faith on September 10, 1946, while on a train. She experienced God's love as the "thirst of Jesus' heart, hidden in the poor." But as early as 1953, and all the way until at least 1995, she seems to have lost contact with God. In her private letters she confesses, "I have no faith. . . . I am told God loves me. . . . Nothing touches my soul." She talked of "an empty place . . .

in my heart there is no faith." She felt a "terrible pain of loss—of God not wanting me—God not being God—of God not really existing." Decade after decade, the darkness lasted, even as she continued in her service. But decade after decade, the longing for faith lasted. In fact, the longing seemed to get stronger as the darkness grew deeper. "I talk of you [Jesus] for hours—of my longing for You." Through all this time, she kept opening houses for the poor, serving the poor, and suffering for them.

During these years her interior life was marked by, as one of my students, Daniel Gordon, put it, "longing in absence." In 1961, an Austrian Jesuit, the Reverend Joseph Neuner, told her she was experiencing the dark night that all spiritual masters must endure, and that the only response was even more total surrender. For reasons that are hard to understand, the lesson hit Mother Teresa with tremendous force. "For the first time in 11 years—I have come to love the darkness," she wrote. According to a biographer, her darkness came from a deep identification with those she served. The poor endured the feeling of being unwanted. She now was called to take on and share their burden. She wrote that "even in darkness the path is sure." She continued, "I just have the joy of having nothing—not even the reality of the presence of God."

As Gordon writes, meaning can be found by the attitude one takes toward unavoidable suffering. Once Mother Teresa understood the meaning of her suffering, it began to feel like a kind of mission. Her faith was not a balm to her; it was often a dark sadness, but she kept her commitment to her faith even after it left her, and enduring this darkness and sharing in the suffering of the poor put her in membership with Jesus.

In other words, a commitment to faith is a commitment to stick with it through all the various seasons of faith and even those moments when faith is absent. To commit to faith is to commit to the long series of ups and downs, to intuitions, learning and forgetting, knowing one sort of God when you're twenty-five and a very different God at thirty-five, fifty-five, and seventy-five. It means riding out when life reveals itself in new ways and faith has to be reformulated once again. To commit to faith is to commit to change. It includes moments of despair, or it is not faith.

By the time he was twenty-seven, Frederick Buechner already had two published novels under his belt. He moved to New York to try writing full-time, but it did not go well. He grew depressed and thought about other careers—maybe advertising. For no clear reason, he began attending a Presbyterian church on Madison Avenue, even though he found that most clergy preach out of their shallows, not their depths. One day, he listened to a sermon comparing the coronations of Queen Elizabeth and Jesus. The preacher said that Jesus was not crowned amid splendor, but "among confession and tears and great laughter."

Buechner writes that at the sound of the phrase "and great laughter," "for reasons I have never satisfactorily understood, the great wall of China crumbled and Atlantis rose up out of the sea, and on Madison Avenue, at 73rd Street, tears leapt from my eyes as though I had been struck across the face."

Buechner came to experience faith as a quest for what he has called a subterranean presence of grace in the world. He came to experience it as a vague sense that life isn't just a bunch of atoms haphazardly bouncing against one another, but a novel with a plot that leads somewhere.

Later in life, Buechner found himself amid young Christians who spoke confidently about God as if they talked to Him all the time, and He talked back. God told them to pursue this job and not that one, and to order this at the restaurant and not that. He was dumbstruck. He wrote that if you say you hear God talking to you every day on every subject, you are either trying to pull the wool over your own eyes or everybody else's.

Instead, he continues, you should wake up in your bed and ask, "Can I believe it all again today?" Or, better yet, ask yourself that question after you've scanned the morning news and seen all the atrocities that get committed. If your answer to that question of belief is "yes" every single day, then you probably don't know what believing in God really means, Buechner writes. "At least five times out of ten the answer should be No because the No is as important as the Yes, maybe more so. The No is what proves you're human in case you should ever doubt it. And then if some morning the answer happens to be really Yes, it should be a Yes that's choked with confession and tears and . . . great laughter."

Commitment to faith, then, is persistence to faith through doubt; it is persistence in faith through suffering and anxiety; it is persistence in faith through struggle and persistence in faith through all the idiots and immoral cretins who speak for faith. It is persistence in faith despite the occasional idiocy of the synagogues, mosques, or churches that are supposed to be the homes of faith. "The church is both my greatest intellectual and moral problem and my most consoling home. She is both pathetic whore and frequent bride," the Franciscan monk Richard Rohr writes. And still faith is the center and joy of his life.

The Exodus is the journey, and the beatitudes and the love that died for us are the sublime beauty to which it all points. I persist toward that point, through all the ups and downs. At some point I began to realize I've inherited a narrative, and I don't want to live a life that isn't oriented toward that sublime beauty. I can't control when I believe or when I don't believe. I can only be faithful to the living stories and to persist in the bet that the sublime is real. At some point I realized that the train of life had taken me into a different country. I believe. I am a religious person. The Bible, open to an infinity of interpretations, is the ground of truth.

What I've really tried to describe here is something we don't talk about in the newspapers—how the process of inner transformation happens. One doesn't really notice it day by day, but when I look back at who I was five years ago it's kind of amazing, as I bet it is for you in your journey. It's a change in the quality of awareness. It's a gradual process of acquiring a new body of knowledge that slowly, slowly gets stored in the center of your being. Cynthia Bourgeault writes that the Kingdom of Heaven is not a place you go to; it's a place you come from. It's a transformed way of looking at the world, which comes about when you move more deeply into God and God moves more deeply into you.

And what you end up with is this grand sense of connection, the sense of metaphysical singleness. There is no such thing as an egoistic self that is separated from everyone and everything else. That's the illusion of modernity. The best part of having taken a weird, strange trip over the past five years of my life is that it reminds me of the possibility that I might take another weird, strange trip over the next five or ten or twenty. So nothing is dismissed as too outrageous. When you've tied yourself to a spirit you can't comprehend, nothing shocks you anymore, but everything brings you into a state of awe and wonder.

TWENTY-TWO

Ramps and Walls

Now I just had to figure out how to live out this commitment. How do religious people live? By now you can probably figure out what part of faith would be hard for me—the blind surrender part. There's a lot of talk, especially in Christianity, about dying to self, surrendering everything to God, taking your hands off the wheel and letting God drive. There's a lot of talk about the utter depravity of mankind, the supposed opposition between spirit and flesh. I used to think that being religious meant that you admit that God is in control of your life, and you surrender to whatever it is God tells you to do. And I can see why I used to think that. There's a lot of talk in all religions that gives you the impression that God demands an absence of agency. God is master, and you are servant.

Fortunately, that kind of blind obedience or total self-erasure doesn't seem to be what God wants. It's certainly true that the will is problematic. It is self-centered. It tends to see all of human existence as something that surrounds me, as something in front of me, beside me, and behind me. There's a selfishness inherent in the normal human perspective.

The will is also narcissistic. As C. S. Lewis observes, every second thought we have seems to be about the self. If you are not thinking about whether you are cold or hot, or hungry or stuffed, you're rehearsing the clever thing you're about to say, or feeling angry about the way some other person didn't treat you right. Even when you do something really humble and good, the self turns around and admires itself for being humble and good.

The will is also voracious. Your will wants popularity and is never satisfied. The great sins come from excessive worship of self and callousness about others: covetousness, injustice, prejudice, greed, dishonesty, arrogance, and cruelty.

"The moment I begin exercising my will, I find that I have put a fox in charge of the chicken coop," the late theologian Eugene Peterson wrote. "My will is my glory; it is also what gives me the most trouble." If you make yourself, as William Ernest Henley's poem "Invictus" put it, "master of my fate . . . captain of my soul," you are headed for the rocks.

But God doesn't seem to want the elimination of the will; He seems to want the training and transformation of it. He doesn't want a lack of will, but a merger between the will of the person and the will of God. Peterson described it this way: When he was a boy he was allowed to work in his father's butcher shop. He started out sweeping the floors and then graduated to grinding hamburger. Then, when he got older, he was handed a knife. "That knife has a will of its own," one of the other butchers told him. "Get to know your knife."

Peterson also found that "a beef carcass has a will of its own—it's not just an inert mass of meat and gristle and bone, but has character and joints, texture and grain. Carving a quarter of beef into roasts and steaks was not a matter of imposing my knife-fortified will on dumb matter but respectfully and reverently entering into the reality of the material."

Hackers—bad butchers—tried to impose their will on the beef. The results were ugly and wasteful. But good butchers learned to cut in response to the beef. They worked with a humility before the materials in front of them.

A believer approaches God with a humble reverence and comes, through study and prayer and the spiritual disciplines, to get a feel for the grain of God's love. She gradually learns to live along the grain of God's love and not against the grain. It is not a willful attempt to dominate life, nor is it complete surrender and self-annihilation. It is an enthusiastic response. It is participation, the complex participation of a person's will into God's larger will.

It is, as Peterson put it, not trying to live in the active voice, which is domination, nor in the passive voice, which is submission, but in the middle voice, which is conversation and response: "We do not abandon ourselves to the stream of grace and drown in an ocean of love, losing identity. We do not pull the strings that activate God's operations in our lives, subjecting God to our assertive identity. We neither manipulate God (active voice) nor are manipulated by God (passive voice). We are involved in the action and participate in its results but do not control or define it (middle voice). Prayer takes place in the middle voice."

Faith and grace are not about losing agency. They are about strengthening and empowering agency while transforming it. When grace floods in, it gives us better things to desire and more power to desire them. When people talk about dying to self, they are really talking about dying to old desires and coming alive to a new and better set of desires. When I was a boy I loved Kool-Aid, a desire that has no appeal to me now. Now I prefer coffee and wine, desires that had no appeal to me then. When I began my career I really wanted to be famous and get invited into the inner rings. Now I have more fame than I really want, and I've seen so much of the inner rings that they have lost their charm.

The love of God and the participation with God's love represent an overthrow of the ego but not a weakening of the self. Gerald May distinguishes between willfulness and willingness: Willfulness is the desire to be captain of your own ship. Willingness is the desire to answer a call with a strong response.

The religious life is not just abstract thinking and feeling. It involves concrete practices, being with actual people, entering actual community. I began to think of my religious journey as the Walk to Chartres. I was on a journey toward God, and I found out pretty quickly along the way that religious people and institutions sometimes built ramps that made it easier to continue my journey, or they built walls, making the journey harder. I found that many of the walls in the Christian world were caused by the combination of an intellectual inferiority complex combined with a spiritual superiority complex. I found that Christians, especially of the Protestant evangelical variety, are plagued by the sensation that they are not quite as intellectually rigorous or as cool as the secular world. At the same time, many of them are inflated by the notion that they are a quantum leap or two more moral.

This combination can lead, for example, to the first wall: the siege mentality. Many Christians notice that there are widening gaps between their values and secular values, especially on matters of sexuality. This can slip quickly into a sense of collective victimhood. The "culture" is out to get us. We have to withdraw into the purity of our enclave. The odd thing is that the siege mentality feels kind of good to the people who grab on to it. It gives people a straightforward way to interpret the world—the noble us versus the powerful and sinful them. We have the innocence of victimhood.

Pretty soon Christianity isn't a humble faith; it's a fighting brigade in the culture war. "Evangelical" stops being an adjective and turns into a noun, a tribe. Pretty soon the ends justify the means—anything to defend the tribe. Pretty soon you get these wild generalizations about the supposed hostility of the outside world. (Every time a pastor begins a sentence with the phrase "The culture," he should interrupt himself and lie down and take a nap). Pretty soon you wind up with what Rabbi Sacks calls "pathological dualism," a mentality that divides the world between those who are unimpeachably good and those who are irredeemably bad.

The second wall is the wall of bad listening. There are a certain number of religious people who come into each conversation armed with a set of off-the-shelf maxims and bumper-sticker sayings. Instead of actually listening to the questions from the people in front of them, they just unfurl the maxims regardless of circumstances.

The third wall is the wall of invasive care. Some people use the cover of faith to get in other people's business when they have not been asked. They tell themselves they are just showing compassion and care. They tell themselves that through prayer they have discerned something important in what's going on in another person's life, which is important for that other person to hear. But really they are just wandering into ground they know nothing about, and where they are not wanted, under the pretext that God wants them to be there.

The fourth wall is the wall of intellectual mediocrity. I teach at Yale. When Yale professors discuss one another's manuscripts, they are brutal. But they are brutal in search of excellence. Sometimes Christians are not brutal to one another. They want to be nice; they want to be affirming, and that softens all discussion. So the jewel of truth is not hardened. Vague words and mushy sentiments are tolerated because everybody wants to be kind. Several years ago, Mark Noll wrote a book called *The Scandal of the Evangelical Mind*—and with some notable exceptions the scandal is still ongoing.

Those are the walls. I also found ramps. The first ramp is the ramp of ritual. Religion is filled with lighting candles, bowing down, standing up, processions, and the rest. These habits are collective enactments of the moral order and a sacred story. They are reminders of certain lessons and truths. In the Torah, the lighting of candles is co-ordinated with the burning of incense because in our lives the illumination of knowledge is connected with the experience of passion and the senses. We are not cold reasoners; we learn with passion.

As the sociologist Christian Smith put it, "Liturgy ritually reenacts a tradition, an experience, a history, a worldview. It expresses in dramatic and corporeal form a sacred belief system in words, music, imagery, aromas, tastes, and bodily movement. In liturgy, worshippers both perform and observe, act out truth and have the truth act on them, remember the past and carry it into the future." It's weirdly powerful to open your arms in worship; the small physical act opens up the mind and makes vulnerable the heart.

The second ramp is the ramp of unabashed faith. You almost never see unabashed faith at a conservative Jewish shul, but you often see it at an Orthodox one, men enclosed in their tallit, rocking and wailing away, giving themselves over to worship. Similarly, you almost never see unabashed faith at a mainline Protestant church, unless it's faith in the Sierra Club. But you do see it at charismatic churches, where the hands are up, the eyes are closed, the hallelujahs are at high decibel. Sure, there's a performance element. But there is something contagious about faith that is unafraid to express itself.

The third ramp is prayer. I'm not a good prayer myself. I often end up directing my words more to the person I'm with than to God. I unfortunately always perform literary criticism on my prayers, while I'm saying them and just after—ugh, that one was boring, that one sort of lost coherence at the end. In *Madame Bovary*, Flaubert writes that "human speech is like a cracked kettle on which we tap crude rhythms for bears to dance to, while we long to make music that will melt the stars." My prayers are like that.

But even a person who is just on the way can pray. Prayer is an encounter and conversation with God. The easiest prayers to say are prayers of thanksgiving, for a meal or some other good thing. Even these easy prayers are good prayers, because gratitude is a soil in which egotism tends not to grow.

Our conversations change depending on whom we are talking to. Talking to God is a confrontation with grace, which is not just His unmerited love, but the kind of love that flows most powerfully to the demerits of the one who is receiving it. The deeper prayers thus have a wonderful quality that are not like conversation with normal people. The emotional tone of that kind of prayer is hard to capture in prose. Many people point to George Herbert's poem:

> *Prayer the Churches banquet, Angels age,*
> *God's breath in man returning to his birth,*
> *The soul in paraphrase, heart in pilgrimage,*
>
> . . .
>
> *A kinde of tune, which all things heare and fear;*
> *Softnesse, and peace, and joy, and love, and blisse,*
> *Exalted Manna, gladnesse of the best,*

Heaven in ordinarie, man well drest,
The milkie way, the bird of Paradise.

Over time prayer reorients the desires. The very act of talking to God inclines a person in a certain way; you want to have a conversation appropriate to Him; you want to bend your desires to please and glorify Him. Just as old couples become more like each other over time, the person who spends years hearing and responding to God's company becomes more like Him, at the secret level, the places only God can see.

The fourth ramp is spiritual consciousness. We in the secular world tend to reduce everything to material cause and effect— economics, voting patterns, international relations. But that lens is constantly getting things wrong, because human beings are not just material creatures driven by narrowly defined economic and political self-interests.

When you are with the best of the faithful, no matter what you are talking about, you are having a richer conversation. Religious communities naturally talk about the whole person, the heart and soul as much as the body and mind. When religious communities minister to the poor, when religious colleges teach their students, they minister to and teach them as whole people, who need not just money but dignity, love, and purpose.

The fifth ramp is the language of good and evil. This language, too, has been largely abandoned in the public world. The word "sin" is now mostly used in reference to dessert. But if you want to talk about the deepest journey, you need words like "sin," "soul," "degradation," "redemption," "holiness," and "grace." If you want to have some conception of life on a vertical axis, you need some conception of the various gradations of goodness and badness. When you walk into the religious world and find even just a few people thinking and talking about these things subtly, intelligently, and carefully, it is tremendously powerful.

The final ramp is the sheer shock of it. Religion is a never-ending surprise. You never quite get comfortable with the idea that creation is alive, and that there is such a thing as universal love. And the biggest shock of all is the way some believers love. Why would Mother Teresa have spent those decades in the slums? Why would Thomas Merton have spent those decades in the monastery? Why would Dorothy Day spend those decades living a life of poverty, giving bread to the poor? Why would Dietrich Bonhoeffer have returned to Germany to resist Hitler—with a good chance that he would get killed in the fight, as indeed he did? Don't these people know there are beach vacations to be taken and nice restaurants to be experienced?

And these are just the famous people. One runs across such people all the time, who have upended their lives to work in hospitals and slums around the world on the belief that God has called them to this hard service.

The natural impulse in life is to move upward, to grow in wealth, power, success, standing. And yet all around the world you see people going downward. We don't often use the word "humbling" as a verb, but we should. All around the world there are people out there humbling for God. They are making themselves servants. They are on their knees, washing the feet of the needy, so to speak, putting themselves in situations where they are not the center; the invisible and the marginalized are at the center. They are offering forgiveness when it makes no sense, practicing a radical kindness that takes your breath away.

Recently there was a documentary about Fred Rogers, the Presbyterian minister who created a TV show on the supposition that the child is closer to God than the adult. Usually adults want to move toward sophistication as they age, but Rogers's show was all about simplicity—the simplicity of tying your shoe, the simplicity of declaring open love. Usually adulthood is about moving to assertiveness and self-sufficiency. But Rogers moved toward vulnerability and dependence. At one point the puppet who is the stand-in for Rogers's inner child sang a song with the lyric "Sometimes I wonder if I'm a mistake." Sometimes he wonders if he is badly made. Usually adulthood means moving from small to big—doing something big in the world—but Rogers wrote a song called "Little and Big" about the loveliness of the little good. Literally, in one show, the washing of feet together. Some people wondered if Rogers could really be that sincere and good. But the movie makes it clear that he was, and by the end everybody in the theater is unexpectedly crying. There is something surprising and powerful and overwhelming in that kind of inverse goodness.

As Augustine put it, "Where there's humility there is majesty; where there's weakness, there's might; where there is death, there's life. If you want to get these things don't disdain those." T. S. Eliot once captured the ideal of religious life: "A condition of complete simplicity / (Costing not less than everything)."

THE SUBLIME

Anne lived in Houston for over three years, and both our lives took many twists and turns while she was there. Then, bowing to a love that then seemed impossible and now seems inescapable, we got married in the spring of 2017, four years after the events described above. That part of the story has had a blissful conclusion.

I've found that being deliriously in love has been good and bad for my faith. In moments of rapturous love, love overflows. It flows from love of this particular woman upward toward a higher and more general love and eventually to the source of love. On the other hand, in my happiness I have left suffering behind, so I no longer have those deep, dark, smoldering spiritual crises I had when I was really in the dumps. (Good riddance.)

Still, the faith part is still radically incomplete. But to be incomplete in faith is not to be unsatisfied. "I prayed for wonder instead of happiness," Rabbi Heschel wrote "and you gave them to me." The Orthodox Jews say that religion is the consecration of the world, seeing the divine spark in everything.

"Astonished reverence" is the phrase people use to describe the presence of God in the world. Astonishment at the infinity of God. Astonishment that He cares for us. "God writes straight with crooked lines," Walker Percy writes. Astonishment at the weirdness. Jesus' first miracle was turning water into wine. Who starts a religion with a party trick?

I hope the journey of faith, thus far, has infused me with a bit more humility than I had before. I'm pretty sure it has infused me with more hope. Today, faith doesn't feel like faith in an old man with a white beard who is separating waters. It feels like faith in wider possibilities than I had imagined and living one's life in the shadow of those possibilities.

Reality shimmers. The person next to you on the subway is never just a body. My friend Emily Esfahani Smith, whom I've quoted a few times, once told me about a time she got in an argument with her husband. They made up, and afterward they went out together to run some errands and stopped at CVS. Emily was still feeling teary and worn out from the fight. As they were checking out, the clerk behind the register asked about their family, if they had kids, where they lived, and so on. At the end of their little conversation, he smiled at them and said, "You know, you two—you two are really good together." It was what she needed to hear at that moment—it was so compassionate and loving, an expression of grace. She had a thought she had never had before: "Wow, maybe angels do exist."

Throughout this book I've been talking about commitments as a series of promises we make to the world. But consider the possibility that a creature of infinite love has made a promise to us. Consider the possibility that we are the ones committed to, the objects of an infinite commitment, and that the commitment is to redeem us and bring us home. That is why religion is hope. I am a wandering Jew and a very confused Christian, but how quick is my pace, how open are my possibilities, and how vast are my hopes.

PART V

Community

The Stages of Community Building I

ONE DAY IN THE LATE 1950S, JANE JACOBS WAS LOOKING OUT HER second-story window at her Greenwich Village street below. She noticed a man struggling with a young girl. The girl went rigid, as if she didn't want to go wherever the man was leading her. The thought crossed Jacobs's mind that maybe she was witnessing a kidnapping. She was preparing to go downstairs to intervene when she noticed that the couple that owned the butcher shop had emerged from their store. Then the fruit man walked out from behind his stand, as did the locksmith, and a few people from the laundry. "That man did not know it, but he was surrounded," Jacobs wrote in *The Death and Life of Great American Cities*.

It turned out to be nothing, just a struggle between father and daughter. But from it, Jacobs drew the right conclusion: that safety on the street in a healthy neighborhood is not kept mostly by the police. It is kept by the "intricate, almost unconscious network of voluntary controls and standards among the people themselves, enforced by the people themselves."

Jacobs goes on to describe the streetscape on her block as an intricate ballet. The ballet starts early in the morning, at about the time Jacobs is taking out her garbage, and parents are taking their kids to school. It goes on through the afternoon, as the proprietors of the shops hang out in front, the postman walks by, and the longshoremen gather at the pub for a beer. Two lovers stroll along. "When I get home after work, the ballet is reaching its crescendo," Jacobs writes. "This is the time of roller skates and stilts and tricycles. . . . This is the time of bundles and packages, zigzagging from the drug store to the fruit stand and back."

It seems frenetic and haphazard, but, Jacobs argues, there is actually a dynamic, organic order here. "Under the seeming disorder of the old city, wherever the old city is working successfully, is a marvelous order for maintaining the safety of the streets."

Jacobs was writing at a time when city planners such as Robert Moses were destroying these sorts of streetscapes. They saw them as old-fashioned and inefficient. Streets should be machines for moving cars, the new thinking went, so urban planners began building highways through neighborhoods, tearing down old tenements and brownstones, and putting up towering apartment blocks surrounded by empty plazas.

Jacobs wanted people to see the old neighborhood streetscapes differently, and to resist these dehumanizing plans. Today, at least in the world of urban planning, Jacobs has won her fight. Everybody now understands the value of dense, diverse streetscapes. But when it comes to the larger issue of what makes a community, which was Jacobs's real subject, the fight is still ongoing.

THE BEAUTIFUL COMMUNITY

A healthy community is a thick system of relationships. It is irregular, dynamic, organic, and personal. Neighbors show up to help out when your workload is heavy, and you show up when theirs is. In a rich community, people are up in one another's business, know each other's secrets, walk with each other in times of grief, and celebrate together in times of joy. In a rich community, people help raise one another's kids. In these kinds of communities, which were typical in all human history until the last sixty years or so, people extended to neighbors the sorts of devotion that today we extend only to family. Neighbors needed one another to flourish and survive—to harvest crops, to share in hard times.

A person enmeshed in a rich community will have a neighbor who helps her get a job interview when she is unemployed. A teenager feels isolated at home, but there's a neighbor whose door is open, so he hangs out there. In a rich community, there's often a "Miss Tompkins," a strong, older lady who seems to be around all the time, who tells teenagers when to turn down the music and tells little children to stop running near the cars, who holds people accountable and enforces community norms. Everybody sort of fears Miss Tompkins, but everybody loves her, too. She's the block mother, effectively the mayor here.

In these kinds of communities, the social pressure can be slightly overbearing, the intrusiveness sometimes hard to bear, but the discomfort is worth it because the care and benefits are so great.

When academics talk about this kind of community, they use the term "social capital." The term is not great. Sociologists sometimes try to borrow the prestige of economists by using hard, economics-sounding concepts. The phrase "social capital" suggests that the thing it measures is quantitative. But care is primarily qualitative. A community is healthy when relationships are felt deeply, when there are histories of trust, a shared sense of mutual belonging, norms of mutual commitment, habits of mutual assistance, and real affection from one heart and soul to another.

THE WAR WITHIN

Not long ago I met an Israeli couple who had moved to an affluent neighborhood in southern California. They told me about a frightening episode that had happened a few months before. The husband was away for work, and called one night to chat with his wife. After they hung up, she went to check in on their four-year-old boy. He wasn't in his bed. She frantically searched the house, unable to find him. She ran out to the pool to see if he had fallen in. He hadn't.

She bolted out of the house and ran up and down her block scream-ing his name at the top of her lungs. It was about 10 P.M. Lights were on in some of her neighbors' homes, but nobody came out to help. By now she was terrified. She ran back inside for one last search of the house and found her son in the family room. He had built a fort with cushions and was sleeping peacefully underneath it.

The next day, she was out walking, and a few of her neighbors po-litely asked her why she'd been screaming her son's name in the middle of the night. She looked at me with incredulity as she told this story. What sort of community is it where people don't help a mother find her son? In Israel, she said, the streets would have been flooded with people in their pajamas frantically searching.

We're not living in Jane Jacobs's America anymore.

That story took place in a neighborhood that has every advantage. In communities across the Western world, the tearing of the social fabric is much worse. Robert Putnam, Theda Skocpol, Charles Mur-ray, Marc Dunkelman, and many others have thoroughly recorded the fragmentation of the social fabric, and I don't need to repeat their work here. I would just refer back to the carnage that results from all this social isolation.

The suicide epidemic is one manifestation of this isolation. The shortened life expectancy is another—the so-called deaths of despair. The contagion of mass shootings are a manifestation as well. These mass killings are about many things—guns, demagoguery, and the rest—but they are also about social isolation and the spreading de-rangement of the American mind. Whenever there's a shooting, there's always a lonely man who fell through the cracks of society, who lived a life of solitary disappointment and who one day decided to try to make a blood-drenched leap from insignificance to infamy. Guys like that are drawn to extremist ideologies that explain their disappointments and give them a sense that they are connected to something. They convince themselves that by massacring the innocents they are serv-ing as a warrior in some righteous cause.

The rising levels of depression and mental health issues are yet another manifestation. People used to say that depression and other mental health challenges were primarily about chemical imbalances in the brain. But as Johann Hari argues in his book *Lost Connections*, these mental health issues are at least as much about problems in life—protracted loneliness, loss of meaningful work, feeling pressured and stressed in the absence of community—as they are about one's neuro-chemistry.

"Protracted loneliness causes you to shut down socially, and to be more suspicious of any social contact," Hari writes. "You become hy-pervigilant. You start to be more likely to take offense where none was intended, and to be afraid of strangers. You start to be afraid of the very thing you need most."

This sounds like a pretty good summary of American politics today—and so, yes, polarization is a product of social isolation, too.

The foundational layer of American society—the network of rela-tionships and commitments and trust that the state and the market and everything else relies upon—is failing. And the results are as bloody as any war.

Maybe it's time we began to see this as a war. On the one side are those forces that sow division, discord, and isolation. On the other side are all those forces in society that nurture attachment, connection, and solidarity. It's as if we're witnessing this vast showdown between the social rippers and social weavers.

And here's the hard part of the war: It's not between one group of good people and another group of bad people. The war runs down the middle of every heart. Most of us are part of the problem we complain about.

Most of us have bought into a radical individualism that, as Tocqueville predicted, causes us to see ourselves as self-sufficient monads and cuts each secluded self off from other secluded selves. Most of us buy into a workaholic ethos that leaves us with little time for community. Those of us in the media know that the way to gener-ate page views is to offer *Pravda*-like affirmations of your tribe's moral superiority. Most of us hew to a code of privacy that leads us to not know our neighbors. Most of us live with technology that aims to re-duce the friction in any encounter, and you get used to that mode of living. But community life—care for one another—is built on friction, on sticky and inefficient relationships.

Community is also under assault because we've outsourced care. As Peter Block and John McKnight argue in their book, *The Abundant Community*, a lot of the roles that used to be done in community have migrated to the marketplace or the state. Mental well-being is now the job of the therapist. Physical health is now the job of the hospital. Education is the job of the school system.

The problem with systems, Block and McKnight argue, is that they depersonalize. These organizations have to operate at scale, so everything has to be standardized. Everything has to follow rules. "The purpose of management is to create a world that is repeatable," they write. But people are never the same.

When there is a loss of care, a neighborhood becomes fragile and so do the people in it. The people are still there but the fluid of trust in which they were suspended has been drained away. If things go bad they have fewer people to turn to. If they yearn for a sense of belonging, which we all do, it's not clear where they can find it. From the outside, neighborhoods like that one in southern California may look the same as healthy communities, but the emotional quality is transformed. Care has been replaced by distance and distrust.

So how is community restored? Basically, it's restored by people who are living on the second mountain, people whose ultimate loyalty is to others and not themselves. Earlier in the book I mentioned Weave: The Social Fabric Project, the group I cofounded at the Aspen Institute. As I write, we've spent a year talking with people who have put relationship building at the center of their lives. Building a community, like building a relationship, is a slow, complex process. It's a lot of things coming together, like Jane Jacobs's ballet. I'd like to walk you through the stages of community creation, which are a bit like the stages of intimacy, but on a larger scale and with more moving pieces.

THE ONES WHO STICK

Community renewal begins, as you can imagine, with a commitment. Somebody decides to put community over self. For example, Asiaha

Butler grew up in Englewood, one of the poorer and most violent neighborhoods in Chicago. Asiaha (pronounced Eye-sha) was robbed there. Gangs controlled the block, and there were killings outside her door from time to time. One night a bullet flew through her front window. There was no decent local school where she and her husband could send their nine-year-old daughter. Eventually they'd had enough. They decided to move to Atlanta, where the streets were safer.

They threw a farewell barbecue for their friends and began packing up their things. It was a Sunday, and Asiaha happened to be looking out her front window at the vacant lot across the street. There are roughly five thousand vacant lots in the neighborhood. In this one some little girls were playing, throwing rocks and broken bottles and playing with abandoned tires in the mud. She turned to her husband and said, "We can't leave that."

Her husband was incredulous. "Oh? Really, Asiaha?"

"If we move, it will be like everyone else who moves. We're not going to be here to show an example of what it's like to have jobs, to raise a family." Asiaha won the argument. They decided to stay. To commit to the neighborhood.

Asiaha didn't know where to start. She didn't know her neighbors. So she Googled "Volunteer in Englewood" and found some neighborhood groups. One of them put her on its education committee. Another local group arranged parties for teens, but adult organizers were in their fifties and sixties and had no idea how to keep teenagers entertained. Asiaha spiced things up with hip-hop and spoken word. Then she realized that she could get neighbors talking if she prompted them with movies, so she set up "Docs and Dialogues." She invited people to get together to watch short documentaries and then have discussions afterward. Within two years, hundreds of people were involved.

Englewood was divided into six wards and had no organization that covered the whole area, so Asiaha created Resident Association of Greater Englewood (RAGE). RAGE holds job fairs and candidate forums at election time. It organizes "cash bombs," where local people gather to shop at locally owned stores. People came out of the woodwork for RAGE—graphic designers, executives, people who can bake and bring cookies. None of this work is heroic or even unusual. Now people know one another. Local shops sell WE ARE ENGLEWOOD and DAUGHTER OF ENGLEWOOD T-shirts. "I love small victories," Asiaha says. It starts with that decision to commit.

THE NEIGHBORHOOD IS THE UNIT OF CHANGE

The next stage of community building is understanding that you have to fix the neighborhood as a whole. It's not sufficient to focus on individuals one by one.

You've probably heard the starfish story. There's a boy on the beach who finds thousands of starfish washed ashore, dying. He picks one up and throws it back into the ocean. A passerby asks him why he bothered. All these thousands of other starfish are still going to die. "Well," the boy responds, "I saved that one."

Many of our social programs are based on that theory of social change. We try to save people one at a time. We pick a promising kid in a neighborhood and give her a scholarship so she can go to an Ivy League school. Social programs and philanthropic efforts skim cream in a thousand ways. They assume that the individual is the most important unit of social change.

Obviously, it's possible to do some good on an individual basis. But with this approach you're not really changing the moral ecologies, or the structures and systems that shape lives.

Maybe the pool story is a better metaphor than the starfish story. As a friend of mine puts it, you can't clean only the part of the pool you are swimming in. You can't just polish one molecule of water and throw it back in the dirty pool.

Rebuilding community involves seeing that the neighborhood, not the individual, is the essential unit of social change. If you're trying to improve lives, you have to think about changing many elements of a single neighborhood all at once.

One of the signature facts of the Internet age is that distance is not dead. Place matters as much as ever, and much more than we ever knew. The average American lives eighteen miles from his or her mother. The typical college student enrolls in a college fifteen miles from home. A study of Facebook friends nationwide found that 63 percent of the people we friend live within one hundred miles. Americans move less these days, not more.

Within the reasonably small radius of our lives, behavior is highly contagious. Suicide, obesity, and social mobility happen in networks as people subtly shape one another's behavior in ways that are beneath the level of consciousness. The work by economist Raj Chetty and others shows that children who grow up in one neighborhood are likely to have different life outcomes than people who grow up in demographically similar neighborhoods nearby. For example, on April 1, 2010, 44 percent of the low-income black men from the Watts neighborhood of central Los Angeles were incarcerated. On the other hand, just 6.2 percent of the men who grew up with similar incomes in the Compton neighborhood were incarcerated on that day. Compton is just 2.3 miles from Watts.

The work by sociologist Eric Klinenberg shows just how important neighborhood is in determining who will survive in a crisis. Klinenberg compared deaths in two Chicago neighborhoods during a heat wave in 1995. More than six times as many people died in North Lawndale as in South Lawndale, even though the two places are demographically comparable and separated by nothing more than a road.

Klinenberg discovered that the key ingredient was the thickness of community bonds. There were more places to meet in one neighborhood than the other, more places for people to establish relationships, and people who are in dense relationships check in on one another in times of crisis. You wouldn't necessarily think that the presence of a neighborhood library would have a big effect on who dies in a heat wave, but it does.

Thinking in neighborhood terms requires a radical realignment in how you see power structures. Does the neighborhood control its own public services? Do neighbors have street fairs where they can get to know one another? Are there forums where the neighborhood can tell its collective story?

Thinking in neighborhood terms means a radical transformation in how change is done. It means you pick a geographic area and throw in everything and the kitchen sink all at once: school reforms, early childhood education, sports and arts programs, and so on. An infinity of positive influences subtly reinforce one another in infinitely complex ways. It means doing away with the way philanthropy is done now, in which one donor funds one program that tries to isolate one leverage point to have "impact." Thinking in neighborhood terms brings home the reality that there is never a silver bullet.

A TECHNOLOGY FOR CONVENING

After you've realized that the neighborhood is the unit of change, it's necessary to find some way to bring the neighborhood together—to replace distance with intimacy and connection.

The third stage of commitment to a community involves inventing a technology for gathering. It means coming up with some method to bring people together and nudge them toward intimacy and trust.

As Peter Block notes in his book *Community*, leaders initiate social change when they shift the context within which people gather. It means inviting new people into the circle, especially people you might have earlier identified as "the problem." It means naming the conversation with powerful questions and then listening to the answers.

Power is created out of nothing when invitations are issued and new people gather and act in new ways. "The future is created one room at a time, one gathering at a time," Block writes. "Each gathering needs to become an example of the future we want to create." In these conversations, people who have been on the margins of society bear special gifts, an outsider's sensitivity to the way things are, a greater awareness of others.

In 2016, Dottie Fromal visited Nelsonville, Ohio, to see some friends. She'd walk down the streets from her friend's house and people would call out to her from their porches and want to tell her about their cat or something. "Some of these people don't have anyone to talk to all day long," she realized. She saw lonely, struggling kids hanging around the squares.

Somehow she never left Nelsonville. She started doing small

things for the people who seemed to need her help. She started knocking on doors and inviting people to community dinners on Thursday nights. It began as a way to feed the kids at the after-school program downtown, who didn't have any food at home. But pretty soon parents and adults started flocking—up to 125 people would show up. She had no funding stream or organization. She would just go to Kroger and buy the food herself. After a few months, as news of the dinners spread, people would stop her in the grocery aisles and hand her twenty-dollar bills, to help defray the costs. Her work is utterly ordinary—feeding hungry people dinner—but somehow nobody had done it before.

There are a zillion ways to do this. There are now hundreds of different dinner organizations that bring people together around tables of different sizes. "Don't let your neighbor drift along in lanes of loneliness," Rabbi Joseph Soloveitchik writes. "Don't permit him to become remote and alienated from you."

Other groups have more elaborate technologies for convening. The Becoming a Man program works with at-risk kids on Chicago's West Side. Small groups of young men gather regularly for "check-ins." Each one has to report how he is doing spiritually, emotionally, intellectually, and physically. If he isn't fully vulnerable, the others get on him.

Diana Westmoreland, who lives in rural Texas, created Bubba Can Cook, which brings teams together to compete in barbecuing chicken, brisket, and ribs—because it's apparently around a barbecue grill that Texans are most emotionally exposed.

Mary Gordon founded the Roots of Empathy project in Ontario, which uses babies to create rich connections in schools. Once a month a parent and an infant visit a classroom. They sit on a green blanket, and the class gathers around them to watch and talk about what the infant is doing. They observe the infant try to crawl to something or reach for a toy. They are learning to put themselves in the mind of a baby, learning emotional literacy, and learning how deep attachment works. In one class there was an eighth-grade boy Gordon called Darren, who had witnessed his mother's murder when he was four and had been bounced around the foster care system ever since. He was bigger than everybody else in class since he was two grades behind. One day, much to everybody's surprise, Darren asked to hold the baby.

He looked scary, and the mother was nervous, but she let him, and Darren was great with the baby. He went over to a quiet corner and rocked the infant while the baby snuggled into his chest. Darren returned the baby to his mother and asked innocently, "If nobody has ever loved you, do you think you could still be a good father?"

A bloom of empathy and connection. A moment when community begins to heal a wound and create a possibility.

One of the most sophisticated methodologies for convening that I have seen is in Baltimore, in an organization called Thread, co-founded by Sarah Hemminger. When Hemminger was a girl in Indiana, her father discovered that their pastor was dipping into church funds. He reported this to the congregation, but instead of firing the pastor, the community shunned Sarah's family. Sarah and her siblings would sit at parties and neighborhood events, and nobody would talk to them. She spent eight years of her childhood ostracized.

In response, she focused her energy in two ways. She became a nationally competitive figure skater, practicing up to eight hours a day. And she focused her energies on schoolwork. She eventually went on to get a PhD in biomedical engineering from Johns Hopkins, and got an offer for a position at the National Institutes of Health.

But, because of the shunning, she always had a special sensitivity to those who were outsiders, those who were lonely. As a freshman in high school, she noticed a boy named Ryan early in his time in school had drifted further and further into isolation and failure, as his own home life crumbled. Six teachers built a support structure around the boy. He turned his academic record around, was accepted into the U.S. Naval Academy, and, finally, years later, married Sarah.

One day, when she was working on her PhD at Hopkins, she happened to drive by Paul Laurence Dunbar High School in Baltimore. She was lonely and wanted to find a way to connect with people she could understand. She thought that maybe she could help students in Baltimore city schools the way people had helped Ryan. She decided she would find volunteers to rally around them, as she and the teachers had rallied around him. She asked the principal to give her the names of the most academically underperforming students at the school. She persuaded them to come see her—mostly by offering them pizza—and then asked if they'd be willing to help her develop a program. Most were happy to join, provided there was more pizza. She then convinced dozens of Hopkins students to volunteer and act as extended family members for the kids: driving them to school, bringing them lunch, driving them back to school when they skipped out, doing homework with them, taking them camping.

Sarah didn't fully appreciate it at the time, but a commitment had been made. Her science career was never going to happen. She formed Thread, which weaves a web of volunteers around Baltimore's most academically underperforming teenagers. Each student has up to four volunteers in their Thread family. Each volunteer is coached by another volunteer, called the head of family, who serves as a support system for family volunteers. The HOF is coached by a still more experienced volunteer called a grandparent. The grandparents are coached by community managers, who are paid Thread staffers. Circling the whole system of relationships are Thread collaborators, who offer special expertise—legal help, SAT tutoring, mental health counseling, and so on. When students first get involved, they sign a contract saying they will be active in Thread for ten years. In this commitment there is no early exit and no dropping out.

The nominal point of Thread is to help underperforming teenagers. The real point of Thread is to build a web of relationships that stretches across the (so far) 415 students and the 1,000 volunteers. The real point is to create a community in which it is possible to fight off loneliness—Sarah's as much as anybody else's.

Often kids are wary as they begin Thread. As a few of them told me, they'd never had anyone consistently and unconditionally show up for them, and so they were suspicious and resentful when it started happening. Their first urge is often to flee, to reject the intrusion. Distrust is their resting state. But the Thread volunteers just keep showing up.

"Unconditional love is so rare in life that it is identity changing when somebody keeps showing up even when you reject them," Sarah says. "It is also identity changing to be the one rejected."

Sarah's commitment is not to the Thread model; she'd change the organization in a minute if she felt it was right. It's to the whole web of relationships. It's to the community. It's to Baltimore. Dozens of cities have asked Sarah to replicate Thread in their town, but she has turned them down. It's better to go deep in Baltimore. There's a pendant featuring a little map of the city on the necklace she wears every day. She is committed not to community in the abstract. She is committed to this one place and hopes that when Thread is big enough, it can change the fabric of the entire city.

Thread is very systematic about the way relationships are structured. There is also a very systematic way of tracking contacts between the people in the community. Thread has created an app called Tapestry, which tracks every time a volunteer has a touchpoint with one of the young people. Tapestry can track how often a young person has touchpoints, who hasn't had a touchpoint recently, and how concentrated touchpoints correlate to other outcomes. Sarah calls it the Fitbit of social relationships. Like a lot of the best community builders, Hemminger combines a yearning heart with an engineer's head. And like a lot of the best community builders, she has no recognition that she is doing anything extraordinary.

THE COMBUSTION STORIES

Gathering people together is the start of community, but it is not yet community. There has to be combustion—that moment when the substrate of one life touches the substrate of another, when, as people say afterward, you go deep.

People generally enter a strange room with distrust and doubt and a feeling of discomfort. But if you gather a group of colleagues to, say, read a passage together, a story like Ursula K. Le Guin's "The Ones Who Walk Away from Omelas," then there's an occasion to go deep.

Some way or another, storytelling begins. Somebody shares a vulnerability and in that way assumes leadership. An ethos is established.

As they say at Thread, everybody is going to "show all the way up." That is, they'll bring their whole mess to the group. There's an expectation in the room that everyone will "call a thing a thing." There will be no evasions and euphemisms. A story follows a story, and soon enough the deepest stories are unearthed. Vulnerability is shared, emotions are aroused, combustion happens.

It's especially powerful when a strong person tells a story of weakness. Carter Davis, who lives in Oregon, has an organization called Lift for the 22, which helps vets struggling with depression and thoughts of suicide. He is quite open about his own attempt. "I remember sitting at my coffee table, looking at my gun, thinking what a joke I was. Here is this veteran who lives two blocks from the VA, who wasn't even a combat veteran and here he is killing himself." His own story opens up possibility for everybody else in the room.

Michelle Leff is a board member at Thread. She is a strong, competent, powerful-seeming woman. She joined to help the young, but the radical honesty of the organization slowly eroded her defenses about herself. She began to tell her fellow board members stories she had never even told her own kids. And then she felt that integrity demanded that she tell her kids what her own childhood had actually been like.

When she thinks of growing up she thinks of pain, bleakness, and shame, she wrote. She thinks of her father's rages, which could be set off by anything. It was her fault that she didn't practice piano enough. It was her fault that she was so stupid she couldn't understand sixth-grade math in first grade. "I remember being in first grade and feeling fortunate that I had thick black hair because it hid the goose eggs from being punched in the head the night before. . . . Anything that frustrated him (and he was easily frustrated) was taken out on either me or my mother. In my young mind, my crime seemed to be that I existed, took up space and cost money."

In ninth grade the pressure became too much. She tried to swallow fifty pain medication pills. She realized that overdosing is not easy. Her throat clenched up. She was both saddened and relieved when she woke up and discovered that her attempt at overdose had failed.

Now she is a successful woman, sitting on an important board. Inspired by the conversations she'd been part of, she decided to share the realities of her childhood—with the board and with her family—for the first time: "Why I show up for Thread," she wrote in a letter to her family. "I remember clearly what it's like to be 14 and feel trapped and powerless. Why I show up. Thread gives me the optimism of future, for the students and myself. Why I show up. Thread has given me this gift of Thread lens. At this point, my Thread lens has allowed me to examine my weaknesses (these biased assumptions and quick judgments I tend to make). Of most value to me, is that this Thread lens has allowed me to recognize the richness of relationships."

Michelle grew up loving Elton John, but never got to see him until about 2011, when he was playing in Baltimore. No one would go to the concert with her but her thirteen-year-old daughter. "When Elton John played songs from his album *Goodbye Yellow Brick Road* I started crying. But I wasn't crying because I was sad, I was crying because I was so overcome with strong emotions as my mind whipsawed between the stark contrast of my bleak childhood memories and my splendid adult life. When I was 13, I listened to Elton John most of the time wishing I was dead; but that night I was listening to his music with my 13-year-old daughter, both of us laughing. My life now is rich with strong, healthy relationships. Life has turned out to be so much better than I ever imagined."

When you are unveiling yourself, it can feel like you are going backward. You realize there is so much trauma around; there is so much blame, and so much forgiveness is required. You realize there are so many people torn between the temptation to deny traumatic events and the desire to proclaim them. Often the struggle comes out as anger, blame, and fury, which can make repair seem impossible.

But, in fact, the honest, brutal story is the kind of story that produces combustion. We spend much of our time projecting accomplishments, talents, and capacity. The confrontation with weakness can have this detonating effect.

The Stages of Community Building II

PERSONAL STORIES ARE POWERFUL. WHEN THEY ARE TOLD AND RECEIVED, trust is created. But in a narcissistic culture, it's easy to stop there. It's easy to sit around one evening, tell a personal tale about yourself, and then, having had a rich experience, go home under the illusion that you've done something good for the world. A commitment to community involves moving from "I" stories to "We" stories. The move, as always, is downward and then outward. Down into ourselves in vulnerability and then outward in solidarity with others.

The next stage of village making is to tell the communal story—a story that links people together. Some places have thick stories and some have thin ones. I'm often in new suburbs in Nevada or Arizona, where not enough time has passed to have a village story, and you can feel the lack. On the other hand, recently I was in Wilkesboro, North Carolina, a town of about 3,500 in the northwestern part of the state. It's 81 percent white with a median income of about $35,000, and it sits in a county where three-quarters of the votes went for Donald Trump in 2016.

Wilkesboro and its neighboring town, North Wilkesboro, were

once thriving business centers. Lowe's, the American Furniture Company, Holly Farms, and Northwestern Bank were there, along with large mirror and furniture manufacturers. But those employers have either moved out, gone bankrupt, or been acquired by someone else. In the early 2000s, the town was hit hard by the opioid epidemic. There was no place for young people to gather and no place for them to work.

The town took its hits, but what's striking about the place is that there is still a strong identity. There is a clear community story.

Part of that identity comes from being Appalachian—having a distinct historic lineage, a culture of scrapping and fierce loyalty to one another. People in Wilkesboro can fight and scream with each other, but if you as an outsider say something critical about someone there, they rise as one to kick your ass. An outsider is defined as anyone not conceived in Wilkesboro. Yankees who move in while in the womb or later don't count.

Part of the community identity comes from what the ancestors accomplished long ago. "We've had a lot of great things created in Wilkes," says Nate, who just opened a coffee shop. "That's what we do in Wilkes, build things out of nothing. There's a passion to do that."

A community is, in part, a group of people organized around a common story. People in Wilkesboro, like many places, tell a redemption narrative: rise, decline, endurance, revival. Part of the revival is spiritual, part is economic, and part is physical.

"How do you create pride again? Everyone's ashamed," says LB, a young local activist. "We're the town of abandoned factories. We're the town that survived that! We're a history of makers. We have made it. We know how to do it."

Then there is the common project. Communities don't come together for the sake of community; they come together to build something together. In Wilkesboro, the common project is place making. We have a tendency to think the social fabric is in tatters because the culture is bad or economic forces are ripping everything to shreds. But sometimes there are just no places for people to get together. Wilkesboro once had a bowling alley in town, but it burned down, and nobody rebuilt it. Today, in response, people from all walks of life are opening coffee shops, health clubs, art galleries, and distilleries, and creating performance spaces, teen nights, and music festivals.

What's fascinating is how cohesive this vision of recovery is, across many people, who, being people, sometimes feud and fuss. A coherent communal story is yet another new form of power.

A town story can be formed in so many ways. When I was living in Chicago, Mike Royko and other local newspaper columnists shaped the city's ethos and definition of itself. They rooted the Chicago story in its ethnic neighborhoods away from the lake (until Royko got rich and moved to the lakefront). In some places, artists form the community story. Diego Rivera's stunning *Detroit Industry Murals* at the Detroit Institute of Arts define the city across four luscious walls. For a few decades, Detroit seemed to have nothing left but its story, but that was enough to keep it together, and now the city rises once again. One of the most important tasks of a community is to create its story.

A community narrative has four parts, says Trabian Shorters, who leads a fellowship group for African American men out of Miami called BMe. There is framing (which defines the context), narrative (where we came from and where we are going), identity (who we are), and behavior (actions that define us). Community stories are almost always cross-generational. They start with the origin of a place, and then tell how it grew.

Edmund Burke argued that people who have never looked backward to their ancestors will not be able to look forward and plan for the future. People who look backward to see the heroism and the struggle that came before see themselves as debtors who owe something, who have some obligation to pay it forward. "The idea of inheritance furnishes a sure principle of conservation and a sure principle of transmission," Burke wrote. "We receive, we hold, we cherish what we have been given and enjoy these things and improve them for others. Respecting our ancestors, we learn to respect ourselves."

Honest communities tell complicated stories, about the times they sinned and inflicted pain as well as the times they endured and showed mercy. Honest American stories talk about slavery and racism. Honest

New York stories tell about the destruction of the old Penn Station and all the grand beauties that have been torn down for the name of commerce. There's always something in every community out of joint, corrupted and unjust in some way. People in community live at a crossroads where their pride of place and anger at injustice meet.

THE CODE OF THE NEIGHBOR

After the community has come together and told its story, there is still the action to be taken: the act of weaving community out of isolation. Community building is done by daily acts of care, room by room. It is done by those who adopt the code of the neighbor.

A neighbor is not on a solitary journey through life, but is one immersed. He sees himself as someone who has been shaped by a tradition of local behavior and place. He feels indebted to that legacy and is happy to pay off that debt. His work, family, and neighborhood lives are not in different silos. They are interconnected pieces of his service to his place. The code of the neighbor revolves around a few common principles:

We are enough. The neighbor doesn't wait for someone else to address the community's problems. He is not just a spectator. As Peter Block writes, "Most sustainable improvements in community occur when citizens discover their own power to act. Whatever the symptom—drugs, deteriorating houses, poor economy, displacement, violence—it is when citizens stop waiting for professionals or elected leadership to do something, and decide they can reclaim what they have delegated to others, that things really happen. This act of power is present in most stories of lasting community improvement and change."

Village over self. A good person inconveniences himself for the sake of his community. A bad person inconveniences the community for the sake of himself.

Initiating the connection. The good neighbor is the one who invites others over for dinner. The good neighbor is the one who is talking to one neighbor and introduces the other neighbor on the other side of the street.

Thirty-year eyes. A neighbor has a different time horizon than an individual. Her actions are not oriented toward making this place better tomorrow. Her actions are geared to make this place better thirty years from now. This child she is mentoring will be a town leader in thirty years. This festival she is organizing will be a tradition going strong in half a century. She plants trees that will bear fruit she will never eat, and cast shade she will never enjoy.

Radical hospitality. Robert Frost wrote, "Home is the place where, when you have to go there, they have to take you in." When someone is in need, the code of the neighbor says hospitality is first, judgment and everything else comes later. The neighbor is like the father of the prodigal son who races out to greet him without asking questions. Grace and forgiveness first, then we can think about what went wrong and heal whatever breach.

The community is the expert. Neighbors know that it's not just the school that educates the child, it's not just the police who keep the town safe, it's not just the hospital that keeps the people healthy. It is the shared way of living. People are safe when the streetscape is active. People are healthy when healthy eating is the norm. Kids are educated where adults talk to and encourage the young. It's the norms and behavior of the neighborhood. It's the people puzzling together to find the best way to live.

Coming in under. Hermann Hesse wrote a short story called "Journey to the East," in which a group of men take a long journey. They are accompanied by a servant named Leo who does the menial chores and lifts the group's spirits with his singing. He takes care of the little things. The trip is going well until Leo disappears. Everything falls into disarray, and the trip is abandoned.

Many years later, one of the men stumbles into the organization that had sponsored the journey and discovered that Leo is, in fact, the leader of this great organization and not some functionary. This story inspired the concept of servant leadership. The lesson is that a community leader is often the person doing the "menial" tasks, the supportive person. As George Eliot observed in the famous last sentence of *Middlemarch*: "The growing good of the world is partly dependent on unhistoric acts; and that things are not so ill with you and me as they might have been, is half owing to the number who lived faithfully a hidden life, and rest in unvisited tombs."

The least are the most. Communities are defined by the treatment of the least among them: the young, the poor, the disabled, or the very sad. Jean Vanier built communities for the mentally disabled. "I come here to tell you how much life these people have given me," he once told an audience at Harvard. "That they have an incredible gift to bring to our world, they are a source of hope, peace and perhaps salvation for our wounded world. . . . If we keep our eyes fixed on them, if we are faithful to them, we will always find our path."

The sin is partly my own. Mutual fallibility is one of the glues that hold community together. We understand that we're all weak and selfish some of the time. We often contribute to the problems we ourselves complain about.

"True community is different because of the realization that the evil is inside—not just inside the community but inside me," Vanier writes. "I cannot think of taking the speck of dust out of my neighbor's eye unless I'm working on the log in my own." Community is a place of pain because it's a place where the truth about one another comes out. But it's also a place of loving through the pain, of disagreement that can be expressed freely precisely because of the unconditional love.

THE VILLAGE COMPACT

In his book *The Home We Build Together*, Rabbi Jonathan Sacks points out that in the Bible the description of the creation of the universe in Genesis is covered in a mere thirty-four verses. But then there is this weird episode in the book of Exodus that takes up an entire third of that book—hundreds and hundreds of verses. It is the instructions for the building of the tabernacle.

Why should the building of this one structure—with specific instructions about the length of the beams and all the different woods and ornaments—require such minute attention? It's because the Israelites are not yet a people. They are an oppressed and disparate group of tribes and individuals. As Sacks puts it, "To turn a group of individuals into a covenantal nation, they must build something together." A people is made by making, Sacks continues; a nation is built by building.

Sacks tells the story of the British diplomat Victor Mishcon. In the early 1980s he was trying to negotiate a peace deal in the Middle East, so he invited King Hussein of Jordan and Israeli foreign minister Shimon Peres over to his house for dinner. They had the meal and a pleasant conversation, and eventually they got up to leave. Mishcon told them they weren't going anywhere. They had to do the dishes. He put King Hussein by the sink and Peres by the drying rack and had them work side by side, washing and drying. This was the point of the evening to him.

Prince Holmes is director of Youth Rebuilding New Orleans. He brings together different kinds of young people and puts them to work building houses. "The community we build is more important than building the homes," he says. "We're big on energy. The fact that you can build a wall with someone that you've never met before creates an instant bond. It's not work to me."

The act of working on common projects redraws the boundaries between groups and redefines where someone is on the hierarchy. Suddenly a guy good with his hands is higher than the guy from the executive suite. In Exodus, the Israelites are never happier than they are when building the tabernacle.

When people come together to build something, they make implied promises to one another. They promise to work things out. They promise to do their fair share or more of the work. They promise to follow through on the intention to build something new.

I sometimes think they should make this moment explicit. Just as a couple make vows to each other at a wedding ceremony, I sometimes think that communities should organize a village compact ceremony. European colonists who came to America in 1620 signed the Mayflower Compact, in which they publicly vowed to "combine ourselves in a civil body politic." A modern ceremony could involve a group of people swearing loyalty to one another, specifying what sorts of projects they are willing to take, what price they are willing to pay. A modern ceremony could have initiation rites, rituals of mutual belonging, the retelling of the community story, symbols that signify common membership, and a sacred meeting spot, where people across generations can make their vows. Then of course there'd be a party.

THE POSSIBILITY CONVERSATION

There is something in our culture that naturally pushes us to think in terms of problem solving. Life is a series of problems to be analyzed and addressed. How do we fix our failing schools? How do we reduce violence? These problem-centered questions are usually the wrong ones to ask. They focus on deficits, not gifts.

A problem conversation tends to focus on one moment in time—the moment when a student didn't graduate from high school, the moment when a young person commits a crime, the moment when a person is homeless. But actual lives are lived cumulatively. It takes a whole series of shocks before a person becomes homeless—loss of a job, breakdown in family relationship, maybe car problems or some transportation issue. It takes a whole series of shocks before a kid drops out of school. If you abstract away from the cumulative nature of life and define the problem as one episode, you are abstracting away from how life is lived. All conversations are either humanizing or dehumanizing, and problem-centered conversations tend to be impersonal and dehumanizing.

The better community-building conversations focus on possibilities, not problems. They are questions such as, What crossroads do we stand at right now? What can we build together? How can we improve our lives together? What talents do we have here that haven't been fully expressed?

A possibility conversation is a conversation that leads to a biography of success. What would a person's biography look like if life started going better? Such a conversation doesn't start with the impersonal question, How do we tackle homelessness? It starts with the personal question, What can we do to help Mary lead a life of stability, safety, and security in a home? When you envision success as biography—as one particular person living on a different life trajectory—you see, in very concrete ways, all the different factors that go into a better future. You see all the different relationships that need to be built. You see how the social and emotional layer has to be acknowledged, even though the issue you are talking about is superficially only physical, like finding the homeless housing.

Modern social scientists unfortunately tend to think in statistical correlations, not in biographical narratives. Randomized controlled experiments seek to tease out distinct cause-and-effect relationships between one input and one outcome. Social science often seeks to disaggregate. But actual lives are longitudinal and relational. Actual lives are lived out amid a thousand different influences that interact in a million different ways over time. It distorts reality to try to chop a life up into distinct cause-and-effect slices, as if a human being were a billiard ball. We tend to understand this when talking about our own lives but we tend to objectivize things when talking about others, or groups of others.

The question in a possibility conversation is not, Who's to blame? It's, What assets can we deploy to make our neighborhood one in which everybody looks out for one another? What gifts can we contribute that we might not yet even see in ourselves yet? In Denver, for example, Nepalese immigrants have trouble integrating into the public school system. Kate Garvin, a local community weaver, realized that village elders were an underutilized source of galvanizing, guiding, and convening power. So she integrated the elders into the school system and liberated an untapped source of community wealth. In Washington, D.C., Sharon Murphy takes in refugees and others who are at some of the lowest points of their lives, yet, she says, "You come to Mary House to become stronger at what you're already doing well." This is possibility thinking. If you want to shift the culture, you've got to have a conversation you haven't had before, one that is about long-term possibilities. What can this place be like in 2049?

THE INVENTION OF TRADITION

When a community begins to build together, they don't just create new stuff; they create new norms. They make a contribution to the community, and over time that contribution becomes the thing everybody is expected to do. For example, my friend Rod Dreher had a sister named Ruthie who lived in a small town in Louisiana. Ruthie was a teacher, one of those people who radiate an inner light. Tragically, she died of cancer at forty. More than one thousand people came to her funeral. Ruthie loved to go barefoot, so the pallbearers, from the local fire department, where her husband worked, carried her casket to the grave barefoot.

Ruthie always thought the dead of her town should be remembered on Christmas, so she created a tradition. Every Christmas Eve she would go to the town cemetery to put a lit candle on each gravestone. Ruthie happened to die just before Christmas, and as the family was sitting around on that Christmas Eve, Rod asked his mother if she would like to do what Ruthie used to do—to light a candle on each gravestone. His mother replied that maybe in other years that would be good, but this year it was just too tough.

That evening Rod's parents attended mass and drove home, early evening, by the cemetery. They looked over and gasped. There were hundreds of lights. Somebody else had put a candle on every gravestone. That's how community works. Somebody starts something. A new tradition is established. Other people step in and carry it on.

A NEW CIVIC ARCHITECTURE

The really difficult community projects don't just require a new organization or new norms. They require an entirely new civic architecture. Not long ago, in Spartanburg, South Carolina, I visited the offices of something called the Spartanburg Academic Movement (SAM). The walls were lined with charts measuring such things as kindergarten readiness, third-grade reading scores, and postsecondary enrollment.

Around the table was just about anybody in Spartanburg who might touch a child's life. There were school superintendents and principals, but there were also the heads of the chamber of commerce and the local United Way, the police chief, a former mayor and the newspaper editor, someone from the healthcare sector, and a bunch of statisticians. This coalition was like nothing I'd seen before. It was private sector and public sector, church and business. It was representatives from nearly every sector in the community, and they were all staring at the same charts.

The people at SAM track everything they can measure about Spartanburg's young people from cradle to career. They gather everybody who might have any influence upon this data—parents, churches, doctors, nutrition experts, and the like. And then together, as a community-wide system, they ask questions: Where are children falling off track? Why? What assets do we have in our system that can be applied to this problem? How can we work together to apply those assets?

This was very different from the way I was used to seeing communities try to achieve their possibilities. In most cases, you have a bunch of organizations who want to do good. They apply to a local foundation or government agencies and compete for grants. A few get chosen, and they go off and do their thing. One donor, one organization, one problem, one program. Then, after a few years, somebody does a study to see if that program had any measurable effect, which most of the time it hasn't. You wind up with a community in which a random spray of programs are competing for a smallish pot of money, working independently and often at cross-purposes, exaggerating their successes and hiding their failures. And you sort of hope it all somehow works out.

But in Spartanburg, the groups I saw weren't trying to compete for money to show they were having isolated impact. They were part of a network working in interdependent ways to have collective impact. When life is going well, it's because these influences are flowing together and reinforcing one another. SAM tries to harness dozens of influences in a way that conforms to the way people and places actually grow.

SAM embodies a new civic architecture that has become known as the "collective impact" approach. SAM is not a lone case. Spartanburg is one of seventy communities around the country that use what is called the StriveTogether method. StriveTogether began in Cincinnati just over a decade ago. A few community leaders were trying to improve education in the city and thinking of starting another program. But a Procter and Gamble executive who was part of the group observed, "We're program rich, but system poor." In other words, Cincinnati had plenty of programs. What it lacked was an effective system to coordinate them.

A methodology was born, and with it, yet another new form of community power: organize around the data; focus on the assets of the community, not the deficits; realize there is no one silver-bullet solution; create a "backbone organization" (like SAM) that can bring all the players together; coordinate decision-making; communicate continuously; create working teams to implement action; share accountability.

At one point the folks in Cincinnati noticed that their students were not coming to school prepared for kindergarten. The data suggested that the private pre-K programs were performing better than the public ones. So the public school system allocated some of its money to support other, private, programs, making Cincinnati one of the first cities to offer universal pre-K. That's a community working as one.

Collective impact structures got their name in 2011, when John Kania and Mark Kramer wrote an influential essay for the *Stanford Social Innovation Review*, in which they cited StriveTogether and provided the philosophical and theoretical basis for this kind of approach.

Collective impact starts with a group of people who are driven, Kania and Kramer argue, by an urgency for change. Maybe they want to extend the local life span by five years. Maybe they want to end homelessness.

They realize the complexity of their problem. They are not going to have a predetermined solution when they start. They're going to engage in a long, iterative process of action and response before they can figure out the right mix of programs—in other words, they're going to have to commit large sums of money and effort before they know exactly what they are going to do with the money, which is an uncomfortable thing to do.

What they're investing in is a learning process. They're getting the whole community to look at a complex problem together from a lot of different vantage points and letting the solutions emerge from the ensuing conversation. The quality of their efforts is defined by the quality of their questions, such as, Why, despite our best efforts, have we been unable to make this situation better?

In effect, they're designing a way to get the whole community to travel like a flock. A flock of birds has the astonishing ability to travel together and shift course without the individual birds bumping into one another. They do it, scientists have learned, because each bird follows three simple rules: maintain minimum distance between you and the neighboring bird; fly at the same speed as your neighbor; always fly toward the center of the flock.

Collective impact requires systems thinking. Systems thinking is built around the idea that if you take the direct approach to any problem, you're probably going to screw things up because you don't see the complexity of the whole system. For example, people used to think the way to solve crime was to throw large numbers of criminals in prison. It seemed to work at first, but over time it became clear that mass incarceration was taking potentially productive men out of the neighborhood; it was subjecting them to a prison experience that, later on, would steer them back toward crime and further destabilize neighborhoods. Over the long term you've ended up making the problem you're trying to address that much worse.

A systems approach means acknowledging that each of us sees only a part of a complex world. If you pull one lever here, you're probably going to produce an unexpected outcome over there. It takes the entire flock, the entire community, to map the whole system and act on all its parts in a continuous way, with continuous feedback conversations.

In a collaborative system, you set up an arrangement in which nobody is punished for an unpleasant fact. For example, many school systems use data as a way to grade schools, close schools, and get them to compete. In Spartanburg they never do that. They want all of the players in the system to be cooperating, not competing. They need to have purity of communication above all and transparency about the data. They don't want anybody hiding data because they're afraid of what punishments may come. They use data as a flashlight, not a hammer. This ethic of contribution (Everybody gives) and this ethic of total collaboration (We're all responsible) is central to community work at its highest level.

THE THICKENING

On the first mountain, the emphasis is on the unencumbered self, individual accomplishment, creating a society in which everyone is free to be themselves. This is a fluid society, and over the short term a productive society, but it is a thin society. It is a society in which people are only lightly attached to each other and to their institutions. The second-mountain society is a thick society. The organizations and communities in that society leave a mark. And so I've been thinking a lot about what makes an organization thick or thin.

The thick communities have a distinct culture—the way the University of Chicago, Morehouse College, the U.S. Marine Corps do. A thick institution is not trying to serve its people instrumentally, to give them a degree or to simply help them earn a salary. A thick institution seeks to change the person's whole identity. It engages the whole person: head, hands, heart, and soul.

Thick institutions have a physical location, often cramped, where members meet face-to-face on a regular basis, such as a dinner table or a packed gym or an assembly hall. Such institutions have a set of collective rituals—fasting or reciting some creed in unison or standing in formation. They have shared tasks, which often involve members closely watching one another, the way hockey teammates have to observe one another on the ice. In such institutions people occasionally sleep overnight in the same retreat center or facility, so that everybody can see each other's real self, before makeup and after dinner.

Such organizations often tell and retell a sacred origin story about themselves. Many experienced a moment when they nearly failed, and they celebrate the heroes who pulled them from the brink. They incorporate music into daily life, because it is hard not to become bonded with someone you have sung and danced with.

They have idiosyncratic local cultures. Too many colleges, for example, feel like one another. But the ones that really leave a mark on their students (St. John's, Kenyon, Wheaton, MIT) have the courage to be distinct. You can love or hate such places. But when you meet a graduate you know it, and when they meet each other, even decades hence, they know they have something important in common.

University of Pennsylvania psychologist Angela Duckworth adds that thick institutions almost always have a clearly defined shared goal, such as winning the Super Bowl or saving the environment. They have initiation rituals; a sacred guidebook or object passed down from generation to generation; distinct jargon and phrases that are spoken inside the culture but misunderstood outside it; a label, such as being a KIPPster for a KIPP charter school student; and they often have uniforms or other emblems, such as flags, rings, bracelets.

Jonathan Haidt of NYU advises that if you want to create a thick institution, you should call attention to the traits people have in common, not the ones that set them apart. Second, exploit synchrony. Have people sing or play or move together. Third, create healthy competition among teams, not individuals. People fight and sacrifice more for their buddies than for an abstraction, so embed people in team relationships.

Thick institutions are oriented around a shared moral cause. They don't see their members as resources to be exploited but as fellow marchers in a holy mission. Thick institutions tear you down in order to build you up. They enmesh you within long traditions and sacred customs that seem archaic a lot of the time. They ask you to bury your own identity in the collective identity. They point to an ideal that is far in the distance and can't be achieved in a single lifetime. "The secret of life," the sculptor Henry Moore once said, "is to have a task, something you devote your entire life to, something you bring everything to, every minute of every day for the rest of your life. And the most important thing is, it must be something you cannot possibly do."

Conclusion: The Relationalist Manifesto

IN THIS BOOK I'VE TALKED A LOT ABOUT TWO MOUNTAINS. AS I MEN-tioned, this device was an attempt to render in narrative form the con-trast between two different moral worldviews. The first mountain is the individualist worldview, which puts the desires of the ego at the center. The second mountain is what you might call the relationalist worldview, which puts relation, commitment, and the desires of the heart and soul at the center. My core argument has been that we have overdone it with the individualist worldview. By conceiving of our-selves mostly as autonomous selves, we've torn our society to shreds, opened up division and tribalism, come to worship individual status and self-sufficiency, and covered over what is most beautiful in each human heart and soul.

In this conclusion, I'd like to bring the different strands of the ar-gument together. But I'd like to bring them together not with quotes from other people and not with stories and parables, but in manifesto form, with all the bluntness, fervor, and conviction that has driven me, with increasing intensity, to write this book.

The world is in the midst of one of those transition moments. The individualistic moral ecology is crumbling around us. It has left people naked and alone. For many, the first instinctive reaction is the evolutionary one: Revert to tribe. If we as a society respond to the excesses of "I'm Free to Be Myself" with an era of "Revert to Tribe," then the twenty-first century will be a time of conflict and violence that will make the twentieth look like child's play.

There is another way to find belonging. There is another way to find meaning and purpose. There is another vision of a healthy society. It is through relationalism. It is by going deep into ourselves and finding there our illimitable ability to care, and then spreading outward in commitment to others. In this manifesto, I try to make the case against the hyper-individualism of the current moment, and for relationalism, a better way to live.

Hyper-Individualism

1. There is always a balance between self and society. In some ages the pressures of the group become stifling and crush the self, and individuals feel a desperate need to break free and express their individuality. In our age, by contrast, the self is inflated and the collective is weak. We have swung too far in the direction of individualism. The result is a loss of connection—a crisis of solidarity.

2. Hyper-individualism, the reigning ethos of our day, is a system of morals, feelings, ideas, and practices based on the idea that the journey through life is an individual journey, that the goals of life are individual happiness, authenticity, self-actualization, and self-sufficiency. Hyper-individualism puts the same question on everybody's lips: What can I do to make myself happy?

3. Hyper-individualism rests upon an emancipation story. The heroic self breaks free from the stifling chains of society. The self stands on its own two feet, determines its own destiny, secures its own individual rights. Hyper-individualism defines freedom as absence from restraint.

4. In this way, hyper-individualism gradually undermines any connection not based on individual choice—the connections to family, neighborhood, culture, nation, and the common good. Hyper-individualism erodes our obligations and responsibilities to others and our kind.

5. The central problems of our day flow from this erosion: social isolation, distrust, polarization, the breakdown of family, the loss of community, tribalism, rising suicide rates, rising mental health problems, a spiritual crisis caused by a loss of common purpose, the loss—in nation after nation—of any sense of common solidarity that binds people across difference, the loss of those common stories and causes that foster community, mutuality, comradeship, and purpose.

6. The core flaw of hyper-individualism is that it leads to a degradation and a pulverization of the human person. It is a system built upon the egoistic drives within each of us. These are the self-interested drives—the desire to excel; to make a mark in the world; to rise in wealth, power, and status; to win victories and be better than others. Hyper-individualism does not emphasize and eventually does not even see the other drives—the deeper and more elusive motivations that seek connection, fusion, service, and care. These are not the desires of the ego, but the longings of the heart and soul: the desire to live in loving interdependence with others, the yearning to live in service of some ideal, the yearning to surrender to a greater good. Hyper-individualism numbs these deepest longings. Eventually, hyper-individualism creates isolated, self-interested monads who sense that something is missing in their lives but cannot even name what it is.

7. Hyper-individualism thrives within the systems of the surface. Consumerism amputates what is central to the person for the sake of material acquisition. The meritocracy amputates what is deepest for individual "success." Unbalanced capitalism

turns people into utility-maximizing, speeding workaholics that no permanent attachment can penetrate.

8. The hyper-individualist finds himself enmeshed in a network of conditional love. I am worthy of being loved only when I have achieved the status or success the world expects of me. I am worthy of love only when I can offer the other person something in return. I am what the world says about me. In the end, hyper-individualism doesn't make people self-sufficient and secure. It obliterates emotional and spiritual security by making everything conditional. It makes people extremely sensitive to the judgments of others and quick to take offense when they feel slighted.

9. Hyper-individualism directs people toward false and unsatisfying lives. Some people lead an aesthetic life. They get to taste a series of experiences which may be pleasant, but which don't accumulate into anything because they are not serving a large cause. Some people become insecure overachievers. They seek to win by accomplishing the love, admiration, and attachment they can't get any other way, but of course no amount of achievement ever gives them the love they crave.

10. When you build a whole society on an overly thin view of human nature, you wind up with a dehumanized culture in which people are starved of the things they yearn for most deeply.

11. The uncommitted person is the unremembered person. A person who does not commit to some loyalty outside the self leaves no deep mark on the world.

12. Hyper-individualism leads to tribalism. People eventually rebel against the isolation and meaninglessness of hyper-individualism by joining a partisan tribe. This seems like relation but is actually its opposite. If the relationalist mentality is based on mutual affection, the tribalist mentality is based on mutual distrust. It is always us versus them, friend or enemy, destroy or be destroyed. Anger is the mode. The

tribalist is seeking connection but isolates himself ever more bitterly within his own resentments and distrust. Tribalism is the dark twin of community. The tragic paradox of hyper-individualism is that what began as an ecstatic liberation ends up as a war of tribe against tribe that crushes the individuals it sought to free.

Relationalism

1. The revolution will be moral, or it will not be at all. Modern society needs a moral ecology that rejects the reigning hyper-individualism of the moment. We need to articulate a creed that puts relation, not the individual, at the center, and which articulates, in clear form, the truths we all know: that we are formed by relationship, we are nourished by relationship, and we long for relationship. Life is not a solitary journey. It is building a home together. It is a process of being formed by attachments and then forming attachments in turn. It is a great chain of generations passing down gifts to one another.
2. The hyper-individualist sees society as a collection of individuals who contract with one another. The relationalist sees society as a web of connections that in many ways precedes choice. A hyper-individualist sees the individual as a self-sufficient unit; the relationalist says, a person is a node in a network, a personality is a movement toward others.
3. As a child, each person's emotional and spiritual foundation is formed by the unconditional love of a caring adult. Each person's attachment style is formed by the dance of interactions between herself and a loving adult. "We" precedes "me."
4. As adults, we measure our lives by the quality of our relationships and the quality of our service to those relationships. Life is a qualitative endeavor, not a quantitative one. It's not how

many, but how thick and how deep. Defining what a quality relationship looks like is a central task of any moral ecology.

5. The best adult life is lived by making commitments and staying faithful to those commitments: commitments to a vocation, to a family, to a philosophy or faith, to a community. Adult life is about making promises to others, being faithful to those promises. The beautiful life is found in the mutual giving of unconditional gifts.

6. Relationalism is a middle way between hyper-individualism and collectivism. The former detaches the person from all deep connection. The latter obliterates the person within the group, and sees groups as faceless herds. The relationalist sees each person as a node in a thick and enchanted web of warm commitments. She seeks to build a neighborhood, nation, and world of diverse and creative people who have made commitments in a flowering of different ways, who are nonetheless bound together by sacred chords.

7. Relationalism is not a system of ideas. It is a way of life. Relationalism is a viewpoint that draws from many sources, from Edmund Burke and Martin Luther King, Jr., from Martin Buber and Dorothy Day and Walt Whitman, from Jacques Maritain, Emmanuel Mounier, Martha Nussbaum, and Annie Dillard to Gandhi and Josiah Royce.

8. The hyper-individualist operates by a straightforward logic: I make myself strong and I get what I want. The relationalist says, Life operates by an inverse logic. I possess only when I give. I lose myself to find myself. When I surrender to something great, that's when I am strongest and most powerful.

The Process of Becoming a Person

1. The central journey of modern life is moving self to service. We start out listening to the default settings of the ego and

gradually learn to listen to the higher callings of the heart and soul.

2. Much of modern social thought, drawing on thinkers such as Machiavelli, Hobbes, and modern economics, sees human beings as fundamentally selfish. Children, Freud wrote, "are completely egoistic; they feel their needs intensely and strive ruthlessly to satisfy them." Most of modern thought was written by men, and often a certain sort of alpha men, who did not even see the systems of care that undergirded the societies in which they lived.

3. Relationalism asserts that human beings are both fundamentally broken but also splendidly endowed. We have egoistic self-interested desires, and we need those desires in order to accomplish some of the necessary tasks of life: to build an identity, to make a mark on the world, to break away from parents, to create and to shine. Our savage impulses to dominate, murder, rape, and pillage are written across the annals of history. But relationalism asserts that there are other, deeper parts of ourselves. There are motivations that are even stronger than self-interest, even if they are more elusive. At the deepest center of each person there is what we call, metaphorically, the heart and soul. There are capacities that can tame the savage lusts and subdue the beasts that remain inside, and those capacities are realized in community.

4. The heart is that piece of us that longs for fusion with others. We are not primarily thinking creatures; we are primarily loving and desiring creatures. We are defined by what we desire. We become what we love. The core question for each of us is, Have we educated our emotions to love the right things in the right way?

5. The soul is the piece of us that gives each person infinite dignity and worth. Slavery is wrong because it obliterates a soul. Rape is not just an assault on physical molecules; it obliterates another soul. The soul yearns for goodness. Each

human being wants to lead a good and meaningful life, and feels life falling apart when it seems meaningless.

6. A child is born with both ego and heart and soul on full display. But for many people, around adolescence, the ego begins to swell, and the heart and soul recede. People at this age need to establish an identity, to carve a self. Meanwhile, our society tells adolescent boys to bury their emotions and become men. It tells little girls that if they reveal the true depths of themselves, nobody will like them. Our public culture normalizes selfishness, rationalizes egoism, and covers over and renders us inarticulate about the deeper longings of the heart and soul.

7. But eventually most people realize that something is missing in the self-interested life. They achieve worldly success and find it unsatisfying. Or perhaps they have fallen in love, or been loved in a way that plows open the crusty topsoil of life and reveals the true personality down below. Or perhaps they endure a period of failure, suffering, or grief that carves through the surface and reveals the vast depths underneath. One way or another, people get introduced to the full depths of themselves, the full amplitude of life. They realize that only emotional, moral, and spiritual food can provide the nourishment they crave.

8. When a person has undergone one of these experiences, which can happen at any age, she is no longer just an individual; she has become a person. Her whole personhood is alive and engaged. She has discovered, down at the substrate, her infinite ability to care. Relationalism guides us as we undertake this personal transformation, surpassing the desires of the ego and taking on a bigger journey.

9. The movement toward becoming a person is downward and then outward: To peer deeper into ourselves where we find the yearnings for others, and then outward in relationship toward the world. A person achieves self-mastery, Maritain wrote, for the purpose of self-giving.

10. An individual who has become a person has staged a rebellion. She rebels against the individualistic ethos and all the systems of impersonalism. Society tells her to want independence, but she has declared her interdependence. Society says we live in a materialist reality, but she says we live in an enchanted reality. Society tells her to keep her options open, but she says, No, I will commit. I will root myself down. Society says, Try to rise above and be better than; she says, No, I will walk with, serve, and come in under. Society says, Cultivate with the self-interested side of your life; she says, No, I will cultivate the whole of myself. Life goes well only when you are living with the whole of yourself.

11. The relationalist doesn't walk away from the capitalist meritocracy, the systems of mainstream life. But she balances that worldview with a countervailing ethos that supplements, corrects, and ennobles. She walks in that world, with all its pleasures and achievements, but with a different spirit, a different approach, and different goals. She is communal where the world is too individual. She is more emotional when the world is too cognitive. She is moral when the world is too utilitarian.

The Good Life

1. The relationalist is not trying to dominate life by sheer willpower. He is not gripping the steering wheel and trying to strategize his life. He has made himself available. He has opened himself up so that he can hear a call and respond to a summons. He is asking, What is my responsibility here? When a person finds his high calling in life, it doesn't feel like he has taken control; it feels like he has surrendered control. The most creative actions are those made in response to a summons.

2. The summons often comes in the form of love. A person falls

in love with her child, her husband, her neighborhood, her calling, or her God. And with that love comes an urge to make promises—to say, I will always love you. I will always serve you and be there for you. Life is a vale of promise making.

3. Or a summons may come in the form of a need. There is some injustice, some societal wrong, that needs to be fixed. A person assumes responsibility—makes a promise to fight that fight and right that wrong.

4. When a summons has been felt and a promise has been made, a commitment has been sealed. The life of a relationalist is defined by its commitments. The quality and fulfillment of her life will be defined by what she commits to and how she fulfills those commitments.

5. A commitment is a promise made from love. A commitment is a promise made without expecting any return (though there will be returns aplenty). A committed relationship is a two-way promise. It is you throwing yourself wholeheartedly for another and another throwing himself wholeheartedly for you.

6. The person makes his commitments maximal commitments. He doesn't just have a career; he has a vocation. He doesn't just have a contract marriage (What's in it for me?). He has a covenantal marriage (I live and die for you). He doesn't just have opinions. He submits to a creed. He doesn't just live in a place. He helps build a community. Furthermore, he is not just committed to this abstract notion of "community." He is committed to a specific community, to a specific person, to a specific creed—things grounded in particular times and places.

7. By committing and living up to the daily obligations of his commitments, the person integrates himself into a coherent whole. Commitments organize the hours and the days of a life. A committed person achieves consistency across time. His character is built through the habitual acts of service to

the people he loves. His character is built by being the humble recipient of other people's gifts and thus acknowledging his own dependency. A contract gets you benefits, but a commitment transforms who you are.

8. Relationalists prioritize those actions that deepen commitment, build relation, and enhance human dignity: giving, storytelling, dance, singing, common projects, gathering, dining, ritual, deep conversation, common prayer, forgiveness, creating beauty, mutual comfort in times of sadness and threat, mutual labor for the common good.

9. A committed life involves some common struggles.

10. It is, for example, a constant struggle to see people at their full depths. In the business of daily life there is the constant temptation to see the other person as an object and not a whole. There is the constant temptation to label and generalize. There is the constant temptation to reduce people to data and to see them as data points. You can count apples with data. You can track human behavior in the mass. But there is something that is unique and irreplaceable about each person that data cannot see. The relationalist tries to see each individual as a whole person—as a body, mind, heart, and soul.

11. There is the constant struggle to communicate well. At every moment there is either a depth of communication or a shallowness of communication. The relationalist seeks conditions that will make communication deep and pure. This is hard because there's something in ourselves that eludes our ability to communicate it. There is something proper about modesty and the slow unveiling of one's self. To achieve I–Thou communication, even to glimpse it, the relationalist sits patiently as vulnerabilities are gradually revealed. She offers safety and respect. Sometimes what is deepest is related in the form of myth, story, and music. When communication fails or is corrupted, the French philosopher Emmanuel Mounier says, I suffer a loss of myself. Madness and misery is a severance of communication with others.

12. There is the constant struggle to live as an effective giver and receiver of gifts. There are millions of people around us whose lives are defined by generosity and service. Personal being, Mounier continues, is essentially generous. But our society does not teach us how to be an effective giver of gifts. The schools don't emphasize it. The popular culture is confused about it.

13. It is a constant struggle to see life through a moral lens. The practical workaday world primes the utilitarian lens. Consumerism calls forth a self that is oriented around material pleasure. Money has an anonymous power and tends to render the person on the other side of a transaction invisible. Workplace rivalries and modern politics require armored individuals—human tanks with no exposure. The effort to fight the utilitarian lens and see daily life through a moral lens is a hard and never-ending struggle.

14. These struggles are not against other people. The line between ego and soul runs down the middle of every person. Most of us, from time to time, buy into a workaholic ethos that leaves us with little time for relationship. Most of us, from time to time, hue to a code of privacy that prevents us from actually knowing the people who live right nearby. Most of us live with technology that aims to reduce friction and maximize efficiency. Relationship, though, is inherently sticky and inefficient. Most of us, daily, slip back into self-absorption, succumb to the hunger for status, and have to recognize that and dive back into relation.

15. The relationalist worldview is not about the forces of good conquering the forces of evil. It's always a competition between partial truths. It's always an evolving conversation between self and society. It's always balancing tensions and trying to live life in graceful balance.

16. The relational life is a challenging life but ultimately it's a joyful life, because it is enmeshed in affection and crowned with moral joy.

The Good Society

1. As T. S. Eliot observed, the chief illusion of modern political activity is the belief that you can build a system so perfect that the people in it do not have to be good. The reality is that democracy and the economy rest upon a foundation, which is society. A society is a system of relationships. If there is no trust at the foundations of society, if there is no goodness, care, or faithfulness, relationships crumble, and the market and the state crash to pieces. If there are no shared norms of right and wrong, no sense of common attachments, then the people in the market and the state will rip one another to shreds as they vie for power and money. Society and culture are prior to and more important than politics or the market. The health of society depends on voluntary unselfishness.

2. In this day and age, our primary problems are at the level of the foundations. They are at the level of the system of relationships. Our society has been spiraling to ever-higher levels of distrust, ever-higher levels of unknowing and alienation. One bad action breeds another. One escalation of hostility breeds another.

3. The call of relationalism is to usher in a social transformation by reweaving the fabric of reciprocity and trust, to build a society, as Dorothy Day put it, in which it is easier to be good.

4. The social fabric is not woven by leaders from above. It is woven at every level, through a million caring actions, from one person to another. It is woven by people fulfilling their roles as good friends, neighbors, and citizens.

5. Whenever I treat another person as if he were an object, I've ripped the social fabric. When I treat another person as an infinite soul, I have woven the social fabric. Whenever I lie, abuse, stereotype, or traumatize a person, I have ripped the fabric. Whenever I see someone truly, and make them feel known, I have woven the fabric. Whenever I accuse someone of corruption without evidence, I have ripped the social

fabric. Whenever I disagree without maligning motives, I have woven it. The social fabric is created through an infinity of small moral acts, and it can be destroyed by a series of immoral ones.

6. Personal transformation and social transformation happen simultaneously. When you reach out and build community, you nourish yourself.

7. The ultimate faith of relationalism is that we are all united at the deepest levels. At the surface we have our glorious diversity. But at the substrate there is a commonality that no amount of hostility can ever fully extinguish, that no amount of division can ever fully sunder.

8. Relationships do not scale. They have to be built one at a time, through patience and forbearance. But norms do scale. When people in a community cultivate caring relationships, and do so repeatedly in a way that gets communicated to others, then norms are established. Trustworthy action is admired; empathy is celebrated. Cruelty is punished and ostracized. Neighborliness becomes the default state. An emergent system, a culture, has been created that subtly guides all the members in certain directions. When you create a norm through the repeated performance of some good action, you have created a new form of power. People within a moral ecology are given a million subtle nudges to either live up to their full dignity or sink to their base cravings. The moral ecology is the thing we build together through our daily decisions.

9. Rebuilding society is not just get-togetherism—convening people in some intellectually or morally neutral way. There has to be a shift in moral culture, a shift in the definition of the good life people imagine together.

10. The state has an important but incomplete role to play in this process. The state can provide services, but it cannot easily provide care. That is to say, the state can redistribute money to the poor, can build homeless shelters and day care centers.

It can create the material platforms on which relationships can be built. But the state can't create the intimate relationships that build a fully functioning person. That can only happen through habitual personal contact. It is only through relationships that we become neighbors, workers, citizens, and friends.

A Declaration of Interdependence

1. A good society is like a dense jungle. There are vines and intertwining branches. There are enmeshed root systems and connections across the canopy. There are monkeys playing at the treetops, the butterflies darting below. Every creature has a place in the great ecosystem. There is a gorgeous diversity and beauty and vitality.

2. A good person leading a good life is a creature enmeshed in that jungle. A beautiful life is a planted life, attached but dynamic. A good life is a symbiotic life—serving others wholeheartedly and being served wholeheartedly in return. It is daily acts of loving-kindness, gentleness in reproach, forbearance after insult. It is an adventure of mutual care, building, and exploration. The crucial question is not, Who I am? but, Whose am I?

3. Most of us get better at living as we go. There comes a moment, which may come early or later in life, when you realize what your life is actually about. You look across your life and review the moments when you felt more fully alive, at most your best self. They were usually moments when you were working with others in service of some ideal. That is the agency moment. That is the moment when you achieve clarity about what you should do and how you should live. That is the moment when the ego loses its grip. There is a sudden burst of energy that comes with freedom from the self-centered ego. Life becomes more driven and more gift.

That is the moment when a life comes to a point.

4. When you see people at that point, you realize they have an interior stronghold of values and devotions against which even the threat of death could not prevail. When you see people at that point, you see a generosity that radiates out into the world. You see people giving of themselves, not even in the grand ways, but just in the small favors and thoughtful considerations. This is how the jungle becomes thick and healthy.

5. When you see a group of people in that state, you see not just individuals but a people, a community, a flourishing society, where people help one another, magnify one another's talents, enjoy one another's creativity, and rest in one another's hospitality.

6. When you see people at the point, you see people with a power that overcomes division and distrust. Distrust is a perversity. No one wants to live in a distrusting place, or be lonely. Distrust comes about because of our own failings of relationship. But love has a redemptive power, Martin Luther King argued. It has the power to transform individuals and break down distrust. If you love a person and keep loving a person, they may lash out at first, but eventually they will break under the power of your care. Division is healed not mostly by solving the bad, but by overwhelming the bad with the good. If you can maximize the number of good interactions between people, then the disagreements will rest in a bed of loving care, and the bad will have a tendency to take care of itself. When trust is restored, the heartbeat relaxes, people are joyful together. Joy is found on the far side of sacrificial service. It is found in giving yourself away.

7. When you see that, you realize joy is not just a feeling, it is a moral outlook. It is a permanent state of thanksgiving and friendship, communion and solidarity. This is not an end to troubles and cares. Life doesn't offer us utopia. But the self has shrunk back to its proper size. When relationships are

tender, when commitments are strong, when communication is pure, when the wounds of life have been absorbed and the wrongs forgiven, people bend toward each other, intertwine with one another, and some mystical combustion happens. Love emerges between people out of nothing, as a pure flame.

ACKNOWLEDGMENTS

This book is about relationship, and it grew out of relationships. Over the past five years, as life took its twists and turns, my old friendships grew deeper and dozens of new friendships came as gifts. One of the things I learned is that if you are in need and you go to your friends for help, they prize the opportunity to help you. It deepens your friendship and sets up a season, later on, when you can help them, after the tables are turned. In the first draft of this acknowledgments I listed out these valuable friends by name, but I was afraid of leaving out somebody who was generous to me. So I just say to my friends—around the country and around the world—you know who you are. You remember the long dinners, the walks, the book clubs and salons, the late-night phone calls. You know how the things we talked about are infused through this book, how I've tried to take the collective wisdom of my friends and plow it into these pages.

Among the people involved most directly in the project, I'm especially grateful to those who read and commented on the manuscript, including April Lawson, James Hitchcock, Emily Esfahani Smith, Shaylyn Romney Garrett, Celeste Marcus, and Pete Wehner. Their advice was brilliant, their counsel invaluable. I'd also like to thank

Maria Popova, whose Brain Pickings blog is a continual source of wisdom and guidance.

I probably haven't written enough in this book about how we are formed by institutions. I've been blessed to have my life intertwined with at least five amazing ones. The first is All Our Kids. I write about my second family in chapter 8. Let me take an extra minute to thank not only David Simpson and Kathy Fletcher, but also Sarah P. and Emilia, not to mention Thalya, Tahrook, Madeline, Kleo, Keyno, Nabil, James, Koleco, Craig, Shaughn, Bella, Kesari, Santi, Bisah, Chyna, Nueta, Azarri, Brandon, Edd, and literally dozens of others. They have provided companionship, an emotional education, and the musical soundtrack for this phase of my life.

The second is *The New York Times*. Working with my fellow columnists is like working in the middle of an intellectual combustion engine. Working under James Bennet and Jim Dao and with James Hitchcock means you know that, despite appearances, the combustion engine won't actually explode. Serving our readers is a constant exercise in humility, in ways pleasant and painful.

The third is Yale University. I taught this book as a course at the Jackson Institute for Global Affairs, with the glowing and forbearing support of its director, Jim Levinsohn. Any professor knows you learn as much from your students as you teach them; I certainly did. I also learned from an array of Yale colleagues, especially Bryan Garsten, Miroslav Volf, Steven Smith, Christian Wiman, Tony Kronman, Stan McChrystal, Charles Hill, and John Lewis Gaddis.

The fourth is the Aspen Institute. Thanks to the trustees of the institute, I have had the chance to spend the past year traveling the country meeting the most inspiring and selfless people I have ever encountered. I'd especially like to thank Daniel Porterfield, Eric Motley, Jim Crown, Bob Steel, Lynda and Stewart Resnick, and, above all, my Weave colleagues: Tom Loper, April Lawson, Shaylyn Romney Garrett, Krystle Starvis, Isabel Soto, Celeste Marcus, and so many more.

Finally, there is Penguin Random House. This is my third book with this house, and I am the rare author who has nothing but good things to say about his publisher. Will Murphy brought me into the house. Andy Ward edited this book with insight and care. Gina Centrello wondered if I was going all woo-woo about eight years ago, but I hope she is satisfied with the Brooks woo-woo phase. Cole Louison is an absolutely amazing fact-checker. Campbell Schnebly-Swanson approached her research work with the verve and flair that marks her life.

I want to acknowledge a few other people. Everybody has a side hustle, and mine is being a pundit on radio and TV. In that role, for the past twenty years, I've had a chance to sit side by side with Mark Shields. It's been one of the great blessings of my life. Mark is rooted in his commitments, generous with his friendship, funny in his manner, and smart, fair, and provocative in our shared work.

My kids—Joshua, Naomi, and Aaron—have had hills and valleys, too, over the past few years, but they have emerged as smart, caring, mature, knowledgeable, and strong young adults. Hanging around them is sheer delight, every time. Every time my kids hit a new stage in life, I always think: Oh, this is the best stage of all. My mother, Lois, died while I was writing this book, and so I was deprived of my best and toughest editor. My father has endured her passing with selfless grace and good cheer.

Finally, Anne. A core argument in this book is that we can be broken open during those times when we are in the valley. We can also be broken open by love. The love that I feel for Anne and receive from her colors everything, warms everything. When people try to describe her, they usually settle on the same word: incandescent. This book has been, and the rest of my life will be, warmed and guided by Anne's light.

Introduction

xv **"I cleaned it so that he could"** Barry Schwartz and Kenneth Sharpe, *Practical Wisdom* (New York: Riverhead, 2010/2011), 10.

xvi **"The load, or weight"** C. S. Lewis, *The Weight of Glory* (New York: HarperOne, 1976), 10.

xxv **"The longer Levin mowed"** Leo Tolstoy, *Anna Karenina*, trans. Richard Pevear and Larissa Volokhonsky (New York: Penguin Classics, 2004), 253.

xxvi **"Words are inadequate"** William McNeill, *Keeping Together in Time* (Cambridge, MA: Harvard University Press, 1995), quoted in Jonathan Haidt, *The Happiness Hypothesis* (New York: Basic, 2005), 237.

xxvi **"A rail-thin man"** Zadie Smith, "Joy," The *New York Review of Books*, January 10, 2013, https://www.nybooks.com/articles/2013/01/10/joy.

xxvi **"If I had written the greatest book"** Nancy L. Roberts, *Dorothy Day and the Catholic Worker* (Albany: SUNY Press, 1985), 26.

xxvii **"Joy is the meeting place"** David Whyte, *Consolations* (Langley, WA: Many Rivers Press, 2015), 127.

xxvii **"For a long moment I'm still in"** Christian Wiman, *My Bright Abyss* (New York: Farrar, Straus and Giroux, 2013), 44.

xxviii **"Whenever I plunge into wilderness"** Belden C. Lane, *Backpacking with the Saints* (New York: Oxford University Press, 2014), 8.

xxix **"As I lay there"** Jules Evans, "Dissolving the Ego," *Aeon*, June 26, 2017, https://aeon.co/essays/religion-has-no-monopoly-on-transcendent-experience.

xxxiii **"Joy is not merely external"** Miroslav Volf, "The Crown of the Good Life: A Hypothesis," in *Joy and Human Flourishing*, eds. Miroslav Volf and Justin E. Crisp (Minneapolis: Fortress Press, 2015), 135.

ONE Moral Ecologies

8 **"Man is a creature"** Iris Murdoch, "Metaphysics and Ethics," in *Existentialists and Mystics* (New York: Penguin Press, 1998), 75.

TWO The Instagram Life

17 **"I am very sure that someday"** Jack O. Balswick, Pamela Ebstyne King, and Kevin S. Reimer, *The Reciprocating Self* (Downers Grove, IL: InterVarsity Press, 2005), 182.

17 **"identity capital"** Meg Jay, *The Defining Decade* (New York: Twelve, 2012), 10.

THREE The Insecure Overachiever

23 **"is a place you can lose"** David Whyte, *The Three Marriages* (New York: Riverhead, 2009), 25.

FOUR The Valley

26 **"I tried to achieve intellectual perfection"** Leo Tolstoy, *A Confession*, in *Pilgrim Souls*, ed. Amy Mandelker and Elizabeth Powers (New York: Touchstone, 1999), 51.

29 **"So there I was, a couple of years after college"** William Deresiewicz, *Excellent Sheep* (New York: Free Press, 2014), 110.

30 **"Something that doesn't have"** David Foster Wallace, quoted in Hubert Dreyfus and Sean Dorrance Kelly, *All Things Shining* (New York: Free Press, 2011), 24.

31 **"Conversation after conversation"** Veronica Rae Saron, "Your Unshakable Stuck-ness as a 20-something Millennial," *Medium*,

December 20, 2016, https://medium.com/@vronsaron/your
-unshakable-stuck-ness-as-a-20-something-millennial-d7580383
e1b0.

32 **Seventy-six percent** Rosalyn F. T. Murphy, "The Fellowship of
The King," *Comment*, June 12, 2018, https://www.cardus.ca/comment
/article/the-fellowship-of-the-king.

33 **"the state of mind that can find a social order"** Robert Nisbet, *The
Quest for Community* (San Francisco: ICS Press, 1990), xxiii.

34 **only 20 percent of young adults** William Damon, *The Path to
Purpose* (New York: Free Press, 2008), 60.

34 **church attendance has declined** Charles Heckscher, *Trust in a
Complex World* (Oxford: Oxford University Press, 2015), 50.

FIVE **The Wilderness**

39 **"You are living through an unusual time"** Henri J. M. Nouwen,
The Inner Voice of Love (New York: Image Books, 1999), 16.

40 **"What happens when a 'gifted child'"** Lane, *Backpacking with the
Saints*, 56.

40 **"Your pain is deep"** Nouwen, *The Inner Voice of Love*, 88.

41 **"If I were called upon"** Frederick Buechner, *The Alphabet of Grace*
(New York: HarperOne, 2009), 87.

41 **"As the darkness began to descend"** Parker J. Palmer, *Let Your Life
Speak* (San Francisco: Jossey-Bass, 1999), 19.

41 **"Trying to live"** Ibid., 5.

42 **"When I venture into wilderness"** Lane, *Backpacking with the
Saints*, 76.

43 **"Your ego prefers certainty"** James Hollis, *What Matters Most*
(New York: Avery, 2009), 95.

SIX **Heart and Soul**

44 **book about a guy who bought a house** Ronald Rolheiser, *The Holy
Longing* (New York: Image Books, 2009), 17.

45 **"To be human is to"** James K. A. Smith, *You Are What You Love*
(Grand Rapids, MI: Brazos Press, 2016), 8.

46 **Because you have this essence inside of you** Gerald K. Harrison, "A Defence of the Soul," *The Montreal Review*, June 2016, http://www.themontrealreview.com/2009/A-defence-of-the-soul.php.

49 **"My fit of illness"** Nathaniel Hawthorne, *The Blithedale Romance* (Boston: Ticknor, Reed, and Fields, 1852), 73.

SEVEN **The Committed Life**

55 **"A man who would say"** Dietrich von Hildebrand and Alice von Hildebrand, *The Art of Living* (Steubenville, OH: Hildebrand Project, 2017), 23.

56 **"Spirituality is an emotion"** Rabbi David Wolpe, "The Limitations of being 'Spiritual but Not Religious,'" *Time*, March 21, 2013, http://ideas.time.com/2013/03/21/viewpoint-the-problem-with-being-spiritual-but-not-religious.

57 **"existential urgency"** Paul Froese, *On Purpose* (New York: Oxford University Press, 2016), 54.

EIGHT **The Second Mountain**

68 **"There is a gravitas"** Richard Rohr, *Falling Upward* (San Francisco: Jossey-Bass, 2011), 117.

71 **"Instead, we saw"** Anne Colby and William Damon, *Some Do Care* (New York: Free, 1994), 70.

75 **"chaotic, extravert"** Patrick Woodhouse, *Etty Hillesum: A Life Transformed* (New York: Continuum, 2009), 7.

75 **"I think my parents"** Ibid., 13.

76 **"My capable brain"** Etty Hillesum, *An Interrupted Life: The Diaries, 1941–1943* (New York: Henry Holt, 1996), 49.

76 **"What I really want is a man"** Ibid., 17.

76 **"All my inner tensions"** Ibid., 7.

76 **"You are my beloved"** Woodhouse, *Etty Hillesum*, 21.

77 **"In other words, I wanted to subject nature,"** Ibid., 33.

77 **"Oh God, take me into Your great hands"** Hillesum, *Diaries*, 33.

78 **"No longer: I want this or that,"** Woodhouse, *Etty Hillesum*, 46.

78 **"The threat grows ever greater,"** Hillesum, *Diaries*, 133.

78 **"What is at stake"** Woodhouse, *Etty Hillesum*, 81.

78–79 **"I no longer believe"** Hillesum, *Diaries*, 84.

80 **"It is just as if"** Woodhouse, *Etty Hillesum*, 105.

80 **"There are many miracles"** Ibid., 120.

81 **"The misery here is quite terrible;"** Ibid., 128.

NINE **What Vocation Looks Like**

89 **"that one can be right and yet be beaten,"** Jeffrey Meyers, *Orwell: Wintry Conscience of a Generation* (New York: W. W. Norton & Company, Inc., 2000), 170.

91 **"It did not really matter"** Viktor E. Frankl, *Man's Search for Meaning* (New York: Pocket Books, 1985), 98.

91 **"When an issue is less central"** Anne Colby and William Damon, *The Power of Ideals* (Oxford: Oxford University Press, 2015), 84.

TEN **The Annunciation Moment**

96 **"A beautiful thing"** Frederick Turner, *Beauty: The Value of Values*, quoted in John O'Donohue, *Divine Beauty: The Invisible Embrace* (New York: HarperCollins, 2004), 55.

97 **"I can still remember"** Walter Isaacson, *Einstein: His Life and Universe* (New York: Simon & Schuster, 2008), 13.

97 **"Music, Nature and God"** Ibid., 14.

97 **"Only those who realize"** Froese, *On Purpose*, 8.

98 **"Let the young soul survey"** Friedrich Nietzsche, *Schopenhauer as Educator*, trans. Daniel Pellerin (self-pub., CreateSpace, 2014), 4.

ELEVEN **What Mentors Do**

102 **Escaping death by crocodile** E. O. Wilson, *Naturalist* (Washington: Island Press, 1994), 31.

103 **"The teacher, that professional amateur"** Leslie Fiedler, *What Was Literature?*, quoted in Deresiewicz, *Excellent Sheep*, 182.

103 **"Moral education is impossible"** Tracy Lee Simmons, *Climbing Parnassus* (Wilmington, DE: ISI Books, 2007), 45.

103 **"The most indispensable viaticum"** Ibid., 44.

104 **"In any hard discipline"** Matthew B. Crawford, *Shop Class as Soulcraft* (New York: Penguin Press, 2009), 65.

104 **"I went in curiosity"** William James, "What Makes a Life Significant?," *Leading Lives That Matter*, eds. Mark R. Schwehn and Dorothy C. Bass (Grand Rapids, MI: Eerdmans, 2006), 15.

105 **"The solid meaning"** Ibid., 27.

TWELVE **Vampire Problems**

107 **Eighty-three percent of all corporate mergers** Chip Heath and Dan Heath, *Decisive* (New York: Crown, 2013), 3.

107 **"You shouldn't fool yourself"** L. A. Paul, *Transformative Experience* (Oxford: Oxford University Press, 2014), 47.

108 **"It is remarkable that I am never quite clear"** Colby and Damon, *The Power of Ideals*, 108.

111 **"Your emotional commitment"** Robert Greene, *Mastery* (New York: Viking, 2012), 180.

113 **a snowball sitting on an iceberg** Timothy D. Wilson, *Strangers to Ourselves* (Cambridge, MA: Belknap Press, 2004), 6.

114 **The share of parents who arrived late doubled.** Samuel Bowles, *The Moral Economy* (New Haven: Yale University Press, 2016), 5.

116 **"the habit of analysis"** Atam Etinson, "Is a Life Without Struggle Worth Living?," *The New York Times*, October 2, 2017.

117 **"I watched her move around"** Mary Catherine Bateson, *Composing a Life* (New York: Grove Press, 2001), 39.

117 **"After an event like that"** Emily Esfahani Smith, *The Power of Meaning* (New York: Broadway Books, 2017), 163.

118 **"One's mind has to be a searching mind,"** Thomas Bernhard, *Old Masters* (Chicago: University of Chicago Press, 1992), 20.

THIRTEEN **Mastery**

124 **"My own particular cover"** Lane, *Backpacking with the Saints*, 41.

125 **Bradley found two long, narrow corridors** Greene, *Mastery*, 79.

128 **"but we also need to learn the virtue"** Galen Guengerich, "One Well Deep Enough" (sermon, All Souls Unitarian Church, New York City, NY, October 5, 2014).

128 **"Something rather intriguing"** Schwartz and Sharpe, *Practical Wisdom*, 87.

129 **the entire architecture of a piece of music** Greene, *Mastery*, 6.

130 **"the greatest album cover"** Bruce Springsteen, *Born to Run* (New York: Simon & Schuster, 2016), 49.

132 **"An artist is conscious"** Wiman, *My Bright Abyss*, 41.

133 **"Here was where I wanted to make my stand"** Springsteen, *Born to Run*, 264.

FOURTEEN Maximum Marriage

140 **"These men came to adulthood"** Judith S. Wallerstein and Sandra Blakeslee, *The Good Marriage* (New York: Houghton Mifflin Harcourt, 1995), 43.

140 **"I was trying to think of the worst fight"** Ibid., 313.

140 **"We need to swap the Romantic view"** Alain de Botton, "Why You Will Marry the Wrong Person," *The New York Times*, May 28, 2016.

141 **"I think what was so refreshing"** Wallerstein and Blakeslee, *The Good Marriage*, 173.

142 **"Expressive individualism"** Eli J. Finkel, *The All-or-Nothing Marriage* (New York: Dutton, 2017), 82.

142 **"we have been living in the era"** Eli J. Finkel, "The All-or-Nothing Marriage," *The New York Times*, February 14, 2014.

142 **"my companion"** Finkel, *The All-or-Nothing Marriage*, 111.

142 **"the savvy, sovereign chooser"** Polina Aronson, "Romantic Regimes," *Aeon*, October 22, 2015, https://aeon.co/essays/russia-against-the-western-way-of-love.

143 **"We must return to an attitude"** Mike Mason, *The Mystery of Marriage* (Colorado Springs: Multnomah, 2005), 107.

143–44 **"Whether it turns out to be a healthy, challenging, and constructive crisis"** Ibid., 10.

145 **"And there's the great problem of marriage"** Timothy Keller and Kathy Keller, *The Meaning of Marriage* (New York: Dutton, 2011), 180.

FIFTEEN **The Stages of Intimacy I**

149 **"A man in this state"** C. S. Lewis, *The Four Loves* (New York: Harcourt Brace, 1991), 93.

152 **About a fifth of adults in Western cultures** Hal Shorey, "Fear of Intimacy and Closeness in Relationships," *Psychology Today*, April 19, 2015.

153 **"Good people will mirror goodness"** Rohr, *Falling Upward*, 155.

153 **I am your match** Whyte, *The Three Marriages*, 50.

SIXTEEN **The Stages of Intimacy II**

156 **"Wife and husband together bless"** Amy A. Kass and Leon R. Kass, *Wing to Wing, Oar to Oar* (Notre Dame, IN: University of Notre Dame Press, 2000), 449.

156 **"Many of the divorced couples I've seen"** Wallerstein and Blakeslee, *The Good Marriage*, 48.

156 **"There is a lovely disarray"** O'Donohue, *Divine Beauty*, 150.

158 **"Thus one might wake the other"** Sheldon Vanauken, *A Severe Mercy* (New York: Harper & Row, 1977), 39.

160 **"He who is devoid of the power"** Martin Luther King, Jr., *Strength to Love* (Minneapolis: Fortress Press, 2010), 44.

162 **"The unrelated human being"** James Hollis, *Finding Meaning in the Second Half of Life* (New York: Gotham, 2006), 119.

163 **"We said, 'If we aren't more in love'"** Vanauken, *A Severe Mercy*, 43.

163 **"Better this than parting"** Lewis, *The Four Loves*, 107.

SEVENTEEN **The Marriage Decision**

166 **The odds are worse** Jay, *The Defining Decade*, 74.

168 **"If you choose some dreamy partner"** Ty Tashiro, *The Science of Happily Ever After* (New York: Harlequin, 2014), 152.

169 **They relax because it feels normal** Ibid., 195.

169 **For people with anxious attachments** Ibid., 203.

170 **"Neurotic individuals"** Ibid., 173.

170 **three types of love** Reimer, *The Reciprocating Self*, 226.

EIGHTEEN **Marriage: The School You Build Together**

175 **"To separate emotionally"** Wallerstein and Blakeslee, *The Good Marriage*, 28.

176 **"We too often act from scripts"** Alain de Botton, *The Course of Love* (New York: Simon & Schuster, 2016), 83.

177 **"The magic of a couple's relationship"** Ayala Malach Pines, *Falling in Love, 2nd Edition* (New York: Routledge, 2013), 183.

178 **"There's a habit of mind"** Emily Esfahani Smith, "Masters of Love," *The Atlantic*, June 12, 2014.

179 **"The sulker both desperately needs"** de Botton, *The Course of Love*, 63.

181 **"It is the deliberate choosing of closeness"** Mason, *The Mystery of Marriage*, 42.

181 **"A marriage lives, paradoxically"** Ibid., 36.

182 **"an ecstasy of deeds"** Abraham Joshua Heschel, *God in Search of Man* (New York: Farrar, Straus and Giroux, 1976), 358.

184 **"You're 82 years old"** Alain Badiou and Nicolas Truong, *In Praise of Love* (London: Serpent's Tail, 2012), 45.

NINETEEN **Intellectual Commitments**

191 **"Joining a radical movement"** Irving Kristol, *Neoconservatism* (Chicago: Ivan R. Dee/Elephant Paperbacks, 1999), 470.

193 **"One is apt to think of moral failure"** Simmons, *Climbing Parnassus*, 43.

193 **"draws our attention away"** Anthony T. Kronman, *Education's End* (New Haven: Yale University Press, 2007), 127.

193 **"For it made the question"** Ibid., 125.

196 **"an endless unrehearsed intellectual adventure"** Paul Franco, *Michael Oakeshott: An Introduction* (New Haven: Yale University Press, 2004), 122.

TWENTY **Religious Commitment**

203 **"And I knew that the Spirit"** Wendell Berry, *Jayber Crow* (Washington: Counterpoint, 2001), 83.

206 **"In reality there was an opportunity"** Frankl, *Man's Search for Meaning*, 93.

207 **"For the first time in my life"** Ibid., 57.

208 **"This tree is the only friend"** Ibid., 90.

209 **"Really? You have never felt overwhelmed"** Wiman, *My Bright Abyss*, 10.

210 **"it is not only as if we were suddenly"** Ibid., 82.

TWENTY-ONE **A Most Unexpected Turn of Events**

212 **"My old ideas were not adequate"** Ibid., 92.

214 **"With a penetrating consciousness"** Avivah Gottlieb Zornberg, *The Particulars of Rapture* (New York: Schocken, 2011), 10.

223 **"When they realize that nobody cares"** Jean Vanier, *Becoming Human* (New York: Paulist Press, 2008), 9.

223 **"Weakness carries within it"** Ibid., 40.

226 **"concrete religion"** Joseph Soloveitchik, *Halakhic Man* (Philadelphia: The Jewish Publication Society of America, 1984), 58.

227 **"Holiness is created by man"** Ibid., 46.

229 **"I just sat there"** Robert Coles, *Dorothy Day: A Radical Devotion* (Reading, MA: Addison-Wesley, 1987), 16.

232 **"Awe is itself"** Heschel, *God in Search of Man*, 74.

235 **"One attitude is alien"** Ibid., 45.

240 **"In Dostoyevsky's novel, this prostitute"** Jaroslav Pelikan, *Fools for Christ* (Eugene, OR: Wipf and Stock, 2001), 76.

243 **"For my part, I can very well describe"** Søren Kierkegaard, *Fear and Trembling*, eds. C. Stephen Evans and Sylvia Walsh, trans. Sylvia Walsh (New York: Cambridge University Press, 2006), 31.

244 **"One can only choose a side"** Vanauken, *A Severe Mercy*, 99.

246 **"Our only truly essential human task"** Cynthia Bourgeault, *The Wisdom Jesus* (Boston: Shambhala, 2008), 106.

246 **"In the Beatitudes something of the celestial grandeur"** Romano Guardini, *The Lord* (Washington: Gateway Editions, 1996), 84.

248 **"Religion is not"** Soloveitchik, *Halakhic Man*, 142.

248 **"then I have to admit"** Wiman, *My Bright Abyss*, 9.

250 **"among confession and tears"** Philip Yancey, *Soul Survivor* (New York: Galilee/Doubleday, 2003), 249.

250 **"At least five times out of ten"** Ibid., 264.

251 **"The church is both my greatest intellectual"** Rohr, *Falling Upward*, 80.

TWENTY-TWO Ramps and Walls

254 **"The moment I began exercising my will"** Eugene H. Peterson, *The Contemplative Pastor* (Grand Rapids, MI: Eerdmans, 1993), 98.

257 **"Liturgy ritually reenacts a tradition"** Christian Smith, *Moral, Believing Animals* (Oxford: Oxford University Press, 2003), 16.

TWENTY-THREE The Stages of Community Building I

265 **"intricate, almost unconscious network"** Jane Jacobs, *The Death and Life of Great American Cities* (New York: Vintage, 2016), 32.

266 **"Under the seeming disorder"** Ibid., 50.

274 **"The future is created"** Peter Block, *Community: The Structure of Belonging* (San Francisco: Berrett–Koehler Publishers, 2008), 85.

TWENTY-FOUR The Stages of Community Building II

286 **"I come here to tell you"** Vanier, *Becoming Human*, 7.

286 **"True community is different"** Ibid., 50.

287 **the Israelites are never happier** Aaron Wildavsky, *Moses as Political Leader* (Jerusalem: Shalem Press, 2005), 111.

Thunderfire

Ralph C. Summers

A Black Horse Western

ROBERT HALE · LONDON

© John Glasby 1964, 2003
First hardcover edition 2003
Originally published in paperback as
Thunderfire by Tex Bradley

ISBN 0 7090 7255 4

Robert Hale Limited
Clerkenwell House
Clerkenwell Green
London EC1R 0HT

The right of John Glasby to be identified as
author of this work has been asserted by him
in accordance with the Copyright, Designs and
Patents Act 1988.

Typeset by
Derek Doyle & Associates, Liverpool.
Printed and bound in Great Britain by
Antony Rowe Limited, Wiltshire

ONE

LEGACY

It was mid-morning when Chris Ranson forded the wide river that cut across the trail. Back in the night, he had made camp among the tall ridges which overlooked the trail into Memphis, had spent long, shivering, uncomfortable hours in the rocks, hungry and angry at having to be there at all. The letter which had brought him all this way across the wilderness of desert and mountain from the warm country south of the Rio Grande, still reposed in his pocket, a strange letter from the lawyer here in Memphis, asking him to come as quickly as possible. What could any lawyer want with him? he wondered as he off-saddled on the far bank of the slow-flowing river, let his horse blow and drink; and why the urgency so clearly implied in the letter? There had been nothing in it to give him any clear indication of why his presence here was so necessary, merely the tersely worded summons to Memphis.

He seated himself wearily on a low knoll of ground, in the shade of a tall tree which overhung the water, took the letter from his pocket, extracted the paper and read it through once again, trying to read something into it. The wind which swept along the river was good, its smell clean and fresh in his nostrils, but he was anxious to get on and ten minutes later, he tightened the cinch and stepped up into the saddle, turn-

5

ing his mount towards the wide Memphis trail. Tall, broad-shouldered, narrow hipped, his face tanned by the hot Mexican sun, his eyes hard and blue like chips of agate, stared straight ahead of him as he rode. At first sight, he might have been one of a hundred saddle tramps who rode these trails, keeping one uneasy jump ahead of the law, doing a little cowpunching here and there along the way but never stopping for very long in one place. But a closer look would have revealed that the clothes he wore, dusty and travel-stained as they were, were of a different cut to those worn by the ordinary trail-riders. There was an expensive quality about them, the way they had been so obviously tailored to fit him. There was, too, one other thing which marked him out from the usual run of trail trash. He carried no gun in his belt and the Winchester thrust into the saddle scabbard was brand new, shining, the metal glinting brilliantly in the hot sun.

It was high noon when Chris Ranson rode into the streets of Memphis. Heat had come to the town. Heat from the sun and the stretching plains around it. It shimmered in the streets and lay in a heavy, oppressive pressure on the tall buildings that flanked the streets. Siesta time and there were few people abroad at this hour. A handful of ponies stood with a stolid patience, tethered to the hitching rail outside one of the saloons, tails twitching at the flies which had settled in swarms around them. A couple of men drifted slowly across the dusty street towards the nearby hotel, paused for a moment to watch the tall stranger who rode along the street, then turned and pushed open the doors, going inside, out of the heat and the flaming sunlight.

Ranson rode slowly, eyes glancing along the rows of build-ings. This was much the same as a score of towns he had seen both north and south of the Rio Grande. Memphis was a town that had been built in a great hurry, sprouting from the desert in the space of a few short months, thrown up by men who were in a hurry to build, to get things done, because the frontiers were pushing south and west and there had to be places such as this to keep things moving, to bring up the freight and the wagon trains, to drive the railroad west, to bring the banks and also law and order into a lawless territory.

He located the livery stable halfway along the street, put in his horse, then turned back, retracing his steps to where he had noticed the lawyer's office, the faded gilt lettering over the doorway peeled off by the action of sun and rain and the driving, abrading dust that blew along the street. He thrust open the door with the flat of his hand, walked in with the assurance of a man used to having things done his way. The office was empty as he entered, and he could feel the tremendous heat of the sun strike his shoulders through the dusty, fly-speckled window that looked out on to the wide street. In spite of the bright sunlight that streamed through the window, the room still contrived to look dark and forbidding. Maybe it was the furniture that did it, he reflected, glancing about him. The heavy, solid, carved woodenness of it, with the huge desk dominating everything.

The door at the back of the room opened and Ranson turned quickly, facing the man who stepped through. Lawyer Sims was a small man, his face lined and wizened so that it was virtually impossible to guess at his real age. He peered closely at Ranson through the rimless glasses perched on the end of his thin nose, then moved to the desk and stood behind it, as if it afforded him some form of protection.

'I'm Chris Ranson.' He took the letter from his pocket and held it out to the other, leaning forward over the desk as he did so.

'You got here fast,' acknowledged the other. He seated himself in the padded chair at the back of the desk, motioned Chris to the other. 'I didn't expect you for some days yet, wasn't even sure that my letter would reach you.' He peered at Chris over the glasses, still holding the letter in his hand. 'You're a very elusive man, you know.'

'Maybe if you'll tell me what this is all about, I'll know whether I've wasted my time or not,' said Chris pointedly.

'All in good time, Mister Ranson. First I must satisfy myself on certain points and make sure that you really are the man I'm looking for.' He surveyed the other for a long moment, peering over the top of the glasses, then bent to take a paper from the lower drawer of his desk, head still cocked at an angle to look up. 'Your father, what can you tell me about him?'

Chris grinned. 'I liked him. They reckon I take after him, that's why neither of us ever went back to the family spread up north, in Cochise County. My father died more than three years ago.' There was an almost defiant tilt to his face as he went on: 'He was shot in the back by some drunken gunman in Abilene.'

'They said he was cheating at poker, wasn't that it?' murmured the other softly as he studied the papers in front of him.

'That's a lie!' In a swift, lithe movement, Chris leaned over the desk and gripped the other around the throat, fingers squeezing inexorably. Desperately, the other pulled himself back, lips working, eyes bulging from his head.

'I'm sorry . . . I—' The other fell back in the chair as Chris released his hold on him, throat muscles working in his scrawny neck. After a moment, he sat up, rubbing this throat. 'I'm only saying what I've heard,' he muttered.

'Then you heard wrong. But you didn't ask me to come all the way to Memphis just to hear about my father.'

The other swallowed thickly. He seemed to have recovered some of his composure. Sitting forward on the edge of his chair, he riffled through the papers for a moment and then said quietly, evenly: 'You're quite right, Mister Ranson. I asked you to come here so that I might read to you the last will and testament of your grandfather, James Ellerton Ranson.'

'My grandfather!' Chris sat tall and very still in his chair, staring at the other as if unable to believe his ears.

He recalled very little of his grandfather; he had been only nine years old when he had left the vast ranch in the north and gone with his father to spend the next fourteen years south of the Texas border in the small towns of Mexico. They had been long, interesting years. He had never asked where his father had got the money which he seemed to spend so freely, not even after his mother had died that hot, sultry summer evening, with the faint rumble of thunder over the low hills in the distance, heralding the rain which would bring a little coolness to the oven-like air. Now that he came to look back on it, he remembered what the doctor had said, that she had died of some obscure coronary disease. It was as good a name for a broken heart as any.

They had buried her on the green hill outside the little town of Santa Rosita, where the deep red camellias lay like fire among the grass, and the air was warm and sweet and the only sound to disturb the deep, eternal stillness was the ringing of the Angelus from the little stone church, half a mile away. His father was now buried next to her in the same churchyard on the hill, and for three years he had been alone, drifting from one town to another on both sides of the border.

During the whole of that time, he had thought nothing of his grandfather. His only memories were of a stern and fine-featured man who ruled his ranch hands with a rod of iron, who had tried to do the same with his family; and this had been the cause of the break-up. Now, it seemed, his grandfather was dead. He leaned back in his chair. Even though his memories were dimmed by the intervening years, it still seemed impossible to believe that the old man was dead, that he no longer ruled over that vast ranch.

'. . . and to my grandson, Chris Ranson, I hereby bequeath all of my property and herd in the earnest hope that keeping it intact will make a man of him and in some way blot out the bad blood that was in his father.'

Carefully, the lawyer laid the paper down on top of the desk and glanced up at Chris, took off the spectacles and polished the lenses with his handkerchief.

'It would appear that you are the only surviving relative of the late James Ranson,' he said finally when Chris made no move to speak. 'The news has come as something of a surprise to you?'

'I scarcely remember him,' Chris rubbed his chin thought-fully. 'He was a queer old cuss from what I do recall.' He straightened on his chair. 'So he's dead at last and the ranch belongs to me.'

'That's right.' The other regarded him keenly. 'Are you accepting it? If so, I feel it only right to warn you that you won't find things easy to handle there, and there may be danger for you.'

'Danger? What kind of danger?'

'All of that greed, all that crazy hate. Your grandfather was a hated man, Mister Ranson. There were more men than you could count who wanted that spread of his. He owned most of the water in the territory, he had the best grassland and the biggest herd and if that doesn't add up to a powder keg just waiting for somebody to step in and light the fuse, I don't know what does.'

'And you figure that if I ride in there and claim the ranch, I'll be ridin' right into trouble.'

'Don't you?'

'You could be right.' Chris frowned. 'Tempers can run mighty high in that part of the country. But if anybody's trying to take over the ranch then it's up to me to go back there and stop 'em.'

'You'll have the biggest fight of your life on your hands if you do,' warned the other. 'Every man in the territory will be gunning for you. From what I've heard, your grandfather was one of the fastest men on the draw and nobody fancied going up against him. But now he's dead, every range wolf in the county will be setting their sights on that land and herd.'

Chris remained silent for a long time, bent forward in his chair, his arms across his knees. He seemed indrawn and sober, a lot of the assurance gone from him as he tried to absorb all of this news, felt the full weight of responsibility which had been suddenly, and unexpectedly, thrust on him. He had scarcely ever considered that one day, the ranch would be his. Most of his life had been spent in the cantinas south of the border, in a carefree existence, wanting little, his father having left him comfortably off. Life had proved to be something of a lazy, idyllic existence for him during those years. Now, quite suddenly, he had been brought up against life as it really was, with a jolt. He needed a little time in which to pause and think things over; but if what the wizened little lawyer said was true, then time was something he had little of. Already, there would be powerful and unscrupulous forces at work, scheming to take over the ranch by fair means or foul.

'Well,' said the lawyer presently, staring at him over the huge, polished desk. 'What do you intend to do? Ride on to Cochise County and take over where your grandfather left off; or take your horse and ride back south of the border, leave the place to the gunwolves.'

Chris pressed his lips tightly together. He gave the other a bright-sharp stare.

'When my father left the ranch all those years ago, took my mother to live with him in Mexico, my grandfather disowned him, cut him off completely. True I had little to do with him then, but he must have had a reason for leavin' the place to me.'

'Evidently he thought very little of your father, even when he died,' said the other evenly. 'He mentions the bad blood in your father, hoping that you'll somehow be able to wipe that out.'

'Maybe he reckoned that I might be shot in the attempt to hold the ranch and he could get back at my father that way.' Chris spoke in a quiet, impersonal way, but there was a touch of bitterness on his face. 'If that was what he wanted, some kind of revenge beyond the grave, then this would be a good way of getting it.'

'A man would have to hate a lot to do a thing like that,' the lawyer reminded him. 'I only knew your grandfather slightly. He was never a man who made a great many friends. They either feared him or hated him and you can't base friendship on feelings like that. But he seemed to me to be a hard, though fair-minded, man. He had an iron will and he would never give in to any man. I think that was why he hated your father so much, because he had the will power to stand up against him and defy him.'

Chris got slowly to his feet, stood for a long moment looking down at the other, then said tightly. 'Reckon I'll step across to the hotel for a bite to eat. I'll come back later this afternoon when I've had time to think this whole thing over and let you know what I've decided.'

The lawyer shrugged. 'That's your privilege, Mister Ranson,' he said stiffly.

Chris crossed the dust of the street to the hotel and signed the register before climbing the squealing stairs to the room on the top floor. He pulled off his shirt and washed the trail dust off his body, filling the washbowl from the tall pitcher of water. His bones ached from the long ride; seven days on the trail, through the tall mountains and over the dry, dusty plains with a waterhole every twenty or thirty miles. Inwardly, he felt like a board that had been left out in the sun for far too long, warped and twisted and dry to the core. Up-ending the pitcher, he poured the rest of the water into the glass that stood on the small table by the bed and drank all he could hold, but he still seemed unable to slake the thirst that was deep in him, or wash all of the trail dust out of his throat. Pulling on a fresh shirt from his saddle roll, he went out into the passage outside his room, passed a couple of other rooms where the doors lay open, saw men seated there playing poker. A couple glanced up at him as he went by, curious, but not over inquisitive. A stranger in town was always likely to attract some attention, he reflected, as he made his way into

12

the dining room, found himself a table by the wall where he could see the other diners, and ordered his meal. When it came, he ate it slowly, savouring the well cooked food which he had missed during those long days on the trail, turning things over in his mind, trying to decide what to do for the best.

Certainly he was now the last of the Ransons and the ranch itself was his heritage no matter what the reason was for his grandfather leaving it to him, clearly knowing the danger there would be. The old man would have known of the envious eyes which were cast on the spread, knew that before Chris could maintain a hold on the place, there would be bad years when the smell of gunsmoke and powder lay thick and heavy over the range and men died with a surprising suddenness. The other rich desert ranchers would try to grab off all the water and the best land for themselves and now that his grandfather was dead, now that the gunhand which had held them in check in the past was stilled in death, they would doubtless renew their efforts and let nothing stand in their way, certainly not a newcomer to the territory who, although he held claim to the ranch, would surely have to fight for it.

Finishing his meal, he sat back, found the makings of a smoke and rolled the tobacco slowly, then lit the cigarette and drew the smoke deep into his lungs. He had been weary when he had stepped down into the dining room, but the meal seemed to have acted as a stimulant and restlessness bubbled up inside him, something he found hard to control. Maybe the urges that moved a man to the wandering from one town to another were beginning to change. Maybe there came a time for every man when he wanted something more lasting and permanent, something to call his own and some place where he could sink his roots and stay for the rest of his days. Maybe a man would even be prepared to fight for such a thing, to fight and to kill if that were the only way he could hold it.

He returned to the livery stable to check on his horse, then made his way slowly to the lawyer's office. The other gave him a brief nod as he entered, motioned to him to be seated.

'Had time to think this over?' he asked.

'I reckon so,' Chris nodded. 'I've decided to ride up into Cochise County and take over the ranch.'

The lawyer gave him a slow look of surprise, as if this had not been the answer he had been expecting. He said: 'You know your own mind better than anybody, I suppose. I only hope that you've made the right, and wise, decision.'

'I guess so. I reckon it's the only decision I can make in the circumstances.' He had surveyed all of the other possibilities during the minutes he had sat over his meal at the hotel, had turned them carefully in his mind while musing through the pale haze of smoke from his cigarette. True, the future was something that had no promise of anything definite for him other than perhaps an uncertain and maybe impecunious hardship. Danger he expected, but he was still far from being free of the nagging uncertainty and that troubled him more than he dared admit, even to himself. As he sat there in that dusty, drab office, he wondered what plans might be being laid against him, even at that moment, for he did not doubt that word of this would already have reached the men who would be waiting to kill him.

He thought about that a lot more throughout the evening, wondering again if he had done the right thing but each time that doubts assailed him, the thought came to him that his grandfather, no matter what else might have been said against him, had made the vast ranch himself, had built it with his own two hands in the hard, old days just before the Civil War, had made it into what it was. He had made it not only for himself, but for the Ranson family so that the name might come to mean something in that part of the territory. He had made this small empire, proclaimed himself the head of it; and now it was up to him to carry on the name.

Bob Dunson dragged his spurs over the yard of the ranch, raking up little snakeheads of dust under his feet. At the porch, he hesitated for a moment, turned to throw a quick glance about him, at the horses moving in the corral and the cattle which were clustered high up on the brow of the hills in the distance. Then he pushed open the door with the flat of his hand and strode inside.

Taking off his hat, he looked about him with wary eyes, swung swiftly as the door opened and Matt Wilder stepped into the room. The other brought his glance to Dunson and looked at him for a thoughtful moment. 'You've been a long time,' he said, thinly, 'what did you find out in Memphis?'

'Jest what you figgered,' muttered the other. He sank down into the nearby chair as the other poured a drink into a glass and held it out to him. 'That lawyer fella managed to locate old man Ranson's grandson. They say he was way down in Mexico, south of the border. Made quite a name for himself down there.'

Wilder's brows went up a little. 'What sort of a name'?' he queried.

'Not as a gunman, that's a fact,' grinned the other. 'I'd guess you'd call him a gambler like his father. Ain't surprised the old man wanted nothing much to do with either of 'em.'

'So it shouldn't be too difficult to get rid of him, one way or another,' murmured the other musingly. He rubbed a hand down his face.

Dunson watched the other steadily over the rim of his glass, trying to guess at the thoughts now in the other's mind. 'You figuring on stopping him before he gets here? Reckon that would be the simplest way of makin' sure.'

'The simplest way, maybe, but not the best way,' countered the other, his face suddenly hard as he turned the possibilities over in his mind. 'This has got to look like an accident. You know as well as I do, that there are still a lot of folk in this territory who thought a lot of old man Ranson. They'll stick by his grandson if he's anythin' like the old man. From what you say, that ain't likely, but we have to play this hand carefully.'

'Better be sure that you don't wait too long before makin' your play,' muttered Dunson. He finished his drink, laid the empty glass on the table. 'There are more than you with eyes on the Ranson spread. If they make their play first, you may find that you're squeezed out.'

'You think I don't know that. I know all about Webber and Diego. I can call twice as many men to my back as they can between them – and they know that. If they step out of line as far as this deal is concerned, they'll be shot to pieces and they'll lose everything they have now.'

'You want me to keep an eye open along the trail? He was still in Memphis when I pulled out, but I reckon if he left the next mornin' he can't be more than a day's ride behind me.'

Wilder nodded tersely. 'Do that,' he ordered. 'Let me know the minute he rides into town. I figure he may head there for a word with Sheriff Maxwell before he moves on to the ranch.'

It was late morning before Chris Ranson reached the long line of timber which reared up on the slopes of the low hills. Down below him lay Cochise County and the vast Ranson spread, and a few moments later, he came upon the trail that wound down through the trees, then through the narrow ravine, at the lower end of which the trail widened, moved across a river and then vanished into the rocks on the far side. He halted his mount, sat tall in the saddle, his eyes fixed ahead, but seeing little, lips tightly compressed. Depression chilled his spirit a little as he struggled with his thoughts.

Finishing his smoke, he went on, crossed a bare bench of ground that opened out like a scar among the trees. There were a few blackened stumps on the edge of the open stretch and it was obvious that fire had destroyed the undergrowth here at some time in the past, possibly during the war, for this was part of the land which had been fought over during the long battle of the Wilderness. Half an hour onward, he came across a narrow footbridge that stretched over a deep gorge

16

with a narrow, swift-running stream at the bottom of it.

He glanced at the creek, running fast and white, creaming with foam where the water splashed and raced among the sharp-pointed boulders which thrust up from the rocky bed, then put his mount to the bridge, listening to the hollowness of its hoofbeats on the wood. Somewhere close by the bridge, but still out of sight, he was able to pick out the sound of the falls which had produced this creek, dropping with a steady thunder down the side of the rock face. The mist from the falls lay in the air with a thin dampness that touched his face and neck and brought a quiet coolness to everything. Even the vegetation here seemed to grow more densely and lushly than anywhere else along the trail.

He turned a sharp corner in the trail just beyond the far end of the bridge and came suddenly on the bare patch which had been cleared away at the very foot of the mountain wall. Here, there was a wooden shack, little more than a lean-to, with the far wall set simply against the bare rock. The contrast between the grey, weathered rock and the tall green-topped pines that marched away in every direction from the hut, was tremendous, almost breath-taking. A couple of mangy dogs came scuffing towards him, stood on top of a small knoll, sniffing the air at him, their tails between their legs.

Chris sat quite still as a man moved into sight from around the side of the cabin, a rifle held loosely in his right hand. He had a thin, stretched face, with wrinkles showing around the eyes and mouth, a face from which it was impossible to tell if he was old or young. Chris reckoned he was about six feet in height, but the slimness of his build made him seem even taller.

For a long moment, the other stared at him through narrowed eyes, suspicious of him. The two dogs came snarling forward, but still keeping a safe distance, as if they too were unsure of him.

'You lookin' for somethin', stranger, or jest ridin'?' asked the other after a long pause.

'I'm lookin' for the Ranson place,' said Chris softly. He eyed the rifle which the other still held in his hand. The man stared at him for a few moments longer and then lowered the hand that held the gun. 'Still quite a ways from here,' he said harshly. 'Reckon you won't make it before evenin'. You look like you've been ridin' for quite a spell. Get down and come inside.'

Gratefully, Chris climbed from the saddle, let the horse go free. There was no place it could wander here and he doubted if it would make the return journey over the narrow bridge above the deep, steep-sided canyon.

'You got any reason for lookin' for the Ranson spread?' grunted the other as he bent his head and led the way inside the shack.

'Some,' said Chris casually. 'I'm Chris Ranson. I got word a couple of days ago that my grandfather was dead and the place had been left to me.'

The other stolidly accepted the information, gave a brief nod of his head as he laid his glance on Chris, the look like the edge of a knife, motionless but ready to cut. Chris guessed he was one of the lonesome sort, a man who came out to this wild wilderness to be away from other men, perhaps preferring the company of the dogs to that of his fellow men.

'So you're Jim Ranson's grandson,' he said. 'Well, I reckon you know what you're up against. There's a mighty lot of men who'd like to get their hands on that spread.'

'So I've been told. You know anythin' about 'em?'

'Some.' The other motioned him to the table, spread with food. 'Jest because I live up here, don't mean that I know nothin' of what goes on down in the valley. Reckon I know more'n most folk. Matt Wilder tried to get the ranch some years ago, but your grandfather wouldn't sell. Wilder's ranch butts on to the Ranson place and he needs more water than he's got. Any man other than Jim Ranson would have been run out of the territory once Wilder started. But your grandfather stood up to him, forced him to pull in his horns like a salted snail.' The bushy brows went up in an expression of mute interrogation. 'You figger that you're the same kind of man, that you can stand up to men like Wilder or Diego?'

His gaze had dropped to the belt around Chris's waist. 'See you ain't carryin' guns. A man needs guns if he's to stay alive around these parts, specially with men like Diego and Wilder gunnin' for him.'

'No reason for anybody to know who I am just yet.'

The other shook his head as he seated himself at the other side of the table. 'You're a danged fool if you believe that. Wilder will know that you're ridin' in already. He'll have had one of his men, probably Dunson, watchin' for you.' The bright, bird-like stare fixed on Chris again. 'Where'd you get the news about the ranch?'

'Memphis. The lawyer there sent word across the border to Santa Rosita.'

'Then I figure you can bet your bottom dollar that Dunson would be there, in Memphis. Reckon that must've been him I saw ridin' hell for leather yesterday along the valley trail.'

Chris gave him a tight look. 'You seem to have got your fingers on a lot of things in these parts for all that you live so far off the beaten track.'

'A stranger ridin' into town will be suspected, particularly now that old man Ranson is dead. They'll know that sooner or later, you'd come ridin' in to claim the ranch. You couldn't fool them even if you tried.'

'Then you figure I'm a fool.' Chris looked directly at the rangy man.

The other shrugged. 'Either that, or there's a heap more to you than I can see right now. I know the sort of man that your grandfather was, but whether you can stand in his shoes or not, I'm not sure.'

'Were you a friend of my grandfather's?'

The other chewed thoughtfully on a mouthful of food for a long moment as if turning that question over in his mind. He said finally: 'Reckon your grandfather had no friends. But he was a straight, honest man and that's why a lot of the folk here respected him. They knew that he'd back 'em in any fight that came between them and men like Wilder and Diego. So long as he was around, they felt safe. Now he's dead, they're not sure of themselves any longer. They know that it's only a matter of time before Wilder starts to move in on them, to take over their spreads.'

'And the men on the ranch,' asked Chris quietly. 'You know anythin' about them? Whether they'll stay and take orders from me, or whether they'll ride on over the hill?'

'Reckon that's up to you. If you're a hard man like your grandfather, then they'll follow you clear to Hell and back. But if not, if you're soft, then they'll pull out and leave you, maybe even go over to the other side.'

Chris was silent for a long moment, staring straight ahead of him. Then he stirred as if aware of the other's presence in the room. 'Thanks for lettin' me know how things are,' he said quietly. 'And thanks for the grub. Maybe I can do the same for you sometime.'

'Mebbe,' acknowledged the other meaningly. 'If you live that long. There's a mighty powerful group against you. But they won't kill you straight out, they'll want to make it look like an accident. That is, until you've shown yourself in your true colours. If you're soft, then nobody is goin' to mind if you're dead or alive, but if you make a stand against Diego and Wilder, you'll have the same kind of respect from the small ranchers as he got.'

'And the law in the territory?'

'You mean Sheriff Maxwell? He's in cahoots with Wilder. Trust him and you're as good as dead.' He looked at Chris with a moment's penetrating attention. 'I don't quite know about you.'

'For you,' said Chris, calmly dismissing the statement, 'I guess it doesn't matter.'

'Mebbe not. This is your business, I reckon. But if you do try to go for Wilder, you'll have to break through a host of gunslingers to get at him.'

Later that evening, Chris left the cabin, picked up his horse and made a wide circle through the timber before striking the trail a couple of miles further down the mountainside. The sun was dipping low towards the western horizon on his left and his shadow grew long and huge on the ground beside him as he rode. The main stage trail lay far below him, down in the valley and he could occasionally make it out through gaps in the trees, a scar of grey against the overall greenness. The sun flamed in a vast haze of red and scarlet as it touched the rim of the world, touching the tops of the tall hills with flame, leaving the floor of the deep valley in hazy shadow. Far below him, he could make out the small township that stood at the junction of the trails from the hills. In the length of time since he had left the small shack to the moment he rode out of the timber belt and came upon the open stretches of rock and huge up-thrusting boulders where the narrow mountain trail dipped to the valley, no rider moved along the wide stage trail. The very stillness of the hills spoke its own voice of tension. It was as if the world was waiting tensely for something to happen, something which had been hanging fire for some time now, but was now about to break. It was the feeling he had whenever a storm lay close to the horizon, with the oven-heat and the stillness hanging like a mighty pressure over everything.

He paused for a long moment at the head of the descending trail, sitting loose and relaxed in the saddle. But it was only his body that was relaxed, muscles loosened a little. His mind was still alert and tensed. He had learned a lot from that man back there in the cabin against the mountainside. What he had learned had not helped to ease the tension in his mind. The thought of this man Matt Wilder, and the others, waiting to move in and grab the ranch, knowing of his coming, disturbed him anew. It was a signal of things to come, of the problems and dangers that faced him in this wide, stretching valley which the deep, quiet hills seemed to heed.

He was half a mile down the trail, his horse picking its way

21

forward with care among the treacherous boulders that lay strewn along the narrow, winding trail, when he heard the first faint whispers of sound in the distance. The sun had gone down behind the western horizon and the redness in the sky had given way to the deep, cool blue and indigo and he reined his mount, listening to the tattoo of sound as the other rider came forward, pushing his mount at a punishing pace. He moved his horse into the shadows of the rocks, looked down at the stage trail, now less than half a mile below him, trying to pick out the shape of the rider.

Seconds later, horse and rider came into view, moving swiftly in a cloud of churned-up dust along the lower trail. It was too dark and the other too far away for Chris to be able to make out his features and the rider's steady echo faded swiftly into the night, presently dying into silence.

By the time he approached the outskirts of the town the starlight laid a faint trembling glow over the trail and there was still the smell of dust in the air, indicating that men were travelling these trails. He felt a sense of uneasiness as he rode into the wide street, eyes alert, watchful for trouble. Tying up the horse in front of the first saloon he came to, he went inside. Six men were clustered around a table in one corner where a poker game was in progress and there were others at more tables, with a couple standing against the bar. As he went over to the bar, all six men playing poker stopped their game and eyed him with a curious steadfastness, then went back to their play as they saw him eyeing them through the mirror at the rear of the long bar.

Resting his elbows on the bar, Chris glanced at the bartender. The other moved slowly in his direction, stood stolidly in front of him, waiting.

'Where can a man eat in this town?' Chris asked.

'You can either get a meal over at the hotel, or take your luck with anything we've got here,' said the man softly.

'I'll take a chance with what you've got,' Chris said. He picked up the glass and bottle which the other had brought

over with him and poured himself a drink, only half filling
the glass. He held the drink between his fingers for a long
moment, staring down at it while the barkeep watched him
for a moment with no expression on his round, red face, then
moved away, disappearing into the room at the back of the
bar.

Drinking, Chris watched the men at his back through the
mirror. One or two of them were still glancing almost furtively
in his direction, sure that he was keeping them under surveillance, but wondering about him. Maybe a stranger in town
was sufficiently rare to evoke such curiosity, he thought
inwardly, but then on the other hand, it might be that this
man Wilder had passed word along to his cronies in town to
keep their eyes open for any stranger riding in, particularly if
he looked as if he had been on the trail for some time.

Ten minutes later, the bartender came back, ran a wet
cloth over the bar, then said quietly: 'Find yourself a table,
friend, and I'll bring your meal across to you. Take the bottle
along with you.'

Chris nodded, gripped the bottle by the neck and carried
it to one of the empty tables, standing a little apart from those
which were occupied. None of the men in the room had
stirred since he had come in. Then, one of them scraped
back his chair, got heavily to his feet, and walked across to his
table, stood in front of it for a long moment, looking down at
him, waiting for the invitation to sit down.

It was some time in coming. Chris was unsure how he
would be able to tell those men who had been on speaking
terms with his grandfather from those who wanted him dead.
There was the feel of danger all about him. He guessed this
town was likely to be the same as a score of others he had
known, full of dodgers, men running from something, be it
the law or others of their kind seeking revenge, and probably
the best trade this saloon got was from men such as these.

'Sit down, friend,' he said at last, waving a hand towards
the chair opposite him. He pushed the bottle towards the

other, eyed him closely. 'You look like a man who has something on his mind.'

'Just curious,' said the other openly. 'You figuring on staying around these parts or just ridin' through?'

'Depends a lot on what I find here,' said Chris easily. His gaze locked with the other's, held fast. 'Might be I'd find myself a spread and settle down.'

'Ain't no land here for the buyin',' grunted the other. 'Most of the smaller ranchers are movin' out, headin' back east.'

Chris raised his brows as if in surprise. 'Could be I'd be able to pick up one of their spreads cheap,' he remarked.

The other shook his head emphatically. 'Not a chance. Either Matt Wilder or Diego will get 'em. Nobody stays long in these parts.'

'Did hear there was a big ranch a couple of miles out of town, to the north.'

'You mean the Ranson place?' The other grinned. 'Mister, if you're figgerin' on tryin' to get a hold of that spread, better forget about it right now.'

'Any reason why?' Chris spoke deliberately, with a casualness that was far from casual.

The other did not seem to have noticed. His smile was a tight-lipped thing that merely deepened the lines around the corners of his mouth and eyes. 'Half a dozen reasons, and all good ones,' he said shortly. 'Old man Ranson died a few weeks ago. Nobody knows what's going to happen as far as the spread is concerned, but both Wilder and Diego and maybe half a dozen more of the big men are after it, and you can be sure one of 'em will get it, even though there'll be gunplay before it's finally settled.'

'That,' said Chris at long length, 'is open to question.' He turned as the bartender came over with the meal, setting in front of him fried potatoes, beans and bacon and a mug of hot, black coffee.

'Well,' murmured the other, 'they do say there's a grandson somewhere, but he ain't lived here for close on twelve or thirteen years. From what I've heard tell, he's a dude, spends all of his time living it up in the cantinas south of the Texas border – and that's a mighty long way from Cochise County.'

Christ finished the rest of his meal in silence, acutely aware of the other's glance, but giving no sign of it. Lighting a smoke, he sipped the hot coffee, felt it burn the back of his throat on the way down. 'This seems to be one hell of a place,' he said softly, blowing the smoke into the air in front of his face.

'It is now,' agreed the other. 'While old man Ranson was alive, there was some kind of law and order about the place. Now that he's dead, that's all gone by the board. Wilder and Diego are runnin' things their way and Sheriff Maxwell is carrying out their orders.'

'A crooked sheriff in town and the beginnings of a full-scale range war out on the prairie,' mused Chris softly. 'Seems I've ridden into trouble here.'

'Better get your horse and ride out tomorrow,' advised the other. He poured a drink from the bottle, gulped it down. 'This is no place for anybody who has no part in this quarrel.'

Chris sat for several moments in his chair, savouring the smoke. 'I'll think on what you've said,' he muttered, getting to his feet.

He tossed a couple of coins on to the bar, then walked out, across to the hotel.

TWO

MARKED FOR VIOLENCE

Chris walked through the small lobby of the hotel, waking the man who lay sprawled in the chair behind the desk, his mouth open, snoring loudly. The man opened his red-rimmed eyes, glanced up, made to close them again, then sat up straight and sudden in his chair before finally scrambling to his feet.

'You got a room?' Chris asked tersely. He still felt jumpy inside and spoke more sharply to the other than he had intended.

'Sure, plenty of room,' grunted the other. He rubbed the back of his hand over his mouth. 'How long are you figuring on stayin'?'

'A couple of days.' Chris turned the register, signed his name with a flourish, then swung it back to face the other. He saw the clerk glance down at the name, saw his gaze flick away without any recognition in it, then suddenly swing back as the significance of what he saw went home. He looked up at Chris with his jaw hanging slackly open. 'Ranson!' he said thinly, as if unable to believe his eyes. 'Say, you ain't no relative of old Jim Ranson who died a couple of weeks ago, are you?'

Chris nodded slowly, his gaze holding the other's. 'I'm his grandson,' he said evenly, casually.

'Well, I'd never have guessed it,' murmured the other. He

26

was wide awake now, moved around the edge of the desk, looking along the lobby for any luggage the other might have brought with him. Disappointed at seeing nothing, he turned. 'This all you have?' he asked, nodding his head towards the saddle roll on the floor behind the desk.

'That's right. Now about that bed, old-timer. I've been more'n two days on the trail and I could do with a good night's sleep.'

'Sure, sure.' The other moved quickly around the edge of the desk, swept a key from the wooden rack on the wall and handed it over to him. 'First floor, at the far end of the passage,' he said quickly. 'If you want anythin' before mornin', just holler. I'm here all night.'

'I'll remember that,' Chris nodded, picked up the saddle roll, slung it over his shoulder and made his way up the creaking stairway, along the narrow corridor on the first floor and opened the door of the room at the end, locking the door behind him. It was cool inside the room and he opened the window a little, peering down on to the street below the hotel. From the window, with no light on in the room at his back, he could see everything that went on down there, hear everything. He had been standing there for less than ten seconds when he heard the faint sound of the hotel doors being opened. Pulling himself back from the window, pressing his body tightly against the wall to one side, he peered down, taking care not to be seen by anyone in the street below.

The dark figure came creeping out of the hotel door almost immediately below him, moved out cautiously into the middle of the dark street and paused there for a long moment, staring furtively about him, then lifting his head to peer up at the window of Chris's room. Finally, he was satisfied that no one was watching him and moved off, across the street, on to the boardwalk on the far side, his body alternately hidden in darkness and alternately hazed by the yellow light from the windows of the buildings on the other side of the street. But by that time, Chris had seen enough to know who it was. There had been no mistaking the small figure of the desk clerk.

Now where would he be running to at that time of night? Chris wondered tightly. Seemed there would be only one answer to that. He was the only man in town who knew who he was and now he was hot-footing it out of town to pass on the news, either to Wilder, Diego, or perhaps Sheriff Maxwell.

He kept the door of his room locked as he went back and stretched himself out on the long, low bed. There was the deep weariness of the long ride along the trail in every fibre and muscle of his body, an ache that had been with him now for many days, something he could neither rid himself of nor forget. A hat for a pillow and the hard, stony ground for his bed; and often no fire to keep him warm through the long, cold, starlit nights when the blackness had crowded in from the far horizons of a vast world and the stillness had been heightened and sharpened by the thousands of pinpoints of brilliant light in the heavens. It had been a deep and bitter loneliness which he had known out there on the trail. The kind of loneliness that had been known by man long before he had become civilised, when he had looked out on the moon and the bright constellations and wondered what it had all meant; a fear-filled, frightening loneliness that had somehow left its mark on him, left him with something he had not known before.

In spite of the deep-seated uneasiness in him, Chris Ranson slept, surrendering to the weariness in his body and mind. When he woke, the pale grey light of an early dawn filtered through the windows and there was the breathless hush that came with it in these frontier towns. A horse whinnied softly from somewhere along the street, but that was the only sound that broke the deep silence. He lay for a moment with his hands clasped behind his neck, staring up at the ceiling, remembering everything that had happened the previous day; the warning he had been given by the man in the saloon; a man who had not known who he was – and the way in which the desk clerk had slipped out of the hotel once he figured that Chris was safely asleep in his room.

By now, everybody who mattered would know that Jim Ranson's grandson had come riding into town, that he had put up for the night at the hotel. Was there a plan being laid against him at that moment, while he lay there doing nothing? The thought stirred him into action. Swinging his legs to the floor, he washed in the basin at the window, listening to the other, faint sounds outside in the street. The town was shaking itself awake, ready for another hot day.

Downstairs, he went into the dining room for an early breakfast. The man behind the desk in the lobby was not the same one who had been there the night before and he guessed that the other had gone off duty. He found a table, waited for the meal to come, then ate ravenously. He had missed good cooking all the time he had been on the trail and he meant to make up for it while he had the chance.

He was on the point of getting up after finishing the meal when he noticed the tall man who came into the diner, standing looking about him for a moment, before turning and coming over to his table. The other was a broad-shouldered, heavy-set man, going to fat now, with broad jowls and thick lips. He paused in front of Chris's table.

'Mister Ranson?' he said harshly.

Chris glanced up, then waved the other towards the empty chair. 'That's my name,' he said easily. He noticed the silver star pinned on the other's shirt, the weight of it pulling the thin material away from the other's vest. 'Won't you sit down, Sheriff. I suppose the desk clerk told you I was here last night.'

The other's eyes narrowed and for a moment there was a dangerous look on his face, then he seemed to pull himself together, the broad lips opened in a wide grin, the right hand dropped from the neighbourhood of his gun butt and he lowered himself slowly into the chair.

'All right, Mister Ranson,' he said quietly. 'Seems you know a lot more than I had given you credit for. So the clerk did happen to mention to me that you'd registered here. But that was only because I'd asked him to do so. I heard that you might be ridin' into town sometime. We figured that you'd get word about your grandfather dying and you'd be ridin' in to take over the ranch and I reckoned it was kind of important that I had the chance to get a word with you before you rode out to the ranch.'

'You got somethin' on your mind, Sheriff?' asked Chris innocently.

'Well, let's say there may be trouble if things get out of hand,' said the other, lips pursed a little. 'And as the sheriff here it's my job to see that there ain't no real trouble.'

Chris leaned back in his chair, eyeing the other closely. 'Sheriff Maxwell,' he said softly. 'All I came here for was to take over where my grandfather left off. I fail to see why that should cause any trouble for anybody.'

'Well, now, let's not rush into this before we know all the facts,' said the other soothingly. 'Things are a little more complicated than that. Your grandfather was a strong man, fast with a gun. Nobody fancied trying to take anythin' from him, land or water, or even cattle. There was some rustlin' from the other spreads, but never from his. He had a way of exactin' retribution whenever it was needed, that usually deterred anybody from tryin' it with him. But he's dead now and I'm wonderin' if you're the right man to take over in his shoes. I ought to warn you here and now that there are powerful men such as Matt Wilder who want to buy that spread. They'll pay good money for it and if any of 'em approaches you with a proposition, then I'd pay it real serious consideration. They'll offer you a fair price and you'll be able to ride back to where you came from a very rich man. Why stay here and stick your neck out for nothin' when you could have all that?"

'Then I take it that you're advisin' me to sell out if I get an

30

offer for the spread and the ranch?' Chris looked at him, open-eyed.

'That's right. Make things easier all round.' The other smiled, obviously well pleased with himself. 'I always say there's a peaceable way to do everythin' if you only take the trouble to look for it.'

'And supposin' that I refuse to sell?' Chris looked the other squarely in the eye. 'Supposin' I figure on takin' over the ranch and runnin' it as my grandfather did?'

The other's lips tightened suddenly. His face grew a mite ugly. 'Then you'd find yourself in more trouble than you've ever dreamed of,' he stated flatly. 'And I wouldn't be able to answer for the consequences.'

'You tryin' to say that if any of these men, Wilder, or Diego, tried to grab that land from me, you'd stand by and do nothin'? I thought you were the law in these parts.'

'I'm the law as far as this town is concerned,' corrected the other stiffly. 'There ain't no law out yonder on the prairie. The ranchers make their own law and until the Rangers move in, there's nothin' I could do.'

Chris smiled thinly. He said: 'You seem to have made your position in this matter quite clear, Sheriff.' A glinting expression showed on his face. 'I reckon it's only fair I do the same. I'll be ridin' out to the ranch tomorrow and takin' it over. There'll be no question of sellin' it, to Wilder or anybody else.'

'That your last word, Ranson?' said the sheriff, pushing himself stiffly to his feet. There was a faint flush high in his cheeks, and his eyes were sharp-bright under lowered brows.

'That's right,' Chris nodded. 'You found that you couldn't run my grandfather out of the territory when he stood up against tyranny and you'll find the same with me.'

'I doubt it,' answered the sheriff. 'Your kind never likes to shoot it out with a man used to handling a fast gun. D'you think we know nothin' about you? We know of the way you used to live down in Mexico, we know the kind of man your father was and they always say: like father, like son. In this case, I'm goshdarned sure that it's true.'

'Then you guess wrong,' said Chris. He did not allow any of the deep, bitter, anger to show in his face. Only the tight-knuckled grip of his hands on the edge of the table showed anything of the emotions in him.

The sharp glitter of tight, angry amusement died out of Sheriff Maxwell's face. He got to his feet, stood for a moment with his gaze held tight on the other man's features as though trying to read what lay deep beneath that hard, inscrutable expression. Then he said in a strained voice: 'Don't try to fight these men, because you just can't do it. Only man who ever could stand up to 'em and make 'em back down, has just died. You're not the kind of man to step into his shoes and I reckon you know it.'

It was the waiter who broke the tension by coming forward until he stood beside the sheriff. 'You want breakfast here, Sheriff?' he asked quietly.

The other shook his head, his face suffused with a dark anger. 'No thanks, I never eat before noon.' Turning sharply on his heel, he stalked out of the dining room. A moment later, Chris heard the front door of the hotel slam as the other left and he caught a brief, fragmentary glimpse of him walking swiftly across the street, shadow long beside him as the sun came up over the hills which lay to the east.

The waiter stood beside the table, glanced down at Chris. 'Seems you set his back up, rubbed him the wrong way, mister,' he said softly. 'He can be a bad man to fall foul of, if you get my meaning.'

'I get it,' Chris nodded. He crushed out his smoke, pushed back his chair and made his way up to his room.

When he went down into the street an hour later, the sun was well up and the heat lay thick and heavy in the air. Not a breath of wind stirred the dust on the wide street and there were few people about. He checked at the livery stable, made sure that his horse had everything it needed. As he was coming out from the rear, the groom stepped out of the shadows and came forward, eyeing him curiously.

'You the fella who just rode in from Memphis last night?' he asked softly, head cocked a little on one side, his eyes bright like those of a magpie.

'That's right,' Chris nodded, paused, stood with his shoulders resting against the thick, wooden upright.

'There's some talk about town that you're Jim Ranson's grandson.' The other had a sly humour on his face and a bright and beady wisdom in his eyes. Here, reflected Chris, was a man who would see everything that went on in town, would evidently know everything, and he wouldn't be likely to have lined up with anyone on either side of the feuding parties.

'And if it's true?' countered Chris. He watched the old fellow and wondered how much he knew about him, whether he would talk, and if he did, how much of it would be factual truth.

'Then I reckon you're either a brave man or a goshdarned fool.' He squinted up at Chris's face in the slanting beams of sunlight that filtered through a wide window in the low, slanting roof of the building. 'You don't look like a fool to me.'

'You know if there were any men my grandfather trusted?' asked Chris tautly.

'You mean apart from those who worked for him on the ranch?' The other rubbed a horny hand over his chin, the stubble rasping under the hard flesh. 'I reckon there's Doc Fordham and Frank Jargens – he owns the local newspaper. You may find Jargens reluctant to help. Now that Jim Ranson's dead, Wilder will have warned him of the consequences if he prints anythin' against him.'

'It figures,' nodded Chris. 'For a lot of reasons. But I reckon I might pay a call on this Doctor Fordham.'

'Me,' said the groom, 'I'm so old that nobody cares a hoot about me. But I know a lot more'n I ever tell. Reckon if I told all that I knew, I'd no longer be an old man, I'd be a dead one.' He threw a quick, meaningful glance at Chris's waist, then lifted his eyes back to the other's face. 'Notice you ain't totin' any guns,' he said, and there was a hopeful curiosity in his tone, his head bent forward a little, clearly waiting for an answer.

'Haven't found any need to carry 'em so far.' Chris rolled a smoke, firmed it between his fingers, then lit it, scraping the sulphur match down the side of the wall beside him. From where he stood, it was just possible to see the street for perhaps thirty yards, but he could not be seen himself unless someone out there was deliberately looking for him and he didn't think that likely at the moment. But the smoke provided him with an excuse for standing there apparently doing nothing and he knew, inwardly, that he needed the answers to one hell of a lot of questions before he would feel himself to be on sure ground in this territory.

There was no doubt that his grandfather had made himself a whole heap of enemies here and it was essential that he should be able to recognise them before he went much further. There were sure to be some folk here who might talk to him, provided he got to them before Matt Wilder, or Diego, did. He could guess at the means these men would use to persuade such people not to talk to him. And as far as the folk in this part of the county were concerned, he was an unknown quantity and no man in his right mind would be willing to risk his life for someone like that.

'Just where do I find Doc Fordham?' he asked at length, dropping the glowing butt of his cigarette on to the stone floor and crushing it out carefully under his heel.

The other stepped forward, pointed along the street. 'Fifty yards along on the other side,' he grunted. 'You goin' to stay here, take over the ranch?'

'It looks that way,' Chris said quietly. There was something in his voice which made the other look up at him in mild surprise. Then the oldster nodded. 'Could be that you are a chip off the old block at that,' he murmured. 'Sure, but I reckon there'll be hell let loose if you are.'

Chris made to say something further, then changed his mind and swung out of the livery stables, out on to the board-walk, ducking his head under one of the wooden overhangs, glancing right and left at the folk who moved past him. A minute later, he stood in front of the doctor's office, an unpretentious place, with very little to mark it out from any of the other buildings on either side of it. He rapped loudly on the door, waited until he heard the sound of footsteps approaching. There was the rattle of a chain and a moment later, the door opened and a tall, white-haired man stood in the opening, peering out at him. Chris had an impression of a kindly, lined face, filled with the character of the man. He guessed instantly that here was a man who would not back down easily, nor run from what he considered to be right.

'Doctor Fordham?' he asked quietly.

The other gave a quick nod, his brow furrowed in thought as he tried to place this stranger. 'That is my name,' he answered, 'but I'm afraid that I—'

'I'm Chris Ranson.' He saw the sudden gust of expression that came over the older man's face, saw the look which the name evoked in the man's grey eyes. Then Fordham had reached out, caught him by the arm, pulling him inside his office, after throwing a quick glance up and down the street. The door was shut behind him, the chain put back into place. Then the other was ushering him along a narrow passage into the room at the back of the building. Chris caught a glimpse of a larger room through an open door which he took to be the surgery.

'Somehow, I never figured that you'd come here,' muttered the other, as he motioned Chris to a chair. 'I heard that you were somewhere in Texas, or maybe even south of there, over the border. But I never thought for one moment that you would come riding back to claim the ranch. I reck-oned it would go to the man who proved himself top dog in these parts, who killed all other opposition and stepped in to take the spoils.'

Chris forced a quick, tight grin. 'It seems that I've made quite a lot of people change their plans,' he said simply. He lowered himself gratefully into the chair, watched the other as the doctor went over to a small, wall cupboard and took out a bottle and two glasses which he set down on the nearby table.

'How did you know to come to me?' asked the other, as he poured the drinks.

'I got to talking with the groom down at the livery stable and he mentioned your name when I asked who was likely to have been my grandfather's friends.'

'Did he mention anyone else?' The other handed Chris the glass, sank down into the chair opposite him.

'The owner of the local newspaper,' said Chris, sipping the whisky.

'Frank Jargens,' Fordham nodded his head slowly. 'He was your grandfather's friend, that's very true. But I'm not so sure of him now. Matt Wilder was in the office yesterday, talking very confidentially with him. I've no idea what they were talking about, but you can be sure Wilder knows you're here in town and he'll be scheming how to get rid of you without making it look too darned obvious.'

'Just what sort of a man is Wilder?' Chris felt the whiskey burning in his stomach.

'Rotten, all the way through,' declared the other without hesitation. 'I've know him since he came here from somewhere back east. That was more'n fifteen years ago. Bought himself a small spread with money he said he got during the war. Then he started lending out to the small ranchers in these parts, taking over mortgages on their spreads. When they failed to meet the deadline with cash on the nail, he simply went in and took over. There was nothin' they could do to stop him. Everything was quite legal and above board.'

'That sounds like the usual thing,' nodded Chris. He held

out his glass at a nod from the other, as Fordham filled it for him. 'And in time, he became one of the most powerful men in these parts.'

'That's it,' acknowledged the other. He gazed at Chris over the rim of his glass. 'Only man he couldn't make back down was Jim Ranson. He tried, but your grandfather took a score of his men and rode out to Wilder's place and shot up several of his boys. Since that time, there was a kind of uneasy truce between the two. Now that your grandfather is dead, Wilder has seen his chance and he means to move in and take over as fast as he can.'

'And now that I've turned up it complicates matters a little for him.'

'It complicates matters a whole lot. This place is a powder keg and it only needs one little spark to set off the fuse, and once that is lit, nothin' is going to put it out until the whole lot goes up in a full-scale range war.'

'A lot of folk have told me I ought to ride back to Mexico and forget about the ranch. Sheriff Maxwell suggested I should accept the offer which he feels sure that Wilder is going to make, then leave this territory. So far, nobody thinks it would be a good thing for me to ride in and take the ranch.'

Doc Fordham looked at him searchingly for a long moment. Then he scratched his lean jaw thoughtfully. 'I'd like to be able to tell you that,' he said softly. 'But even if I did, I don't know whether it would be the best thing to do. It needs a man as good as, or better, than your grandfather to tame this country. A man has to be quick and sure on the draw – and I notice you got no guns.'

'Might be that I figure there's another way to keep the ranch without havin' to resort to gunplay,' said Chris soberly.

The other shook his head emphatically. 'There's no other way here, believe me,' he murmured fervently. 'I know these men. I've seen them grow from nothing to what they are now. They only did that by the law of the gun and they know that's the only way they can stay as they are. They'll fight tooth and nail, not only to keep what they've got, but to get hold of more.'

'I came all the way from Santa Rosita to claim this ranch and I don't aim to back down now,' said Chris tightly.

'You'll stay and fight men like Wilder, men with more than sixty hired gunslingers at their back, ready to ride in and grab what they can at a moment's notice.'

'That's right.'

'Well, I wish you wouldn't, but I know that you will,' said Fordham. Again, the long, slender-fingered hand rubbed over his jaw.

'It's a safe bet that Ranson will stay in town until he's sure of himself,' opined Dunson sombrely, 'and we can ride in there any time and take him.'

Wilder said nothing for a long moment, turning the news over in his mind. It had come as no surprise to him to hear from Maxwell that Ranson had put up at the hotel in town, nor that he had been asking a lot of questions around the place.

'You want me to arrest him on some charge or other?' put in the sheriff, standing by the windows in the front parlour of the Wilder ranch house.

'If we try to frame some charge against him and put him in jail, just what do we achieve?' frowned Wilder. He stirred himself in his chair. 'Very little. We'd have to fix it so that we could string him up from the nearest tree and that wouldn't be easy, not with everybody in town probably knowing who he is by now. There are still too many folk there who remember Jim Ranson and they'll back his grandson if we try that.'

'Better if we have the showdown right here and now,' muttered Dunson thinly. He touched the butt of the gun at his waist. 'If we wait much longer, he'll he able to collect some of the old bunch to him and we'll not find it so easy then.'

'Precisely, and I believe this can be done.' Wilder rose to

his feet, crossed to the window. 'Better saddle up men. We're ridin' into town. From what I've heard, this *hombre* is somethin' of a dude, spent most of his time carousin' south of the Texas line. Carries no guns and probably figures that this is goin' to save him if he comes up against a gunslick.'

'You reckonin' on gettin' somebody to shoot him down?' mused Dunson. He gave a smoothly vicious grin.

'I'm reckonin' on nothin' of the kind,' snapped Wilder. 'But I do know that he's the kind of man who doesn't like anythin' said against his father. Now if we was to get somebody to speak up against him in the saloon, within Ranson's hearin', and there was to be a fist fight, I reckon we might be able to arrange it so that Ranson came off worst.'

'You talkin' about Brander, your foreman?'

'Why not? He's killed a couple of men in a fist fight that I know of. No reason why there shouldn't be a third.'

Dunson grinned broadly, nodded in agreement. He followed Wilder and the sheriff out into the courtyard, then over to the corral where their horses were waiting. Minutes later, they had ridden out of the ranch yard, leaving behind them the long, slowly-settling streamers of grey dust in the still air.

Chris Ranson felt the tension in the air the minute he thrust open the doors of the saloon and stepped inside, out of the direct heat of the noon sun. The air over the town held the heat-head in it as if unwilling to let it loose, trapping the oven-like quality of it until it brought the sweat boiling out of a man's skin and a dull, throbbing ache to the back of his eyes, an ache brought on by the long staring at the brightly, glaring sunlight.

There were several men already in the saloon, a small group standing at the bar talking together in low tones. He recognised the sheriff with them and two other men he hadn't seen before. One, a tall, frock-coated man with side whiskers and a handsome, if cruel face, threw him a quick, searching look as he walked in, a glance that made to brush over his face, but clung, probing, as if trying to see what lay behind the expression on his face. Chris met the other's hard stare and it was the other's gaze that slid away as Chris walked slowly to the bar, rested his elbows on it, ignoring the group, although still conscious of their presence.

There was a look on the barkeep's face which indicated that he expected trouble and Chris felt the tension rise a little more in him. These men had seen far too many fights in the saloon not to know when one was about to break, but he was still a little unsure of the direction from which the danger would come. It was as if events had begun to crowd him from the moment he had stepped through the door of the saloon and this was something he didn't like, this feeling riding him. He lifted a finger to the barkeep and the man came over with the bottle and a glass, poured the drink for him, took the coin he flipped on to the bar, then stood back, resting his shoulders against the shelf lined with multi-coloured bottles, just below the long mirror.

Silhouetted in the glass, Chris was able to watch every one at his back. The men seated at the tables scattered throughout the room were pointedly ignoring all that went on at the bar, and this was so obvious that he knew, with a sudden certainty, that trouble would come from the group not far from him on his left. Already, there was a sharp burst of hoarse laughter from the frock-coated man as one man said something in low tones.

Chris sipped his drink slowly. The talk from nearby was beginning to get louder.

Suddenly, the tall, broad-shouldered man, with his back to him, said sharply, loudly, 'I don't care what you say, Sheriff. Jim Ranson may have been tough, fast on the draw, but his son was a yeller-livered coward. He ran away to Mexico the minute things got tough and nobody seen hair nor hide of him since then.'

Chris felt the fingers of his hand tighten convulsively

around the glass in front of him. There had been a taunting ring to the other's voice which told him, more than the words, that the other had intended he should hear.

The sheriff said something in a low tone, motioned with his thumb in Chris's direction. Chris caught the movement with the edge of his vision, knew that this was also just part of the act, felt the tightness grow in him again, tensing the muscles of his body.

The big man said hoarsely: 'I ain't carin' who's listenin' to me, Maxwell. I'm sayin' exactly what I know to be the truth. Will Ranson ran away because he was scared. He never dared carry a gun in his life for fear that he might have to use it. All he was good for, was as a card-sharp, cheatin' folk at poker and—'

Chris swung around to face the others. His voice was as cutting as the lash of a whip. 'Maybe you're just shootin' off your mouth, mister,' he said thinly. 'But you're a liar. My father was no coward and no cheat.'

The big man turned slowly, eyed him up and down, with a sneering look on his face. He was a tall, solid shape, burned a dark brown by weather and sun; a hard one, scarred by trouble, looking for trouble, evidently still wanting it. During the past ten years, Chris had seen many men like this one, hard and restless, born killers, narrow of mind and governed by passion, hungering for a chance to use their fists and beat a man into a senseless pulp. There was that bright shine in the man's eyes and that twisted look about his thin-lipped mouth that told Chris all that he wanted to know about the other.

'You callin' me a liar, mister?' There was menace in the other's tone as he took a step away from the bar, his hands clear of his body. His gaze swung up and down Chris's body then he looked aside and a glance passed between him and the tall, frock-coated man.

Chris moved slowly forward. The men at the tables had moved away, stumbling to get out of the way, not sure whether or not bullets would begin to fly at any moment.

41

'I say that you're a liar if you call my father a coward and a cheat,' Chris repeated tightly.

The other's brows lifted a little as if in mild surprise. 'So you're Ranson. I figured you might be from the way you act. I see you carry no guns. But like your father, that ain't goin' to save you. I can take you apart with my bare hands.' Moving slowly and deliberately, the other unbuckled the heavy gunbelt from around his middle, handed it over to the sheriff. He squared himself at Chris, moving forward in a low crouch, balanced on the balls of his feet.

As he came towards Chris, the other said softly: 'Seems nobody had the chance to take care of your father, but this is where you get what's comin' to you. We don't want the likes of you around here and—' He never finished what he meant to say. His talk had been merely a feint to cover up his next move. His right hand swung all the way from his belt, aimed for Chris's jaw, but the other was ready for the move. His head scarcely seemed to shift at all, but it was not there when the blow should have landed and the man swayed off balance, falling against Chris, arms outflung as he tried to steady himself. He caught Chris round the middle, hung on to protect himself and brought the top of his head up hard under the other's jaw. Chris felt the shock of the blow roar up into his brain and he was carried back against the bar with the weight of the other, thrusting against his chest, threatening to crush all of the wind from his lungs. With an effort, he shook the ringing sensation from his head, clearing it a little, twisted his body swiftly and instinctively, to one side, knowing what the other intended to do next. He guessed that this man would be a dirty fighter, that he had been brought up in the rough-and-tumble school. The blow which the other aimed with his knee for his crotch, glanced harmlessly off the side of the thigh and the big man uttered a sharp bleat of pain as his knee caught the solid, unyielding wood of the bar.

The pain of the impact forced the other to slacken his grip slightly around Chris's waist and he whirled free of him, swinging a short, hard jab to the gunman's jaw as he moved back. His knuckles rasped along hard flesh, glanced off the cheek bone with a jarring numbness. But the other staggered back under the force of the blow, arms flailing wildly.

Dimly, Chris was aware of the frock-coated man's voice saying: 'Make sure you do a good job on him, Brander. I don't want him walkin' around after this.'

So that was it! A savage anger burned through Chris at the other's words. They had deliberately staged this so that they might get rid of him without having any awkward questions asked. There would be no gunplay. There would be no shooting down of an unarmed man in cold blood. He guessed that the man in the black coat was Matt Wilder. He cursed himself for not having realised that before. The man he faced was undoubtedly a killer with his fists otherwise they would not have been so sure of themselves as to do this in public.

Chris stood away from Brander, facing up to him, waiting for the other to move in. The anger that boiled up inside him was held in tight control as he kept his gaze fixed hard on the man's face, watching his eyes. This was a man who was so sure of himself that he gave a forward indication of what he meant to do, so utterly confident that he would be able to beat any man to a bloody pulp. Snarling fiercely, Brander regained his balance, came stalking forward, arms swinging slightly by his sides, lips drawn back tightly over his teeth, fingers hooked into claws as if he already had Chris's neck in them, was squeezing the life out of him.

Savagely, he swung with his left, throwing all of his weight behind the punch. It grazed Chris's cheek as he swayed back out of reach and before the other could check his onward rush, Chris had sent in two hard jabs to the man's stomach, felt his doubled fists crush into the other's belly, heard the breath gasp out of him in a shrill bleat of agony.

By now, there was a hush on the room. The men standing around the tables could scarcely believe their eyes, that the great Brander, the man who claimed to have already killed two men with his bare hands, was being whipped like this by a man they had considered to be nothing but a dude. Eyes wide, they watched as two more ramrod blows burst against Brander's temple, hitting a little too high up to do any real damage, but stopping him in his tracks, jolting him back on his heels and making him pause in his bull-like rushes.

Chris waited calmly for the other to come in once more. There was hardly a mark on him, apart from the flush on his neck where the top of the other's head had hammered against it during the first ten seconds of the fight. In contrast, Brander's face bore several marks of the punishing battle. There was an angry flush down one side of his face and a puffiness under his eyes which had not been there a few moments earlier. His lower lip, too, seemed to have become more swollen where Chris's fists had hammered a brief, squashing blow against it, where Brander's teeth had bitten deeply into it, bringing the taste of blood into his mouth.

Brander came forward again, marked but seemingly not badly hurt by the blows. Built solidly, any blows to the chest had little effect on him and Chris had wisely decided to concentrate on the other's belly and face. Crowding him, trying to use all of his tremendous advantage in weight, Brander thrust himself forward, caught out at Chris's arm, swung him round savagely. Wisely, Chris went with the blow – to have tried to withstand it would have meant a broken arm – but as he slid along the polished front of the bar, Sheriff Maxwell thrust out a foot, tripped him so that he fell backward, his shoulders striking the hard, sawdust covered floor of the bar with a stunning force. For a second, all of the air was driven from his chest and he felt as though his lungs had been caved in under the blow. Through a blurring of tears, he saw Brander leap forward with a savage grin of triumph on his face, aiming the kick for the small of Chris's back. Desperately, he tried to roll clear of the blow, but the toe of the other's heavy boot struck him on the side and a savage burst of pain exploded inside his body, lancing up through his chest and into his brain.

For a moment, he lay there, utterly unable to move, aware of the grinning faces of the men standing by the bar, leering down at him, vaguely hearing the sudden roar from them as they urged the other on to the kill. But it was this supreme confidence, the feeling that nothing could stop him now, which proved to be Brander's undoing. He drew back his foot for the death-dealing kick, aiming it for the prostrate man's kidneys, lips showing the uneven teeth.

But the other's pause had given Chris the chance he wanted, those few precious seconds in which to clear his head of the bursting, throbbing ache which had threatened to overwhelm him. This time, instead of trying to wriggle away from the blow, he moved towards it, hands reaching up, fingers grasping around the other's ankle, holding on with all of his strength, pulling sharply to one side.

With a wild yell, Brander teetered on one foot for a moment, then fell sideways, crashing on to the floor beside Chris. Ignoring the pain which lanced through his body, forcing air down into his aching, tortured lungs, Chris forced himself onto his hands and knees, releasing his hold on the other's foot as he struggled to get upright, knowing that he had to get to his feet before the other could collect his scattered wits.

Standing back, resting himself against the bar, knowing that the other men would not dare to shoot him down, not with so many of the townsfolk looking on, he took advantage of the brief respite to breathe slowly and evenly, forcing his thudding, racing heart into a more normal beat inside his ribs. His body felt bruised and battered, and there was that sharp, shooting agony in the lower part of his back. But his vision was clearing and he stared down at the inert figure of the man in front of him, wondering if he would get up again.

Slowly, Brander was clawing himself upright. When he finally swayed erect, arms hanging by his sides, his face was a bloodied mask. It trickled from his nose and the broken lip, smeared over his face, mingled with the sawdust that had formed a mask. His eyes, puffed by the effect of earlier blows, stared at him with a feral hatred and he still came on, prompted only by the savage passion, the desire to kill.

Grinning a little, Chris stood and waited for him, noticing how the other was breathing more slowly now, his great barrel chest heaving with the effort. Too late, he saw that the other held something in his right hand. Even as he moved away from the bar, Brander threw the handful of sawdust into his face. There was no time to move away, no time to think or close his eyes instinctively. The sawdust hit him full in the face, blinding him. With a wild yell, Brander lunged forward, throwing his arms around Chris's waist. Desperately, the other tried to blink the sweat and sawdust from his stinging, tear-filled eyes, unable to rub them as his arms were pinned to his sides.

He could feel the other's foul breath on his face, in his nostrils, as the man tightened his grip around him, locking his fingers around the small of his back, crushing the air and then the life out of his body. This was the kind of fighting the other liked, what he had been trying to do ever since the fight had started, using his superior weight and strength to crush Chris. Desperately, Chris tried to loosen the anaconda-like grip around his body, knowing that his spine would only take so much before it snapped like a rotten twig. The other was beginning to force him back, bending him inexorably. The sheriff yelled something, but the words simply roared through Chris's brain, making no sense. All that he was aware of, was the terrible pressure which was beginning to make his senses reel, the tremendous pain in his back. He knew inwardly that he had somehow to break that hold very soon, or he would be finished and these men would have won. There would be no one to stop them from taking over the ranch and all of that grassland, and the name of Ranson would be finished here, gone from Cochise County.

The thought gave him a sudden surge of angry strength.

He relaxed a little in the other's clinging arms, felt the man shift his stance slightly for that last surge of strength which would finish him. In that same second Chris dropped, bending his knees, felt the other's grip loosen at this sudden and unexpected move, then surged upward, thrusting out with his arms as he did so.

He brought his knee up, felt it hammer against the other's stomach, heard the explosive rush of air from the broken, bleeding lips as Brander staggered back, clutching at his stomach, retching with the pain.

This time, Chris did not pause to give the other a chance to get back his breath, but moved after him, lifted his right arm and brought it down with all of his might across the back of the other's neck. It was a blow that would have killed most men. As it was, there was a bone-jarring crack and Brander dropped without a murmur on to his face at his feet, lay still on the floor, utterly knocked out by the savage force of the blow.

Slowly, sucking air down into his starved lungs, Chris swung to face the men at the bar, his lips drawn back thinly over his teeth. Harshly he said: 'I reckon that takes care of this killer. Any of you figuring on startin' somethin' more?'

For several seconds, there was no move from any of the men there. Then with a harsh grunt, Wilder swung around, pulled a Colt from the holster at his waist and levelled the long barrel on Chris's chest. There was a fanatical glint in his eye as he hissed: 'If we don't finish you one way, I'm damned if I won't make sure with this.' His finger whitened with the pressure he was exerting on the trigger and Chris knew that he was facing a man who would do exactly as he said, who would stop at nothing now that his original plan had failed.

Nothing, he thought numbly, could stop the other from pulling that trigger and sending him into eternity; nothing at all.

Then, quite abruptly, a voice from the doorway said sharply: 'Put up that gun, Wilder, or by God, I swear I'll kill you. The people of this town will stand for a lot from men such as you, but cold-blooded murder is somethin' different.'

For a second, the thought of trying to turn and beat the other to the shot, lived in Wilder's face. Then he evidently decided better of it, lowered the gun, then thrust it back into the holster, pulled the heavy black coat back over it.

'I'll finish this little episode with you later, Fordham,' he said tightly. He whirled away from the bar, moving towards the door, brushing past the tall figure of Doc Fordham who stood there with the ancient Colt still held firmly in his right hand, his eyes watchful. Reaching the door, Wilder turned in the opening and said harshly: 'Bring Brander along with you, boys. We'll finish this some other time.'

The sheriff and the other man with him bent and picked up the still unconscious man from the floor and staggered out with him. The doors swung shut behind them and Chris leaned back with his elbows propped up on the bar at his back, surveying the scene in front of him. Most of the men went back almost sheepishly to their tables, taking care to avert their gaze from Chris's as he eyed them tightly. The doctor came over and motioned to the barkeep.

'Better drink this up,' he said quietly, handing the glass to Chris. 'You look as though you need it. How did that start?'

'It was all framed, a trap for me to step right into. They'd brought that man with them for the express purpose of killin' me. Like a fool I walked right in with both feet.'

'That's the way these men work. They didn't dare shoot you down without any warnin'. Too many of the people still remember your grandfather and they wouldn't let a thing like that pass. But being killed or badly mauled in a fist fight is somethin' different, even if it was a fight with Brander. He's killed two men like that so far as I know and there may have been more.'

'And I was set up to be number three,' grunted Chris harshly. He drank the whiskey down in a single gulp, almost choked as the raw spirit hit the back of his throat, but it shocked some of the feeling back into his bruised and battered body and a moment later, he was able to think more clearly.

'I guess that now you know a little of what you're up against if you persist in goin' through with your plan and stayin' here,' murmured the other. He poured them both a second drink, then led the way over to one of the tables. 'Get that inside you,' he said quietly, 'and then I'll take you along to my place and strap you up. Wouldn't surprise me none if you ain't got a couple of ribs broken – or at least, cracked, after that brawl. But I guess you're luckier than most. Never figured I'd see the day when Brander was bested in a fist fight.'

'What made you step in like that?' asked Chris tightly. 'This is no quarrel of yours and you said that a man should-n't take part in another man's quarrel.'

'Let's say that I don't like to stand by and see another man shot down without any chance at all of defending himself.'

Chris drank the second whiskey more slowly than the first. The pain in his body had now subsided into a diffuse ache that had spread to every part of it so that it was impossible to say that it was now located in any particular limb. If anything, this ache was even more difficult to bear than the pain.

When he had finished his drink, the other took him by the arm, gave the bunch of men at the nearby table a quick, almost scathing, glance, and helped him out of the saloon, along the street, to his surgery. Once inside, he locked the door and got to work, washing and bandaging Chris's chest and back.

'You're lucky,' he said finally, when he had finished. 'No bones broken, and only a couple of ribs bruised. I doubt if the same can be said for Brander. You know that you must have nearly killed him.'

'He had it coming,' grunted Chris. He lay back on the low bed, staring up at the ceiling of the room, lips pressed tightly together.

'He'll make a powerful and dangerous enemy,' warned the other, fastening the bag which contained his surgical instruments. 'He'll do anythin' that Wilder asks of him now, just to get even with you. You've beaten him in public and he'll never forget that.'

'At least I know where I stand with him,' nodded Chris. He made to swing his legs to the floor and get up, but the other pushed him back, gently but firmly.

'Where do you think you're goin'?' asked Fordham.

'Back to the hotel,' protested Chris. 'Where else?'

'You'll be doin' no such thing,' muttered the other in a tone that brooked no argument. 'You'll be stayin' here for the next couple of days until those deep lacerations have healed. Then I might consider lettin' you go back there.'

'But you don't understand. I have to ride out to the ranch tomorrow, otherwise there may be—'

'Surely the ranch has got on all right without you for three weeks since your grandfather died. I reckon it can go without you for another two days.'

Chris sighed, then nodded, giving in. What the other said made sense, of course, but there was still that deep-rooted sense of urgency riding him, an urgency which had been heightened by what had happened in the saloon, the incident bringing home to him the need for speed if he was to take the ranch and hold it, because he felt certain that Wilder did not intend to stand still now. He would be formulating fresh plans, seeking to put them into operation.

'I'll get somebody to come along and look after you,' promised the other. 'All you have to do is lie here and get some rest. If anythin' happens, I'll let you know right away.'

It was later that evening, when Chris heard the outer door of the office open. Doc Fordham had been out seeing his patients most of the day and Chris guessed that this was the other returning.

'That you, Doc?' he called loudly. He felt a trifle unsure of himself. It hadn't sounded like the other's heavy footfall in the passage outside the door of the room. There was a pause and then the door of the room opened and a girl stepped inside. Chris lay back on the bed, watching her curiously. She walked over and stood beside the bed, looking down at him. There was a faint smile on her face. 'I'm sorry if I startled you,' she said in a low, musical voice, 'but Doctor Fordham asked me to look in and see how you were. I'm Rosalie Blane.'

'I suppose you already know who I am,' he said quietly, sinking back on to the pillow.

She nodded, unperturbed. 'You're Chris Ranson.' She spread the sheets more evenly over the bed, her manner of crisp assurance returning a little. He knew that she had been a little unsure of herself the moment she had stepped into the room, but no longer. 'They're saying that you fought Brander, the Wilder ranch foreman, and beat him. That must have been something.'

'You seem mighty interested in this,' murmured Chris. The light from the lamp on the nearby table threw shadows over her face, high-lighted the glints in her blue-black hair and the darkness in her eyes. Her lips moved slightly as they curved into a warm smile.

'There's been a lot of talk about you in town and it started long before you rode in. They reckoned that you were just a dude, that even if you did come here you'd simply sell out the ranch and go back south.'

'And would it have made any difference to anyone here if I had?' he inquired.

She nodded, brought him a glass of water, lifted it to his lips. 'It would have meant a lot to the small ranchers in the territory. They looked to your grandfather to protect them against killers like Wilder and Diego. He was the only man here they could really trust, the only man big enough to stand up to them. Without him, they would have been forced off their land many years ago. When he died, they didn't know what to do. There was talk of banding together and forming themselves into some sort of fighting force, knowing that separately they were finished. Then they figured it might be best to wait and see what sort of a man his grandson turned out to be.'

'I see.' He looked at her close and careful, puzzled. She was something of a mystery to him at the moment, not smiling at him now but deadly serious. 'And once they've made up their minds on that score, what do they mean to do?'

'Fight Wilder and Diego. It's the only thing they can do if they want to keep what they have. If they don't, they'll be run out of the territory.'

'And they're lookin' to me to fight their battles for 'em?' He tried to keep the tight bitterness from his voice, but the girl looked up sharply and he saw her lips go tight together.

'All they ask is that you should help them as your grandfather did,' she retorted. 'My father was one of those small ranchers. We had maybe five hundred head of cattle and a couple of hundred acres of land. It wasn't much, but we built a ranch there and it was all that we asked out of life, just to be left alone to live there in peace. But Matthew Wilder wasn't content to let things stay like that. He claimed that we had water on our land that he needed to raise his own cattle. My father said he could have as much of the water as he needed, but that wasn't enough for him. He wanted the land, and the cattle, offered a sum of money that wouldn't even have bought the house and when my father refused point blank to sell, he sent his men early one morning. They fired the barns, and then the house, drove off the cattle and shot my father in the back when he ran out to try to stop them. They would have killed me too but I was trapped in the barn and only managed to get out by the skin of my teeth.'

'Then I can understand why you want to see them finished,' said Chris evenly. 'I can see why you would use every means you could to get revenge on these men.'

'Revenge?' There was a faint note of scorn in her voice and she took a step back from the bed. 'Is that what you think it is? You think I'm just wanting to use you to get revenge on these men.'

'At the moment,' Chris said quietly, 'I don't know what to think. I've been warned so many times that if I don't get my horse and ride out of here, go back to where I came from, my life won't be worth a plugged nickel. You want me to stay but only, it seems, to prevent Wilder and Diego from running the small ranchers off their land.'

The girl remained silent over the long minutes, her face indrawn and sober as she looked into his face. When she finally spoke, her voice held a drag of sadness. 'I thought when I heard what had happened in the saloon, that here was a man who was so like his grandfather that we had nothing more to worry about. I was so glad when I thought that perhaps we now had the chance we've been waiting for to clean up this place, to bring law and order, and justice, back into this part of the territory.' She drew herself up to her full height. Then she turned on her heel and moved towards the door, pausing as she opened it. 'It seems I was wrong,' she said wearily. A moment later, she was gone. He heard her move softly along the passage and then the street door closed quietly behind her. Only the faint, subtle, perfume of her still hung in the room.

Wearily, Chris lay back on the bed and scowled up at the ceiling. He felt angry, not only at himself, but at the fact that there were so many people here who only wanted to use him to gain their own ends, to get something for themselves for which they seemed unwilling to fight and risk their own lives.

He was asleep when the doctor came back, an hour later, and the other did not disturb him, knowing that in his present condition he needed all of the sleep and rest he could get.

It was morning when he woke, the bandages across his ribs making his movement stiff but most of the ache had gone from his body and his mind seemed clear.

THREE

GUN THUNDER

On the second morning, Chris rose early. The night's chill still lay on the room and in spite of himself, his teeth chattered as he dressed as quickly as he could, conscious of the bruising and battering his body had received. There was a pan of warm water which the doctor had brought for him and he shaved with it, the tough whiskers on his face pulling hard against the edge of the razor. There was no other sound of activity in the house and he guessed that Doc Fordham had left on one of his errands. In a town such as this, with only the one doctor, there were bound to be plenty of patients calling him out in an emergency.

Outside, the street was empty and there was the dimness that came before the dawn lying over the town. As he turned the corner and made his way toward the livery stable a man seated on a long, low buckboard, shoulders and head hunched forward against the biting cold, rode by, and there were two others at the far end of the street, loading bags of grain on to other wagons from one of the warehouses. He passed the saloon where Brander had tried to kill him and walked on, shivering as the air bit deep into his bones. He had lain too long in that bed to be able to come out into this without it having this effect on him.

A couple of dogs, their ribs showing like washboards, ran out of the stables as he came up to them. For a moment, he paused to make a smoke and light it up before going in. There was activity inside the stable. Chris saw nothing of the man he had given his mount to when he had arrived, but a gaunt-faced, unkempt man came shuffling out from the stalls at the back, looked him up and down with a brief glance that held nothing of curiosity, then walked over with the horse he was leading and stood by the water trough while it drank.

'Clem ain't here yet,' said the other without turning his head.

'He the groom?'

'That's right.' The other finished watering the horse, turned. 'You must be Jim Ranson's grandson. Heard about what you did to Brander in the saloon the other day. Wish I'd been there and seen it for myself. Always wanted to see that *hombre* get what he deserved, but never figgered I would.' He grinned slyly. 'Reckon you'd better have eyes in the back of your head, mister. He'll shoot you down the first chance he gets and he won't give you any warnin'.'

'So I've been hearin'.' He followed the other as the hostler led the watered horse back to the stall. Putting the horse in one of the stalls, the other slid the long wooden bolt into place, then turned to face Chris.

'You wantin' your own horse?' he asked perkily.

'Not right now,' Chris said. 'I'll be needin' him around noon. How long will it take me to ride out to the ranch?'

'I figger you could make it in an hour,' said the other musingly. His eyes were of the palest, watery blue that Chris had seen and he had the habit of not looking straight at you when he spoke, letting his gaze slide away as if afraid to face you.

'I hear tell that there are a lot of men after that ranch.' Chris rested his arms along the edge of one of the stalls, drawing the smoke from his cigarette down into his lungs. 'Powerful men.'

'That's right. Wouldn't surprise me if they ain't gettin' ready to ride right now.'

Chris said nothing. He had hoped that there might be time in which he could make some plans of his own to meet these men, but it seemed that time was at a high premium as far as he was concerned.

The heat struck him with a savage, built-up intensity as Chris rode out of town and took the trail that led through the low hills which lay to the north. The powdery dust of the trail hung in the air, churned up by the hoofs of his mount and others that had gone before him. He followed the trail as it led up the rising curve of a hill and on its far slope found himself looking down into a wide valley which stretched away almost as far as the eye could see, certainly beyond the wide river to the blue hills that lifted on the far horizon.

The river glinted brilliantly now in the hot sunlight and he could just make out the vast herd of cattle grazing peaceably on the gently rising ground on the far bank. The ranch buildings were visible in the sun-hazed distance, clustered together within sight of the river.

He halted his mount on the rocky outcrop of ground that jutted out from the side of the hill, sat tall and straight in the saddle, feeling the heat on his back and shoulders, listening to the afternoon's great silence, conscious more than ever of the vast blue reaches of the sky over his head; a deep blue vault in which only the glaring disc of the noon sun burned and, looking down at the land which he only vaguely remembered from a dim and distant past, he felt the deep stirrings of emotion within him. Close to him, on the slope, shaded by the outstretching arms of the big cottonwood trees, a narrow creek tumbled noisily over the flat, smooth stones that glistened and shone whitely on the bed of sand. Nothing seemed to ever disturb the utter peace here and he felt that one had

56

only to stand there long enough to be able to hear the Voice of God speaking out over the vastnesses of the great country.

Gripping himself, he pulled his mind away from the majesty of the scene, forced himself to concentrate on the nagging worries that tugged at the back of his thoughts and kept the tautness in him. Maybe, after all, his mission here would prove to be pointless. He had learned much since he had ridden into this territory. It was a land divided with Matt Wilder on one side of the fence, Diego on the other – and nothing in between for the lesser men now that his grandfather was dead. He knew they were looking desperately to him to fill the vacuum left by the old man's death, to step in and take over where he had left off. But killing other men was a big thing as far as he was concerned; a problem that a man could deal with only as he saw fit.

He raked the rowels over the flanks of his mount, pulling its head around sharply, let it take its own time and find its own way down the twisting, rocky trail. There was smoke rising from the chimney of the ranch house as he rode into the courtyard, slid from the saddle and let his mount run into the corral, closing the gate after it. Who would be there at this time of the afternoon? he wondered; unless it was someone who knew of his coming and had wanted to put the place into some kind of shape for his homecoming.

Making his way over the dusty courtyard, he paused for a moment outside the door, feeling all of the memories which he had thought were long since forgotten, come flooding over him again in a tremendous wave. This was the place he had known intimately for the first nine years of his life. Had it not been for the bitter quarrel between his father and grandfather, he might have stayed there for the rest of his life, instead of running off to Mexico.

Opening the door and stepping inside, he found himself in the well-remembered hallway with the old pictures on the wall. Nothing seemed to have changed in the slightest. It was as if he had left home and then returned the next day, instead of there having been almost thirteen years in between. There was a movement in the room which led off the corridor and he swung round sharply as the door opened, then stared in amazement. The girl stepped out into the passage, gazing frankly at him.

The moment's tension reacted strongly and sharply in Chris. He spoke half-angrily. 'I thought that I'd given you to understand—'

'I know what you're going to say, and I'm sorry for what I said the other day,' put in the girl quickly. 'I came here to see if there was anything I could to do help. Since your grandfather died, this place has had nothing done to it and—'

Once again, Chris stared in surprise. The silence lengthened and he found himself thinking how cool it was in here, in contrast to the tremendous heat in the air outside. Forcing a faint smile, he moved forward and followed her into the large parlour. The knowledge of how he had spoken so roughly to her on their last meeting rested heavily on him.

Crossing to the window, he stood for a long moment with his back to her, peering out into the courtyard, out to the corral where more than a score of work-broke horses moved between the circular fences.

'I think I know how you feel about this place,' said the girl from behind him. She came over and stood beside him, looking out towards the distant hills which marked the southern boundary of the spread. 'Your grandfather and my father were friends, perhaps each was the only real friend that the other had. When they both died, I came here to try to look after the place. I'd come to look on it as my home. Believe me, I've had a hard time keeping hired hands here. They seem to have heard a lot of stories about you – and they never bothered to check on whether there was any truth in them or not. Whenever any of Wilder's men started spreading rumours, they were readily believed.'

'And what do you think?' he asked, his voice strangely cold and distant. He saw her looking at him and he had the idea that she wanted desperately to trust him but was not sure whether she could.

'Running away from responsibilities is a pretty small thing for a man to do,' she said finally, weighing her words with care. 'You'll find that if you ride out and leave the small ranchers to the tender mercies of Wilder and Diego, you can never run far enough to get away from your own conscience.' She shrugged her shoulders. 'Never mind, though. It's your business, I suppose; and nothing really to do with me. But you can see how things are going, can't you?'

'The ranchers would be strong enough to stand up to these killers, if they only had the sense and the courage to bunch together and force the issue.'

'These people did not come here with the idea of having to fight for what they bought legally, and which they've built over the years with their bare hands. All that they've ever asked is to be left in peace. But Wilder hates all of the small people, believes that this country can never thrive properly unless it's ruled by one man, a strong and ruthless man.'

'Namely, Matthew Wilder.'

'Exactly. He's a greedy man who wants wealth and power more than anything else in this world and he doesn't care how he gets it.'

'All men are greedy in one way or another,' said Chris musingly.

She gave him a sharp, keen glance, suddenly arrested by that remark, then turned away from the window, walking back into the room and standing in front of the small table. 'I wonder just how deep that hatred of violence really goes in you?' she murmured. 'How much it is going to take before you see things as they really are, before you discover that to be any sort of man at all in this country, you have to fight and risk your neck. You don't have the face of a man who seeks only pleasure out of this life. Are you sure that you're as dead set against violence as you would have everyone believe?'

'Does that really matter so much to you?'

'Yes, I think it does,' she said, her voice a little too casual. 'I knew your grandfather very well. He might have been my grandfather instead of yours; and all his life, he tried to do what he could for men less fortunate than himself. Oh, I know he tried never to show it. He, too, believed that doing good was a show of weakness that was unbecoming of a man. But nevertheless, he stood behind these men, facing up to Wilder and the others whenever they tried to move in. I hoped that for his memory, you would turn out to be the same kind of man, that you wouldn't simply stand by, doing nothing, while these men have their homes and spreads burned down about their ears, their wives and families shot by gunmen, because they refused to sell their ranches at a ridiculously low price.'

She bit her lower lip in indecision, for a moment, then went on: 'I can remember the time, not long ago, when I could ride out across the range and up into the hills without carrying a gun, without any fear at all. But that isn't so now. I always have to expect the worst from every bend in the trail.' She paused and looked up curiously. 'You would ride along the hill trail out of town when you came here?'

He nodded. 'That's right. But I never saw anybody there who represented any danger to me.'

'But don't you agree that this is one of the most beautiful, clean stretches of country that you've ever seen?'

He said: 'I don't think there's any point in denying that.'

'Yet you'd stand by, willingly, and see this terrible evil come to so beautiful a stretch of land.'

Once again, Chris felt himself caught by surprise. Quietly, he said: 'I'll attend to any chores I have, but I fail to see why I should carry out those of any other man.' He felt a wave of bitter anger in him, directed more against himself than against the girl. After all, he thought inwardly, she had lived here all of these years and knew what was happening.

He went back to the table where she stood, then glanced down at what lay on the smoothly polished surface. For an instant, there was a touch of ice trailing down his spine.

The girl said softly: 'Those are your grandfather's guns, Chris. He always wore them when he rode around the ranch, or into town. They've killed men but all in fair fight. I thought you might like to have them, seeing as you have the right to them.' She twisted her lips into a faint, half-hearted smile, as if unsure of herself and what she had done.

Chris stared down at the guns in their leather holsters, at the smooth metal that shone in the bright sunlight which streamed through the open window. They spoke to him with their own voices and told of things that he did not like.

'I don't see why you should—' he began, then stopped abruptly at a sudden sound outside. Thinking back, he realised that he must have been vaguely aware of the sound of riders coming closer to the ranch, cutting in over the stretching grassland, but he had paid little attention to it, supposing that there were still plenty of men around, waiting to see how events would turn out, men who had served under his grandfather. Even as he started for the window, he heard a man outside yell, loud and long, in warning and a second later, there came a sudden flurry of gunshots, sharp and angry in the quietness outside the ranch house.

'What is it?' asked the girl quickly. She came forward, then pressed herself against the wall of the room as a shot came splintering through the window and bedded itself in the wall of the other side. The move outside had taken Chris completely by surprise. The firing swung round, seemed to be concentrated near the big barn some fifty yards from the house itself. It was a savage destruction that seemed to have flared up within moments. Risking a quick look through the smashed glass of the window, he caught sight of the group of men on horseback, milling around at the far end of the court-yard. They were emptying their guns into the barn where some of his own men were trapped. Even as he watched, he saw the three men break away from the main, milling bunch, the lighted torches in their hands, racing their mounts past the narrow opening in the barn, hurling the torches through on to the straw that lay piled high inside.

'They're going to burn those men out,' gasped the girl. She had pushed herself forward, oblivious of the danger she faced, was staring open-mouthed and white-faced, in the direction of the long barn, her eyes wide in horror.

Whirling, Chris ran out of the room, along the passage and threw open the front door. Behind him, he heard the girl shout a quick warning.

Ignoring it, he stepped out into the courtyard, walked purposefully in the direction of the tightly-bunched riders. He was within twenty feet of them before his presence there was noticed. Then one of them gigged his mount forward, pulling out from the others and Chris recognised him immediately; the same black frock-coat, the same handsome but sneering expression.

'I figured you might need a little persuasion, Mister Ranson,' said Wilder sarcastically. 'Here, we don't bargain with dudes or men who don't wear guns. I made your grandfather an offer for this place. Ten thousand dollars. He wouldn't accept it, even went so far as to threaten me.' The sneering lips parted a little more. 'Seems to me that the ranch is in a worse condition now than it was then. You just seem to have lost one of your barns, so my offer is now eight thousand dollars and you can take it or leave it. Only don't expect the offer to stay open for too long. I'm an impatient man and I like to get things done quickly.'

'I gave my answer to that crooked sheriff of yours,' Chris said through tightly-clenched teeth. He fought to keep the savage anger from breaking the bounds of his tight control. 'I don't make bargains with cold-blooded murderers.'

For a moment, he thought the other meant to shoot him down there and then. The long-barrelled Colt in Wilder's right hand levelled on his chest and he saw the finger tighten on the trigger, saw the look of deep anger suffused in the other's face. Then Wilder jerked back his head and laughed harshly. 'Then in that case,' he said thickly, 'we've got nothin' more to discuss. It would be a pity if I had to burn down all of this and shoot every man who works for you, but that's what I'll do if you haven't seen sense in the next couple of days. Forty-eight hours, Ranson and then I'll be back for my answer.'

He pulled hard on the reins, wheeling his mount away. Turning, he paused and looked down. 'Somehow, I don't think you'll get anybody to back you up if you try to stop me. My advice to you is not to waste your time. Ride on out of here while you still have a whole skin.'

Raking rowels across his mount's flanks, he raced the sorrel away over the dusty courtyard, calling to his men to follow him. Even as they rode along the winding trail that led up the side of the hill in the distance, Chris ran for the burning barn. One glance was enough to tell him that there was no chance of saving the building; the fire had gained too firm a hold and the straw there was as dry as tinder. There was scarcely any smoke, only the quivering of the superheated air in the harsh, strong sunlight as the invisible flames licked upward, soaring irresistibly towards the roof. Here and there, flames were beginning to sprout from the roof and it was only a matter of minutes before it fell in.

A wall of flame met Chris as he moved towards the blazing doorway. He knew that there were still men trapped inside, caught by the barrier of flame, possibly wounded men who had taken refuge there when those killers had started slinging lead. Swiftly. he tore off his jacket, thrust it into the trough beside the barn until the water dripped from it into a small puddle around his feet, then held it in front of him as a shield, before running through the wall of flame. Heat singed his hair and face, burning his arms. But in a few seconds, he was through, trying to see through the heat haze that brought tears into his eyes, blurring his vision as he strove to make out the figure of any of the men. One lay on the blazing straw less than four feet away, but even as he turned the other over, felt the limp looseness of the man's body, he knew that there would be no need to try to get this man out. The bullet had caught him high in the chest, on the left side, had probably nicked the heart, killing him almost instantly.

Coughing, struggling to breathe, he rushed on into the barn. A blazing beam fell from the roof and crashed on to the floor only a couple of feet in front of him and glancing upward, he saw the huge gap in the roof, the sagging, twisted beams which would fall within a few more moments. Desperately, he tried to hang on to his buckling consciousness. His chest felt as if it were on fire and every breath that he took, sucking it down into his aching, tortured lungs, seemed to be adding fuel to the fire that roared inside him. His lungs seemed to be unable to extract sufficient oxygen from the air to supply his body with its needs and his heart was pumping and racing inside him so that it threatened to burst asunder at every single beat. He knew that he could not stay here much longer, that if he did not get out soon, he would be overcome by the heat and flames and have little chance of getting out alive, even if the roof did not collapse and crush him entirely.

He was on the point of turning back in the direction of the door, when he caught a fragmentary glimpse of the figure over by the far wall, crouched against it, one arm thrown over its face, as if trying to shield the eyes from the searing heat. Reaching the man, he caught at him by the shoulder, saw the other lower his arm as if in surprise, then try to get to his feet, but his leg gave under him as though unable to bear his weight. Glancing down, Chris saw the stain of blood on the other's pants, gritted his teeth, thrust one arm under the injured man's shoulder and half-dragged, half-carried him through the flames. It was impossible to see the door. Tears blinded him and he was forced to narrow his lids until he could see very little. Somehow, he managed to get the other to the door, felt the strength leave him. There were only three more feet to go. Dimly, he could see daylight through the quivering flames, could just make out the confused shouting outside. Then his senses left him. He fell forward, unable to hold up the other any longer. He was not aware of the beams which crashed down behind him, adding their heat to that already inside the barn. He was not aware of the two men who ran in through the open doorway, grasping him and the injured man, lifting them and staggering with them outside.

His first impression was of coolness on his face, of water trickling down his cheeks, dripping from his chin and on to his neck. There was a faint crackling in his ears which he could not recognise and the dull murmur of voices nearby. When he tried to open his eyes, the glaring brightness forced him to close them again. For several moments he lay still, then felt the coldness of glass against his lips as they were gently forced open and something raw and hot was poured down his throat. Coughing and spluttering, he shook his head in an attempt to clear it and this time when he opened his eyes, he forced them to stay open, squinting up at the sun. He turned his head to one side, found himself looking at the girl and the two men with her. The man he had brought out of the blazing barn lay a few feet away.

'Better lie still for a little while,' said Rosalie softly, 'until you've recovered. Then we'll get you into the house.'

He shook his head, pushed himself up on to his hands. There was still a dull throbbing in his forehead, but now that he was able to breathe down great lungfuls of clear, clean air, he felt better. Groggily, he got to his feet, swaying a little as the blood rushed, pounding, to his aching forehead, but waved away the two men as they took a step forward to help him.

'I'm all right now,' he said harshly. He turned a little and threw a black look in the direction of the barn, now almost completely gutted and destroyed. A few beams smouldered in the centre of the ruin and here and there a tall column of red-edged flame leapt upward as it fed momentarily on a pile of unburnt straw or wood.

He knew that the others were watching him closely, wondering what he intended to do, he felt their eyes on the back of his neck as he turned and walked slowly towards the house. Rosalie made a quick move to follow him, but one of the men put out a restraining hand and shook his head and she fell back again, watching him wonderingly.

The silence that lived in the parlour pounded in Chris's chest as he went in through the open door. The tiny shards of glass from the broken window glittered brilliantly on the carpet under his feet; but he gave them only a cursory glance as he walked, stony-faced, to the table in the middle of the room. He stared at the strange gunbelt on the table, with the twin Colts resting snugly in the leather holsters, the material polished hard and smooth and shiny from the constant rub of metal against it. Any feeling of guilt, of reluctance, which had once been in his mind seemed to have been burned away by the flames inside the blazing barn, seared by the anger that had flooded through him in a savage wave. Reaching out, he ran his fingertips over the hard, cold metal; then his fingers curled about the smooth leather. Slowly and methodically, he put it around his waist and fastened the heavy buckle into place.

Night reached in from the east and the reds and scarlets in the west were swiftly swamped by the encroaching darkness that spread itself over the sky. As Chris rode down the twisting mountain trail into town, there was the faint sound of other riders moving in the hills, the dull murmur of hoofbeats reaching out of the clinging, all-enveloping stillness which seemed to come to the country at this hour of the day. Once clear of the crags and boulders, he rode on without hurrying, still trying to put his thoughts into some kind of order. The trail widened where it met the main stage route into town, but he passed no one on the way and there were few people abroad on the boardwalks as he rode along the main street, not pausing until he reached Doc Fordham's office.

Dropping from the saddle, he hitched the reins over the

post, climbed up on to the sidewalk and knocked softly on the door. It opened a few moments later and Doc Fordham peered out into the darkness, recognised him, and opened the door wider for him to step inside.

'Glad you came, Chris,' he said genially, opening the door into the parlour. 'I was worried about you when you moved out in spite of my objections. How are the cuts and bruises?'

'Well enough, Doc. But it wasn't about that, that I came to see you.'

The other moved around to the far side of the table, peered closely at Chris in the lamp light. Then his eyes widened just a shade and he nodded to himself as if in secret understanding. 'I think I'm beginning to get the picture,' he said, and he nodded his head slightly towards the guns slung low at Chris's waist. 'Are those your grandfather's guns?'

Chris nodded in silence.

'I thought I recognised 'em. Somethin' has happened, hasn't it?'

'Wilder and some of his hired killers rode into the ranch this afternoon, shortly after I arrived there. They killed two of the men and wounded another, after they'd trapped 'em in the big barn. Then they fired the barn, just as a warnin' to me of what would happen if I didn't give in to them, and sell out at a ridiculous sum.'

'So you've finally come to your senses,' nodded the other. There was a hard glint in his deep-set eyes. 'Do you intend to use those guns? Or are they there just for ornament?'

'If they force me to use 'em, then I will,' said Chris harshly. 'That's why I carne to see you. I need your help.'

The other shrugged. 'If you want me to strap on a pair of guns and stand at your shoulders, then I'll do it, but I reckon I ought to warn you that I'm a pretty poor shot and—'

'That isn't the sort of help I want from you,' Chris told him. 'But it seems to me there's only one way to fight Wilder and his crew of hired gunslingers, and that's by usin' force, the same way as they do.'

'Then where do I come in?' asked the other, glancing up at him, the light from the lamp throwing his face into deep shadow.

'Who elected Maxwell as sheriff of the town?'

'Why, we did, I reckon. I mean, the townsfolk. To be quite honest, I think he was the only man for the job. Nobody else would have it. This place had the name of a pretty lawless town in those days and I guess everybody was thinking of their own skin. The only reason Maxwell has lasted so long is that both Wilder and Diego use him.'

'But you could get rid of him if you wanted to, couldn't you, elect another man in his place?'

The other pursed his lips tightly, considering that. 'Wilder isn't goin' to like it if we did that.'

'Damn Wilder!' snapped Chris tightly. 'If there's to be law and order around here, then we've got to make a start somewhere. And the sooner we get rid of that crooked sheriff, the better.'

'You got any suggestions as to who we ought to elect in his place?' The other lifted thick, bushy brows, drawing them into a tight, interrogative line.

'I'll take that job,' said Chris flatly. 'And if it brings things to a showdown quickly, so much the better.'

'And Maxwell – he won't like it either. What do you mean to do with him?'

Chris smiled mirthlessly. 'I reckon that the best place for a crooked lawman such as Maxwell will be in his own jail. There should be plenty of charges we can bring against him, enough to keep him locked away for several years, if not to put a noose around his neck.'

'Now you're talking like that grandfather of yours,' said the other with a trace of enthusiasm in his voice. He reached for his hat hanging near the door. 'Let's get around and have a little talk with Haycock, the banker, and one or two of the others. I figure this oughtn't take long.'

In the Grand Union saloon, it was the dead hour of the

evening, the hour when most of its customers were in the hotels, eating their supper, thankful of the evening which had brought coolness to the air, replacing the oven-rawness of the day. Inside the saloon, the bar-room was almost empty. A swamper ran the broom over the floor, clearing away the refuse of the afternoon, ready for the usual influx of men which would begin in less than half an hour's time. He finished his brushing, laid the broom in one corner and pulled the rag from his pocket, wiping down the stains from the bar with a mechanical, half-hearted movement, his actions dull and lethargic, mind blurred from lack of fresh air, the atmosphere inside the bar-room filled with the stale odour of cigars and spilled whiskey. Tossing a couple of empty bottles into the box under the counter, he reached the end of the bar, glanced up at the long mirror on the wall at the back of the room, then swung his glance around quickly as the doors were pushed open and the two men came in.

In the dim light, he recognised Sheriff Maxwell and Brander, Wilder's ranch foreman. For a moment, he busied himself with stacking up the empty glasses that had lined the bar, then glanced up as the two men moved across to him, stood with their elbows hooked on to the bar.

'You're in early tonight, Sheriff,' he said quickly.

Maxwell gave out with a surly scowl, took the bottle from the other with a sharp movement and poured out drinks for Brander and himself. 'You heard that there was a burnin' at the Ranson place?' he asked casually.

The barkeep shook his head. 'I ain't heard nothin' about that,' he said thinly. 'Nobody's been here yet to tell me anythin'. Much damage done?'

The barkeep was a man who had no leanings either way in this duel that was shaping up on the range outside of town. He meant to ensure that he remained neutral, knowing that there would be plenty of money coming into the saloon, whichever side won in the end, and no actions of his would influence either side until the outcome was clear. He did not doubt, for one moment, that with all of the men he had at his back, and the fact that if the stories which he had heard about this grandson of the old man's were true, then Wilder would have little difficulty in running the other off the range and out of the territory. That was, if he did try to stand up and face Wilder. The most sensible thing for him to do, if he valued his skin at all, would be to get his horse and ride back to where he had come from. But even though the outcome did seem to be a virtual certainty, there was still that nagging little suspicion at the back of his mind that perhaps this stranger had more to him than met the eye, and that being the case, he would stay sitting on the fence until he knew for sure which way to jump.

'The boys fired the big barn and shot up a few of the ranch hands there,' declared Brander thickly. He gulped down his drink and poured himself another, tossing it down his throat in a single, swift motion, screwing up his lips as the bite of the raw liquor hit the back of his throat. 'I reckon that should make him realise he's not wanted here.'

'And if he don't feel like runnin'?'

'Then by God, we'll stop him permanently,' put in Maxwell. He lifted the glass of whiskey to his lips, then paused with it halfway there, as if frozen into stone, his wide-open eyes fixed on the mirror at the back of the bar, on the reflection of the men who had stepped into the saloon, the swing doors closing softly at their backs.

'For your trouble, Maxwell,' cut in Chris's voice thinly, 'you can have the chance to finish me permanently right here and now.'

Maxwell whirled, his back to the bar. Brander turned more slowly. If he felt any surprise at hearing Chris's voice behind him, he gave no outward sign. Only the dark eyes narrowed into mere slits and there was hardness to his features, a look of malevolent hatred in his gaze. His face still bore the marks of the beating he had taken from Chris some days before and he put up one hand to his cheek, feeling it instinctively,

70

gingerly, as he faced the other. Then his gaze dropped to the guns at the other's waist and his lips pulled back in a faint sneer.

'You come dressed with guns this time, dude,' he called thickly. 'You sure don't think much of life.'

'I've come to arrest Maxwell,' said Chris flatly. 'On a charge of working in cahoots with Matthew Wilder. There may be more charges when we get around to 'em, but I reckon that should be enough to keep him locked in jail until certain other matters have been taken care of.'

'You ain't got no right to arrest me,' snarled Maxwell. He took a step forward and moved his hand towards the badge on his shirt. 'I'm the law here and I—'

'Not any longer,' broke in Chris tightly. He eased back his jacket a little, to show the star on his own shirt. 'You see, the townsfolk here figured that they want somebody as sheriff who takes his orders from nobody, certainly nobody like Wilder. So they decided you were no longer sheriff here and they elected me in your place – as of now.' His words bit across the clinging silence in the bar-room like the lash of a whip.

'You can't do that,' shouted Maxwell in harsh protest. 'I'm sheriff here and no two-bit tinhorn is goin' to ride in and take over. I'll see you all in Hell first.'

'If you make any move towards your guns, that's where you'll be goin',' cut in Chris.

At that, Brander began a slow drift to one side, keeping his shoulders pressed against the bar, his eyes never once leaving Chris's face. He kept his hands in full view all of the time, but Chris knew that this was a deliberate move on the other's part, that it was as if a pre-arranged signal had passed between these two men, and they were making their move to box him in from two sides when it came to the showdown. Deliberately, he eyed them with an unfocused gaze, his eyes taking in both of them so that any sudden movement by either of them would be seen at once.

'That's far enough, Brander,' he snapped harshly. 'Now, Maxwell, do you intend to come quietly, or do you want this thing done the hard way?'

'You wouldn't dare draw on me,' said the sheriff. 'You know damned well that you don't stand a chance of getting the drop on us and even if you tried, there are two of us, three if we count the barkeep. I reckon he knows where he'd better stand in this and he always keeps a shotgun just below the counter.' From the way the other spoke, stressing his words, Chris guessed that this was as good as an order to the barkeep, that if he knew what was good for him, he would do exactly as he was told and make a dive for the shotgun – and use it – whenever he, Chris, made his play.

Chris flickered a glance towards the stocky, stolid-faced man behind the bar. The other still stood there, unmoving, his hands in sight on top of the bar in front of him. Chris prided himself on his knowledge of what other men were likely to do in circumstances such as this and he felt pretty certain that the barkeep would make no move until he saw how things were going. He could discount the other and keep his attention glued to the two men facing him at the bar.

'Somehow, I don't think that man behind you is goin' to take any sides in this little argument,' Chris said finally, as the silence in the bar-room grew long. 'Now I'm tellin' you once again. Toss down your guns and move out of here in front of me. The same goes for you, too, Brander. I've got a charge of murder hangin' over you.'

'You ain't got nothin' on me,' snarled the other. Each finger of his hands was thrust wide, pushing outward like the spoke of a wheel, the hands held inches above the butts of his guns. His eyes were now locked with those of the man who faced them. Waiting, watching, probing for the sign that would indicate that death was on its way. Silence crowded down on the room.

Then, as if at a signal, both Maxwell and Brander went for their guns. Hands swept down, plucking the Colts from leather. But their draw was no match for the man who faced them. Down and up, Chris lifted the long barrels in a sweeping draw that brought the muzzles inches above their line of fire. A single, swift snap of his wrists and sound bucketed through the bar-room. Brander stood upright for a moment, as if stretching up on his toes, head thrust forward, a look of stunned wonder and surprise on his features, his eyes striving to hold life in them. Then he toppled forward, the guns slipping from nerveless fingers, dropping with a clatter to the floor seconds before his huge body crashed down on top of them, to lie unmoving in the newly-swept sawdust.

Beside him, Maxwell lay back, half over the bar, his arms by his sides. Neither gun had cleared leather when the bullet had hit him high in the shoulder. His face was contorted into a spasm of shocked, stunned agony and the red stain on his shirt was beginning to widen slowly as the cloth soaked up the blood which welled slowly and continuously from the wound.

Chris moved forward, paused in front of the other, thrusting one of the Colts back into its holster, the other lined up on the wounded man's chest.

Without being told again, the other released his hold on the guns and they fell into the sawdust at his feet. Sweat showed on his forehead and trickled down the folds of skin on his flabby cheeks. His eyes were wide, staring, with fear showing deep in them. Reaching forward, Chris grasped the star on the other's shirt as he cringed back, then ripped it off with such force that it tore the material, leaving a gaping rent in the shirt.

'All right,' he said thinly, 'let's go. Over to the jail.'

'You won't get away with this,' muttered the other, as he stumbled forward, out through the swinging doors and along the dark street. 'When Wilder hears about this, he'll send his boys into town to get me out and they'll shoot you down like a dog, whether you're wearin' that badge or not. You don't think the townsfolk here have got any say in what happens, do you?'

'Maybe they hadn't in the past, but we've decided to change a few things as from tonight,' muttered Chris as he prodded the other forward. 'And this is one of those things. Now I reckon you'd better get inside that jail and keep quiet, or this gun may go off. If there's one thing I hate it's a crooked sheriff, a man who hides behind a badge and sells out the people he's hired to protect.'

He thrust the other into one of the small cells at the rear of the jail building, stepped out into the corridor and locked the door behind him.

With an effort, Maxwell got to his feet and came forward, fingers hooked around the metal bars of the door. 'You're not goin' to leave me in here like this, are you?' he muttered hoarsely. 'What about this slug in my shoulder? You want me to bleed to death in here before mornin' ?'

'Wouldn't worry me particularly if you did,' grunted Chris harshly. 'I'll get the doctor to take a look at you as soon as I can get him here.'

When Matthew Wilder came in from the corral, the sun had just lifted itself clear of the eastern skyline and shadows were long in the courtyard as he made his way over to the ranch house, spurs raking up the dust on the ground. The horse that stood near the water trough had been ridden long and hard during the night, its coat streaked with dust, the lather of sweat still on its neck and legs. He gave it a quick glance, then went inside. He went quickly along the narrow passage to the door at the end, thrust it open and stepped inside. Four men were seated in the room. Garvey, Wendell and the two Matson brothers. Wendell got to his feet as Wilder strode into the room, his gaze flicking to each man in turn.

'Somethin' happened?' he asked tersely. He rolled himself a smoke and seated himself in the chair that Wendell had just vacated.

'That's right,' nodded Wendell. 'Somethin' we've got to take care of right away.'

Wilder eyed him in momentary surprise. 'Well,' he asked dryly. 'What's on your minds? Not worried about what Ranson might do after that lesson we taught him yesterday, are you?' He lit the cigarette, blew smoke into the air. 'If you are, then forget it. He'll be running out of the territory any day now with his tail between his legs like a whipped cur.'

Garvey shook his head. 'Ranson ain't goin' to run, Boss,' he said with conviction. 'He's already started to make trouble for us – big trouble.'

Wilder sat up straight in his chair at that, the cigarette forgotten between his fingers, the smoke curling up and lacing painfully across his eyes, but he did not seem to notice. 'What sort of trouble?' he demanded, his voice hard.

'Brander's dead,' put in Wendell. 'Seems this *hombre*, Ranson, put on his grandfather's guns and rode into town shortly after we burned down the barn. He went straight to the townsfolk and got them to elect him sheriff and cut Maxwell out altogether. Then he went to the saloon, threatened to run Maxwell into his own cell on a charge of being in cahoots with you and sellin' out the town. He called 'em both and the barkeep swears that they drew first, but that this *hombre* is like greased lightning with a gun. He shot Brander before he could squeeze off a single shot and plugged Maxwell in the shoulder before his guns had even cleared leather. Maxwell's in jail right now and like I said, Brander's dead.'

A sudden heat showed briefly in Wilder's hard stare. He made to push himself out of the chair, arms braced beside him, then lowered himself down again, forcing himself to relax. 'You're right. We've got to finish him – and fast. Before he can rally any of the others to him. There are several men who remember his grandfather and they might figure on joinin' up with him now that he's shown that he's not such a dude as we reckoned. We made a mistake and it's up to us to rectify it as quickly as we can. Where is he now?' His look challenged Wendell.

'Back in town,' nodded the other. 'I figure he'll stay there until the circuit judge gets here to try Maxwell.'

'That's all the better for us. We've got to get Maxwell out of there before he cracks and does a heap of talkin'. He knows too much of our plans. If he spills it all to Ranson, we may not find it easy to get rid of him.'

'How do you figure we ought to do it?' asked Garvey.

In answer, Wilder jerked a thumb towards the Matson brothers. 'That's your chore, boys,' he said softly. 'You know what to do.'

They nodded. 'Sure thing, boss. If he's as fast as they say he is, maybe a shot from a dark alley would—'

'Do it any way you like,' retorted the other heatedly. 'All I want now is that Ranson is dead before the mornin' tomorrow.'

Wendell shook his head swiftly. 'It ain't that easy,' he put in. 'Even though he's only been here a few days, already a lot of folk are beginning to swing round to him. We spread that story about his father and that satisfied most of the folk here and they seemed prepared to accept that Chris Ranson was made in the same mould. When he first came here, that impression stuck, but since this happened yesterday, I figure they'll be thinkin' differently. He's a tougher proposition than we figured. A shot in the back – yes, I'd go along with that, but not in any way that could connect it with us.'

'Why not, once he's dead, we've got nothin' to worry about,' snapped Wilder harshly. 'He's mortal like the rest of us and a bullet can kill him as quickly as any other man. If we wait, we may lose more men and with Diego ready to move in once we show any sign of weakness, that's somethin' we can't afford.'

'But if we arranged it so that it appeared one of Diego's men had done it,' muttered Wendell, 'that ought to solve both of our problems.'

'You make sense,' Wilder acknowledged eventually. 'You got any idea how that can be done?'

'Me and Garvey have it figured,' he claimed with conviction in his voice. 'Just leave it to us and you can be sure this *hombre* Ranson won't be any more trouble after tonight.'

'All right. Have it your way. But if there's any slip-up, then—'

'There won't be,' promised the other tightly. He eased himself to his feet from where he had been seated on the arm of Garvey's chair. Motioning to the other, they went out and a few moments later, Wilder heard them ride out of the courtyard and take the trail that led into town. In spite of their assurance that everything would be taken care of, he still felt uneasy in his mind. This news of Brander's death and Maxwell's imprisonment had come as a tremendous shock to him. It was the last thing he had ever expected Ranson to do. That burning down of the barn on his spread and the killing of those men of his must have forced his hand. Certainly that was the only explanation he could offer to himself at the moment.

But if all this were true, and at the moment he saw no reason to doubt it, it meant that he was facing an opponent at least as hard and as fast on the draw as old man Ranson had been. When the other had died, he had expected to be able to move in and take over that ranch without any trouble. If he had been able to do that, he would have become so much bigger and more powerful than Diego, that he might be strong enough to force the other out of the territory. Then he would be the undisputed ruler of this part of the country, his empire would stretch much further than the eye could see in any direction and even the town would be his.

Now he had been forced to rearrange all of his carefully laid plans. If Wendell and Garvey succeeded in what they had set out to do, all so well and good – and his worries would be over. But if not, if they failed as Brander and Maxwell had so clearly failed, then the time would have come for a showdown.

For an instant, he even considered the possibility of team-ing up with Diego, until they had rid the place of Ranson, recognising him as a common enemy; but he doubted if Diego would trust him sufficiently to agree to this. He wasn't sure that he could trust Diego.

His glance fell on the Matson brothers and he nodded towards the door. 'Better get back to work,' he said tonelessly, 'and if I need you, I'll call on you.'

When they had gone, he sat stiff and straight in his chair, staring straight out ahead of him, turning his thoughts over in his mind. Why in God's name did this Chris Ranson have to come back and claim this ranch? After all, he hadn't been to this place, hadn't been within several hundred miles of it, for close on thirteen or fourteen years. Now, somehow, the lawyers had succeeded in tracing him and giving him the news of his grandfather's death and he had decided to take the place and begin where his grandfather had left off. It was beginning to look as though the raid on the Ranson spread the previous day had been a big mistake. It might have been better if he had held his hand for the time being, and gone out there to parley with Ranson. At least, it would have been possible to gain time in which to formulate some other plan which might have had a higher chance of success. There was, of course, one possibility that he hadn't considered, but which was obviously worthy of consideration. That girl, Rosalie. She had been hanging around the Ranson place for some years now, even before the old man had died. If she was to be kidnapped, it might force Ranson to change his mind about a lot of things; especially if the other were sweet on the girl, and Wilder thought that to be entirely possible. He kept the idea in the forefront of his mind. If Garvey and Wendell failed in their mission, it was something he had to fall back on.

Doc Fordham came out of the small cell for the second time that day, set down his bag on the desk in the sheriff's office, and lowered himself gratefully into the chair, taking out a thin, black cheroot and placing it carefully between his lips, rolling it around his mouth for a few moments as if savouring the firm feel of it before lighting it. Then he lit it and sat back in his chair, looking over the top of the desk at Chris.

'Well?' Chris asked. 'Do you reckon he's goin' to live?'

'He'll live,' stated the other, glancing down at the redly glowing tip of the cheroot. 'A slug in the shoulder never kills that kind. The devil looks after his own, they reckon, and I think that applies in his case. He'll be fit enough to be strung up when the time comes.'

'I'm glad to hear it.' Chris broke open the shotgun that lay on the desk and pushed the two large cartridges home, then closed the weapon with a snap that jarred loudly in the silence of the office.

Fordham noticed the other's action, gestured towards the shotgun with his left hand. 'You expectin' trouble?'

'I guess it's likely. Wilder will know about this by now, probably knew first thing this morning and he knows he's got to get Maxwell out of here before he talks and tells us a lot of things that he ought not to tell.'

'When do you reckon he'll come?'

'I don't think he'll ride into town and try to take him by force. There are too many people in town who know how Maxwell has been in cahoots with Wilder. If he's either shot down to stop him from talkin', or they try to bust him out of jail, they'll play it a subtle way, maybe try to make it look as though some of Diego's men have had a hand in it. That way, they'll kill two birds with one stone.' Chris's smile was cold, tight.

'You want me to stay with you? Two extra guns are better than none at all.'

'I don't reckon there's any reason why you should get mixed up in this,' Chris said quietly. He checked the chambers of the twin Colts, spinning the chambers quickly, then thrust the guns back into their holsters. Outside, the town seemed quiet. It was not late and he would have expected more activity on the streets, but it was as if the townsfolk had sensed that something was about to break loose at any moment, and they were keeping off the streets.

Getting to his feet, Chris walked to the door and opened it carefully before stepping through, standing a little to one side on the boardwalk, so that the light that streamed through the open door, spilling on to the dusty ground, was not directly at his back, silhouetting him there for any gunman to see and kill. The air that blew along the street, sighing down from the hills in the distance, was cool and pleasant on his face and in his nostrils. Tonight, the town was showing its quietest face for some time; yet for all of this comparative, apparent peace, he knew with a sudden certainty that it was merely an illusion, that there was danger out there in the dark-thrown shadows on either side of the street, danger that would come unexpectedly and from virtually any direction.

FOUR

NIGHT HAWKS

The steak which Rosalie brought him from the hotel was tender and fried to perfection. She seated herself in the chair facing the long desk and watched him as he ate. Despite the tension in him, he worked his way through the meal with gusto, eating with relish. Seated in the chair by the door, tilting it back against the wall, Doc Fordham said harshly: 'You look worried, Chris. Expectin' more trouble?'

Chris glanced up from his plate, gave a brief nod. 'I'm always expectin' trouble in a town like this. Too quiet for my likin'. Besides, our friend Wilder won't be standin' still now that he knows we've got Maxwell locked up here in jail.'

'But we ain't sure that he does know,' pointed out the other tersely.

'He knows, and he has to do somethin' about it – and soon. It's been quite a hectic two days. Another thing that worries me, is what Diego is goin' to do about this. So far, he hasn't put in an appearance and that surprises me.''

'Diego is a strange man. Maybe it's because he's a Mexican. Nobody knows which way he'll jump.'

'Eat up the supper I brought you and don't try crossing your bridges until you get to them,' said Rosalie quickly. 'Did you manage to get word to any of the other ranchers?' She glanced at the doctor as she spoke.

81

He pursed his lips, shrugged his shoulders a little. 'They were all for it,' he muttered. 'Some of 'em had heard about Brander and Maxwell. But they still weren't too sure about you, Chris. They figure that you might be forced to back down if Wilder decides to move in with all of his men and ride on the town.'

Chris pressed his lips tightly together, then drank down the scalding hot coffee. It was what he had expected. These men were not going to risk their lives, their ranches, everything they had built up over the years, just on the chance that he might be able to lead them against Wilder and possibly Diego. He pushed the empty plate into the middle of the table, fumbled for the makings of a smoke, then got to his feet and walked over to the window. Glancing out, he noticed that his mount was no longer standing at the hitching rail immediately outside. Puzzled, a tiny alarm bell ringing at the back of his mind, he motioned to Rosalie to put out the lamp, then opened the door, standing a little to one side before going out on to the wooden boardwalk, his right hand hovering close to the butt of the gun in its holster. The silence was enough to warn him that there was something wrong, very wrong. He had been too absorbed in his own thoughts to have noticed it before.

Narrowing his eyes, he glanced about him. His horse stood in the dust in the centre of the wide street, the reins trailing loosely on the ground. For a moment, he considered the possibility that the leather might have slipped, but he knew within himself that he had made the hitch properly, that it would not have been pulled loose by the horse.

'Get back inside the office,' he called as the girl made to come outside to join him.

He heard her step back into the room, then a swift movement at the edge of his vision caught his attention. The shadowed shape moved quickly across the face of the narrow alley on the far side of the street. There was the faint sound of boots in the muffling dust, then the brief, clearly-heard clatter of them as the man darted on to the boardwalk opposite him, running in a low crouch. The other darted across the beam of light from one of the windows and Chris caught a brief glimpse of a drawn gun. He let his gaze drift swiftly to either side, probing the shadows. There had to be another man somewhere around, with a gun lined up on him from the dark alleys.

Ducking back towards the barrel outside the sheriff's office, he threw himself down behind it, the Colts whispering from their holsters, his fingers bar-straight on the triggers. A couple of shots rang out from the far side of the street and he saw the bright lances of flame from the muzzles of the guns, pinpointing the hidden marksman. The slugs tore wood from the upright close by, went screaming off into the night, in murderous ricochet.

He snapped a quick shot at the gunman but it was impossible to tell if it had hit or missed its target. All the time, he felt the uneasiness in his mind as he tried to locate the second gunman. He had neither seen nor heard anything of this man but he knew with a strange certainty that this attack was following the classic pattern and the man across the street would never have given himself away like that if it hadn't been for the purpose of drawing attention to himself, while his companion moved into position.

'Better give up, Ranson,' yelled a harsh voice from the shadows on the other side of the street. 'We've got the place surrounded. If you turn Maxwell loose, we may consider letting you off with your life. If not, then we'll move in and make sure we finish you.'

Crouching down, keeping his head low, Chris waited, trying to get a clear glance of the other. There was a movement a little to one side of him and he half turned, then stopped as he recognised Doc Fordham's voice, yelling harshly from the window of the office.

'You got the rest of us to contend with,' he yelled, and punctuated his words with a sudden blast from one of the shotguns. The lethal hail of lead went bucketing across the street and Chris was able to hear it quite clearly as it peppered the walls and uprights there, tearing through the wood, smashing one of the windows into a thousand pieces.

'Keep your head down,' roared Chris harshly. Although there was no light in the office window, he knew that the old doctor would make an excellent target for the bushwhacker directly across the street. Scarcely had the warning left his lips than there came another roar of sound, this time from the mouth of the narrow alley some twenty yards to his left. He narrowed his eyes, threw himself flat, then wriggled swiftly along the boardwalk, hugging the uprights, making as little noise as possible. Now that he knew the location of the other killer, it made things a little simpler. Pulling himself the full length of the walk, he slid snake-like over the dust, arms thrust out in front of him.

There was a wagon standing by the side of the street a few yards down from the office and he reached this in less than twenty seconds, swung up behind it and paused for a moment, waiting for the whining slug that would tell him he had been spotted by one of the others. But there was no sound from further along the street and he guessed they were still crouched in the shadows, looking for him. Bent slightly forward, he eased his way across the street, crouched down on the far side and balanced himself on the balls of his feet, eyes probing into the pitch blackness of the nearby alley. A moment later, his prying eyes had picked out the grey, blurred shape of the killer, his body pressed into the wall of the building that stood on the corner of the two streets, where they intersected.

'You heard what we said, Ranson?' yelled the man on the boardwalk. Chris listened to the voice carefully. He placed its source somewhere halfway along the front of the building and swung a little, waiting to see what the other man would do, letting the silence drag, finally growing weary of it, his finger itching on the trigger. As he waited, he remembered those two men who had been killed in the barn on the ranch and the wounded man he had somehow managed to get out of the blazing inferno before it had collapsed in ruins about him; and he felt the anger pour through him in a cold wave, chilling him. Patience made rock out of him so that he felt he could outwait these men no matter how long it took to break them down.

At last, he saw the man close to him begin to move forward, evidently not liking the stillness and silence at all. It was the sudden need to do something, to ease the tautness in his limbs which had prompted the killer to move; and he seemed to know that by doing so, he had given himself away, for he began to fire swiftly and with complete recklessness, raking the boardwalk in front of the sheriff's office with shots, clearly hoping that if he pumped in enough lead, some of it was bound to find its mark.

Chris stepped away from the wall, bringing up the guns as he did so. They bucked swiftly against his wrists as he sent two shots crashing into the darkness, saw the man stumble and give up a great shout as his legs went from under him, pitching him forward on to his face in the dust. His companion turned suddenly, began throwing lead. Chris heard the vicious hum of it close to his head and slugs struck the ground near his feet as he planted them wide. There was a part of a crowd on the street now, keeping in the background while the gunfight lasted.

Running forward, he reached the corner of the alley, pushed himself up right against the wall, keeping one eye on the man who lay face-downward in the dust, watching him closely for several seconds before he decided that there would be no more trouble from him. His breath quickened and drew deeper in his lungs as he pulled himself upright, then thrust his body forward, around the corner of the tall building. A slug blasted wood from the wall. Another missed his body by inches. But the gunslinger had given away his exact position and Chris pulled up his gun, pointed it at the place where the muzzle flash had lit up the boardwalk and fired. He heard the bullet smash through brick and wood, heard the other suddenly shift direction, knowing that he had been seen. Chris fired again. The bloom of the burned powder was blue-crimson in the pitch blackness and above the gun thunder, he heard the man cry out, his voice lifted in a shrill yell. Then the cry faded, the echoes of the gunshots drifted into silence around him and he heard the harsh, slow guttering of the man's breath as he lay flopped against one of the doorways.

Cautiously, his gun ready in his hand, Chris went forward, coldly and patiently waiting to put another shot into the man's body if he tried to move. But the other was finished, there was no more fight left in him, his body twisting and threshing slightly against the wooden uprights. From the other side of the street, Doc Fordham came forward, the shot-gun hefted in his right hand, his face puckered a little as he hurried over. He stopped in front of the dying man, went down on one knee, laying the weapon down carefully, out of reach of the gunhawk.

Chris said: 'I aimed to kill him, Doc. He'd have shot one of us if I hadn't.'

The other nodded, turned and yelled at the small crowd in the street. 'One of you bring a light over here.'

A few moments later, one of the men shuffled forward, with a lantern in his hand. He stood on the boardwalk, holding it close to the man's body as the other bent to examine him. The gunslinger had been stirring slowly on the wooden slats, but now his body lay still and his breathing was so quiet that Chris had the feeling he was already dead, but after a few moments, he stirred and muttered something under his breath, the words so soft and slurred together that it was impossible for Chris to make them out.

'Must have cut across his lungs,' grunted Fordham. 'Nothin' I can do for him. He won't last long.'

'Reckon we ought to get him inside, Doc?' asked one of the men gruffly.

Doc Fordham shook his head. 'No need for that,' he

muttered. 'He can die out here as well as in there.' It was a callous outlook, thought Chris, glancing sideways at the doctor, but he knew that it was not this that had prompted his answer. The man at his feet twisted a little, then his head dropped back on to the boardwalk with a faint thud and his breathing stopped with a long sigh that gushed out of him. Chris bent over the man, lifted his arm, felt the humped looseness of it and let it drop on the other's chest. He straightened, looked about him at the faces of the men clustered around the building.

'Anybody seen either of these killers before?' he asked harshly.

'Sure.' One of the men stepped forward, glanced down at both men, then nodded. 'I know 'em. Wendell and Garvey. They work for Wilder.'

'I figured that might be the way of it,' nodded Chris. He turned and made his way over to the office. He felt the hardness grow in him as he made his way along the narrow passage to the cells at the back, paused in front of the one which was occupied and stared through the bars at Maxwell. The other sat nursing his arms, glanced up with a faint grin on his fleshy features.

'Some shootin' out there, Ranson?' he asked innocently. 'Reckon the town ain't used to havin' you around.'

'Mebbe not,' muttered Chris. 'Seems Wilder must be plain scared at havin' you locked away in here. Sent along two of his hired killers to try to finish me and bust you out.'

Maxwell raised his brows at that, said nothing.

'Two fellas by the name of Wendell and Garvey. Could be that you knew 'em.'

'Never heard of either of 'em,' protested the other mildly.

Chris shrugged. 'I wouldn't let that bother you none. They're both lyin' out there in the street. They ain't goin' to worry anybody now.'

For a moment, Chris felt sure that he saw the first faint flicker of doubt show on the other's fat face. Then it was gone as if it had never been, wiped away, and he was no longer sure that it had even been there.

'Reckon you'll be safe enough here until the circuit judge comes around. Then you'll stand your trial on as many charges as I can bring against you.'

'You'll never bring me to trial, Ranson, and you know it. If Wilder doesn't come ridin' in to get me out, Diego will. You can't fight the two of 'em, no matter how big you figure you are, or how many men you reckon you can count on from the other ranches or the town.'

'We'll see about that,' muttered Chris. Turning on his heel, he made his way back along the passage and into the outer office, lowering himself wearily into the chair behind the desk. Rosalie came over and stood with her hands resting on the top of the desk, looking down at him, a worried frown creasing her forehead.

'You're worried about Wilder, aren't you?' she murmured softly, glancing up as the outer door opened and Doe Fordham came in.'

'Not particularly Wilder. It's this *hombre* Diego I'm worried about at the moment, because I can guess pretty closely what Wilder's next move is goin' to be; but I know nothin' about Diego.'

'Then I reckon this is where you get the chance to find out about him,' said Fordham pointedly. 'He's ridin' along the street with a bunch of his men. Looks to me like there might be trouble.'

Chris heaved himself from his chair, walked quickly to the door and thrust it open, looking out into the shadowed street at the tightly-packed bunch of men who rode at a slow walk along the street. The group of riders halted in front of the sheriff's office and for a long moment, there was no movement. Chris was aware of the squat, dark-haired man who sat the large, black stallion, watching him from beneath the rim of the wide sombrero.

'Senor Ranson?' inquired the other, after a long pause, the

flash of white teeth showing clearly in the shadow of his face.

'That's right,' said Chris clearly. 'And you must be Miguel Diego.'

'I am Diego.' Again the flash of a smile on the other's face. 'I wish to talk with you, Senor Ranson.'

'Better step down and come inside,' Chris said tightly. He threw a quick, sideways glance at the men the other had brought with him. Diego noticed this, and said something harshly in fluid Spanish. The men swung down from their saddles, hitched their mounts to the rail and then moved off in the direction of the nearby saloon. Diego waited until they had gone, then swung easily from the saddle, and came forward. 'Now we can talk alone, Senor Ranson,' he said smoothly, his dark eyes never once leaving Chris's face.

Chris stepped to one side, allowed the other to precede him, then closed the outer door. The Mexican glanced at Rosalie and Doc Fordham for a moment and some retort seemed to be balanced in his mind; then he shrugged his shoulders and walked over to the chair in front of the long desk, sat down in it and turned to face them.

'I have heard of the trouble there has been with Matthew Wilder,' he said softly, smiling broadly. 'I came into town to see if you needed any help. He is a very bad *hombre*, Senor. Very bad. He tries many times to take my ranch from me and it is only because I have many men with me, that he has not been able to do so. But he will try again, once he has taken your place from you.'

Chris squared round and looked across at him, eyes narrowed a little. With the other's back to the light from the lantern on the table, he could make nothing of the Mexican's expression beyond the broad twist of his smile. 'Just what do you expect of me?' he asked suddenly.

'Nothing, Senor. You have very few men on the ranch who will back you in any fight against Wilder. He has many gunmen, thirty, perhaps forty. You will need men to ride with you and I have such men.'

'I see. So you're willin' to throw in your hand with me in an attempt to finish Wilder?' Chris pressed his lips tightly together. This was something he had not expected. But now that he came to look at things objectively, he ought to have figured that something like this might happen. Diego would want to get rid of Wilder by any means that he could, even if it meant throwing in his lot with him.

Diego spread his hands wide on top of the desk, leaning forward. 'I have heard that you have locked up Sheriff Maxwell in the jail and you have taken his place. It is good that there should be law and order here, but so long as Wilder is alive, that cannot be. Believe me, Senor, I have lived here for many years and I know him. He is a man who desires power and wealth more than anything else in this world. He will kill for it, destroy for it.'

'And you – what do you expect to get out of it?' Chris grinned thinly. 'I don't suppose that you'll do this for nothin'.'

'But of course not. When this is finished, I shall take over Wilder's ranch. That is fair exchange, is it not?'

'Perhaps.' Chris nodded slowly. He was still unsure of the other. There was something in his story which did not ring quite true. He reckoned that Diego was more than capable of pitting one side against the other, standing in the background until the fighting was over and then stepping in and taking over all that was left, knowing that neither side had enough men to oppose him. 'I'll think it over,' he said finally.

The other gave him a studying glance and for a moment, the smile slipped and there was a hard tightness on his features. Then he shrugged negligently, took out a thin cheroot and lit it slowly. 'I would advise you not to wait too long, *amigo*. Matthew Wilder is a very impatient man and when he learns of the shooting tonight, he will seek revenge. Can you stop him if he rides into town, or against your ranch, with forty gunmen at his back?'

'I'll still think over your offer, Diego,' he said firmly. When the Mexican was gone, he leaned back in his chair and forced himself to relax, not aware until then that his body had been taut, every muscle pulled tight inside him.

'You're not goin' to trust that snake, are you?' muttered Doc Fordham, standing by the side of the desk, glancing down at him. 'He's only waitin' for you to move in on Wilder and you'll find that there'll be no men at your back. When you're all done, he'll move in and scoop the jackpot.'

'That possibility had occurred to me,' Chris murmured. He rolled himself a smoke and pulled the cigarette smoke down deep into his lungs. 'But can I afford not to take him up on his offer? He knows that he's got me in a cleft stick. He can always use his men to aid Wilder and there's no force in the whole State could stand up to both of 'em if they joined forces.'

Rosalie watched him, her face shadowed and soft. 'The ranchers will stand by you if you steer clear of Wilder and Diego,' she said, forcing conviction into her tone.

'Will they?' Chris shook his head slowly. 'Even if you're right, they don't have enough men among the lot of 'em to face up to Wilder and Diego. I reckon we have to accept Diego's offer of help. We've got no other choice.'

'If you do, none of the ranchers or the townfolk will lift a finger to help you,' warned the girl. 'I'm sure of that.'

Chris sighed, blew smoke into the still air. He knew that the girl was right. He was supposed to represent law and order here in the town, and he could not do that if he allied himself with men such as Miguel Diego. There were several ways of enforcing law and order, but they did not include working hand in glove with killers, even if that seemed to be the only way left open to him.

'I reckon you'd better grab yourself some sleep,' broke in Fordham, changing the subject abruptly. 'You might be able to think things over a lot more clearly in the mornin'.'

'And Maxwell? What happens if Wilder decides to try again durin' the night?'

'I'll stand guard,' declared the other positively. 'There won't be any more trouble, but if it'll make you feel easier in your mind, I'll act as your night man. If there's any sign of trouble, I'll waken you.'

Chris wanted to protest, but he knew that at the moment, he needed sleep more than anything else and he was only too grateful to accept the other's offer. He finished his smoke, checked the twin Colts and the Winchester, took them with him into the back room and stretched himself out on the cold bed, the weapons close beside him, where he could reach them within seconds.

Outside, the town was quiet. The shooting had stirred it up a little, but it was not long before it had gone back to its usual stillness. Lying back, stretching himself out full length on the low bed, he closed his eyes and fell asleep almost at once.

Early the next morning, Matthew Wilder stood on the wide, back porch of the ranch house and watched the oncoming storm develop. It had begun as a high piling of the thunderheads over the distant mountains, the black masses of cloud building up from the horizon, dark and brooding, promising the threat of rain. He felt a responding tightness grow within him as he contemplated the news which had been brought to him two hours before, while it had been still dark, with only a thin, grey line showing where the dawn was about to break. The fact that Wendell and Garvey were dead, shot down by Ranson in the streets of town, scarcely affected him. Both men had clearly been fools, but they had claimed they would finish Ranson and he had been forced to let them have their chance, knowing only too well what the price would be if they failed.

But the additional item of news, namely that Diego had been to visit Ranson and the two had talked together in the sheriff's office for close on an hour that evening, had brought a sense of fear and apprehension to him, something he had not known for a long time now. If Diego had offered to throw in his lot with Ranson, and the latter had accepted that help, then he could see all of his dreams and carefully laid schemes coming to naught. There had to be something he could do, but until this storm blew itself out, he would be unable to ride out with any of his men and force a showdown.

The stillness that hung in the air had lasted for more than an hour now, while the thunderheads had increased their piled-up intensity, threatening and black. Then, the wind struck. It came suddenly and unexpectedly, whining over the smooth prairie at the rear of the ranch, flattening the grass and within moments, the rain came hard on its heels, wind-driven water that hammered at the roof of the porch over his head, searching out any unsuspected openings in it, pouring from the roof on to the ground around the house, flattening the mud, turning it into a quagmire, large puddles forming in it. The windows had been shuttered, but even so, they banged and crashed against the walls of the house as the wind caught at them, threatening to tear them from their hinges. All work on the ranch had stopped and the men were huddled in the comparative safety of the bunkhouse. Out on the hill, in the lee of the rounded promontory of ground, the cattle lowed in abject misery, their tails turned to the wind and rain as it blasted past them, showing no mercy to anything that stood in its way.

One of the men came over from the bunkhouse, feet splashing through the muddy puddles of the courtyard, a long poncho trailing down to his ankles and the tall, wide-brimmed hat already funnelling water down over his face. He paused in front of Wilder, lifting his face, the water streaming down it, his eyes narrowed to mere slits.

'Goin' to last most of the day, boss,' Matson said.

Wilder forced a curt nod. Impatience was riding him, but he tried not to show it in front of the other. 'We'll wait until it blows itself out and then get ready to ride,' he said sharply. 'How many men do we have here?'

For a second, there was surprise on the other's coarse,

bluff features. Then he caught the drift of the other's reasoning, and his thick lips split in a snarling grin. 'Enough to take Ranson,' he said harshly.

'And Diego too?' queried Wilder thinly. The colour of his face was stronger and more marked than usual and pride caused him to keep his worry hidden deep within him, his eyes half-shut as the wind howled around his tall body. He deliberately held himself erect.

'You figure that Diego may go in with Ranson?'

'Perhaps. We know they were seen talkin' together last night. They wouldn't be discussing anythin' else, now would they?'

'I guess not,' said the other, his voice spare and dry. 'But it ain't likely that Ranson will accept help given by Diego. He knows what sort of a man that Mex is by now.'

'If a man is in a tough spot, he'll take help from whatever quarter it's given,' said Wilder ironically. 'Honest people will always try to turn the devil against himself.'

Wilder said no more, but went inside, closing the door quickly behind him. A blast of cold air swept past him and caused the fire in the wide hearth in the parlour to blaze up with a sudden, renewed fury as the draught caught at it. As he went into the parlour, he caught a glimpse of his reflection in the long mirror that stood between two lamps, eyed it critically. He was tall and broad, but with the beginnings of a paunch that sagged over the belt around his middle. He had known that this was the first sign of his physical degeneration and tried to hide it by pulling himself in consciously.

Events along the forty-five years of his life had hardened him, had given him that cold assurance and arrogance which was obvious to all who met him; but he liked to look upon himself as a man with an acute perception, the ability to see where his destiny lay and to take all steps necessary to see that he attained it. He had built up one of the largest forces of men in the state, killers, cardsharps, men on the run from the law, offering them safety and sanctuary in return for their allegiance.

Thoughts of having all of his plans slip away from him, disturbed him more than he cared to admit and he shook out his tobacco pouch and sifted some of the long, fine strands on to a creased paper and rolled a smoke, running the tip of his tongue over the paper. Thrusting it between his lips, he struck a match and applied it to the tip of the cigarette, pulling the smoke deep into his lungs, forcing himself to think clearly, turning over the problem that faced him in his mind.

Outside, the storm was sending rain down fit to beat hell. He heard it slashing at the windows beyond the stout shutters and a few moments later, the thunder rolled like the beat of a vast drum, hammering across the heavens.

Sinking into one of the chairs, he continued to smoke the cigarette, his thick, heavy brows bunched forward, drawn down tightly over his eyes, showing his displeasure. When he had first come to this place, the Civil War had just rolled over this land, leaving it stripped and bare, a place where little would grow and from which all of the beef had been taken to feed the hungry mouths of the fighting men. They had said that nothing would ever grow there again, that no one in his right mind would try to start a herd in this country. But he had seen the tremendous potential here and there had only been old Ranson there with the same vision as he had himself. At first, they had managed to survive side by side. There had been good summers and bad ones, when the drought had lain over the land and cattle had died in their hundreds, without water in their bellies, nor grass to feed them.

Somehow, he had managed to survive and his one aim in life had been to climb so far from that state of chaos that there would never be another period when he would have to fight to survive. The ruthlessness had been born in him then. But he had met his match when he had tried to go up against

Jim Ranson. There had been a man as hard as he himself, a man who had refused to back down in spite of everything he had been able to do. But there had been the others, small men who had faced bad times and not been able to repay the mortgages on their ranches. He had frozen them out without any feelings at all, taken over their places and built up a position for himself in this territory. Now he was damned if he would let himself be driven out like those men by this young whelp, Ranson, even if the other had somehow managed to link up with Diego in an all-out attempt to drive him from the territory.

The anger that seized him, remained with him all of the morning, while the fierce storm raged outside, lightning forking the beserk heavens and thunder rumbling, primitive and raw, bucketing off in whiplike echoes over the plains to all of the far horizon. There was a savagery in the storm which found answer in Wilder's mind. And then, as suddenly as it had come, the storm broke, passed away to the east. Wilder moved out on to the porch, felt the returning coolness in the air and watched the dark clouds rolling away, leaving the sun shining brilliantly in the blue heavens.

He stood for a long moment, watching the steam rise from the wet ground, lifting in wavering streaks from the backs of the horses in the corral. Soon, he knew, the heat would return and they would begin to wish that another storm might rise over the mountains to bring rain and coolness into the parched ground.

Matson came out of the ranch house, stood beside him, looking off over the stretching plains, quartering the horizon with his eyes. He stood quite still for a long moment, then said gruffly, 'You still goin' ahead with your plan to finish Ranson?'

Wilder hesitated for a moment, then nodded his head. 'But I've been thinkin' things out and I reckon it would be just plain stupid to try to crowd him out right now.'

'Then you ain't ridin' into town with the boys?' There was

surprise in the gunman's tone. He swung squarely on to Wilder, gazing at him with a wrinkled brow.

Wilder sighed and shook his head. 'That could be what Ranson is expectin' us to do,' he explained. 'And we might ride into town just to find that there was a trap laid for us.'

'Then why not ride for the Ranson spread? If Ranson is in town, lookin' after Maxwell, we could take the ranch and finish things that way.'

Wilder breathed heavily and gave the other a bitter, killing glance. 'I figure I should have shot him down in the saloon that day when I had the chance, but I never figured he'd give us this much trouble. I thought it would be easy to run him out of the territory.'

'I always said it was a mistake to ride on to the ranch and fire that barn. It only served to put his back up and now we've got a wildcat by the tail. He's already killed three of our best men and Maxwell is in jail, locked up in one of his own cells. He ain't any good to us there.'

'He never was any good anyway,' snapped the other thinly. The other made him feel sour and embittered. He drew his heavy lips back from his teeth. 'I want you to ride into town – find out all you can about this deal between Ranson and Diego. I want to know exactly what I'm lettin' myself in for when I do decide to ride.'

Sunlight filtered into the streets of the town, following swiftly in the wake of the storm that had swept over the area that morning. It touched the blistered paintwork of the stores and the hotel, fell on the steaming dust where all of the moisture that had fallen with the storm was being sucked avidly out of the ground by the heat. Doc Fordham made his way slowly along the boardwalk from the sheriff's office. Yawning, he stopped off at the small store, went into the tiny diner and ordered a late breakfast, eating it slowly. He had been on watch all night, while Chris Ranson had slept like a dead man. Nothing had happened, just as he had told the other, but perhaps, he reflected, there had always been the chance, and there was no sense in taking unnecessary risks as far as Wilder was concerned. That man was as tricky and as cunning as a desert coyote and would have to be watched every minute of the day and night. He drank his coffee black, hoping it would bring some of the life back into his weary bones. He was getting just a little too old for this sort of game, he decided, sitting up all night and then going back to his surgery, ready to tackle all of the many patients he had waiting for him. Swallowing the last morsel of food, he drew a cheroot from his pocket, lit it and sat back in his chair, relaxing. Chris Ranson had seemed a lot better for the long night's sleep and there had been no trouble so far. Maybe Wilder had realised that here was a man as good as his grandfather, a man who would never back down in the face of trouble, but would go forward and meet it halfway. Once Wilder got that through his thick skull, he might decide to leave well alone and things would return to what they had been when old Jim Ranson had been alive, keeping the peace in the territory. It had been an uneasy truce between the two feuding parties, that was true, but it had been a lasting one; and that was really all that mattered.

Outside, a dog lay in the dust, panting a little. He could make it out through the open doorway. It lay there for a long moment, then pulled itself up on to its haunches and dragged itself lazily out of the direct sunlight, moving back into the shadows. One solitary rider came into town. Fordham caught a brief glimpse of him as he rode slowly past the dusty, fly-speckled window. The man had the brim of his Stetson pulled well down over his face, his head hunched forward a little as he sat in the saddle so that it was impossible to see his face.

Tossing a couple of coins on to the table, Doc Fordham got slowly to his feet and walked out of the diner. He would have liked to stay there a lot longer, letting his weary bones relax, but he knew there were people waiting for him and he was not the sort of man to let things slide just because he had been awake for most of the night.

Pushing open the door of the surgery, he stepped inside, closed it behind him and threw a swift glance along the corridor. There was only one man waiting for him. He heaved a faintly audible sigh of relief. There was the chance that things might be easy for the rest of the morning. Usually, there were at least half a dozen patients waiting to be attended to. Going into the room, he pulled off his jacket, went over to the basin and poured the pitcher of water into it, then washed his face and hands, letting the cool water trickle down his neck. He rubbed himself dry with the rough towel, felt the blood begin to circulate in his veins. He needed to shave, but there was not time for that. Perhaps later in the afternoon, he might be able to find time in which to—

The door opened softly behind him and he whirled to find the man he had seen waiting in the corridor pushing his way into the room.

'I'll be with you in just a moment,' he said coldly. 'In the meantime, if you would care to wait outside, I'll call you when I'm ready to see you.'

'I think you'll see me now, Doctor,' said the other thinly. He closed and locked the door at his back and Fordham found himself looking down the barrel of the gun which the other held at his hip. The barrel was still, stone-steady, pointed at his chest. No use to gamble on the chance of bringing up his own gun from its holster, although for a moment, the thought lived in his mind. With an effort, he forced himself to relax and stand quite still.

'Damn it all,' he said harshly. 'Put that gun away.'

'Not until you've given me the answer to some questions.' muttered the other sharply. He moved closer, reached out and pulled the ancient Colt from Fordham's holster, thrusting it into his belt. 'Now sit down and don't try any tricks. I ain't got no real likin' for you and I won't think twice about using this gun.'

Fordham lowered himself into the nearby chair. Not once did he allow his gaze to wander from the other's face. He knew that he had seen this man before, but he couldn't place him. One of Diego's men – or one of Wilder's? It was difficult to tell. Either man would be wanting to know the answers to some questions before they committed themselves to any course of action that might mean using all of their men in one all-out effort.

'When did Diego and his men pull out last night?'

'Diego, I never saw that *hombre*. You know he won't ride into town openly like that and—' The lash of the gun butt across the side of his head stopped any further flow of words, sent him reeling back in his chair, so that he half fell from it. Blood began to trickle down his cheek from the cut above his right eye and the searing pain of the blow lanced into his brain.

'Reckon you figure I'm playin' games with you, Doc,' grunted the other. His pale eyes snapped angrily. 'I happen to know that Diego came into town last night and that he rode across to the sheriff's office to have a parley with that *hombre* Ranson. I want to know what they talked about. Is Diego plannin' to link up with Ranson and the ranchers? When are they figurin' on doin' it, and how many men have they got at their backs?'

'If you know so much, then there ain't nothin' more I can tell you.' Somehow, Fordham got the words out through shaking lips. He knew that this man would kill him without any hesitation, whether he got the information he wanted or not. And he knew too, that this was one of Wilder's men, probably one of the Matson brothers he had heard about, men who rode with Wilder,

'There's plenty.' The other leaned forward, thrusting the muzzle of the gun hard into Fordham's stomach. The doctor winced as a further stab of pain went through him and sweat mingled with the blood that trickled down his face. He ran the tip of his tongue around his mouth, tasting blood. 'You

100

goin' to tell me the easy way, Doc, or do I have to get rough?'

'All right, so Diego rode into town yesterday. He tried to get Ranson to go in with him, but he refused.'

Suspicion and disbelief flared in the other's eyes. 'You expectin' me to believe that Ranson refused Diego's offer of help, when he knows that without it he doesn't stand a chance in hell?'

'I reckon you don't know what kind of man Chris Ranson is. How could you? He's a man who believes in the law, a man who hates those outside the law, and that goes for Diego as well as you and the man you ride for.'

A sudden heat showed in Matson's face and for a moment, the pressure of the gun muzzle into Fordham's chest increased, forcing the other back into the chair until he could move back no further and the sweat popped out on his forehead and began to trickle down his face, twisted into a grimace of pain. Matson's lips were pulled back in a sneering grin. 'So Diego won't be ridin' with Ranson? Reckon that's all Wilder wants to know.' He got to his feet, thrust the gun back into his belt as if recognising that there was no danger from the doctor now. He made a gesture of impatience.

'Let's move,' he said shaprly. 'Out the back way!'

'Where are we goin'?' asked Fordham harshly. He put up a hand and gingerly felt the wound on the side of his face.

Matson grinned widely. 'You don't reckon I'd be fool enough to leave you here to go runnin' across to that jumped-up sheriff, do you? We're goin' to have a talk with Wilder. Reckon he'll know what to do with you.'

He made Doc Fordham move ahead of him, through the store room at the back of the building and out into the narrow, rubbish-filled alley. A mangy cat ran howling from behind a pile of boxes, vanished along the alley at the far end. Where the alley linked up with the side street, there were two horses waiting. Fordham eyed them narrowly. It was clear that Matson had planned this well, had made sure of everything. He experienced a sinking feeling in the pit of his stomach as he swung himself up wearily into the saddle. Matson climbing up smoothly and easily on to the other horse, keeping a wary eye on him in case he tried to make a break for it.

Nodding curtly along the street, Matson indicated that the other was to ride in front of him. There were few folk about in the street and none of them paid the two men a second glance.

The first sun was high above the rocky shelves of the distant mountains as they headed out of town, but in the valley, the air was still cold and grey, still in shadow. Turning off the main trail, Matson led the way into the thick brush that grew along the side of the hill. The thick carpet of pine needles muffled the sound of hoofbeats and Fordham knew with a sick certainty that anyone on the trail would be unable to pick out the sound of their horses, even though they might be only a hundred yards or so away. The almost solid mat of interwoven branches over their heads trapped the sunlight, allowing little of it to filter through and they rode in a deep green silence which seemed to have been unaltered for a thousand years.

'I suppose you know that Ranson will come ridin' out after me as soon as he discovers I'm gone,' said Fordham softly, breaking the silence that had existed between them since they had left town.

Matson sneered. He pale stare sharpened. 'Maybe that's just what Wilder is hopin' he'll do,' he declared flatly.

Fordham eyed him steadily for a long moment as they rode along the narrow, twisting trail through the tall pines. Then he shook his head emphatically. 'If you're figurin' on getting him to ride into a trap, you're wrong. He's too smart for you, or Wilder.'

'If he's reckonin' on the ranchers ridin' with him, he's due for a big surprise and he'll soon find out he ain't quite as smart as he figures he is.'

FIVE

DAWN ATTACK

The Wilder ranch, built against the lee of a small, smooth-rising hill, seemed on casual appraisal to be a single-storey affair, smaller than the Ranson place. Actually, at the rear, due to the slope of the hill, there was an additional section to the building, a sort of step-up, which Matthew Wilder used as a store room. Here it was that Doc Fordham found himself imprisoned after arriving at the ranch. They were taking no chances with him, had tied him tightly to the chair in which he sat, the thin ropes biting tightly and painfully into his arms and wrists. The knots had been tied by an expert and no matter how he twisted and struggled, it was impossible to loosen them at all. In the end, exhausted by his attempts to free himself, he sank back in the chair and tried to find a comfortable position, to relieve the agonising spasms of cramp which threatened to knot every muscle in his arms and legs.

The room was dull with dingy light and full of stale odours which assailed his nostrils and he made no effort to hide the grimace of distaste as the door opened and Wilder came in, followed by the two Matson brothers. They took up their position on either side of the door, leaning nonchalantly against the wall, grinning viciously as Wilder walked forward and stood to front of him, staring down out of bleak, cold eyes.

'I'm sorry it had to be like this, Fordham,' Wilder said. 'I hadn't meant that you should be brought here. All I wanted was information, but it seemed that you or Rosalie were the only ones who could supply that information, except for Ranson himself, of course, and it's not likely that he would have talked so easily. But you have to realise that we couldn't leave you in town, ready to run to Ranson and warn him of what had happened. You'll have to stay here as our – guest, until this little affair has all been sorted out.'

'Just what is it you're planning to do, Wilder? Take over the whole town just to bust that no-good Maxwell out of jail?'

'Maxwell!' Wilder grinned thinly. 'He means nothin' to me. He was just a fool to let himself get caught like that. Trouble is that we all seem to have figured this *hombre*, Ranson, wrong.'

'You reckoned he'd be easy to run out of the territory, like his father.' Fordham stared straight at the other, knew that he had touched a tender spot. 'I guess you'll find that you've underestimated him, and overplayed your hand this time; because he'll never stop until he's finished you for good.'

'Could be that he'll never have that chance,' said the other with a cold, calm assurance. 'I hear that he's trying to whip up the ranchers into getting their men behind him and run me out of the territory. Even now, he's in town, waitin' for me to ride in and force a showdown.'

Fordham nodded, but said nothing. For a moment, he struggled again against the ropes that held him, then gave up.

Wilder said tightly: 'We'll be leavin' you here in a little while, Doc. Come nightfall, we're ridin' out and headin' for the Ranson place. Reckon we can take it without any trouble while Ranson sits in town waitin' for us. When we don't show up, he might get around to thinkin' that maybe he's wrong and we ain't coming into town; but by that time, it'll be too late for him. With the Ranson spread in our hands, he won't stand a chance, even with the rest of the town behind him.'

Doc Fordham tightened his lips, glared up at the other,

trying to keep the coldness in his chest from showing through on to his face. He knew that Chris had decided to stick around in town and wait for Wilder to show up there, that he had already decided to get the rest of the men from the ranch to ride out into town and meet him there and this would leave the ranch itself virtually unprotected. Somehow word had to be got to him to warn him of this new danger.

'Do I get somethin' to eat?' asked Fordham, playing for time. He had to get to know something more about Wilder's plans if he could, and he guessed that the other would not be averse to talking if he considered that there was no possibility of his prisoner getting away from this place in time to warn Chris.

Wilder considered that, then nodded, turned to one of the men at the door. 'Get him somethin' to eat,' he said tightly. 'Untie his hands, but keep his legs tied. When he's finished, be sure that you tie him up again.' Wilder stood eyeing the prisoner with a look of satisfaction and vicious, savage triumph. He had obviously not forgotten the humiliation he had suffered at the hands of Chris Ranson, the way his men had been shot down in front of many of the townsfolk, and now he was determined that this would not happen again, that he would have his revenge on the other, would show him who was the top man in this part of the territory,

Going over to the door, as one of the men slipped out, he said to the other: 'Get the rest of the boys rounded up. We're moving out tonight, and I reckon we ought to reach Ranson's spread by dawn. Then there'll be no trouble taking over the ranch.'

With food inside him and a smoke thrust between his lips, Fordham felt a bit better than before. The throbbing pain inside his head where the blood had crusted over the deep gash, had eased, allowing him to sit and think things out logically, but for a long while, there had seemed to be little profit in his thinking. Bitterly, he could only sit there, his hands free of the ropes while he finished the smoke, reflecting on how the cards were stacked against both himself and Chris Ranson. Maybe he ought to have chanced getting away from his captor while he had been in town. Now that he was here, there was little chance at all of getting to warn Chris Ranson in time. There was an inevitability about Wilder's plan that was almost frightening. His one hope was that he could outwit the man left to guard him once the others had ridden away. There was bound to be a spare horse around, and Wilder's evident assurance that everything would go his way, would mean that they would travel relatively slowly along the trail to the Ranson place. Wilder himself had maintained that they would not launch their attack on the ranch until dawn.

Outside the store room, there was the sound of heavy footsteps coming closer and a moment later, the door was unlocked and one of the Matson brothers stepped inside. He eyed Fordham casually from beneath lowered lids. clearly sure that there would be no danger from this old man.

He stood leaning against the wall for a moment, a sneering grin on his craggy features. Then he pushed himself upright, walked over to the chair, his eyes wary, and picked up the rope which had been used to tie Fordham's arms. 'Reckon it's time I made sure you're safely tied up,' he said harshly. 'The boss will be ridin' out soon with the rest of the boys and then there'll be just you and me here, so I figure we should make ourselves comfortable. You're goin' to be here for quite a while, at least until Wilder gets back with the news that he's taken the Ranson place. Then, maybe, he'll decide to let you know '

Reaching forward, he wrapped the rope tightly around Fordham's arms and chest, pulling it more tightly than was necessary until the other groaned with pain.

'Reckon that ought to hold you,' he said thinly. His big face twisted into a scowl. 'If you don't give me any trouble. you won't come to any harm.' He placed the lighted paraffin lamp on the table a few feet away, then went out of the room, closing and locking the heavy door behind him.

Fordham let his breath go in a long sigh, his gaze flicking around the room. The sense of urgency was rising in him, urging him to do something. He tested the ropes around his shoulders once more, but they had been tied as tightly as before and there was no way of loosening the knot. Exhausted, he sank back, feeling the sweat break out on his forehead and the palms of his hands. He did not doubt that without warning, Chris would stay in town and would lose the ranch to Wilder and his bunch. Outside, he guessed that the shadows were already beginning to lengthen. It was impossible to guess at the passage of time, but he had been questioned for more than an hour after arriving at the ranch and more than three hours had passed since then. Besides, it was getting dark beyond the solitary window set in one wall. The lee of the hill would get the shadows first, he reasoned and that meant these men would be riding out soon, if they had not already gone.

Fordham's eyes were searching desperately now for some means of escape. He saw it at last, although he knew that it would mean taking a desperate risk. The lantern on the table was his only hope. Gritting his teeth, he began to move his bound legs, inching the chair over the rough floor towards the table. Pain jarred through his limbs, but somehow, he forced himself to keep moving, lips pressed tightly together to prevent any sound from escaping through his clenched teeth. He could hear nothing happening outside now and guessed that his jailer had decided to remain in the house, rather than in this room watching him.

The minutes slipped by and the feeling of urgency in him grew. Once, the chair tilted under him, threatening to pitch him to the floor and he stopped his movements while the sweat spilled out of him. Thrusting his body and the chair forward, almost at the end of his strength, he finally reached the table, and steadied himself against it, the edge catching him across the chest. He felt his strength oozing away, felt the breath raw and harsh in his lungs and throat, but all the time, the knowledge of what would happen if Wilder managed to go through with his plans drove him on, gave him a strength that he had never known he possessed. Gasping air down into his heaving, tortured lungs, he forced himself to sit upright, thrusting down with his legs, straining against the ropes that bound him to the chair. The lantern was balanced near the edge of the table and he began to rock the long table back and forth, thankful for the bumpiness of the floor. The lantern began to shake, the glass rattling in its frame, the flame flickering as the oil began to slop around inside the metal container.

Gritting his teeth, Fordham continued to thrust against the heavy wooden table. He knew what the consequences of his action might be. If that oil were to run all over the floor once the lantern fell and if it were ignited by the flame, the whole room would become a blazing inferno within minutes. There would be little time in which he could cut himself free and get out.

He tried to lift himself even higher in the chair, but the ropes held him fast, made it almost impossible to move. Then the lantern tilted far over, slithered a few inches to the very edge of the table and went over, hitting the floor at his feet with a crash. There was the sudden flare of flame as the oil ignited. Without pausing to think, he thrust his bound feet forward, straining the ankles as far apart as possible, feeling the fire burn and singe the bottom of his trousers. Some part of his mind, detached from the rest, told him that he did not have a chance, that he would be burned before the ropes gave way. Sweat poured from his face as he held his feet there, tensing his muscles, ignoring the pain that lanced through his limbs. He tried to bend himself lower, twisting the cumbersome weight of the chair to one side as the fire started to catch at the table and the legs of the chair. His movements were awkward and the smell of smoke hit the back of his nostrils, bringing a rising nausea into his stomach. The ropes still held, binding his feet together, his ankles purple and swollen. Smoke drifted up from the floor of the room where the oil from the smashed lantern had run in a wide circle under the table. Fortunately, there had been only a small amount of oil in the lamp, otherwise the whole floor might have been a mass of flame by that time.

When it seemed that he could bear the pain no longer, he felt the frayed ropes begin to slacken their grip on his ankles and a moment later, with a wild, savage surge of strength, they snapped and he tottered shakily to his feet. There was a pounding agony in his forehead as the blood rushed to his head, but somehow he succeeded in remaining upright, backing away from the fire in the middle of the room, feeling the heat on his face, knowing that by now it had gained a firm hold there and within minutes it would have engulfed everything. Something glittered on the floor at his feet and he bent, managed to get a hold on it in his fingers and backed away into the corner of the room nearest the door, holding the fragment of sharp-edged glass from the lantern between his feet as he sawed at it with the rope binding his wrists. The rope which had held his arms to the sides of the chair had burned through in the flames which had leapt up the side of the chair.

His clothing was singed and smouldering, his lips drawn back over his teeth as the agony of singed flesh tore into his brain. Only the knowledge that he had to get away from this place enabled him to go on sawing the rope against the glass until the bonds fell away from his wrists. He rubbed them for a moment to restore the circulation, noticing the deep red marks where they had bitten deep into his flesh. Now there was no time to be lost. Snatching up the heavy wooden rod that lay propped in the corner, he commenced yelling at the top of his voice. Behind him, the fire was spreading rapidly through the room. If Matson didn't come running to see what was wrong, there was a good chance of him dying in this blaze before he had a chance of getting out.

Seconds later, however, there was the clatter of footsteps

outside the door and Matson's harsh voice yelling: 'What the hell's goin' on in there, Fordham?'

'The lamp,' he yelled back. 'It fell from the table. Hurry, man! The whole place is burning.'

Some of the smoke must have been drifting under the door, confirming what he had said, for he heard the other mutter something savagely under his breath, then there came the metallic rattle of keys as the other fumbled for the one which fitted the lock. Tensing himself, ignoring the pain in his body, Fordham stood pressed against the wall beside the door, the heavy rod held high over his head. Swiftly, the door was thrust open. He caught a glimpse of Matson standing in the passage outside, staring into the room, open-mouthed and wide-eyed, peering at the blaze which was already beginning to lick up the far wall. The other gave a quick yell, started forward into the room, turning his head wildly from side to side. He sensed Fordham's presence there beside him, swung round, one hand clawing for the gun at his waist. But he was too late. It had still not cleared leather when the heavy weapon in Fordham's hands thudded with a sickening force against the back of his skull. Any lesser man might have died instantly under the crushing impact. As it was, Matson fell forward with scarcely a whimper, arms and legs folded under him. Swiftly, the doctor bent, hooked his hands under the other's armpits and hauled him outside into the corridor. Then, straightening up, he ran along the corridor, stumbling and falling, recovering his balance, running on until he was outside in the wide courtyard, sucking the clean, cold air down into his chest, feeling it like a soothing balm on his face and body. There had been nobody else in the house and he guessed that Wilder and his men had already ridden out. There was no telling how long he had to warn Ranson but he knew there was no time to wait and try to get his breath back. Every minute might he precious now.

There were three horses in the corral. They had obviously smelled the smoke which was drifting up from the back of the house and whinnied sharply as he moved over to the gate, pulled it open It was hard work getting any of them to come to him, but finally, he succeeded in getting one of the saddles across one of the horses, tightening the cinch with hands that ached and burned. It took all of the strength that was left in him to haul himself up into the saddle, fingers scrabbling for the leather of the horn and clinging on with a desperate strength. The horse whinnied again, then plunged forward as he touched spurs to its flanks. The sudden jolt as it cleared the gate of the corral almost unseated him and he lay low in the saddle, clinging to the bucking animal with all the strength that was in him.

The horse veered sharply around the front of the house and pounded across the courtyard. Smoke, mingled here and there with licking tongues of flame, rose up from the rear of the building. Fordham thought for a moment of the man lying there outside that blazing room, but swiftly, he put the thought out of his mind. The other would have done exactly the same to him had the positions been reversed and at least, he had given the other a chance of life by pulling him out into the corridor where the through draught of air would keep the fire away from him for sometime, until the rest of the building caught.

There was a grim sense of triumph in him as he rode away from the ranch. He did not doubt that Matson, when he did recover his senses, would catch one of the horses still in the corral and flee the area, rather than stay and try to put out the fire. By the time Wilder got back, if he ever did get back, he would find that he had no ranch to return to. It would be nothing more than a burnt-out, blackened shell.

The horse headed out over the desert trail while Fordham clung to the saddle tenaciously, giving the animal its head, not trying to rein it for the moment, trying to get his wind back, to clear his throbbing head. A whiplike branch of thorny mesquite struck savagely against his shoulder and twisted him in the saddle, almost throwing him. He tried to bend his head even lower but the long thorns raked the horse's flanks, sending it thundering forward, half-crazed by the pain, and lanced across his own exposed flesh. A wall of chapparal reared up in front of them. He could see no trail through it and the horse plunged onward without pausing, tossing its head, snorting, fighting, pawing at the dense mass of vegetation until it had somehow forced a way through. The long branches ripped and tore at Fordham's coat until it had been almost completely shredded on him. There was nothing he could possibly do now but try to dodge the upthrusting bushes, thorn and mesquite, that dotted the plains. Reeling weakly in the saddle, it was all that he could do to hold on as the animal twisted away instinctively from a patch of Spanish bayonet grass, avoiding the upthrusting needle-like points that reached for its legs and soft underbelly.

Ten minutes later, he felt consciousness begin to slip away from him. Somehow he managed to force himself up in the saddle, sucking air down into his lungs, fighting to clear his head, forcing his stultified vision to clear so that he could see where he was heading.

Only another quarter mile, he reckoned, and he would be out of this hell and on to the trail. He glimpsed it in the distance, winding away over the brown-and-green country, towards the low foothills in the distance which stood immediately outside the town. Once he reached them, he would feel comparatively safe. Then his nightmare journey would be almost over.

It was dark as Chris Ranson made his way across the wide street of town, with the cold night air beginning to flow down from the distant hills, striking into his body. Brow puckered in worried thought, he stamped into the sheriff's office and lowered himself into the chair behind the desk. Knowing that Doc Fordham needed his sleep after being on watch all night, he had delayed in going over to see him until mid-afternoon. When he had found that the other's place was empty and there was no sign of him, he had thought little of it at first. Knowing that as the only medical man in town, the other had plenty of work on his hands, he had figured that perhaps Fordham had been called out on an urgent case which had demanded instant attention. But when he had tried to find anybody who had seen the doctor since morning, it had become increasingly obvious that Fordham had left his office early that morning without bothering to get any sleep and had not been seen around since.

It wasn't like the other to ride out without telling someone where he was going, in case a patient needed him in a hurry and the more Chris thought it over in his mind, the more convinced he was that something was wrong. He glanced up as the door opened and Rosalie came in. Chris managed to dig up a weary smile. The sight of the girl was a heart-warming tonic.

'I've talked with some of the men who run the small ranches around town,' she said, a little breathlessly as if she had been hurrying. 'They're willing to throw in their men behind you if you decide to move against Wilder or Diego.'

'I'm glad to hear it.' He nodded slowly, thoughtfully. 'I didn't like the idea of accepting Diego's help, even to use it against a man like Matthew Wilder. But at the time when he made me the proposition, there didn't seem to be much alternative.'

The girl sat down in the chair facing him, eyeing him seriously. Then she said softly: 'You look troubled, Chris. Something on your mind?'

'Yes. I've been lookin' all over town for Doc. Nobody seems to have seen him since he left here first thing this mornin'. He called in at the store along the street and had a bite to eat, but that's the end of his trail. It ain't like him to go ridin' out of town without leavin' word with somebody.'

'You think something's happened to him?'

'I don't know. I only wish I knew where he was this minute.'

His head jerked up at the sound of a lone rider coming along the street outside. He had heard several riders head into town, but this one was different. This was somebody in a hurry, and acting on impulse, he pushed back his chair, got to his feet and crossed over to the street door, jerked it open and went out on to the boardwalk. The rider stopped in front of the office. For a moment, Chris peered out into the darkness, trying to make out the identity of the man who leaned forward in the saddle. The next moment he had moved quickly down the steps into the street and was reaching up to help Fordham from the saddle as the other sagged weakly to one side and would have fallen had he not been there.

Bending, Chris took the other's inert body across his shoulders and carried him up on to the boardwalk and into the office, laying him down on the couch against the wall.

'It's Doctor Fordham,' said Rosalie quickly. She peered down over Chris's shoulder. 'Has he been hurt?'

Gently, Chris examined the barely conscious man, noticing the red marks on his wrists, others on his ankles and the burns which had blackened and scorched his clothing.

'He's been tied up somewhere, kept a prisoner,' he said thinly, rising to his feet and staring down at the other. 'Get me some hot water, Rosalie. I'll try to bring him round. I want to know what's been happening. I've an idea this is something important and the sooner I know about it, the better.'

The girl went through into the back room, came back in a few moments with a bowl of water and a towel. Pushing Chris to one side, she bathed the doctor's wounds, washing the blood from his forehead, exposing the deep gash just above the right eye.

'Whoever it was, they seem to have done their best to kill him,' she said, as she finished. 'I think he's coming round now.'

Chris went down on one knee beside the other, as the doctor stirred on the couch, his eyes flicking open. For a moment, he stared about him, with no sign of recognition in

his eyes, then his gaze fell on Chris and the girl and a long
sigh escaped him. He turned his head a little, his tongue flicking out, licking the dry lips. Chris went over to the desk,
pulling the whiskey bottle from the drawer, filled a glass and
brought it over, holding it to the other's lips. Most of the raw
liquid dribbled down the other's chin, but he managed to get
some of it down, coughing and gasping as it hit the back of
his throat.

'Feelin' any better?' asked Chris quietly,

The other swallowed thickly, then nodded slowly, wincing
as pain jarred through his head. He reached out and caught
at Chris's sleeve with his right hand, fingers clawed into the
cloth.

'Who did this?' Chris asked tensely. 'Take your time and lie
still. You're safe now.'

'Wilder.' Fordham spoke thickly. 'He's ridin' out to the
ranch with his men. He knows you're waitin' here in town for
him and he figures he'll outsmart you.'

'You sure of this?' In spite of his concern for the other,
there was a certain roughness in his voice. 'Was it Wilder who
took you?'

'Matson. One of Wilder's men. They kept me tied up at
the ranch after they'd questioned me about you and Diego.
He was afraid that you might have thrown in with Diego, and
if you had, he wouldn't have a chance of defeating both of
you. Now that he knows you didn't, he's ridden out to the
ranch. He's figuring on attacking it at dawn. You'll have to get
your men together and ride out fast if you're goin' to stop
him.'

Chris drew in a deep breath. So that was the plan. 'We'll
stop 'em all right,' he said tightly. 'You'd better stay here with
Rosalie. You'll be safe here.'

Fordham gave him a bright-sharp stare, then nodded
weakly. 'Watch yourself, Chris,' he said warningly. 'Wilder has
men in the hills, watching every trail, every move you make.
He's no fool.'

'He's got to be stopped,' said Chris and there was ice in his tone. He lifted his glance to Rosalie. 'When can those men meet me at the edge of town?'

'Half an hour,' she said without hesitation. 'Most of them were friends of my father. They'll do this if I ask it of them.'

'Tell them to come ready to ride hard,' he said. 'I'll be waitin' for them at the edge of town.'

He walked over to the desk, picked up the heavy gunbelt that lay there and buckled it on. Strange, he mused worriedly, how it had now become a part of him. It felt as if he had been wearing these guns, ready to use them, all of his life, instead of just a handful of days. Was this how it got a man, turned him into a hardened killer? That was the fear which had always been in him. He had tried to stop from wearing guns, hoping that he would be able to take over the ranch and run it without having to resort to violence of any kind. But he had not been here very long before he had discovered, in no uncertain terms, that this just wasn't possible. If a man was not prepared to stand up and fight for what he had, then he would not last long in a place as lawless as this. Strength came only in the form of the sixgun, and the right of might was supreme.

Outside, he climbed wearily into the saddle, pushing all thought of what lay in front of him to the background of his mind. Overhead, the sky was bright with the brilliant powdering of stars and there was a round, yellow moon lifting clear of the eastern horizon, throwing long shadows over the quiet street. From the direction of the nearby saloon came the sound of a tinny piano and booming voices yelling out one of the marching songs of the war.

He rode past the lighted windows, past the narrow alleys whose black, empty mouths looked out into the street. The road was a solid streak of dust in front of him, touched with the pale moonlight which gave everything an eerie appearance. A horse stood sway-backed and sleepy in front of the hotel and near the outskirts of town, a couple of men sat on

the boardwalk, staring in front of them, the tips of their ciga-
rettes glowing redly, on and off, in the dark shadows as they
smoked. Apart from them, and a drunk lying in one of the
alleys, this part of town showed no life. The fact struck him
forcibly and he fell to watching the side streets more closely.
The thought of leaving Maxwell in the jail, unguarded,
disturbed him anew; but in the circumstances, there was
nothing else he could do.

It was almost thirty minutes later, before he heard the
sound of riders approaching, some from the middle of the
town, and others from the direction of the low hills which
bordered it to the north. A moment later, they came in sight,
two tightly-packed bunches of men, riding tall in the saddle,
merging as they came up to him. Chris threw a quick glance
over them, recognised one or two of the men as ranchers
from the nearby hills. Paul Denver and Hank Rannigan, men
who had came out here to settle this land with their families.
Now they faced a common enemy and they had realised that
there was only one way to destroy it, to make sure that it was
finished for good; and that was to band together and ride
with any man who would lead them. They had found this man
in the grandson of Jim Ranson.

Rannigan said sharply: 'Rosalie said that Wilder was headed
to your place, Ranson. You figuring on stopping him there?'

Chris gave a quick nod. 'I reckon we can get to the ranch
as fast as they can if we take the mountain trail. They'll be
headin' over the plains, takin' their time.'

'You got any men at the ranch?'

'A dozen. Not enough to hold off Wilder and his bunch
for long, but maybe long enough for us to get there and take
'em from behind. They won't be expecting anythin' like that.'

'Sounds like a good plan,' agreed Denver. 'I like it.
Whatever happens, we have to finish it soon. I reckon dawn is
as good a time as any.' As he spoke, he wheeled his mount
and rode up alongside Chris, his face hard in the moonlight
which flooded the scene.

Chris gigged his mount, urged it forward. The rest fell in behind him, forming a long column, the mass of men beginning to shift and sway as they moved on out of town. Presently, the road turned upgrade, became rougher as they passed through a short belt of timber, on over the brow of a hill and up into the short switchback courses that led up and around the out-thrusting curve of the mountains, higher and higher, through belts of vegetation that shone silver in the drenching moonlight, then over belts of rough, open ground covered with rocks and thin scree. In places, the trail was little more than three feet wide and they were forced to ride in single file, walking their mounts. There would undoubtedly be some delay along this trail, Chris reasoned, and felt the urgency rise in him once again, riding him, forcing him to keep his mount moving more quickly than he really intended, for here the ground dropped away swiftly to one side, falling in a steep, sheer-sided precipice for many hundreds of feet down into the floor of the ravine.

The land was deceptive. In places, the trail ran along the edge of the chasm at a breakneck angle and his mount's feet slipped and slithered dangerously where he could no longer see the course in front of him. In the end, he was forced to cease pushing it to the limit, letting it find its own pace. It was a good horse and he had full confidence in it, but always, at the forefront of his mind, driving him on was the knowledge that with every minute that passed, Wilder and his men were drawing closer to the ranch, protected by only a handful of men who would certainly be taken by surprise.

It took them more than seven hours to clear the hills, to climb over the tall summits and down the other side, down fresh slides of earth where part of the trail had dropped away from the cliff face. By the time the grey band of light in the east began to dim the stars, they were riding across the smooth plains in the direction of the ranch, now less than three miles away. They had seen no sign of Wilder and his men, had heard nothing in the deep stillnesses on the mountain in the night. He had thought that they might possibly have picked out the sound of other riders in the distance, knowing how far such sound would travel at night under the cold, frost-sparkling stars and the fact that they had heard nothing worried him more than he cared to admit, even to himself. The other men kept up the punishing, breakneck speed, not hesitating to sacrifice their mounts to keep up with him, knowing what was uppermost in his mind. The trail ran across the river and they forded it without pausing, pulling up on the far side, water running from their horses. Gaining the shelter of the grove of trees on the other side, they slowed their mounts to walking pace. Now, they were almost within sight of the ranch and Chris held his breath until it hurt his lungs, sitting tall in the saddle, motioning the others into silence as he strained his ears to pick out the faintest sound. It scarcely seemed possible that they had succeeded in getting here before Wilder and his crew. They would have made good time over the plains, while they had been forced to pick their way carefully across the mountain trail.

'You hear them?' asked Rannigan tightly. He turned in the saddle to face Chris, features tight in the dim light.

'Nope. Don't hear a goddarned thing. They're probably down there right now, creeping up on the ranch.'

He dismounted, pulled the Winchester from its scabbard and moved up into the trees, waving the others to follow him. There was the soft murmur of the river in the near distance, but that was the only sound that disturbed the deep, clinging silence. Then, suddenly, sharply, shattering the quietness into a million shrieking fragments, sending the harsh echoes bouncing over the hills, came the report of a rifle from the direction of the ranch. Chris felt the sudden tightness in the pit of his stomach, knotting the muscles into a hard tautness. He pushed his way through the brush, ignoring the thorns that raked their needle-tipped fingers over his flesh. More firing broke out, the sound bucketing in every direction.

Swiftly, not turning his head, he waved the men behind

him forward, dropped behind one of the smooth rocks as he peered down in the direction of the cluster of buildings in the low hollow. The flashes of muzzle fire were easily seen, and he saw that Wilder and his men had gained their positions all around the ranch, although the main concentration of fire seemed to be in the area of the corral.

Answering fire came from several of the windows of the ranch, and there were also some men holed up in the one barn that was still standing, not far from that which had been deliberately burned by Wilder's men some time before.

Every muscle in him was so tight that his whole body began to ache intolerably. He waited impatiently, until the men with him had spread themselves out, in a wide circle behind Wilder's crew. He did not want to tip his hand to the other until he was certain he had him just where he wanted him, with no possibility of escape. He already knew where Wilder had left his horses and he reckoned it would be possible to stampede them before any of the gunmen had a chance of reaching them and riding clear of the area.

The firing below had swung round as the gunhawks threw lead into the buildings. Dimly, Chris heard the sharp tinkle of splintered glass as one of the windows was caught by the blast and a man cried out in the overall dimness that lay over the scene. Time to be making his own play, he decided. A swift glance to right and left told him that Rannigan and Denver were in position with the rest of their men, just waiting for his signal to open fire. From their vantage points, they were able to look down and see most of Wilder's men stretched out on the ground near the barn or in the corral, where they were able to fire at the house without exposing themselves to the return fire.

He grinned viciously to himself for a brief moment as he realised how the tables would be turned in the next few moments, then sighted his Winchester on the dark shape that lay some fifty yards below him, his finger taking up the slack on the trigger. Before he squeezed it, he yelled loudly: 'All right, Wilder! Tell your men to get to their feet and throw down their weapons. We've got a bead on the lot of you.'

For a long moment, there was no movement at all from any of the men down below them. Then he saw several of them squirm around, bringing their guns to bear on any targets they could see behind them. Pulling back his lips, Chris squeezed the trigger and saw the man in his sights, suddenly jump and then flop back as the bullet found its mark. As if it had been the prelude to an overture of utter destruction, the entire hillside racketed with volley after volley of gunfire. The thing was terrible. Lead flailed through the air from more than a score of points all around the house and outbuildings. He heard more of Wilder's men shout and drop as they were caught in the withering crossfire that tore into them, cutting them down as they tried desperately to get to their feet and run for the horses. Chris drew back and away, pulled himself forward, down the slope, to the point where Wilder's mounts were tethered. Two men came blundering forward from the direction of the ranch as he rose up from the thin brush and moved in. Both saw him at the same instant.

He heard one of them yell something to the other, saw their hands come up, clutching their weapons. His own hands scarcely seemed to move, but in an instant, the twin Colts were in his fists and the two shots sounded as one. Both men staggered as the hot lead tore into them, remained poised upright for a few tense seconds and then tottered forward on the toes of their feet before pitching down in front of the frightened horses. Running forward, Chris loosened the reins which tethered them to the branches of the low trees, fired his Colt three times into the air, yelling at the top of his voice. Madly, the horses panicked, rearing and plunging as they stampeded into the distance.

The shouting and yelling went on, running at random around the buildings. In the grey dawn, it reminded Chris of nothing so much as the continual howl of a racing wolf pack.

Firing continued to break out, first at one spot and then another as Rannigan and his men moved in for the kill. A man came running out of the dimness directly in front of Chris, crouching low, firing as he ran. Chris felt the passage of hot lead past his face, heard it strike the rocks near him and ricochet into the distance with the whine of tortured metal. Chris snapped a shot at him, saw the other swerve. It was impossible to tell if the slug had hit or not. The man went down behind one of the rocks, remained out of sight.

Slipping to one side, Chris came up against Denver, said harshly: 'Where is Wilder?'

The rancher shook his head. 'Haven't seen him since we got here. Reckon he must be down there somewhere.'

'Keep up your fire. I'm goin' down to look for him. I don't want him to slip through our fingers this time and in all this ruckus he's liable to do just that.'

He crept to the edge of the trees, stopped to listen to the firing, judging its position and intensity before moving on. Most of the men inside the ranch house were firing now, their fire cutting into Wilder's men as they floundered in the grey dimness, striving to get away from the terrible crossfire that grew in intensity, cutting them down as they ran headlong for cover which no longer seemed to exist for them.

Chris let his breath fall away, then rush into his lungs, only to exhale it again as he plunged down the slope, heedless of the slugs that tore through the air around his body. Reaching the side of the long barn, he paused, looked about him through narrowed eyes. Most of the gunhawks had moved well away from the house and were trying to escape into the hills. Leaderless now, they ran in little groups, seeking to get away, but running into Rannigan and his men on the lower slopes of the hills.

Carefully, Chris edged around the edge of the barn, then paused suddenly. A familiar voice out of the dark opening where he had expected to find no one but perhaps a few of his own men, said sharply: 'Let that gun drop, Ranson. I've got a bead on you and I'm just itchin' to pull this trigger. But I want you to see who's sendin' you into eternity.'

Chris turned slowly. Matthew Wilder was standing with his back to the wall. There was a tight expression of triumph on his fleshy face, his teeth showing in a snarl, his deep-socketed eyes glowing in the dim light. The air here was thick and heavy with the smell of gun smoke.

'Don't try to be a hero, Ranson. Maybe you've killed most of my men, but I'll see that you don't live to get anythin' out of it.'

For a moment, the thought lived in Chris's mind that he might be able to swing and beat the other to the shot, but one quick look at Wilder was enough to tell him that to try such a move would be utter suicide. There was a cold glitter in the deep-set eyes. Chris saw the hammer lift on the other's gun. The round black hole of the muzzle was pointing directly at the middle of his body. He reckoned he had only a second or so to go.

Back in his head was the knowledge that he had been badly caught off guard by the other. He ought to have known that Wilder would have stayed around, hoping to get a shot at the man who had engineered all of this, destroyed his force. Even the remnants of Wilder's outfit would never ride solid behind him again unless he at last brought some kind of order out of this chaos and destroyed the man who had been responsible for it.

All of these thoughts raced through Chris's mind in the split second that he stood there, the Colt beginning to slip from his fingers at the other's sharp command. He knew that Wilder expected him to try to make a fight of it, even at that last moment, but he did the one thing that the other did not expect. He dropped, a split second before the gun roared in Wilder's fist, and lunged forward with his shoulder as he went down. The lead whined an inch over his head and smashed against the upright of the door. Wood splintered on Chris as he hit Wilder's feet, throwing him back against the wall. A loud gasp came from the other's lips as his head struck the thick timber with a sickening crack. Savagely, Wilder tried to twist away, to bring up his gun again. Chris had released his hold on his own weapon the moment he had hit the ground. Now he grabbed at Wilder's wrist, thrusting it away as the man heaved with all of his strength, trying to twist the gun so that the muzzle pointed at Chris's head. Another shot bucketed out as Wilder pressed the trigger, but the bullet went high.

Smashing down with the side of his hand, Chris knocked the gun from the other man's fingers, sent it hurtling into the dirt. Wilder uttered a choked cry, then his hands clawed up at Chris's throat, getting a throttling grip. The strength in those long talons of fingers shocked Chris. He could begin to feel the effect of the strangling fingers as the other tried to heave himself upright and his eyeballs bulged as if they would jump from their sockets. The pain was making him dizzy and there was a roaring in his ears that drowned out every other sound, the constricting band of agony around his chest growing tighter with every passing second as his lungs were starved of air. He knew that he had to break the other's hold soon or die. With a surging effort, he got both arms free and slammed them against the side of Wilder's head. The man gurgled in pain and the grip on Chris's throat slackened fleetingly. In that second, he jerked his head back, feeling the nails tear at his flesh. The other's grip did not loosen completely, but his head and shoulders were lifted clear of the ground by the sudden movement. Chris seized his chance, thrust forward with his own head and a groan was forced from Wilder's lips as his skull crashed against the hard ground under him. Tearing his bruised throat free of the other's hands, Chris swung his fist, sending it crashing against Wilder's unprotected jaw and the man, with a pulping groan, went limp. Sucking air down into his tortured lungs, Chris managed to get to his feet, stood swaying as he stared down at the other through tear-blurred eyes. Wilder lay where he had fallen for several seconds, then shook his head as if to clear it and tried

124

to push himself on to his hands and knees, head hanging down between his arms. All of the fight seemed to have been hammered out of him. Then he moved forward in the direction of Chris's gun, lying in the dirt a couple of feet away. One hand reached out, clawing for the weapon. He scarcely seemed to know what he was doing, or of Chris's presence there. Almost, he had his fingers curled about it. Then he collapsed on to the ground as Chris kicked him in the head and stood back, drawing himself upright. There was the pounding of feet in the near distance and a moment later, Denver came running around the corner of the barn, his drawn gun wavering a little as he sighted the two men.

'Hold your trigger,' Chris said sharply. 'I reckon he's finished.'

'Wilder?' asked the other tightly.

Chris nodded. 'He tried to bushwhack me from inside the barn. Would have done it, too, if he hadn't been too sure of himself.'

'The rest of his outfit are finished too,' grunted the other, thrusting the Colt back into its holster. 'The boys are rounding up any strays who might be tryin' to work their way through the trees.'

Chris nodded, picked up his gun and slipped it into leather. 'We'll take him back into town with us,' he muttered, jerking a thumb at the unconscious man lying at his feet. 'I reckon we can always find a rope to hang him once the judge has passed sentence.' He rubbed his throat tenderly with his fingertips, found it hard to swallow.

'I reckon this is somethin' that Wilder never expected,' grinned the other man. 'He must've figured it would be the easiest thing in the world to take your ranch, imaginin' you were more'n thirty miles away in town.'

'Thanks to Doc Fordham,' said Chris solemnly. He wondered how the old doctor was and a twinge of conscience touched him. True they had taken care of Wilder, and he would bother them no more. His men, what few of them were still alive, were scattered to hell and beyond, leaderless, representing no further danger to the territory; but Diego was still around some place, a man of a different calibre to Matthew Wilder, and possibly twice as dangerous. What was the Mexican doing now, while the town was unguarded? The thought troubled him, made impatience grow in him, but he knew that these men who had ridden with him were saddle weary and some of them had been hurt.

'Better get the men together and we'll have a bite to eat, and rest up the horses before we ride on back into town,' he said. The sun was just beginning to lift, colouring the sky a deep crimson in the east.

Denver glanced at him curiously. 'You ain't reckonin' on more trouble, are you?' he asked pointedly.

Chris drew in a short, swift breath. He looked closely at the other, trying to sort out the immediate things in his mind. 'I'm not sure,' he murmured finally, as they turned towards the house. 'Diego is still around and he wanted as much as Wilder did, but maybe he has a more subtle way of goin' about it.'

'Diego!' Denver gave him a sideways glance. 'Certainly he and Wilder were at loggerheads. Both wanted this spread when your grandfather died and as you say, Diego is a ruthless killer, maybe more dangerous than Wilder. He's like a rattler, coiled and ready to strike when you least expect it.'

'How many men has Diego got behind him?'

'Thirty maybe. Not as many as Wilder. And when he knows that Wilder is finished, he may think twice about tryin' to fight. He may back down rather than risk the same thing happenin` to him. He's no fool and it could be that he'll be content with what he's got, rather than lose everythin'.'

'Maybe.' There was little conviction in Chris's voice. He led the way into the house, turned for a moment and watched the rest of the men straggling in from the low hills and around the corral, saw them make their way over to the bunkhouse. He reckoned they would be ready to ride again at high noon. There would not be as many of them as had ridden out with him during the night. Some had been killed, others wounded. But would they be enough to stop Diego? He knew he would never feel easy in his mind until Diego was finished too, as Wilder was finished.

When high noon came, with the burning heat of the sun lying over everything, they rode out of the ranch and headed for the trail over the plain, back towards town. As he rode, Chris felt a sense of growing alertness in him, something which overrode the weariness that was deep inside him. The trail ran dog-leg fashion through clumps of cactus and mesquite, then out on to the broad, stretching plain which lay between the town and the ranch, with only the river to break the flat monotony of it. The sun pressed on them with a heavy, oppressive heat that burned through their clothing, and the harsh light flashed off the metal of their bridles with painful stabs of light. Dust was a silver screen all about them, hazing the men who rode with him and heat rolled back from the punished earth on either side of the trail, making a thin, unseen turbulence all about them, rising up and touching the shimmering hills in the distance, where they rose in great, undulant shapes on the skyline. The smell of the day was a burnt-out scent of dried grass and sage and the bitter alkali smell of the dust that was everywhere.

By the time they came within sight of the town, the middle-down sun was a glaring disc that shone directly into their eyes, even under the lowered brims of their hats and the horizons were burned a deep blue-yellow. Nothing had relieved the piled-up intensity of the heat and the day's ride had been a punishment for all of the riders and their mounts. Caked with dust and sweat, every breath was a labour, a tightness in their chests which turned them nervous.

A little before five o'clock, they crossed the narrow bench of land that fronted the town and rode into the wide street. The town was quiet and as he turned his gaze from one side to the other, Chris felt a little of the nervous tightness draw out of him and he relaxed his tight-fisted grip on the reins.

Drawing rein in front of the sheriff's office, he slipped from the saddle and went inside, heels rapping a hollow tattoo on the boardwalk. The outer office was empty and there was a stillness there that he didn't like, a waiting silence that ate at his nerves. Stepping through the far door, he made his way along the passage to the cells.

For a moment, he paused in front of that which had held Maxwell when he had left town the previous night. Then with a muttered curse, he ran back into the outer office for the keys, saw in a single, sweeping glance that the rack was empty, ran back to the cell and blasted the lock into jangled ruin with a single shot. Thrusting the door open, he knelt beside the bound and gagged figure that lay on the low bunk, ripped the gag from the man's face and found himself staring down into Doc Fordham's weather-beaten features.

SIX

LONG VENGEANCE

It took Chris only a minute's examination to determine that the doctor had been merely knocked out and then bound and gagged. The wound on the side of his head had been re-opened and had bled a lot while he had been lying there and he groaned in deep agony as he stirred and came round. There was the clatter of feet in the corridor outside and Denver came running into the cell, taking in everything in a single glance.

Chris bit back a curse as he stared at the grey-haired rancher. 'I knew it was a mistake to ride out and leave this place unguarded, but I never figured that Maxwell would be able to trick Fordham into anythin' like this. He must've feigned illness and got the doc to go into the cell and then knocked him cold. But where's Rosalie? She should have been here.'

'Could be that she went for help,' suggested the other. He bent beside the doctor. 'He may be able to tell us when he comes round fully.'

Fordham muttered something under his breath, his head twisting from one side to the other, lips drawn back over his teeth. Then his eyes flicked open. For a long moment, he stared up at Chris and Denver, his gaze devoid of all expression.

'You'll be all right, Doc,' said Denver quietly. 'Just lie there and try to tell us what happened. Where's Maxwell? Did he make a break for it?'

Fordham swallowed thickly, then shook his head, wincing as the movement sent pain jarring through it. With a tremendous effort, he forced himself into a sitting position in spite of Chris's move to restrain him. Reaching out, he caught the other's arm, his fingers biting in with a steel-like, urgent strength. 'Diego!' he mumbled. 'I blame myself for this, Chris. I should've known that double-crossin' Mexican might try something' while you were out of town.'

'Diego!' Chris stared at the other in sudden shocked surprise. He felt the coldness draw tight within him.

'What time is it?' grunted the doctor, ignoring the other's sudden exclamation.

'Nearly five-thirty,' muttered Denver. 'We caught up with Wilder and brought him back to town for trial.'

'Where is Diego now?' asked Chris sharply. 'Did he come here just to bust Maxwell out of jail?' Deep inside, he knew that this had not been the case, but he had to live with that single hope for as long as he could, afraid of what he might hear from the other's lips.

'Maxwell?' Fordham shook his head. 'Diego claimed you'd run into an ambush, that you needed help and I was to try to get some of the townsfolk to ride out with me. No sooner had I turned towards the door than a gun was jabbed into my back. They pushed me into this cell after they'd turned Maxwell loose. Then they grabbed Rosalie and said . . .' He broke off suddenly, as if unable to continue.

'Go on,' said Chris demandingly, the sudden fear crystallising into a deep conviction inside him. 'What about Rosalie?'

'Better give him time,' said Denver quietly, forcing Chris's grip on the old doctor's arm to relax. 'He's come through hell and it won't be easy for him to—'

'But don't you understand?' Chris turned on him almost savagely. 'Diego must have taken Rosalie with him when he rode out of town with Maxwell.'

He turned back to Fordham, saw the slight, almost imperceptible nod of the man's head. 'That's what they did all right,' grunted the other. He tightened his lips. 'Diego said that you'd get her back only when you signed the ranch over to him and rode out of the territory.'

Grim faced, Chris got to his feet, sucked in a deep breath, his eyes very hard and still, pinched down as he looked across at Denver. He caught the rancher's steely look and jerked his head towards the door. Denver nodded, stepped out into the corridor and moved back into the outer office.

'Get some of your men to help Doc,' said Chris tightly. He took the Colts from their holsters, one by one, loaded shells into the empty chambers, then pushed them back into place. Denver looked sharply at him.

'You're goin' after them, despite the fact that you don't even know which way they're headed?'

Chris's jaw muscles bunched and his eyes flashed in swift, sudden anger. 'You know damned well that question don't need any answer.'

The other shrugged his shoulders swiftly. 'Only wanted to know,' he grunted. 'I'm comin' with you. Rosalie's father was a friend of mine. I can get more than fifty men who'll ride with us and—'

'No,' Chris snapped, tight-lipped. 'This has to be handled by me alone. A whole bunch of men on the trail will be spotted at once and I know enough about Diego to know that he'll kill the girl rather than let us get our hands to her again. He's got nothin' to lose in this affair.'

'Then I'll ride with you alone.'

'Two of us might be one too many,' said Chris, 'but thanks for the offer. I know how you must feel.'

Denver ran a hand across his mouth, brow drawn deep in thought. 'Somethin' you forget, Chris,' he said slowly, evenly. 'I know this country far better than you do. I know Diego too, know how his mind works. And I figure that I can read a trail as well as any man in these parts. Besides, we don't know how many men he has ridin' with him. I figure he won't have many. He'll need most of 'em to watch his own spread, knowing that when this is discovered, we'll ride against him, no matter what you plan on doin'. But if he was to head for the mesas to the south, there are plenty of places where they could hide out and hold off an army of men, just the two of 'em.'

'Then you reckon that Maxwell is ridin' with him?'

'Could be,' mused the other. 'Maxwell will be lookin' after his own skin now. He knows that if we get him and bring him back here, he'll stand trial, so he'll stick with Diego.'

Chris stared levelly at the rancher, then gave a brief, terse nod. 'All right. We'd better get started. There's no way of tellin' when they did this and the trail is goin' to get pretty cold durin' the night.'

Denver swung away. 'I'll get us a couple of fresh broncs,' he said harshly, then paused: 'Just one thing, Chris. When we do finally catch up with Diego and Maxwell and get a chance to nail 'em without endangerin' the girl, that's what we do?'

Chris's lips were drawn back into a thin, compressed line. 'I don't trust that Mexican one little bit,' he said coldly, keeping his anger under tight, rigid control. 'He'll kill the girl rather than hand her over to us, whether I agree to sign over the ranch to him or not. He knows that I won't stop until I've destroyed him.' Unconsciously almost, his right hand dropped to the gun butt in his belt, fingers touching the smooth wood. 'When we get them, we drop them any way we can. We shoot them in the back or through the head, without any warnin' at all. Just one thing though, Denver.'

The rancher paused with his hand on the handle of the door, stared across at Chris with quizzically-lifted brows. When he finally spoke, Chris's tone was soft and filled with menace. 'When we finally locate 'em – Diego is mine.'

One last wave of red sunlight washed over the high hills, breaking into the deep purple of twilight, and then it was gone and darkness descended swiftly on the land. The pines which massed on the higher reaches of the hills stood in deep shadow as they thrust themselves up, tall and straight, arrowing towards the heavens. Here the air was thin and clear and cool on Rosalie's face as she sat high in the saddle, her gaze flicking from Diego's dark, swarthy features, to the sagging cheeks of the man who had once been sheriff, before he had been tossed into jail by Chris Ranson. The thought of Chris stirred some emotion deep in her mind and she fell to wondering what he would do once he rode back into town and discovered what had happened.

Would he guess where these men were taking her – or would he do as Diego had said and sign the ranch over to the Mexican in return for her life? Diego had wasted no time in making his move, once Chris and the others had ridden out of town to hunt down Matthew Wilder and his gunmen. He must have been planning this for some time, perhaps even when he had gone to Chris and offered to throw in his men, to help him against Wilder.

Diego's voice broke in on her thoughts: 'We should reach the mesas by dawn if we ride all night.'

'Don't you reckon we can rest up somewhere?' muttered Maxwell sullenly. 'These horses are mighty tired and there ain't much chance of anybody ridin' after us.' He seemed anxious and nervous, the sort of man who was eager to make sure of this chore, hoping that it would go off without a hitch, knowing Diego's reputation as a gunman and killer, but also unsure of what Chris Ranson, who had also shown himself to be something of a gunfighter, meant to do.

'Why don't you relax, *amigo*,' said Diego harshly. 'We've covered our trail pretty well and it's goin' to be dark within minutes. Besides, Ranson knows nothin' of this part of the territory.'

'Some of the others with him may,' put in Maxwell, unconvinced.

'Ranson won't follow us, you goshdarned fool,' Diego

hissed. 'He's got more sense than that. He knows he'll never get the girl back alive if he tries to track us down.' He sat his saddle squarely, cuffed his hat back on to the dark, curly hair and then tilted his head back, looking at the towering range that rose up in front of them.

'Heavy timber,' grunted Maxwell thickly. 'That will slow us down a lot.'

'It'll down the same for them, *amigo*,' said Diego thinly. 'And if they were to follow us and tried to work their way around it, they'd lose many hours before they hit the trail again.'

While the two men were eyeing the pines which rose in ordered array above them, Rosalie pulled the silk handkerchief from her pocket, bent low in the saddle, keeping her gaze on the two men as she let it drop among the rocks on the edge of the trail. This done, she urged her mount forward until she was level with the others. Neither man glanced behind her and in the darkness, the tiny square of silk would have been difficult to pick out from the boulders, but she could only hope that if Chris was following, that if he had, somehow, picked up the trail further back, he might spot it and know that he was moving in the right direction; for once up there among those tall pines, it would be virtually impossible for anyone but an Indian scout to follow them.

'All right,' said Diego thinly. 'Let's get moving.' He looked anxiously at the shadowed bank of the low foothills to either side, then urged his mount forward, with the girl behind him and Maxwell bringing up the rear.

Once they were well clear of the town, Denver slowed his mount, moved forward with an undue care, eyes scanning the ground in front of him, flicking from side to side, missing nothing. It was still sufficiently light for them to make out most of the details of the ground. They had crossed the wide river ten minutes before and Denver had spent several minutes walking his mount up and down the bank before pausing and pointing in satisfaction. The prints of three horses were just visible in the soft ground. There were also the scratches of a branch in the dirt and a few crushed leaves which told of the attempt which had been made by someone to obliterate the trail.

'I reckon they didn't make a good job of it,' Chris said tightly. 'Leavin' those leaves behind is a give-away. Ain't no branches near here.'

Catching up the reins, he urged his mount forward. Denver rode up beside him, his face tight and grim in the fading light. He stared directly ahead of him, up at the great, brooding weight of the mountains that lifted in front of the sunset. Only the expression on his face gave any indication of the thoughts that were running through his mind at that moment; but Chris could guess at them, the same thing had occurred to him. Once Diego got into the mountains, into the dense pines which covered the lowermost slopes, they would find it difficult, if not quite impossible, to trail him. All they knew at the moment was that three riders had passed this way recently. Everything pointed to it having been Diego and Maxwell, taking the girl with them, but if they were on a wild goose chase . . . .

He let the idea drift swiftly out of his mind. It was no good thinking along those lines. They had to keep on following this trail in the hope that, at some time, the girl managed to leave some sign behind while the others were not watching, which would confirm for them that they were following the right trail and not riding in the opposite direction. Certainly Denver's idea that the Mexican was heading for the rising spires of the hills, seemed plausible. Any other trail would have merely taken him through low foothills, or out on to the stretching plain, and there would be little or no cover there where they could hole up with the girl. He fell to wondering, as he rode, how Diego intended to get word through to him to sign over the ranch. It would all have to be done legally, otherwise Diego would have no claim to it. It was more than likely that he would take Maxwell and Rosalie up into the mountains somewhere and leave the crooked sheriff to watch the girl while he rode back into town, knowing that Chris dared do nothing so long as he had the girl well hidden.

Darkness came down swiftly as they rode on, eyes continuing to search the ground. There was a winding trail that led up into the foothills, the only trail they saw, and it was unlikely that Diego would be foolish enough as to try to force his way over unbroken ground, thereby slowing himself up more than was necessary. The cliff face was rock and earth, a very thin skim of earth which grew little here except for rough patches of coarse grass that clung to the sheer wall of dirt, sucking a precarious existence from the dry soil. The pathway dropped along the side of the cliff at breakneck speed, running higher and higher as they forced their way up to where the solid wall of pines marched grandly around the side of the mountains. From the look of it, there was no way of telling how recently this trail had been used. The solid rock would leave few hoofmarks for them to follow and they could only ride the trail to its end and then backtrack at first light if they had not come across anything definite which would give them a lead.

The steep slope soon began to tell on the horses and no amount of urging would make them increase their gait. There was water flowing at the bottom of the chasm which lay on their left and the cold dampness of it began to rise to them now that darkness had fallen. They had been on the ascent for more than two hours and Chris was beginning to feel the strain of it tell on him, and he thought that he heard other echoes of sound above the murmur of distant water and the muffled hoofbeats of their own mounts as they toiled slowly upward. Vague murmurs of sound that came up to them from the lower reaches of the trail, and others which seemed to sink from above them, from the broad, uprearing summits, still more than two thousand feet above their heads. He had the impression of the whole solid weight of the mountain crushing down on him from above. At a sharp bend in the trail, they stopped and sat loosely in the saddle, listening for the vague, indefinable sounds but unable to make anything of them. Chris still felt dissatisfied, then reached for his tobacco and rolled a smoke as he sat there, listening to the gale of his mount's breathing, loud in the stillness that clung about them. He held the match in his hand for a long moment, ready to light, then caught himself. The flare of a match could be seen for almost a mile, might bring a bullet. He put the match away again, nursed the dry smoke between his lips, getting no satisfaction from it, then moved ahead behind Denver.

The other seemed to know his way intimately, even in the pitch blackness that had descended on them. The night was bright with thousands of brilliant stars and there was the faint indication of moonlight far below them, but it did not shine on them, the vast bulk of the mountain shutting it off completely, hiding the moon from sight.

It was not until a couple of hours later that the moon finally drifted into sight directly ahead of them as they turned a wide bend in the trail, edging up to the timber belt. The black mass of the sky-rearing pines lay less than half a mile from them, dark and forbidding.

Denver pointed a finger upward. 'They must have taken the trail through the pines,' he said softly. 'It's the only way over this shoulder of the mountain and it would take the best part of a day to work around it. They wouldn't waste precious time like that, not with weary horses.'

'So we go ahead through the trees,' murmured Chris musingly. There was still the savage, bitter anger in him, coupled with a rising impatience. The long journey up into the mountain reaches had taken them the best part of six hours and all the time, there had been a memory in his mind which had haunted him every minute of the way. The memory of Diego's face when he had seen him in the sheriff's office, when the other had come to offer his help against

Wilder. He had had the other at his mercy then, even though there were more than thirty of the Mexican's men drinking in the saloon. He ought to have put him into one of the cells along with Maxwell, or shot him down while he had had the chance. At that moment, he had been on equal terms with the other, which was more than could be said now.

The thought of Rosalie, riding with those two men threatened to swamp out everything else in his mind. They must have a tremendous lead on them by now, he thought grimly. Then he remembered that the others would have been forced to ride slowly up that treacherous and steep trail. He glanced sharply about him. This part of the trail was ideal for a bushwhacker.

'Good cover here for a dry-gulcher,' he said brusquely.

Denver snapped his head around. 'You figure they might lay for us along the trail?'

'Could be – one of them at least. If they reckon they're bein' followed, that's exactly what I'd expect Diego to do. He might decide to leave Maxwell behind to cover his trail while he rides on with the girl.'

Denver's gaze ran over the thick brush ahead of them. He pursed his lips and edged his mount forward a little, then paused and stared down at something in the rocks nearby. A moment later, he swung out of the saddle and went forward. Chris swung up to him, looked down with a feeling of excitement in him as the other bent and picked up something white, holding it up to him.

'Recognise this?' asked the rancher.

Chris took it, felt the smoothness of silk. Then he nodded quickly. 'It looks like one of Rosalie's handkerchiefs,' he said tensely. 'You figure she dropped it for us to see?'

'Sure looks that way to me,' murmured the other. He climbed back into the saddle. 'If she did, then it means we're on the right trail this time. Maybe we can make better time knowing that.' A quick glance at the trees and he went on quietly: 'There's goin' to be no dust yonder and the undergrowth will muffle the sound of the horses.' He seemed to have dismissed the idea of a bushwhacker lying in wait for them.

It was well into the early hours of the morning when they rode through into the heavy timber. Most of it was first-year pine, the trunks tall and straight for more than thirty feet before they spread out into a thick and impenetrable blanket over their heads, shutting out even the faint, shimmering starlight and the pale moonglow. The smell of moist earth was in their nostrils now and there was scarcely any sound all about them. Only the breathing of their horses disturbed the quiet stillness. Chris knew none of this land and yet he felt no inward concern. Denver obviously knew exactly where he was, had possibly ridden this particular trail on many occasions in the past.

They came out into the open a couple of miles further on; a wide break in the trees where the trail ran alongside a deep chasm, the ground falling away into pitch blackness on the very edge of the trail. As they came out into the open, Chris reined his mount. Far away, there was a single starved echo, fading swiftly. Denver turned in the saddle, looked across at him tightly.

'Sounded like a gunshot,' Chris said thinly. 'Far way.'

'Could be,' nodded the other. 'Trouble is that sounds are deceptive in the hills at night.'

Riding on, they listened for any repetition of the sound, but there was nothing more. The silence descended like a sable cloak all about them, the deep and utter silence of the mountains. The pines ran solemnly before them again, shutting out the rest of the world, rising in a flawless line towards the lower limits of the mountain crests. By degrees, the country became rougher. Huge boulders were scattered over the trail and they were forced to edge their way forward slowly and carefully, inching around the tall rocks, loose stones sliding under them and bouncing off down the slope. The trail seemed to hold to the crests of the ridges most of the way, then they were over its topmost point, dipping down again in a series of switchback courses to a levelling off place among the tall hills. Here the rocks were so numerous, dotting the slopes, the brush so thick among them, that Chris knew that if either of the two men had stayed behind to cover the trail, this was surely where it would be.

The going was tough now, really tough, and in some places, Maxwell and Diego had to dismount and lead their horses and the girl's through the sharp-edged boulders that studded the trail, where it twisted and wound in a series of almost terrifying curves towards the narrow, rocky valley that lay surrounded entirely by the tall mountains.

Rosalie was kept in the saddle all of the time, her body bruised and sore. They had ridden all night without a stop, Diego forcing them on with muttered curses whenever Maxwell suggested that they should halt, if only for a little while to give the horses a chance to blow and get their wind. He seemed to have now become obsessed by the idea of getting to their destination as quickly as possible, regardless of the discomforts they were forced to endure on the way.

Maxwell rode the short stretches of the trail in silence now, his flabby features twisted into a permanent scowl. Rosalie guessed that he was never a brave man even at the best of times – certainly he had shown nothing of courage during the time he had been sheriff – and he seemed to be on the very edge of panic now, his nerves stretched almost to breaking point. She caught him glancing back over his shoulder more often now, as if certain that someone was following close on their heels, ready to exact retribution for what they had done.

Forcing away the little tremor of fear in her own mind, she wondered whether she might not be able to turn the other's increasing nervousness to her own advantage.

'They're not far behind, Maxwell,' she said softly. She saw the other whirl in the saddle, glaring back at her. 'And when

140

they do catch up with you, nothing is going to save you.'

'Shut up,' snarled the other. He made a swift, instinctive move towards his gun, his face twisted in sudden savage fury. For a moment, the thought of killing her lived in his mind. Then he dropped his hand away. 'Keep ridin',' he snapped, 'and keep your mouth shut.'

Rosalie knew that she was courting disaster, but she had to keep on, trying to play one man against the other. If she didn't succeed in that, there was just the chance that she might slow down their pace and allow anyone who might be following their trail a chance to catch up on them before they reached their destination.

'You know that Ranson is following you, don't you,' she went on remorselessly as the other reined his mount, moving up beside her, his face contorted with fury. 'And it's only a matter of time before he catches up with us. Then you're as good as dead and—'

'Damn you, I warned you to shut up!' snarled Maxwell. His right hand clawed to draw the gun from its holster. It had half cleared the leather when the sound of a shot drove everything from the girl's mind. Maxwell reeled back in the saddle, clawing at his smashed wrist.

'I do not warn you again, *amigo*.' Diego thrust the smoking gun back into its holster. His face hard, he swung on Rosalie. 'As for you, *senorita*, I shall not hesitate to tie you to the horse and gag you if you try anything like that again.'

The girl recognised the menace in his tone, knew that he would do exactly as he said and fell silent, pressing her lips tightly together. But even as she rode forward again, aware of the murderous glance that Maxwell gave her, she felt an inward thrill of exultation. If Chris was following, if he was anywhere within ten miles at that moment, he would surely have heard the sound of that shot, echoing from the hills and mountains . . . .

Dawn greyed the eastern heavens as they moved out of the

pines and on to a stretch of rough trail. Here and there, it was possible to make out the marks of horses and men in the dust, recent marks, where the men had been forced to dismount and lead their horses.

'They can't be far ahead now,' murmured Denver. He lifted himself high in the saddle and glanced down into the narrow valley that opened out in front of them.

'You know this place at all?' Chris asked tautly.

'Heard about it,' corrected the other. 'Used to be some old mine workings in this part of the territory. Worked out long before the war. Nobody comes here now, except for men like Diego. Makes a good retreat for any *hombre* who's running from the law.'

'Sounds like just the sort of place Diego would head for,' agreed Chris. 'Like you said, a couple of men with plenty of ammunition could hold off a whole army here. How do you figure on getting close enough to 'em for a killin' shot?'

'There are plenty of short trails in these parts. I doubt if Diego knows 'em all. But it'll be rough ridin' and in places we'll have to climb without the horses.'

'But you reckon we can come on 'em unawares?' Chris eyed the other closely.

Denver hesitated, then nodded slowly. 'I reckon so,' he agreed. 'Trouble is that they may be watchin' this part of the trail. If they are, they could spot us long before we get down into the valley.'

They made their way forward over some of the roughest footing that Chris had ever encountered. In several places, they were forced to dismount and lead their horses, breaking forward through tangled vine undergrowth, working their way around vast boulders and great masses of fallen rocks and earth. New slides of dirt were everywhere, blocking the trail in several places and it was here that they found the signs they were looking for; three horses had come this way very recently, certainly not more than a few hours before. Denver nodded in satisfaction.

'Like I figured,' he said softly, 'they're evidently headed for the old mine workings. Once they hole up in there, we'll have a job to smoke 'em out without runnin' the risk of shootin' the girl.'

'My guess is that Diego will leave Maxwell there to keep an eye on the girl and then head back to town.'

'Why do you reckon he'll do that?' asked the other. 'He'd be a hell of a sight safer here.'

'Sure he would. But somehow, he has to get back to make sure that I carry out my part of the bargain, even though it's certain that he won't keep his. Once I sign that place over to him, you can be sure that he'll kill the girl. His life won't be worth a plugged nickel from then on. He'll have to get rid of me if he's to take over the ranch and run it with his own men.'

Denver nodded his head bleakly. In the pale dawn light, his grey hair glistened under the wide-brimmed hat. 'I get your point, Chris,' he said tightly. 'So we have to take care of 'em both here?'

'That's right. We've got no other choice. If we can drop Diego when he rides out of the mine workings, it'll mean that we have only Maxwell to take care of and he'll be a scared man by now.'

'And if Diego sends Maxwell into town, refusing to risk his own skin, and stays with the girl himself?'

'Then we may have to alter our plans.' Chris clamped his teeth tightly together until the muscles of his jaw lumped under his flesh. 'Right now, our problem is to get sufficiently close to them without being spotted.'

A mile from the old workings, Diego reined his mount, grasped the saddle, and leaned back, staring along the way they had come. From where they were, it was possible to see for several miles along the winding, twisting trail that led back up the bleak side of the mountain. The pale light of the early dawn picked out the shapes and angles of the rocks, the rising

spires of the mesas, silhouetted against the slowly, brighten-
ing heavens.

The feeling that maybe Maxwell was right and Ranson had
decided to follow them after all, had been growing within
him during the past three hours. As he sat there, he recalled
the moment along the trail when he had been forced to shoot
the gun from Maxwell's hand before he could shoot the girl.
The sound of that single shot would have carried many miles
back along the trail and he cursed himself soundly for not
having realised that before. Narrowing his eyes, he peered
back into the dim distance, trying to pick out anything that
moved along the trail, any cloud of dust which would indicate
that they were being pursued. He could see nothing, but his
uneasiness did not fade. Instead, the tightness in his mind
crystallised swiftly into a near certainty.

'Somethin' wrong?' muttered Maxwell sullenly.

'Just checkin',' murmured the other evenly. He glanced
back in the direction of the small cluster of shacks which
marked the position of the old mine workings. 'Could be that
you were right when you figured Ranson might try to follow
us. I think we should be careful and watch the trail, just in
case.'

'You said yourself there wasn't anythin' to be afraid of, that
Ranson would never dare to follow so long as we have the
girl.'

Diego nodded. There was a bright, cold glitter in his eyes
as he glanced at the other speculatively, let his gaze wander
from the man's bloodied wrist, then back to his face again. 'I
figure you could use a rifle, even with that wrist of yours,' he
said softly, 'and I want to make sure this time. Better take
cover along this stretch of the trail where you can spot 'em
some ways off. If they do head this way, drop 'em all. You
understand?' His lips drew back in a tight smile. He ignored
the girl's sudden, sharp gasp.

Swiftly, she swung on him. 'You can't do that!' she said
quickly, the words tumbling over each other as she forced

them out. Her face seemed drained of all colour as the knowledge of what the other intended to do penetrated her mind. 'You promised that if he made over the Ranson place to you and rode out of the territory, you would let me go.'

'So I did,' murmured the other. His smile broadened, grew more menacing. 'But I did not say that he could follow me. A man has to protect himself when anyone pursues him. I am merely taking precautions. If he is not following our trail, then there is nothing to worry about, is there, *senorita*. On the other hand, if he has disobeyed my orders and is trying to trail us, then I fear that I must have him killed. That would be a pity. It would mean that I shall have to get my men and take over the Ranson place by force, because some of the men there will fight, even if this man himself is dead.'

'You want me to dry-gulch anybody who comes along this trail?' muttered Maxwell thinly. 'If there are too many for me what—'

'There won't be,' snapped the other, wheeling his mount away. 'They wouldn't risk coming up with too many men. That would be taking too big a risk as far as the girl is concerned. Nail them all and then make your way to the mine workings where we will be.'

Maxwell waited for a long moment, staring dumbly at the Mexican and then, when there were obviously no further instructions forthcoming, he gave a low grunt and moved off into the rocks that overlooked the trail at that point. As he rode off, he slid the rifle from its scabbard, held it balanced over the saddle horn.

No sooner was he out of sight, than Diego leaned over, grabbed the bridle of Rosalie's mount, held it tightly in one hand, as he led them forward, around the tortuous, twisting bends in the trail. All the time, they moved downgrade and in places, the descent was so steep that only their weight in the saddles, prevented their horses from sliding headlong down the slope.

An hour later, they reached the mine workings. There were

several wooden huts all clustered together in front of the sheer, rising wall of the mountain where the deep shafts had been driven into the solid rock. The rusted rails had not seen any movement of the wagons which now stood in a long line, for more than a score of years, and the deep silence of an abandoned place lay over everything there, causing a slight chill to come into Rosalie's mind, as she looked about her, eyes wide. The sun had risen now, but this part of the mountain still lay in shadow and the coldness of the night was in the air. Not until midday would the sun have worked its way around the outjutting lip of rock, shining on to this bare stretch of rocky ground.

Diego motioned her to alight, sat holding her bridle as she did so. Pain jarred through her as cramp seized her legs and she almost fell headlong with the sudden stabbing pain. Biting back the cry that rose unbidden to her lips, she drew herself up to her full height and faced the other as he swung down, slapping the horses on the rumps, sending them cantering towards the edge of the rocky plateau.

'There'll be food inside one of these shacks,' he said quietly. 'I reckon you ought to be able to rustle up some breakfast.' He eyed her soberly as she made to move forward, caught at her arm, fingers biting in as he pulled her around so that she faced him. 'And one thing, *senorita*. Do you hope that your friends will ride in and rescue you? If they succeed in getting past Maxwell – and he will shoot straight from ambush because he knows what waits for him back in town if he's taken alive – you will die before they can rescue you. I promise you that.'

She pulled sharply away from him, her eyes snapping. 'I might have known that you would do that, you – killer,' she said through thinned lips.

Lifting his hand, the Mexican struck her across the face. The impact of the blow sent her reeling and she almost fell, knocked off her balance. Backing away, she put a hand up to her cheek. Diego raked a cold stare over her. 'Now get some food ready.'

146

Stumbling, she made her way over to the largest of the wooden shacks. There was the musty odour of decay in the air as she thrust open the door and stepped inside. It assailed her nostrils, making her cough and choke. Diego came in close on her heels, slammed the door behind him and took up his position by the window, where he could look back along the trail and see all that went on along the whole length of the plateau.

As she worked, Rosalie felt the sinking sensation of defeat in her mind. The other seemed to have thought everything out, even before they had reached this place and the knowledge strengthened the idea in her mind that Diego had been planning this kidnapping for a long time, possibly from the moment that Chris Ranson had showed up in town and intimated that he would take over his grandfather's ranch and fight to hold it. But Diego had not gone at this thing blindly, as Matthew Wilder had, relying on brute force to achieve his ends. He had waited for his chance, had played his hand cunningly, striking where Chris would be hurt most. Now, it seemed, he had succeeded . . . .

As they headed down into the valley, following the winding trail, Chris was especially alert, his hands very close to his gun butts. The chance of spotting any dry-gulcher's rifle before it spat death towards them from the piled-up rocks was pretty remote. This was an ideal place for a man to hide, to watch the trail and shoot down a man from under cover. He drooped his shoulders forward, forced himself to concentrate on the ground ahead.

There were no words between the two men now as they rode. It was as if both recognised that they were nearing the end of the trail, that the showdown lay just around the corner and at any moment all hell could break loose around them.

Half a mile further on, Denver stopped abruptly and motioned to Chris to halt as he slipped from the saddle and bent to examine the patch of dry ground in front of him, hunking forward on his haunches. Then he looked up, pointed at the dry, powdery earth.

'They stopped here for a while,' he said tightly. 'There are plenty of marks and then one of 'em rode off in that direction—' He pointed off into the rocks to the right, '—while the other two went straight on along the trail.'

Thoughtfully, Chris glanced up into the rocks. Here they lay in tumbled confusion, piled high where they overhung the trail. 'You reckon that one of 'em moved off to cover the trail around here?'

'I'm pretty darned sure of it,' murmured the rancher. He eased the Colt from its holster, checked it carefully. He did not put it back, but held it in his hand, ready for instant use. 'I figure we ought to split up, trail him over those rocks. He's sure to be up there somewhere and I'm bettin' that it's Maxwell. Diego won't want to let the girl out of his sight for a single moment. She represents a lot to him.'

Chris gave a brief jerk of his head in answer. What the other said had the ring of truth about it and he had no doubt that this was indeed the case. Bending, he moved over to the high wall of rock at the edge of the trail, peered up to where the first rays of the morning sun were throwing the rocks into light and shadow. Maxwell was somewhere up there, he thought grimly, waiting among the rocks for the chance to draw a bead on them, shoot them down without a chance to defend themselves. He recalled what he had told Denver shortly before they had set out from town. Once they came upon these men who had taken the girl, they would shoot them down in any way they could, even if it meant shooting them in the back or in the head, just so long as they killed them without giving them a chance to harm the girl. He knew that if it came to the point, he would go through with that, no matter how it went against the grain to shoot a man in the back without warning, but these murdering polecats deserved nothing better. He sucked air down into his lungs, let it go in short pinches. Denver had already slipped away into the boulders, moving swiftly and silently with a surprising agility for a man of his age, climbing the steep side of the trail, working his way up and behind any man who might be up there watching the trail.

With a careful slowness, he began moving along the floor of the trail until he reached a narrow passage that led up through the rocks. Cool wind sifted down the natural channel as he edged forward, eyes alert, starting at every sudden sound or movement. Halfway along the channel, he pondered the wisdom of this move. If Maxwell was there, then he would have to draw the other's fire so that Denver might move in on him from behind.

He began moving laterally along the face of the nearer slope, looking for a gentler pitch and in the end he found one and made better progress. Pausing often to keen the dark shadows thrown by the low sun, he climbed upward, moving like a cat, smoothly and silently, in spite of the stiffness in his limbs and the tiredness that pervaded his whole body. He came out of the rocks at a point higher than where he reckoned any man would hide and a moment later, peering down, he spotted Maxwell, some distance below him, his back to him. The other lay on a flat rock, a rifle thrust out in front of him. He had evidently chosen the spot for its excellent and commanding view over the trail and it came to him then, even before he noticed the other's obvious nervousness, that Maxwell must surely have spotted them long before they had reached the trail immediately below him. Several times, the other lifted his head, peering down at the winding scar of the trail below him, trying to make out where they were. He clearly knew that they had stopped for some reason down there and he was obviously puzzled. Chris grinned savagely to himself, feeling the hot sunlight touch his neck and shoulders as he crouched down behind the rocks. Maxwell had not wanted to take any chances. He had deliberately withheld his fire during their approach along the trail, meaning to shoot them in the back once they had ridden past him. What he had not allowed for, had been the sharp eyesight of the rancher, the fact that Denver could read trail as well as any Indian and had seen quite clearly, written there in the dust, the story that had told, as plainly as any words, that he had left the trail and ridden up into the rocks.

Now Maxwell kept twisting his head in every direction, even glancing behind and above him at times, eyes flicking from side to side, warily, probing every shadow for anything that moved. Worse still, he had discarded the rifle and held his sixer in his hand. The rifle would have proved to be a more cumbersome weapon to use in a confined space and Chris had hoped that the other would have retained it, thereby giving Denver and himself the edge on him. A sudden movement over to his left attracted his attention. Glancing round, he made out the tall figure of the rancher as the other pulled himself up over the smooth rock, lay for a moment clearly getting his breath back before continuing. Swiftly, Chris's glance flickered back to Maxwell. The other had also heard the faint sound as Denver had pulled himself up over the outcrop of rock. He had swung round, the Colt held tightly in his hand, his finger on the trigger, every limb poised as he peered into the shadows among the rocks, trying to discover the source of the sudden sound.

Denver moved again, dragging himself forward. He had evidently come out on to a difficult part of the climb and was forced to heave himself up hand over hand, with his guns still in their holsters. Chris emptied his lungs in a sudden exhalation. Maxwell pushed himself up to his full height, swung to face Denver and lowered the muzzle of the gun on him. With a sudden start, Chris realised that the rancher must now be in full view of the other. The shot whiplashed at the very instant that he brought his own weapon to bear on the man below him. Dimly, he heard the shriek as the bullet richocheted off a rock. Then the Colt bucked and hammered in his own fist, twice, three times it was triggered. He saw Maxwell rear up on his toes, try to turn to face him. Then the other was smashed back by the solid, jarring impact of lead. His gun exploded once as he pressed down on the trigger with the last ounce of strength in his body but he was already going backward when he fired and the slug soared high into the air over his head as his body crashed against the rocky ledge at his back. For a moment, he hung there, then he overbalanced, his body falling down the steep slope, bouncing from one rocky ledge to another until it crashed with a sickening, bone-shattering thud on the trail below.

Slowly, Chris made his way towards Denver, leaping from one rock to another until he was level with the other. The rancher was just getting to his feet, rubbing his temple where an ugly bruise was beginning to show.

'Did he hit you?' asked Chris quickly.

'Nope. Guess I must have fallen and hit my head on the rock. But he came damned close to gettin' me. I never figured he was that close.'

'He must've seen us a mile back along the trail. He was lyin' there waitin' for us to move on and then he'd have shot us both in the back.'

They made their way down to the trail. Maxwell lay face-downward under cover of the huge overhangs. Going forward, Chris turned him over with his toe, stared down into the man's fleshy face. The lips were drawn back in a snarl almost of defiance, even in death.

'I reckon he must've quarrelled with Diego somewhere along the trail,' said Denver, pointing to the other's smashed wrist. 'That would likely be the shot we heard durin' the night, back along the trail.'

Chris nodded. 'Trouble is that Diego will have heard the shots and he'll know that Maxwell wasn't shootin' at shadows. He'll be ready for us, just in case we did get past Maxwell.'

Denver laughed harshly. 'Then we'll just have to show that we're smarter than he is, Chris.' He moved towards the horses still standing in the shadow of the rocks. Swinging up into the saddle, he led the way forward. The trail wound and dipped in front of them for another quarter of a mile and at the end of that time, they were able to sight the cluster of long wooden shacks that stood in front of a tall wall of solid rock, the ground there still in shadow.

'There are the shacks,' said Denver, nodding towards the mine workings. 'If I've guessed right then he'll be holed up in one of them. The only other thing he could do would be to move down the shaft into the rock.'

'You reckon it's likely he'll do that?' asked Chris.

'Nope, I don't reckon so. If he did that, there would be too many ways we could reach him without him being able to see us. Those workings go clear back into the rock for nearly a mile. But there's nothing at the end of 'em and if he went there we could sit tight and starve him out, and he ain't such a fool that he don't know that. In the shacks, he could pick us off quite easily if we tried to pet him.'

'So he's holed up in one of those shacks,' repeated Chris tautly. 'But that ain't goin' to help us none. There are probably half a dozen shacks there and he could be in any one of 'em. Not only that, but they seem to be built on some kind of plateau. It won't be a simple matter getting close enough to him, even if we do find out where he is. He could cover the whole stretch of ground from any one of those huts.'

'You're right. We have to circle around and come up against the rock face.'

'Can we do that?' Chris looked at the other in surprise. 'I thought you didn't know these parts.'

'Ain't been here myself, but I did know an old miner once who worked these diggings. Told me quite a heap of things about this place. If what he said was true, there should be a hidden trail leading up to the rock wall at the back of those shacks.'

'And you reckon you can find it?' Chris felt a new hope beginning to stir in him at the other's words. If there was such a trail and they succeeded in getting behind Diego without the other being aware of it, then there was a good chance of taking the other by surprise before he had a chance to harm the girl. As it was, this was the only chance they had and he had to follow the other from there on.

They rode for another half mile before Denver reined his mount to a sudden halt. Chris glanced about him, but saw nothing out of the ordinary. Then the rancher pointed to their left. There was a narrow gap in the rocks on that side of the trail. To the casual eye, it would have passed unnoticed. But now that he came to look at it more closely, he saw that whereas it was little more than a two-foot wide gap in the rocks there, where it fronted the trail, it widened out appreciably only a few yards at the back of the rocks, formed a kind of natural wrinkle in the ground, a long chute of rock.

'We'll leave the horses here,' said Denver quietly. He slid from the saddle and waited for Chris to do likewise.

Rock caught at Chris's arms and shoulders as he squeezed through the gap in the rock. Passing around tall chunks of weather-carved stone, he discovered the trail that wound between the worn walls of sandstone and eventually, they came out on to an area of bald, open rock. Here, they made better time and the sun had scarcely climbed to the zenith when they came upon the sudden sharp turn and found themselves ascending once again. Directly ahead of them, clearly seen now, was the great rearing face of rock that stood at the back of the shacks they had noticed earlier from the main trail.

Chris brought his mind back to Diego as he followed Denver through the tumbled, massive boulders that thrust themselves up in front of them at every turn. He tried to put himself in the place of the other, tried to think out what Diego might do once he heard those shots from back along the trail, once he knew for sure that he had been trailed this far, even though he would not be certain whether Maxwell had stopped them or not. By now, he might be waiting for Maxwell to show up with news of what had happened. When he didn't show, he would know that Maxwell had been killed and that this part of his plan had somehow come unstuck. Would he decide that the girl was too great a liability to have around? Would he try to make a run for it, heading out for New Mexico, as far as possible from this place, hoping to keep one jump ahead of him, knowing what would happen if Chris managed to meet up with him?

Ten minutes later, they found themselves facing a sheer wall of rock that rose for the best part of a hundred feet in front of them, with not even a solitary handhold in sight.

'How do you expect us to climb that?' muttered Chris, staring up at the rock face that towered over them. 'There's no way up there.'

'But there has to be a way. That old miner was so sure that—'

'You think maybe that he was wanderin' a little when he spun you this yarn?' grunted Chris. 'Don't look to me like there's any way up.'

Denver walked along the base of the rock face, peering up, squinting against the glaring sunlight that was reflected from the smooth rock. He moved slowly to the far end, then turned and shook his head in puzzlement, began to move back. Halfway back, he paused, darted forward. Chris moved up to him, saw the opening in the rock, a sort of natural tunnel. Once, in some long past age, there had been a subterranean river here, flowing out of the solid rock and down into the valley which lay some hundreds of feet below them, a natural waterfall, washing its way down the rock. Now the river was gone, dried up these countless thousands of years, but the water course that it had laid was still there, set in the rock. The gap was wide enough and high enough for a man to stand with his head just touching the rocky roof of the tunnel.

Quietly, Denver said: 'This must be it. A natural tunnel that leads into one of the shafts. That's what he must have been talkin' about.'

Before Chris could stop him, he had plunged into the darkness of the tunnel, his head lowered. For a second, Chris stood there irresolute, then ducked his head and followed the other. The metallic sound of their boots on the hard rock struck vibrating echoes ahead of them. How long they moved forward, it was impossible to tell. The darkness here was absolute and they were forced to move on by sense of touch only. Rough outcrops of rock tore at their feet and hands until they were cut and bruised.

Denver stopped suddenly a while later, stopped so quickly that Chris bumped into him from behind.

'What is it?' he asked tightly, his voice carrying and echoing from the rocks.

'There's fresh air coming in from straight ahead,' murmured the other, his voice reaching back to Chris. 'That must mean that one of the main tunnels is only a little way ahead.' He began to move forward again and less than five minutes later, they were standing in one of the large mine shafts, the metal rails gleaming faintly in the pale glimmer of light that filtered into the workings from the opening less than fifty yards away.

Chris felt winded, his fingers bleeding from that long climb through the narrow tunnel. As they came out into the open, he felt the cold anger in his mind rise up until it threatened to choke him. The shacks were silent less than twenty yards away and from where they stood it was impossible to tell in which one Diego was hidden with the girl. Then there was a sudden movement close to the largest of the shacks. Slitting his eyes against the glare of the sky, he saw the Mexican move out, dragging the girl with him. The other was moving slowly in the direction of the trail, evidently wondering where they were, worried, but clearly confident that there was no one at his back. Crawling swiftly forward, Chris angled over the open ground towards the nearest hut, threw himself against it, the breath rasping harshly in his throat. He was not worrying about Denver now. Diego was to be his, although he knew the rancher was ready to back up any move he made.

His gun in his hand, he moved around to the edge of the

shack, feeling the anger in him as he saw the other dragging the girl forward, then thrust her down behind one of the rocks which overlooked the end of the trail. His teeth clenched and his eyes slitted against the glare, Chris moved out from behind the shack, the gun in his hand pointed at Diego's back as the other moved across towards one of the small gullies.

'Hold it there, Diego,' he called sharply. He saw both the girl and the Mexican whirl at the sudden sound of his voice. For a moment, there was a look of stunned, incredulous surprise written all over the Mexican's swarthy features. Then he dived for the rocks, gripping his gun and bringing it up to cover, not Chris, but the girl. Triggering the Colt, Chris saw Diego stagger and jerk as the slug took him in the shoulder, knocking him to one side. The girl had thrown herself down, aware of her danger, and the slug which had been intended for her, whined harmlessly off the rock close to her head, showering her with chips of stone.

Even though he had been hit, Diego was far from finished. Rolling over on his side, he brought up his weapon again, loosed off a couple of shots at Chris. Something scorched along Chris's upper arm and he gritted his teeth as the burst of agony ran up into his shoulder. Somehow, he managed to steady himself, levelling the gun on the prone body of the Mexican. The hammer fell only once but it was enough, Diego tried to get to his feet, tried to hold life in his eyes and hand long enough to get off another shot, but the gun slipped from his nerveless hand and clattered on to the hard rocks in front of him a split second before he toppled forward on to his face and lay still, a motionless figure in the hot sunlight that was just beginning to show around the tall edge of the mountain.

The gun smoke cleared slowly as Chris went forward to where the girl lay against the rock. Denver came over from the mouth of the mine workings and stood looking down at Diego's body for a long moment. Then he shook his head slowly and moved over to them, his face grim.

'I reckon it's all finished.' said the rancher slowly. 'Without Diego, his men will ride on over the hill and never come back. He was all there was to hold them together. Wilder's finished too. He'll hang for sure.'

Chris nodded, placed his arm around the girl, felt the warmth of her against him. There was a feeling in his mind that he had just woken from some terrible nightmare to find that it had all been nothing more than a dream and that life was good and fresh and clean again. Together, the three of them made their way down the winding trail to where the horses were waiting less than a quarter of a mile away.